# THE NEW YORK SCHOOL

## The Painters and Sculptors of the Fifties

# IRVING SANDLER

ICON EDITIONS
HARPER & ROW, PUBLISHERS
NEW YORK, HAGERSTOWN, SAN FRANCISCO, LONDON

FIRST EDITION

*Designed by Gloria Adelson*

Library of Congress Cataloging in Publication Data

Sandler, Irving, 1925
  The New York School.

  (Icon editions)
  Bibliography: p.
  Includes index.
  1. New York School.  2. Art, American.  3. Art,
Modern—20th century—United States.    I. Title.
N6512.5.N4S26 1978     709′.747′1     77-82357
ISBN 0-06-438505-1        84 85 86 10 9 8 7 6 5 4 3 2
ISBN 0-06-430094-3(pbk)        89 90 91 92 10 9 8 7 6

# THE NEW YORK SCHOOL

# Contents

Acknowledgments     vii

Introduction     ix

1   The Milieu of the New York School in the Early Fifties     1

2   The Community of the New York School     29

3   The Colonization of Gesture Painting     46

4   Frankenthaler, Mitchell, Leslie, Resnick, Francis, and Other Gesture Painters     59

5   Gestural Realism     90

6   Rivers, Hartigan, Goodnough, Müller, Johnson, Porter, Katz, Pearlstein, and Other Gestural Realists     103

7   Assemblage: Stankiewicz, Chamberlain, di Suvero, and Other Junk Sculptors     140

8   The Duchamp-Cage Aesthetic     163

9   Rauschenberg and Johns     174

10   Environments and Happenings: Kaprow, Grooms, Oldenburg, Dine, and Whitman     196

11   Hard-edge and Stained Color-field Abstraction, and Other
     Non-gestural Styles: Kelly, Smith, Louis, Noland, Parker,
     Held, and Others                                              214

12   The Recognition of the Second Generation                      256

13   The New Academy                                               278

14   Circa 1960: A Change in Sensibility                           290

     Appendix A: First-Generation Painters, Dates and Places
     of Birth                                                      321

     Appendix B: Second-Generation Artists, Dates and
     Places of Birth, Art Education, and One-Person Shows in
     New York, 1950–1960                                           322

     Bibliography                                                  326

     List of Illustrations                                         345

     Index                                                         355

     *A section of Color Plates follows page 210.*

# Acknowledgments

I wish to express my gratitude to many artists, critics, curators, and others in the art world who generously provided me with information in both formal interviews and informal conversations. Among those who were particularly helpful were Alice Baber, Leland Bell, Ronald Bladen, Nell Blaine, Norman Bluhm, Paul Brach, Ernest Briggs, Rudolph Burckhardt, John Cage, Charles Cajori, Nicolas Calas, Leo Castelli, John Chamberlain, Herman Cherry, Edward Dugmore, Elaine de Kooning, Willem de Kooning, Edwin Denby, Jim Dine, Mark di Suvero, Lois Dodd, Friedel Dzubas, John Ferren, Perle Fine, Louis Finkelstein, Sam Francis, Helen Frankenthaler, Jane Freilicher, Sidney Geist, Ilse Getz, Michael Goldberg, Robert Goldwater, Robert Goodnough, Sidney Gordin, Clement Greenberg, Stephen Greene, John Grillo, Red Grooms, Philip Guston, Grace Hartigan, Sally Hazelet (Drummond), Al Held, Thomas B. Hess, Hans Hofmann, Harry Holtzman, Malcolm Hughes, Angelo Ippolito, Paul Jenkins, Alfred Jensen, Jasper Johns, Lester Johnson, Wolf Kahn, Howard Kanovitz, Allan Kaprow, Alex Katz, Robert Kaupelis, Ellsworth Kelly, Michael Kidner, William King, John Krushenick, Nicholas Krushenick, Fay Lansner, Ibram Lassaw, Philip Leider, Alfred Leslie, Landis Lewitin, Douglas MacAgy, Nicholas Marsicano, Knox Martin, Mercedes Matter, Joan Mitchell, Kyle Morris, John B. Myers, Brian O'Doherty, Frank O'Hara, Claes Oldenburg, George Ortman, Stephan Pace, Raymond Parker, Patricia Passloff, Phillip Pavia, Philip Pearlstein, Jackson Pollock, Fairfield Porter, Robert Rauschenberg, Ad Reinhardt, Milton Resnick, Larry Rivers, James Rosati, Barbara Rose, Harold Rosenberg, Robert Rosenblum, Ludwig Sander, Miriam Schapiro, Jon Schueler, George Segal, William C. Seitz, David Smith, Tony Smith, Richard Stankiewicz, Joseph Stefanelli, Frank Stella, Sylvia Stone, George Sugarman, and Jack Tworkov.

I am also deeply grateful to Jerome J. Hausman, Howard Conant, and Gert Schiff who read the Ph.D. dissertation (New York University 1977) on which portions of this book are based; Joan McDermott-London, whose help in the preparation of the manuscript was invaluable; Ronni Baer and Mikki Carpenter of Rights and Reproductions, and Lamia Doumato, Daniel Pearl, William Feldman, and Rich Shallenberger of the Library of the Museum of Modern Art; Anita Duquette of Rights and Reproductions, and Helen Ferrulli of the Education Department of the Whitney Museum of American Art; R. C. Kenedy of the Victoria and Albert Museum; Dean Robert Gray, Abe Ajay, Michael Torlen, and John Cohen of State University of New York at Purchase; The Archives of American Art; Debbie Taylor and Janelle Reiring of the Leo Castelli Gallery; and Suzanne Vanderwoude of the Virginia Zabriskie Gallery.

Very special thanks are due to Cass Canfield, Jr. and Carol E. W. Edwards of Harper & Row; to my friend Gilbert S. Edelson; to Otto and Frances Freeman; to my wife, Lucy, for her constant encouragement; and to my daughter, Catherine Harriet, for her diligent proofreading.

# Introduction

FROM 1947 TO 1951, more than a dozen Abstract Expressionists achieved "breakthroughs" to independent styles.[1] During the following years, these painters, the first generation of the New York School, received growing recognition nationally and globally, to the extent that American vanguard art came to be considered the primary source of creative ideas and energies in the world, and a few masters, notably Pollock, de Kooning, and Rothko, were elevated to art history's pantheon. Younger artists who entered their circle in the early fifties—the early wave of the second generation—such as Larry Rivers, Helen Frankenthaler, Grace Hartigan, Allan Kaprow, Joan Mitchell, Robert Rauschenberg, and Richard Stankiewicz (to list some of the better known), were also acclaimed, but with a few exceptions, their reputations had gone into decline by the end of the fifties. In the following decade, the second generation was eclipsed by a third generation, the innovators of Pop, Op, Minimal, and Conceptual Art. (Any notion of a generation of artists is necessarily arbitrary, of course. The term "generation," as it is used here, refers to a group of artists close in age who live in the same neighborhood at the same time, and to a greater or lesser degree, know each other and partake of a similar sensibility, a shared outlook and aesthetic.)

From 1960 to the present, critical attention has been focused on the first and third generations of the New York School, largely overlooking the one in between. This second generation has been dismissed as derivative, as the "school" of de Kooning or of Tenth Street, and as the insignificant tail end of Abstract Expressionism. The rich, varied, and complex ideas and insights that shaped fifties art, its particular attitude, have been almost disregarded or forgotten. Thus, the few artists of the period who continued to command interest after 1960 rarely have been treated with reference to the aesthetic context in which they developed. Indeed, even those successful few have often been numbered among sixties artists, so forgotten has the milieu of the earlier decade become.

The disregard of the second generation also has given rise to distorted interpretations of sixties art, which owed more to that immediately preceding it than is commonly accepted. Until the art of the fifties is adequately dealt with, subsequent styles cannot be considered in proper perspective. Consequently, the major questions to be posed in this study are: How did the art of the second generation evolve from that of the first and what did it pass on to the third? What did younger artists of the fifties accomplish that was significantly different from the first-generation Abstract Expressionists who preceded them and from the Pop, Op, Minimal, and Conceptual artists who emerged later and seemed motivated by a different complex of attitudes?

Members of the second generation did develop distinctive new artistic tendencies. Among them were novel styles labeled Neo-Dada at the time and generally influenced by the thinking of Marcel Duchamp and John Cage. These included assemblage (a mixture of painting, collage, and construction) exemplified by the works of Stankiewicz, Jean Follett, and Rauschenberg; a new kind of realist painting initiated by Jasper Johns; and the Environments and Happenings of Kaprow, Red Grooms, Jim Dine, Claes Oldenburg, and Robert Whitman. The fifties also saw the emergence of the hard-edge abstraction of Ellsworth Kelly, Leon Polk Smith, and Myron Stout—which was unlike earlier Cubist-inspired geometric styles of the twentieth century; the color-field stain paintings of Morris Louis, Kenneth Noland, and Jules Olitski, influenced by but markedly different from the abstractions of Pollock, Rothko, Still, and Newman; and other forms of new abstraction such as those of Al Held, Raymond Parker, and Frank Stella.

The above tendencies appeared in the second part of the fifties and are clearly novel. In their novelty, they differ from the dominant tendency of Abstract Expressionism: second-generation gesture painting, abstract, like that of Frankenthaler, Mitchell, Michael Goldberg, Alfred Leslie, and Milton Resnick,[2] and figurative, like that of Rivers, Hartigan (for most of the decade), Lester Johnson, Jan Müller, and Fairfield Porter, and also Alex Katz and Philip Pearlstein who would later innovate a new realism. It was this gestural or painterly or "unfinished" manner of painting in the vein of de Kooning, Hofmann, Kline, and Guston that distinguished the image of fifties art as a whole, constituting the period style as it were. And it is the role of gesture painting and the sculpture related to it that will provide the point of departure for this book.

# Notes

1. Among the first-generation Abstract Expressionists are James Brooks, Adolph Gottlieb, Philip Guston, Hans Hofmann, Franz Kline, Willem de Kooning, Robert Motherwell, Barnett Newman, Jackson Pollock, Ad Reinhardt, Mark Rothko, Clyfford Still, and Bradley Tomlin. For an extensive discussion of these artists, see Irving Sandler, *The Triumph of American Painting: A History of Abstract Expressionism* (New York: Harper & Row, 1976).

2. Questions have been raised as to whether Milton Resnick should be considered in the first or the second generation of the New York School. See Henry Hopkins, Introduction, *Milton Res-*

*nick: Selected Large Paintings*, exhibition catalogue (Fort Worth, Texas: Fort Worth Art Center, 1971), unpaginated. Born in 1917, he was older than most second-generation artists. Moreover, he was on the Federal Art Project of the WPA from 1938 to 1939 as were many in the first generation. However, from 1940 to 1948, he was away from New York, in the U.S. Army and after that he lived and worked in Paris. He therefore missed the germinal period of Abstract Expressionism. Furthermore, he did not have his first show in New York until 1955, later than most second-generation artists. During the fifties, critics such as Thomas B. Hess grouped Resnick with the younger artists, and I too will consider him in this context.

# THE NEW YORK SCHOOL

# 1

# The Milieu of the New York School in the Early Fifties

AROUND 1950, the first generation of the New York School attracted a small group of young artists who formed the early wave of the second generation. It was natural for these newcomers to be drawn to Abstract Expressionism, so struck were they by its expressive power, high quality, freshness or radicality, and aspiration. Moreover, the older artists' passionate and serious commitment to art, their perseverance, often in the face of great personal deprivation, their audacity in painting only what they needed to, each relying on himself or herself as the sole authority, impressed young artists, even striking many as heroic. Frank O'Hara, a poet-curator-critic, recalled: "Then there was great respect for anyone who did anything marvellous: when Larry [Rivers] introduced me to de Kooning I nearly got sick . . . besides there was then a sense of genius. Or what Kline used to call 'the dream.' "[1]

The New York School constituted a loose community which was primarily an open network based on personal relationships, more social than aesthetic in nature. John Ferren accurately defined it as "a state of friendship. Not necessarily love or agreement but, definitely, respect and the personal recognition of the other and yourself being involved in the same thing. That thing is conveniently labeled Abstract-Expressionism by the critics. It isn't quite so simple. If Abstract-Expressionism is the largest vortex, the antithesis, the rejections, the yet unmade developments are also there."[2] Ferren went on to say: " 'He should be in' " really meant " 'He is involved somewhere in the tensions and polarities of our thinking and, through his work, has made us see it.' "[3]

These polarities, as the early wave saw them, were in the realm of gesture or painterly or action painting, ranging from abstraction to representation. The artists who worked within these broad limits all believed themselves to be in the vanguard, for the style was both open to original developments and also the butt of considerable art-world and public hostility.

De Kooning and Hofmann, innovators of gestural Abstract Expressionism, interested the early wave most. Both were available to their juniors to a greater extent than such contemporaries as Pollock, Still, Rothko, and Newman, who by 1951 had largely removed themselves from the "downtown" art scene (south of Twenty-third Street in Manhattan). A newcomer could enroll in Hofmann's school on Eighth Street; meet de Kooning and other painters stylistically related to him, e.g., Kline, Jack Tworkov, and Esteban Vicente, almost any night at the Cedar Street Tavern or at the Wednesday and Friday meetings at the Club (organized by the first generation in 1949), or casually on East Tenth Street, in the center of the neighborhood where most New York School artists lived and worked at that time.

Moreover, both de Kooning and Hofmann were inspirational figures. With his first one-man show in 1948, de Kooning was established as a major Abstract Expressionist, second only to Pollock in reputation, and soon to be the most influential artist of his generation. De Kooning was admired for his integrity and dedication to art—qualities which were thought by many (including me) to be embodied in his painting. He was also a brilliant conversationalist, passionate and convincing in his insights into art and contemporary experience, his persuasiveness augmenting the impact of his pictures. Hofmann's painting was not regarded as highly as de Kooning's, but he was widely considered to be America's greatest art teacher.[4] As a man, he was robust and warm; enthusiastic, expansive, and assured; able to play a commanding paternal role and simultaneously to treat his students as colleagues. Furthermore, he possessed the impressive aura of history. Born in 1880, Hofmann had lived in Paris from 1904 to 1914—the heroic decade of twentieth-century art—had been a friend of the innovators of Fauvism and Cubism; had learned of their ideas at first hand, possibly even contributing some of his own; and as early as 1915, had opened his first school in Munich, which in the twenties began to attract American art students who would broadcast at home his abilities as a teacher.

There were sharp differences between the attitudes of Hofmann and de Kooning, Hofmann more systematic, basing his aesthetics on a belief in universal laws which governed nature and art, although he also affirmed the primacy of the artist's spiritual and intuitive feeling into both; de Kooning strongly anti-doctrinaire, rooting his painting in the immediacy of his experience here and now. Hofmann taught that painting at its highest should reveal spiritual reality, an aspiration that appealed to many of his students. His aesthetics were geared to the creation of suggested depth or space which, not being a tangible pictorial property, was transmaterial or spiritual.[5] De Kooning's complicated, restless and ambiguous, raw and violent painting appeared to be shaped by urban living—the total feeling of the city rather than its appearances—conveying his existential reaction to the world outside and inside the studio. Moreover, the gestures composing de Kooning's pictures were painted directly, implying "honesty"; their final aggregation seemed "found" in a forthright struggle of creation. His work struck young artists as unnervingly "real" and emotionally genuine—and this inspired emulation.

There was also the sense in de Kooning's work that he was perpetually taking "risks," that is, refusing to lapse comfortably into an habitual style, and instead, was venturing courageously beyond the already known, aspiring to paint something that could not be predicted and ultimately, to the unattainable. "Going for broke" as an ambition was powerfully appealing, as a recollection of Friedel Dzubas revealed, even though he was appalled at the psychic costs of de Kooning's effort. "I was aware to what degree he was torturing himself, really, in forever trying to create some sort of absolute answer, an absolute masterpiece. . . . I saw him in East Hampton starting something, and after the first week, people would sneak in to take a look. 'Beautiful,' they'd say, it looked absolutely right. And then over the next two months, day by day, whatever was right he would slowly destroy, out of this incredible pride."[6]

Despite their differences in outlook, de Kooning and Hofmann shared a number of basic conceptions of what a painting ought to be, the ideas of the one reinforcing those of the other in the minds of young artists. And these ideas presented challenging difficulties and opened up enormous opportunities for individual development. In brief, both older artists believed in the viability of subject matter, that is, recognizable images in pictorial depth; of Cubist-inspired relational design; and of masterly drawing and painting.

The two Abstract Expressionists insisted that to be modernist, art need not be abstract. Figuration offered a genuine option. Indeed, their paintings, even the most abstract, have a source in nature. Moreover, Hofmann demanded that his students begin with observable phenomena; the main activity in his classes was drawing from a live model or still life. De Kooning also made a strong case for subject matter, and naturally so, for he was painting his *Woman* series, which in itself was a strong stimulus to figurative art. The first of these canvases was acquired by the Museum of Modern Art and was one of the most reproduced pictures by a painter identified with Abstract Expressionism during the fifties. In a lecture at the museum in 1950 (published the following year), de Kooning ridiculed aesthetician-artists who made an issue of abstraction-versus-representation, and who wanted to "abstract" the art from art. In the past, art had

> . . . meant everything that was in it—not what you could take out of it. . . . For the painter to come to the "abstract" . . . he needed many things. These things were always things in life—a horse, a flower, a milkmaid, the light in a room through a window made of diamond shapes maybe, tables, chairs, and so forth. . . . But all of a sudden, in that famous turn of the century, a few people thought they could take the bull by the horns and invent an esthetic beforehand. . . . with the idea of freeing art, and . . . demanding that you should obey them. . . . The question, as they saw it, was not so much what you *could* paint but rather what you could *not* paint. You could *not* paint a house or a tree or a mountain. It was then that subject matter came into existence as something you ought *not* to have.[7]

De Kooning concluded that the non-objective aesthetician-artists, in trying to make "something" from the "abstract" or "nothing" quality that had always inhered in specific things, lost the aesthetic quality they sought to the exclusion of everything else.

1  Willem de Kooning, *Woman I,* 1950–52.
75⁷/₈″ x 58″. The Museum of Modern Art, New York.

Both de Kooning and Hofmann insisted that contemporary artists approach subject matter in a way different from past artists. For de Kooning, today's "reality" could only be apprehended in sudden "glimpses" all at once in a total experience, and this could not be achieved by painting the appearance of things. Hofmann taught: "There are bigger things to be seen in nature than the object."[8] Visual phenomena could not be copied dumbly by modernist artists. Nor could they continue to use academic conventions. The primary problem that Hofmann posed to his students was to translate the volumes and voids of what was seen in the world into planes of color, in accord with the two-dimensional character of the picture surface—a "modernist" approach. And then the crucial action was to structure these planes into "complexes," every component of which was to be reinvested with a sense of space—depth or volume—without sacrificing flatness. To achieve this simultaneous two- and three-dimensionality, Hofmann devised the technique of "push and pull"—an improvisational orchestration of areas of color, or as he liked to put it, an answering of force with counterforce. "The essence of my school: I insist all the time on depth. . . . No perspective [or modeling which violates two-dimensionality] but plastic depth."[9]

As Hofmann's former student, Allan Kaprow, summed it up, all paintings, despite their diversity,

> . . . submit to certain basic laws. Each picture is an organic whole whose parts are distinct but relate strictly to the larger unit. Since the painting surface, being flat, is only a metaphoric field for activity, its nature as a metaphor must be preserved. That is to say an exact balance had to be struck between the planar uniformity of the canvas and the organic (i.e. three-dimensional) nature of the event set into operation on it. This, we found out, was not easy at all . . . So this part-to-whole problem occupied the class continually and further broke down into the study of certain special particulars of all painting; color, that is, hue, tone, chroma, intensity, its advancing and receding properties, its expansiveness or contractiveness, its weight, temperature, and so forth; and in the area of so-called form, the way in which these act together in points, lines, planes, and volumes.[10]

And yet, despite Hofmann's concern with systematic picture-making, he warned against allowing preconceptions of any kind to govern creation. As he said in 1949: "At the time of making a picture, I want not to know what I'm doing; a picture should be made with feeling, not with knowing. The possibilities of the medium must be sensed."[11]

Like Hofmann, de Kooning painted in depth, for the human anatomy, which was the source of most of his imagery no matter how abstract, is bulky and exists in space. He refused to deny its volume, even though at the same time he insisted on maintaining the picture plane, his painterly brushstrokes asserting the physicality of the canvas which supported them. Moreoever, de Kooning scoffed at making flatness a modernist dogma, calling it old-fashioned. He said: "Nothing is that stable."[12]

Given Hofmann's emphasis on drawing with nature in mind, and the challenge of de Kooning's *Woman* series, it is not surprising that many artists in the early wave

2 Hans Hofmann, *Fantasia in Blue*, 1954.
60″ x 52″. Whitney Museum of American Art, New York.

adopted figuration, and even took the step to a more explicit representation. But they also heeded the lessons of modernist art learned from the paintings of the Abstract Expressionists and of older masters, e.g., Matisse, Bonnard, and particularly Picasso, Braque, and other Cubists.

Cubism was the modern movement that appealed most to Hofmann and de Kooning. Hofmann treated it as a kind of basic grammar of modern art.[13] De Kooning admired its stress on firm design and its poetic qualities. His work generally is based on a Cubist infrastructure, but at the same time it is radically different from the earlier style in that it is more dynamic, ambiguous, and painterly, calling to mind Expressionist facture, e.g., that of Soutine. Furthermore, de Kooning drew with a paint-loaded, meaty brush, which enabled him to render the bulk of the human anatomy in a convincing manner, rarely, if ever, achieved by Picasso, Braque, and their contemporaries, either in the open scaffolds of the Analytic phase or the planar diagramming of the Synthetic period. Hofmann's painting was also founded on a stable quasi-geometry deriving from Synthetic Cubism, but he tried to synthesize this with Fauve brushwork and explosive color, thereby transmuting Cubist design. That is, Hofmann arrived at his composition primarily through the interaction of color, by pitting planes of color against each other to create a sense of volume, of "plastic" color. This approach had its source in the art of Cézanne and the Fauve Matisse (always exemplars to Hofmann). It must be pointed out

3   Hans Hofmann, *Magenta and Blue,* 1950.
48″ x 58″. Whitney Museum of American Art, New York.

that a "push-and-pull" forming with color is the opposite of filling in linear diagrams with color, producing a bright Cubism, as Kaprow termed it, in which color is subordinate to drawing.[14]

Hofmann insisted on painterliness, on totally activating the picture plane, as Clement Greenberg remarked, addressing it "as a responsive rather than inert object, and painting itself as an affair of prodding and pushing, scoring and marking, rather than simply inscribing or covering. . . . His paint surfaces *breathe* . . . And it is thanks in part to Hofmann that the 'new' American painting in general is distinguished by a new liveliness of surface."[15]

And yet, Hofmann's instruction was focused on drawing. Indeed, Carl Holty recalled that for a time in the middle twenties, Hofmann "was so engrossed with the beauties of drawing . . . that he went so far as to remark on one occasion 'that once we had gotten into the whole world of drawing, we wouldn't even want to paint for a long time.' "[16] Kaprow, a student in the late forties, wrote: "Drawing was to painting as nature in the long run was to Art, a preparation and the source."[17] De Kooning, too, the painterly and coloristic quality of his line notwithstanding, was primarily a draftsman in the lineage of the Cubists and of their classical predecessors who depicted the human image.

It is noteworthy that de Kooning's drawing occasionally quotes Rembrandt and Rubens, signifying his regard for the master draftsmen of the past. Hofmann believed that his aesthetic principles had been followed, whether consciously or not, by all great artists, and he illustrated that in class by analyzing reproductions of old and modern masterworks, thus immersing his students in the stream of Western art, opening up all of it for potential cultivation—and, as important, using it as the model of standards of quality.

Indeed, both Hofmann and de Kooning encouraged "good" or professional drawing and painting, although paradoxically, they valued spontaneity or direct expression and mistrusted calculation and artifice. Thomas Hess wrote that Hofmann "convinces his pupils . . . [that] there is such a thing as the Good Painting; a novice's efforts should aspire to it. . . . In the best meaning of the term, the Hofmann School is an Academy—a temple in which mysteries and standards are preserved."[18]

The regard for professionalism and the consciousness of history both point to a deep-grained traditionalism in the artistic outlook of de Kooning and Hofmann, a traditionalism that was also manifest in their painting, revealing as it did references to nature and to Cubist structure, shallow depth, and apparent painterliness. Indeed, the two artists believed themselves to be the heirs of modern European art, and it is significant that both were born and educated in Europe. This attitude set them apart in the minds of young artists from Pollock, Still, Newman, Reinhardt, and to a lesser degree, Rothko, who were considered anti-traditional. Still and Newman even claimed to repudiate Western culture and spoke of their painting as American, infused with the spirit of the New World.

De Kooning ridiculed what he considered their vanguardist and chauvinistic stance

as eating John Brown's body. He said: "They stand all alone in the wilderness—breast
bared. This is an American idea. I am a foreigner, after all. I am different from them
because . . . I feel myself more in tradition. I have this point of reference that I have to
do something about. But I am also interested in my environment. I change the past. I
don't paint with ideas of art in mind. I see something that excites me. It becomes part of
my content."[19]

It was precisely de Kooning's striving to assess past achievements from the vantage
point of his present, of the immediacy of his urban life-style, that inspired the artists of
the early wave, for his experience approximated theirs. He provided them with a pictorial model of seeing what most felt but could not articulate, a model which organized
while it stretched thinking, feeling, and experiencing. Also stimulating was the inclu-
siveness of his painting, its openness to manifold possibilities and extensions. Indeed,

4  Willem de Kooning, *Gotham News,* 1955.
69″ x 79″. Albright–Knox Art Gallery, Buffalo, New York.

de Kooning welcomed complexity; he wrote in 1950: "I'm not interested in 'abstracting' or taking things out or reducing painting . . . I paint this way because I can keep putting more and more things in it—drama, anger, pain, love, a figure, a horse, my ideas about space."[20]

To achieve complexity, de Kooning employed a variety of pictorial approaches and devices. The difficulty of synthesizing multireferential ideas challenged young artists. Furthermore, his virtuosity in resolving the welter of pictorial problems impressed them, particularly because his extraordinary skills were not used to convey expected things. Indeed, de Kooning's direct painting was so unconventional or new, so unvarnished to the point of rawness that it appeared to deny what was commonly thought to be "good" painting, the prime example of which was the abstraction of such leading Parisian artists as Jean Bazaine and Alfred Manessier. Both de Kooning's ties to the great tradition of the School of Paris and his denial of the enervated and contrived, refined and "finished" looking "taste" of his French contemporaries appealed to the early wave, at once traditional and avant-garde minded—and proud of the attainment of its elders.

Like de Kooning, Hofmann referred constantly to past art. His ambition for more than two decades was to arrive at grand syntheses of Cubism and Fauvism while em-

5   Mark Rothko, *Four Darks in Red,* 1958.
102″ x 116″. Whitney Museum of American Art, New York.

ploying the novel and "risky" method of gesture painting. His pictures were also open to new experiences. This can be seen in the variety of styles in which he worked simultaneously. To sum up, the traditionalism of de Kooning and Hofmann, as their admirers saw it, was not academic, for the two artists introduced original and radical approaches and insights into life and art that transformed received ideas. Newness for its own sake or for the sake of shock was not the intention. Rather, it emerged from being true to their own felt experience in the process of painting. Honesty was prized above novelty.

Compared to the gesture paintings of de Kooning and Hofmann, the allover "drip" canvases of Pollock, the extremely abstract, flat, open color-field paintings of Still, Rothko, and particularly Newman, and the reductionist, purist abstractions of Reinhardt appeared unprecedented—so revolutionary that all links to the past seemed severed. But such radicality was only partly in their favor. To be sure, they were admired (often somewhat condescendingly) for their audacity, but they were thought to offer little promise for development. That is, they struck the early wave as too "narrow," "exclusive" rather than "inclusive," too "cerebral" and "vanguardist."

The early wave believed that the primary aim of a Newman or a Reinhardt was to make the "next" move in art, in the process, denying all other options, particularly traditional ones. In contrast, the pictures of de Kooning and Hofmann were thought to open up rather than close off possibilities. They provided the choices of painting representationally and/or abstractly; in depth and/or flatly; Cubist-inspired relational design and/or Impressionist-inspired non-relational fields; with reference to past art and/or in reaction against it. Indeed, the early wave conceived of their enterprise much as de Kooning wrote of Cubism's: "It didn't want to get rid of what went before. Instead it added something to it."[21]

Not only was gesture painting capable of new formal extension, but it also appeared to relate to the complex, changeable texture of an artist's own experience, his humanity. Non-gestural art, on the other hand, was viewed as simplistic and excessively "idea" bound. Indeed, the work of de Kooning and Hofmann looks back to and proceeds from the humanist tradition in its cultivation of masterliness; its retention of figuration and three-dimensionality. Certainly, abstraction was to be accepted, and the "box" associated with Renaissance painting was to be flattened and thus rendered modern, but the picture plane was also to be made *cubic*. It was in this cubic quality, this illusion of mass and space, suggestive of visual reality, that the humanist tradition—or what could be saved of it—was perpetuated.

Perhaps the strongest attraction of gesture painting for the early wave was its painterliness, at once a metaphor for human action and an indicator of quality, whether high or low. The signs of painterly articulation were more or less suppressed in the abstractions of Newman, Reinhardt, Rothko, and Still, and this made them unappealing. So did the seeming lack of design. In comparison to gesture painting, Still's abstraction looked "unformed." As Raymond Parker recalled, "those very large ragged areas seemed intentionally to be *not* drawn . . . There was no line. No gesture except the repeated trowelling of the color and the edges were just the result of that paint appli-

6 Clyfford Still, *1950-A, No. 2,* 1950.
109" x 93". Hirshhorn Museum and Sculpture
Garden, Smithsonian Institution, Washington, D.C.

7 Barnett Newman, *Covenant,* 1949.
48" x 60". Hirshhorn Museum and Sculpture
Garden, Smithsonian Institution, Washington, D.C.

cation, . . . It was a rejection of the kind of drawing which is implicit in the painting of Bill (de Kooning), say, or Franz (Kline) . . . None of the opposition of form, you know, that one used to expect in those days."[22]

Exemplifying the general lack of sympathy to non-gestural painting were the reviews of Newman's exhibitions in 1950 and 1951 written by Hess in *Art News*. In the first, Hess remarked: "Barnett Newman . . . one of Greenwich Village's best known homespun aestheticians, recently presented some of the products of his meditations . . . Newman is out to shock, but he is not out to shock the bourgeoisie—that has been done. He likes to shock other artists."[23] In the second review, Hess wrote that Newman "again wins his race with the avant-garde, literally breaking the tape." Dubbing him a "genial theoretician," Hess went on to say that Newman presented "ideas," implying that they were not really paintings.[24]

Some twenty years later, Hess justified his misunderstanding of Newman's work, recalling that as a young critic, he was associated through friendship more with the downtown bohemian group (close to de Kooning) than with the uptown intellectual circle. "I read the pictures as didactic attacks on established esthetics plus a demonstration to the New York painters on how far art was permitted to go. As a strong believer in the 'ethical' commitment of the artist, I did not think that a painter was 'permitted' to go anywhere. Rather, he was stuck with his 'truth.' . . . I would be more ashamed of this lapse of taste, except that everyone else had it, too."[25] And most did, so much so that in 1952, Greenberg came to the concusion that any artist as widely disparaged as Newman could not be all bad.[26]

Newman was the chief whipping boy, but the abuse leveled at him reflected a general attitude toward Still and Rothko as well. Those who shared de Kooning's point of view simply did not take color-field abstraction seriously. When they dealt with it at all, they mistook it for an exercise in aesthetics rather than, as Newman, Still, and Rothko believed, as an embodiment of transcendental experience, an incantation to the sublime. But aside from the issue of content, there was little understanding of the formal attributes of color-field painting, probably because its departures from the main traditions of Western art were so extreme.

It was not until 1955 that the premises of color-field painting were first fully presented, in an important article by Greenberg entitled " 'American-Type' Painting."[27] Greenberg related the work of Still, Rothko, and Newman to that of the late Monet and counterposed this Impressionist tendency to that of Cézanne and the Cubists, whom he considered the progenitors of de Kooning and Hofmann. Notwithstanding the publication of Greenberg's article, it still took some three or four years for Newman to be dealt with seriously by more than a handful of advanced artists. Still and Rothko fared somewhat better.

The abstractions of Reinhardt, a participant in both the uptown and downtown art scenes, were ridiculed almost as much as Newman's, but more to the point, for they were about purist aesthetics—what art ought to be—and the abuse was softened by a grudging esteem for his obvious abilities as a painter.[28] Skill was necessary since Rein-

8  Ad Reinhardt, *Number 87, 1957.*
72″ x 40″. The Museum of Modern Art, New York.

9  Jackson Pollock, *Number 27, 1950,* 1950.
49″ x 106″. Whitney Museum of American Art, New York.

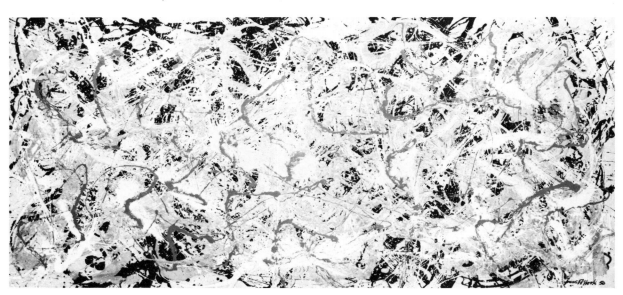

hardt had to realize his pure idea through the impure means of painting, calling the viewer's attention to his finesse.

Pollock was a special case. His reputation, indeed notoriety, was greater than that of any other Abstract Expressionist. For the second generation, he was a symbol of liberation and independence and an exemplar of the passionate commitment an artist ought to have. Yet the early wave did not believe that his style could be followed without yielding counterfeit Pollocks. (Nonetheless, many young artists were influenced by him, although only a few, such as Frankenthaler, Dzubas, and Paul Jenkins, acknowledged it.) Jane Freilicher summed up Pollock's role as the guide to freedom, asserting that "his achievement brought a glamor and authority to American painting which inspired younger painters . . . If you could bring it off, 'make it work,' it might be possible to do anything." [29]

Many artists of the early wave visited Pollock at his home in East Hampton, Long Island. Although he was of a taciturn temperament, he made an enormous impact on them. As Robert Goodnough described it in 1951:

> To enter Pollock's studio is to enter another world, a place where the intensity of the artist's mind and feelings are given full play. . . . At one end of the barn the floor is literally covered with large cans of enamel, aluminum and tube colors—the boards that do show are covered with paint drippings. Nearby a skull rests on a chest of drawers. Three or four cans contain stubby paint brushes of various sizes. About the rest of the studio, on the floor and walls, are paintings in various stages of completion, many of enormous proportions. Here Pollock often sits for hours in deep contemplation of work in progress, his face forming rigid lines and often settling into a heavy frown. A Pollock painting is not born easily, but comes into being after weeks, often months of work and thought. At times he paints with feverish activity, or again with slow deliberation. [30]

But Pollock's personality had another side which alienated young artists, a side that he exhibited increasingly after 1952, when he resumed drinking heavily. On his trips to New York he invariably visited the Cedar Street Tavern, got drunk, and was often violent. Pollock's abusiveness affected the attitude of fellow artists toward his painting. Rivers recalled: "What I had seen in his work as depth of involvement . . . [by 1954] seemed narrowed simply to his point of view. My devotion to Art and a life of Art had taken on a distinctly anti-Pollock tone. What was obviously gorgeous in his work was becoming infused with a mindlessness impossible to separate from his social personality." [31]

Rivers's opinion of Pollock was also affected by a rift in the Abstract Expressionist movement, the emergence of two camps, one centered on Pollock, the other on de Kooning—so it seemed at the time. John B. Myers recalled that you had to choose. [32] In retrospect, it appears that there was only a de Kooning coterie; those who did not wish to be in it or were not welcome tended to favor Pollock or Still. [33] Myers also remarked that de Kooning and Pollock represented the opposing poles; the differences were personal and aesthetic. De Kooning represented the broad view, and Pollock, the narrow. De Kooning stood for tradition, and Pollock for modernity. De Kooning would say: I feel very close to Ingres and Tintoretto, and Pollock would say: I am nature.[34] Pollock would denigrate de Kooning as a Renaissance painter, and de Kooning, equally derogatory, would imply that Pollock had only a process and was not much of a painter. (It should be noted that this rivalry stemmed in part from the mixture of respect and envy that the two artists felt for each other's work.[35])

Because de Kooning was the charismatic figure in the downtown art scene, he and other tradition-oriented, painterly painters in his circle exerted strong pressures on the early wave. But in all probability, young artists appreciated de Kooning more than the other founders of Abstract Expressionism because of dispositions and needs which were different from those of the older artists. The newcomers were the *inheritors*, not the *initiators*, of a revolution, and a successful one at that, and they thought of themselves as a second generation (although it was not always clear who came first or second).

The task of the fifties, as many young artists (and a significant number of their elders) saw it, was to extend the gesture painting of the first generation—toward figuration, for example—while consolidating it, by striving more consciously for aesthetic quality (although there was little agreement on criteria for judgment). Or, to state the aim more modestly perhaps: if you could not be first, then you could still be "good," or professional. As Joseph Stefanelli summed it up in 1956: "Young painters are no longer concerned with newness. . . . Now painting and painting alone counts. . . . Technical carelessness and aesthetic adventures are over. . . . Now we must consolidate."[36]

What had been "the unknown" to the innovators was becoming "the known" to the inheritors who followed aesthetically as well as chronologically. Growing familiarity gave rise to changed ways of seeing. For example, a young painter in 1954 might employ "drips" to create a personal, felt style. But his accidental effects could not appear as radical, full of risk, original, liberating, or even as passionate, as they had some half-dozen years earlier. Other values were naturally brought into consideration: sensuousness, perhaps, or elegance, or proficiency.

The innovators of Abstract Expressionism did not entertain the possibility of consolidation; in this respect, their outlook was in marked contrast to that of their followers. Accountable in part for the differences was the fact that the newcomers regarded their elders as heroes to be emulated and not, as the first generation had regarded the leaders of the School of Paris, as masters to be gotten around or past. Moreover, the early-wave's heroes lived in New York and were available, and not, as formerly, inaccessible across an ocean in Paris. Indeed, few young artists felt the need to go to Paris or even to follow closely current art there, so indifferent had they become to what had been the center of world art, although their interest in the French old masters of modernism remained as strong as ever. The second generation was caught up in the triumph of American painting, and there was a touch of nationalism in its pride.

The differences in the outlooks of the two generations may have resulted in part from the different social, psychological, and material conditions that shaped their formative years. It had taken more than a decade for the pioneers of Abstract Expressionism, in the face of intense art-world and public hostility, to break through the barriers of provincialism; to situate themselves within the mainstream of international art; and finally to attain confidence in their achievements. The early wave was nursed on that accomplishment and was instantly self-confident. It had entered an established art scene that it knew to be the center of global art and a loosely organized community in the life of which it could participate, find support, comfort, and the like. In addition, the first generation smoothed the way to success for the second, providing it with a small but growing, sympathetic audience, including influential critics, museum curators, gallery owners, and collectors. Young artists were almost immediately given shows which were reviewed—or at the very least, taken seriously by the art-conscious public as a whole. The public at large remained hostile to the New York School, but that was becoming more gratifying than threatening since it certified avant-garde status.

For the older artists and generally for the newcomers, public recognition in the forms of museum shows, coverage in the art and mass media, or sales of art was not as important as the opinion of fellow artists. In time, recognition of the New York School by the outside world was increasingly forthcoming—for both generations at roughly the same time. The situation had changed because of the growing aesthetic sophistication and affluence of ever-larger segments of the public willing and able to buy art, and the consequent burgeoning of the art market. A good indicator of growing public acceptance was the increase in the sale of art. *Fortune* magazine reported in 1955 that the "art market is boiling with an activity never known before," and predicted that this market would not only grow but would turn increasingly to modern and contemporary art. "Against the rising demand for art, the available floating supply of Great Art is an ever shrinking quantity." The magazine then listed "speculative or 'growth' painters," among them de Kooning, Pollock, Baziotes, Motherwell, Still, Reinhardt, and Kline, and younger artists, Rivers and John Hultberg.[37]

Financial success became a possibility for New York School artists, but whereas it came late in life to the first generation, it came relatively early in the careers of many of the second. In fact, for the older artists, monetary rewards were not only virtually non-existent but were thought to be in the realm of fantasy, unobtainable in the future as well as in the present. This difference in potential expectations is probably of little significance. However, those who pursue a career in art when few or no worldly rewards are to be gained, either monetarily, or in power and prestige, are less likely to experience any pressure, even inadvertently, from those in a position to confer rewards, and more likely are self-motivated to create art for its own sake, excitement, and satisfaction. With little to lose, they may dare to risk more—and this seemed to be the case with the first generation for it was more venturesome than the second.

Moreover, the newcomers while still young found security in teaching jobs, just beginning to open up in considerable numbers, and in the GI Bill (a law which provided educational subsidies for veterans of World War II)—the kind of security that their elders did not obtain until late in life, and often, never. The GI Bill may have given rise to another difference in generational attitudes. Required to attend school to collect stipends, a proportionately greater number of young artists than their elders received a systematic, formal education, often at colleges and universities—this perhaps helping to inculcate them with traditional and professional values.

The changing social situation in America was also responsible in part for differences in point of view between the two generations. The thirties, when the older Abstract Expressionists began their careers, were very unlike the late forties and fifties, during which the early wave matured. The thirties was the decade of the Great Depression at home and a series of calamitous events internationally that led to World War II. The social urgencies of the time pressured artists to adopt Social Realist and Regionalist styles, but even the relatively few artists who ventured into abstraction tended to claim a social relevance for their painting and sculpture. Art-for-art's-sake and art-for-pleasure's-sake were spurned. During the war, modernist artists began to think of their art as being in crisis. Given the terrible social situation, they asked: What can one paint? Can there be art at all? A number of Abstract Expressionists sought to transcend the crisis, first by turning for inspiration to primitive art and mythology; then by striving for a visionary art of the sublime. Others, influenced by Existentialism (introduced into America from France at the end of the war), asserted that in a catastrophic world only the struggle for self-creation was of value. The artist was transformed into a victim-hero.

During the fifties, the social situation, dominated by prosperity at home and cold (rather than hot) war abroad, exerted different kinds of social and political pressures on artists. They still felt alienated, but the sense of crisis so diminished that they could avoid being caught up in it, and most retreated from politics and turned inward, each on himself—his own needs, feelings, experiences; his art and its traditions; and collectively, on his colleagues, forming a community of artists. In fact, history-minded art consciousness and psychiatry replaced social consciousness as major interests after World War II. Proof of this change was the almost total absence of political discussions at the Club.

Art was still thought to possess an ethical content, but, as Schapiro remarked, it was based on a "concern with self-development and the evolution of art. This belief in a common historical role, dramatized by the opposition of a static, conservative art, gave the artists a solidarity and collective faith, a creative morale, that sustained them at a time when they were most cut off from the public and institutional life."[38]

Later in the fifties, Schapiro justified a disengagement of artists from social action. "If the painter cannot celebrate many current values, it may be that these values are not worth celebrating. In the absence of ideal values stimulating to his imagination, the artist must cultivate his own garden as the only secure field in the violence and uncertainties of our time. . . . maintaining his loyalty to the value of art—to responsible creative work, the search for perfection, the sensitiveness to quality."[39] As artists in the fifties withdrew from social involvement, they withdrew from the pressures that prompted the existential expression of "crisis content." As *angst* lessened, artists felt freer to give rein to hedonistic and aestheticist impulses.

Hess pointed to this shift in sensibility in 1954, in a review of a large show organized by artists of the New York School and dubbed the Stable Annual. He noted the general "absence of shock values and violence," and the predominance of professionalism and of "impulses toward elegance and the civil elaboration of possibilities."[40] In a later article, Hess affirmed his assessment of early-wave art, stressing the cultivation of references "understood by friends, and in such an intimate dialogue it is rude to appear overreaching, explicit or anxious. Manners are deliberately cultivated, irony and parody are the permitted vents for explosions of exasperation."[41] John Ferren came to a similar conclusion in his review of the Stable Annual in 1955: "This is a family affair, . . . We are rebellious at times, heedful of the wisdom of our elders when it suits our needs, loving at times to the point of plagiarism, and sometimes slightly incestuous."[42]

The creation of a "family art" by artists who felt the need to organize themselves into a kind of community can be viewed in a larger social context as a reaction against the social climate in America during the fifties. This in part may have prompted artists to undertake an interior immigration, turning in on themselves and their colleagues, on their art and, to a degree, on the entirety of art through the ages, the "museum without walls" becoming an alternate world to the one outside. Artists were contemptuous of what they believed American society and its dominant culture had become after World War II (and very much as a result of the war), that is, a mixed welfare and garrison state in which a huge new middle class was achieving the American dream of affluence and, in the process, was embracing conservative, corporate, and suburban values with so little critical questioning that the nation seemed to be in the throes of a massive social conformity.

As the standard of living rose, the quality of the life of the spirit was thought to decline. The ever-greater numbers of "average" Americans, who in their work seemed to have become cogs in vast bureaucracies, in their leisure seemed to have become passive consumers of pseudo-culture packaged by corporations indifferent to human and aesthetic values. A proliferating vulgar and shallow mass culture was being manufactured for a mass audience as an aid to the primary business of huckstering mass-produced commodities. This reading of American society in general was confirmed by respected scholars: social scientists, psychologists, philosophers, for example, David Riesman, with Nathan Glazer and Reuel Denney in *The Lonely Crowd*; C. Wright Mills in *White Collar: The American Middle Class*; and William H. Whyte, Jr., in *The Organization Man*.[43]

Artists alienated from society had in the past turned to leftist causes—even creating art on their behalf—but that no longer seemed an attractive enterprise. During the thirties, many had gravitated to the Communist Party, joining or becoming fellow travelers. Most left in disgust when it became clear that Communism had degenerated into Stalinism, and their repugnance did not diminish even when the Soviet image improved during World War II.

After the war, artists of the New York School increasingly lost interest in politics, but fellow intellectuals, mainly of a literary bent, who remained "engaged," came to believe that the Soviet Union was intent on world domination, proofs of which were the fall of China and the invasion of South Korea by the Communist North. Moreover, the enemy possessed the technology to make the Bomb and Sputnik (ahead of us)—a shocking and fearful prospect. International affairs were thought to be so urgent as to eclipse the deficiencies in American society and its mass culture. Indeed, there seemed to be only two choices: democratic capitalism, whose world champion was the United States, and Stalinist totalitarianism. In the face of this apparent either/or alternative, only a "politics of necessity" was deemed feasible. What remained of the revolutionary and utopian thinking of the thirties was dismissed as futile and no longer realistic in an era of cold war. Besides, it seemed to many ex-radicals that the American Way was achieving the goals they had striven for—the abolition of poverty and inequality. The crusade for freedom had its dark side, a paranoid anti-Communism—manifest in Senator Joseph McCarthy's Congressional hearings or Representative George Dondero's linking of modern art with Communism—that generated a mood of repression, suspicion, and fear, aggravating the pervasive social conformity.

Nonetheless, the acceptance of American foreign policy by hitherto dissident intellectuals prompted many to call for a rapprochement with Middle America, even extolling its stability, propriety and other bourgeois values. This was the theme of a widely publicized symposium entitled "Our Country and Our Culture," published in *Partisan Review* in 1952. Its editors and most of the contributing writers and literary critics noted that a large number of intellectuals had come to recognize in American democracy intrinsic, positive values, "not merely a capitalist myth but a reality which must be defended against Russian totalitarianism. . . . [They] no longer accept alienation as the artist's fate in America; on the contrary, they want very much to be a part of American life."[44] Not only had intellectuals "ceased to think of themselves as rebels and exiles," but many proclaimed that American culture had come of age. However, the participants in *Partisan Review*'s symposium did not indicate how or why this was so; paradoxically, they claimed to be confounded by the enormous growth of mass culture, the primary cause of alienation, which makes the artist "feel that he is still outside looking in."[45]

Much as the artists of the New York School were opposed to Communism, waging the cold war did not inspire any enthusiasm. Foreign affairs were much too abstract; as artists, they were far more concerned with the texture of their immediate experience. This caused them to find incredible any motion of accommodation with Middle America—on its terms. Indeed, artists who passionately prized individuality, self-realization, and artistic freedom, and who insisted on accepting only those standards they each devised, saw Middle America's conformist values—and the mass culture that they spawned—as totally repugnant.[46] Moreover, the New York School could not conceive of a rapprochement with Middle America in the face of its intense hostility to modernist culture, exemplified by the suppression of exhibitions and public commissions of so-called unintelligible art by philistine governmental and "patriotic" agencies in the cause of anti-Communism.[47]

And yet, vanguard artists were of a mixed mind. Beneath the resentment, there lurked the hope that Middle American taste was redeemable, that in time an ever-larger public would recognize their contribution, and even more, would see that the values embodied in their art could transform society. Against the values (or absence of them) of the conformist and despirited organization man and his depersonalized, hackneyed pseudo-culture, the advanced artist offered the values of individualism and self-discovery, freedom of belief and action, and autonomous, honest creation. Art could function, in Lewis Mumford's words, "to engender creativity in the observer and participant, releasing him from habit and routine, deepening his feelings and emotions, focusing more sharply his perceptions, clarifying his inner nature, bringing into existence a meaningful unity out of what seemed in the act of living a contradictory or a bafflingly incomplete experience, lacking in value and significance."[48]

But artists would not provoke social change by taking an active role in public life; quite the contrary, they would refuse to join—welcome alienation for the privacy and freedom it guaranteed—in order to concentrate on their own art, cultivate their own gardens, as Schapiro said they should.[49] By inference, the artists' lives would become models of social behavior. As Schapiro wrote, in his consciousness of the personal and the spontaneous, and in his commitment to creation and excellence, "the artist is one of the most moral and idealistic of beings, although his influence on practical affairs may seem very small. Painting by its impressive example of inner freedom and inventiveness and by its fidelity to artistic goals . . . helps to maintain the critical spirit and the ideals of creativeness, sincerity and self-reliance, which are indispensable to the life of our culture."[50]

Artists believed that their ethical obligations to a future, better American society were to preserve, each "in his life but above all in his art, these 'true' values on which society (hopefully temporarily) had turned its back."[51] It is noteworthy that artists believed that their experimental, subjective art could be socially beneficial; their reasoning was that American society in the fifties had become so atrophied that it might have to look for other than the dominant norms to revitalize it, and they were to be found in its artists' subculture. But the general public did not look for social guidance to its artists, and although the New York School's audience grew as the fifties progressed, it did not reach mass proportions. Future yearning did not overcome existing reality, and the mood of many artists was one of alienation. However, there was another cause of estrangement that was not at all idealistic, but had to do with lack of worldly success. Many artists yearned for the "good life" as avidly as any Middle American. Their malaise was aggravated by the fact that a growing number of their colleagues were beginning to sell their works. In the end, it was surprising how readily alienated artists could become "men of the world."[52]

Aside from fellow artists, the most enthusiastic supporters of the New York School were among the avant-gardes in the other arts: for example, Edgard Varèse, Stefan Wolpe, Virgil Thomson, John Cage, Morton Feldman, Lucia Dlugoszewski, and David Amram in music; Merce Cunningham, Merle Marsicano, Erik Hawkins, and Midi Garth in dance; in literature, Frank O'Hara, John Ashbery, Kenneth Koch, James Schuyler, Barbara Guest, and others who were so close to the artists that they came to be called the New York School of poets; Charles Olson, Robert Creeley, and Joel Oppenheimer, associated with Black Mountain College; and somewhat later in time, the Beat writers, Jack Kerouac, Allen Ginsberg, and Gregory Corso.[53]

It was natural for vanguard artists in every field to gravitate to the world of the New York School because the painters and sculptors were geographically concentrated and sufficiently organized to provide a potential audience. This they did, for they were open to fresh ideas in a way that the milieus for literature, music and dance of the time, dominated as they were by academic bores, were not. The art world also generated social and intellectual energies that made being in it exciting; poets, composers, and dancers often entered into artists' perpetual dialogues, drawing sustenance for their own enterprises, and often contributing significantly to the artists' thinking, particularly Cage, whose ideas will be discussed in full subsequently, and O'Hara, Ashbery, Guest, and Schuyler, all of whom wrote art criticism.

Dissident visual artists, poets, composers, and dancers sought each other out because all were repelled by cliché-ridden culture, by what Edmund Wilson called the "classics and commercials."[54] But of greater significance, they shared certain basic attitudes, summarized by Martin Duberman: "The determination to break the hold of previously accepted models in behavior and art, the outcry against penury and politesse—and the attendant *épatez*-frenzy—. . . There was a search on simultaneous fronts for the personal voice, for the immediate impulse and its energy, for the recognition of (even surrender to) process, to the elements of randomness, whimsy, play, self-sabotage. Those elements are hardly new in the arts, but had recently gone either unrecognized or been dismissed as peripheral."[55]

For example, avant-garde artists and writers shared a concern with the *process* of writing—a kind of conversing in the first person that aimed to reveal directly, naturally, and honestly an autobiographical content. They tried to ignore preconceived notions of what poetic form and content ought to be (meaning what it had been) in order to convey the sense of their immediate, individual life experience—at the risk of self-indulgence.

This is clear from the following remarks, selected from among many similar ones. Creeley recalled that in 1950 Olson "gave me access at last to that which I had so hungered to have, a way of thinking of the *process* of writing that made both the thing said and the way of saying it an integral event."[56] Creeley went on to say "that a number of American painters had already made the shift I was myself so anxious to accomplish, that they had, in fact, already begun to move . . . to a manifest directly of the *energy* inherent in the materials, literally, and their physical manipulation in the act of painting itself. *Process*, . . . was clearly much on their minds."[57] The painters in person were often as appealing as their pictures. Creeley remarked:

> Possibly the attraction the artists had for people like myself—think of O'Hara, Ashbery, Koch, Duncan, McClure, Ginsberg; or Kerouac's wistful claim that he could probably paint better than Kline—has to do with that lovely, usefully uncluttered directness of perception and act we found in so many of them. I sat for hours on end listening to Franz Kline in the Cedar Bar, fascinated by literally all

that he had to say. . . . Kline could locate the most articulate senses of human reality in seemingly casual conversation. . . .

It may also have been simply the *energy* these people generated, . . . The subtlety with which they qualified the possibility of *gesture* was dazzling. So Michael McClure speaks of having "totally bought Abstract Expressionism as spiritual autobiography."[58]

Black Mountain poets were influenced by Olson's theory of projective or open verse, published in 1950. Olson wrote that if poetry was to advance, it had to be based on the breathing of the writer while composing. As his student, Joel Oppenheimer said, a poem should have the writer's breath in it—much as a painting should have the artist's idiosyncratic gesture in it. It "should read on the page as if Joel Oppenheimer were reading it to you, or Charles Olson were reading it to you."[59] Olson also conceived of a poem as an open field of energy which at all points discharged energy—a conception of field composition that called to mind Pollock's "drip" painting. Olson taught that "FORM IS NEVER MORE THAN AN EXTENSION OF CONTENT," that "ONE PERCEPTION MUST IMMEDIATELY AND DIRECTLY LEAD TO A FURTHER PERCEPTION," that the poet must write spontaneously and swiftly, "keep it moving as fast as you can, . . . USE USE USE the process at all points, in any given poem always."[60]

O'Hara's contribution to poetry was characterized by Peter Schjeldahl as "a form of uncommon common speech, urbane and at the same time passionately attached to the everyday . . . He seems to have had that most dubious and enchanting of gifts, the ability to romanticize reality, for oneself and others, as it is happening."[61] O'Hara himself was so intent on poetry as confessional conversation that he imagined another person to whom it was addressed, a kind of one-to-one communication, or better still, communion. In 1959, he announced this as the basis of a movement he called Personism.[62]

Kerouac embraced an aesthetic of spontaneity in order to express, as he said, "the way the consciousness *really* digs everything that happens."[63] In 1951, he originated a new method of improvisational writing which he called "sketching," during which he tried to confess his thoughts about his experiences in his own unique voice. And to him that meant writing impulsively, ecstatically, without self-conscious revision in ordinary (American) speech. Like Olson, Kerouac believed that his inner stream of experience would find its form in the rhythm and measure of his breath. This was the method of his exemplar, the jazz musician, "in the sense of a, say, a tenor man drawing a breath and blowing a phrase on his saxophone, till he runs out of breath, and when he does, his sentence, his statement's been made . . . that's how I therefore separate my sentences, as breath separations of the mind . . . Then there's the raciness and freedom and humor of jazz instead of all that dreary analysis."[64]

Kerouac collaborated with second-generation artists in one venture. He improvised and narrated the screenplay for the film *Pull My Daisy* (1959), whose working title was *The Beat Generation*. It was produced and directed by Leslie and photographer Robert

Frank with music by Amram. The cast, including Rivers, Ginsberg, Corso, Richard Bellamy, Alice Neel, and others in the circle of the New York School, enacted a zany confrontation of Beatniks (playing themselves) and Middle America personified by a white-suited bishop, his mother, and sister.

Influenced by Kerouac, Ginsberg wrote in an article titled, "when the mode of the music changes the walls of the city shake": "Trouble with conventional form (fixed line count & stanza form) is, it's too symmetrical, geometrical, numbered and pre-fixed—unlike to my own mind which has no beginning and end, nor fixed measure of thought (or speech—or writing) other than its own cornerless mystery—to transcribe the latter in a form most nearly representing its actual 'occurrence' is my 'method.' "[65] This urge to personal discovery which he considered poetry's primary value led him to free his mind of arbitrary, preconceived patterns "unless discovered in the moment of composition."[66] Ginsberg also based his spontaneous writing on breath notation: "Ideally each line of *Howl* is a single breath unit. My breath is long—that's the Measure, one physical-mental inspiration of thought contained in the elastic of a breath. . . . it's a natural consequence, my own heightened conversation."[67]

If a writer is genuinely concerned with finding his or her own voice, going so far as to examine breathing, then it follows that each would evolve an individual style, and the best of the above writers did, ranging from O'Hara's slangy, intimate, and cosmopolitan wit to Ginsberg's apocalyptic *Howl* or Kerouac's manic and populist *On the Road* vernacular.

The daily music of gesture painters almost without exception was jazz, particularly Bop, so much so that the famous jazz club, the Five Spot Café (whose walls were covered with announcements of artists' shows) was sustained initially by an artist clientele. Moreover, a number of artists, e.g., Rivers and Howard Kanovitz, themselves played the music. Jazz was attractive because it was open and energetic, the improvisation of the creative individual rather than the interpretive group, and because it was an urban music, reflecting the tempo, tension, and energy of the city, particularly New York.

The relation of jazz to gesture painting is evident (although exaggerated) in the remarks (fairly representative of his generation) of Ted Joans: "I want my paintings to swing, like good jazz solos. . . . American painters like Joan Mitchell, Kline, de Kooning . . . are wailing real great stuff. . . . with painting I just want to swing and be me, all me, bad or good. . . . Man I never know beforehand what I'm going to paint, I just start wailing and later on when it gets good, I slow down and put it together—then the climax."[68]

# Notes

1. Frank O'Hara, "A Memoir," in Sam Hunter, *Larry Rivers* (New York: Harry N. Abrams, 1969), pp. 51–52.

2. John Ferren, "Stable State of Mind," *Art News*, May 1955, p. 22.

3. Ibid.

4. For a discussion of Hofmann's commanding role as an art teacher, see Irving Sandler, "Hans Hofmann: The Pedagogical Master," *Art in America*, May–June 1973, pp. 48–55.

5. For a comprehensive analysis of Hans Hofmann's aesthetics, see William C. Seitz, *Hans Hofmann*, exhibition catalogue (New York: Museum of Modern Art, 1963).

6. Max Kozloff, "An Interview with Friedel Dzubas," *Artforum*, September 1965, p. 50.

7. Willem de Kooning, "What Abstract Art Means to Me," *Museum of Modern Art Bulletin* 18 (Spring 1951): 5–6.

8. Frederick S. Wight, *Hans Hofmann*, exhibition catalogue (Berkeley: University of California, 1957), p. 23.

9. Ibid., p. 24.

10. Allan Kaprow, "Hans Hofmann," an obituary, *Village Voice*, 24 February 1966, p. 2.

In his classes, Hofmann focused on the pictorial mechanics of suggesting pictorial depth through the interaction of flat planes of color. But in the greater part of his writing, he focused on the spiritual synthesis of his aesthetic dialectics; he wrote that "the relation of two given realities always produces a higher, a purely spiritual third" (Hans Hofmann, "Plastic Creation," *League* 5 [Winter 1932–33]: 14).

11. Elaine de Kooning, "Hans Hofmann Paints a Picture," *Art News*, February 1950, p. 40.

12. Interview with Willem de Kooning, New York, 16 June 1959.

13. Glen Wessels, answers to a questionnaire on Hofmann's role as a teacher devised by William C. Seitz in 1963, referred to as *Hofmann Students Dossier*, on file at the Museum of Modern Art, New York.

14. Allan Kaprow, interviewed by Dorothy Seckler, New York, 10 September 1968. Transcript in the Archives of American Art, New York.

15. Clement Greenberg, "Hans Hofmann: Grand Old Rebel," *Art News*, January 1959, pp. 29, 64.

16. Carl Holty in *Hofmann Students Dossier*.

17. Kaprow, "Hans Hofmann," p. 2.

18. Thomas B. Hess, "U.S. Painting: Some Recent Directions," *Art News Annual* 25 (1956): 92–93.

19. Interview with Willem de Kooning, 16 June 1959.

De Kooning was outspoken about his ties to tradition. When in 1958 he was asked whether he was with or against the past, he answered: "They called us drippers and paint-slingers. I don't think our pictures look violent any more. The big Pollock [at the Metropolitan Museum of Art] seemed very lyrical and calm. Going through the other rooms, Rembrandt and Rodin are near each other. Although they're centuries apart, in the museum they seem part of the same thing. . . . Being anti-traditional is just as corny as being traditional." ("Is Today's Artist With or Against the Past?" *Art News*, Summer 1958, p. 27).

20. Willem de Kooning, statement in caption of illustration of untitled painting, *New York Times Magazine*, 21 January 1951, sec. 6, p. 17.

21. De Kooning, "What Abstract Art Means to Me," p. 7.

22. Mary Fuller McChesney, *A Period of Exploration: San Francisco 1945–1950*, exhibition catalogue (Oakland, Calif.: Oakland Museum Art Department, 1973), pp. 39–40.

23. T[homas] B. H[ess], "Reviews and Previews: Barnett Newman," *Art News*, March 1950, p. 48.

24. T[homas] B. H[ess], "Reviews and Previews: Barnet [*sic*] Newmann [*sic*]," *Art News*, Summer 1951, p. 47.

25. Thomas B. Hess, *Barnett Newman* (New York: Walker and Company, 1969), p. 43. Hess also remarked on the split in the Abstract Expressionist milieu between the "bohemians" and the "intellectuals." The "bohemians," exemplified by de Kooning and Kline, were largely self-educated, the products of art schools rather than colleges, whose social life was in and around Greenwich Village lofts and who showed at the Egan Gallery. The "intellectuals," among them Newman, Rothko, and Gottlieb, were more articulate, gravitated uptown socially, lived in apartments, and showed at the Parsons and Kootz galleries (pp. 42–43).

26. Clement Greenberg, "Art Chronicle: 'Feeling Is All,' " *Partisan Review* 19 (January–February 1952): 100–101.

27. Clement Greenberg, " 'American-Type' Painting," *Partisan Review* 22 (Spring 1955): 179–96.

28. For an example of the ridicule aimed at Ad Reinhardt, see Elaine de Kooning, "Pure Paints a Picture," *Art News*, Summer 1957, pp. 57, 86–87.

29. "Jackson Pollock: An Artists' Symposium, Part 2," *Art News*, May 1967, p. 72.

30. Robert Goodnough, "Pollock Paints a Picture," *Art News*, May 1951, pp. 39–40.

31. "Jackson Pollock: An Artists' Symposium, Part 1," *Art News*, April 1967, p. 32.

32. John B. Myers, interviewed by Barbara Rose, New York, no date. Typescript in Archives of American Art.

33. Interview with Helen Frankenthaler, New York, 24 May 1973.

34. Myers, interviewed by Barbara Rose.

35. See James T. Valliere, "De Kooning on Pollock," *Partisan Review* 34 (Fall 1967): 603–5. De Kooning said: "A couple of times he [Pollock] told me, 'You know more, but I feel more.' I was jealous of him—his talent. But he was a remarkable person. He'd do things that were so terrific."
Grace Hartigan, in a conversation with the author, Baltimore, Maryland, 14 January 1974, recalled meeting Pollock around 1948 and asking him who the "really good" artists were. He answered that apart from himself there was only de Kooning, and he urged her to meet him.

36. Joseph Stefanelli, remarks at a Club panel, "Valid Motivations for the Artist Today," 24 February 1956 (notes taken by me). The panelists were Angelo Ippolito, Kyle Morris (moderator), Al Newbill, Richard Stankiewicz, and Joseph Stefanelli.

37. Eric Hodgins and Parker Leslie, "The Great International Art Market," *Fortune*, December 1955, pp. 119, 152, 158.

38. Meyer Schapiro, "Rebellion in Art," in Daniel Aaron, ed., *America in Crisis* (New York: Alfred A. Knopf, 1952), p. 219. Schapiro's essay was first presented as a public lecture at Bennington College, Vermont, in the winter of 1950–51.

39. Meyer Schapiro, "The Liberating Quality of Avant-Garde Art," *Art News*, Summer 1957, p. 42.

40. Thomas B. Hess, "The New York Salon," *Art News*, February 1954, p. 57.

41. Hess, "U.S. Painting: Some Recent Directions," p. 174.

42. Ferren, "Stable State of Mind," p. 23.

43. David Riesman, with Nathan Glazer and Reuel Denney, *The Lonely Crowd* (New Haven, Conn.: Yale University Press, 1950); C. Wright Mills, *White Collar: The American Middle Class* (New York: Oxford University Press, 1951); William H. Whyte, Jr., *The Organization Man* (New York: Simon & Schuster, 1956). See also Herbert Marcuse, *Eros and Civilization* (Boston: Beacon Press, 1955); John Kenneth Galbraith, *The Affluent Society* (Boston: Houghton Mifflin, 1958); and Vance Oakley Packard, *The Status Seekers* (New York: David McKay Company, 1959).

44. "Our Country and Our Culture: A Symposium," *Partisan Review* 19 (May–June 1952): 284.

45. Ibid.

46. American society in the fifties struck the New York School much as it did John Clellon Holmes, a Beat writer, who wrote of

> . . . its suspicion of any distinct personal identity; its sickening Eisenhower piety and equally revolting Nixon cant; its constant referral in all matters of taste to hypothetical twelve-year-old girls, . . . its absolutely straight-faced insistence that all this was somehow mature, responsible, healthy and American.
>
> It was a decade when the patronizing, whipped-cream sentiments of Oscar Hammerstein and Norman Vincent Peale wafted through a nation stupefied under the pall of millions of barbecue pits, automobiles the size of gun boats, golf carts with built-in massagers, and rotisseries on which to cook precooked meals. It was a time when sane people seriously believed that rigged quiz shows at least indicated a new respect for the intellectual life; . . . It was a decade during which . . . most professionals secretly subscribed to Lenny Bruce's mock motto, "Be a man. Sell out," and the public sat hypnotized, as before a crazy-house mirror, happily watching themselves pictured on TV as so many dumb but lovable husbands, canny but well-meaning wives, and fiendishly mischievous children who were wiser than Socrates—the whole travesty bathed in moral pap, intellectual sloth, and the baldest banshee-commercialism (*Nothing More to Declare* [New York: E. P. Dutton & Co., 1967], pp. 244–45).

47. See William Hauptman, "The Suppression of Art in the McCarthy Decade," *Artforum,* October 1973, pp. 48–52.

48. Lewis Mumford, quoted in Bernard Rosenberg and Norris Fliegel, *The Vanguard Artist: Portrait and Self-Portrait* (Chicago: Quadrangle Books, 1965), p. 32.

49. Willem de Kooning believed that society's indifference to art was beneficial to the artist. In a class paper, "Subject Matter of the Artist," New York University, 1950, unpaginated, Robert Goodnough remarked that "to those who bemoan the situation of the artist today, he [de Kooning] answers that he finds the artist to be in a fortunate position. There is no one to limit his freedom since few understand the frontiers where he walks."

50. Schapiro, "The Liberating Quality of Avant-Garde Art," p. 42.
The point of view advanced by Schapiro was also held by such Existentialists as Jean Paul Sartre, who was widely read by New York School artists. Sartre maintained that art which was extremely subjective could be intra-subjective, that is, apprehended by others, and ethical. As he saw it, the individual who chooses himself and creates the man he wants to be, creates an image of man as he thinks man ought to be, that is, he chooses for all men, for mankind. For a further analysis of this Existentialist hypothesis, see Terence Smith, "Abstract Expressionism: Ethical Attitudes and Moral Function" (Master's thesis, University of Sydney, Australia, 1974), pp. 129–41, 291. Smith elaborated on the " 'indirect moral effect' " desired by the Abstract Expressionists which

> . . . is not incidental to their aims, but neither is it their sole and major objective in painting at all. Unable to countenance any form of universal ethics, their communication objective would be something like: if I am to paint in the most ethically good way possible, this striving has a metaphorical consonance with other men attempting to act ethically in their form of life, and may have an actual effect on their lives, but I cannot sacrifice my individual struggle to the kind of generalization required for guaranteed direct moral effect on their lives.

See also Dore Ashton, *The New York School: A Cultural Reckoning* (New York: Viking Press,

1973), pp. 181–82, which relates how Sartre's opinions helped the New York School justify its art.

51. Smith, "Abstract Expressionism: Ethical Attitudes and Moral Function," p. 147.

52. See Allan Kaprow, "Should the Artist Become a Man of the World?" *Art News*, October 1964, pp. 34–37, 58–59.

53. Kindred poets in San Francisco were Lawrence Ferlinghetti, Gary Snyder, Philip Whalen, and Michael McClure. The Beat movement and the San Francisco Renaissance are often dated from the evening in 1955 when Ginsberg first read *Howl* at the Six Gallery in San Francisco. The general public became aware of the Beats in 1957 with the publication of Kerouac's *On the Road* (written in 1951).

Poets generally sympathetic to the New York School were anthologized in Donald Allen, ed., *The New American Poetry, 1945–1960* (New York: Grove Press, 1960).

54. Edmund Wilson, quoted in Renato Poggioli, *The Theory of the Avant-Garde* (Cambridge, Mass.: Belknap Press of Harvard University Press, 1968), p. 124.

55. Martin Duberman, *Black Mountain: An Exploration in Community* (New York: E. P. Dutton & Co., 1972), p. 337.

56. Robert Creeley, "On the Road: Notes on Artists and Poets," in Neil A. Chassman, ed., *Poets of the Cities New York and San Francisco 1950–1965*, exhibition catalogue (New York: E. P. Dutton & Co., 1974), p. 57. Avant-garde writers were all inspired by Walt Whitman, Ezra Pound, and William Carlos Williams. They also wanted to free poetry from the established literature promoted by the *Kenyon Review* and *Partisan Review*, their differences notwithstanding.

57. Ibid., p. 58.

58. Ibid., p. 59. Michael McClure considered Pollock the exemplar of "gesture painting," a term he used in "Ode to Jackson Pollock," *Evergreen Review*, Autumn 1958, pp. 124–126.

59. Duberman, *Black Mountain*, pp. 390–91.

60. Charles Olson, "Projective Verse" (1950), reprinted in Donald Allen and Warren Tallman, eds., *The Poetics of The New American Poetry* (New York: Grove Press, 1973), pp. 148–49.

61. Peter Schjeldahl, "O'Hara—Art Sustained Him," *New York Times*, 3 March 1974, sec. 2, p. 21.

62. Frank O'Hara, "Personism: A Manifesto," (1959), reprinted in Allen and Tallman, eds., *The Poetics of The New American Poetry*, pp. 353–55.

63. Ann Charters, *Kerouac: A Biography* (New York: Warner Paperback Library, 1974), p. 123.

64. Jack Kerouac, "The Art of Fiction LXI," *Paris Review* 43 (Summer 1968), p. 83 (Interview by Ted Berrigan, Aram Saroyan, and Duncan McNaughton).

65. Allen Ginsberg, "when the mode of the music changes the walls of the city shake," *Second Coming Magazine* 1 (July 1961): 40.

66. Ibid., p. 41.

67. Allen Ginsberg, "Notes Written on Finally Recording Howl," *Evergreen Review* 3 (November–December 1959): 33.

68. Ted Joans, "Tape Recording at the Five Spot," in Seymour Krim, ed., *The Beats* (Greenwich, Conn.: Gold Medal Books, 1960), pp. 211–13.

# 2

# The Community of the New York School

NEW YORK CITY's appeal to artists is well known. Among its attractions are museums and private art galleries; the concentration of artists in all of the arts and the challenge, pressure, and stimulation of the newest and liveliest culture; the existence of an art-conscious audience; and the availability of part-time jobs in sizable number and variety which enable artists to survive without taking too much time from their art-making.

Given the concentration of artists, it was reasonable for a New York School to have emerged. There appears to have been little design in its formation.[1] Artists of an avant-garde disposition who met fortuitously more often than not developed a loose network of acquaintances. This in time led to the organization of a "scene," which centered on a number of semi-public and public meeting places. Stimulating the growth of an artists' "ghetto," as Motherwell called it, was "the enormous pressure of the social world around us," as Dzubas recollected. "You had a feeling . . . of you and your friends against everyone else on the outside."[2] However, artists drew together for reasons other than their alienation from American society. They shared a more or less common sensibility, an awareness of what was dead and alive in art. Therefore, they provided the primary audience for each other's work. They also gathered frequently because of a simple desire to socialize; every memoir of the period dwells nostalgically on the frequent parties, and shared meals—the fun, esprit, and communion. Furthermore, there was a collective need for assurance, a need to talk out one's insecurities with one's peers; Robert Rauschenberg recalled that appearing at artists' gatherings was valuable because it allowed one to show one's face in the hope of being identified as an artist.

Most important was the need to exchange ideas, to defend and promote one's aesthetic premises—and one's existential stake in them—for "confession," that is, the revelation of one's inmost feelings and ideas, was the verbal style (and aggressiveness its tone). Dzubas remembers this process as "a mutual kind of search. The search was conducted individually, but when you were together with people, you felt that there was a dynamic process of growth . . . It was that which really connected us. . . . this not yet definite or channeled pushing."[3] The constant face-to-face encounters and exchanges of strongly held ideas gave rise to a milieu of constant feedback, mutual awareness, and, of course, vehement controversy. This running commentary by artists and persons respected by the artists made the work *count*, at least because it indicated that the work was seen, taken seriously, and had repercussions. So urgent was the need for discussion that private conversations in the studios and homes of artists, or even in the bars and restaurants that they frequented, did not seem adequate, and the artists established forums where they could address audiences, composed mainly of themselves, but also of critics, curators, dealers, collectors, professors, advanced art students, and the avant-gardes of the other arts.

This audience *by paying attention* (and it did so enthusiastically) bolstered the artists and contributed to the intensity with which they worked. The energies that gave rise to, and were generated by, semi-public dialogue and the sense of vital community it implied were so elating to the participants that most recognized that they were witness to a rare phenomenon: a living culture and American at that.

Vanguard artists in New York organized themselves with relative ease because most lived in the same neighborhood in Manhattan: a low-rent area downtown in and around a belt between Eighth and Twelfth streets on the south and north, and First and Sixth avenues on the east and west. Indeed, the section came to be called Tenth Street, since the stretch of that street between Third and Fourth avenues was roughly the center. On that one city block alone in 1956 were the studios of some dozen artists including Goldberg, Guston, Kohn, de Kooning, Resnick, and Vicente.[4] When in the middle and late fifties young artists organized cooperative galleries, most were located on the same block: the Tanager, Camino, Brata, Area, and March galleries. Not only did significant numbers of artists live, work, and show in the vicinity of East Tenth Street, but within easy walking distance were to be found the primary gathering places: the Cedar Street Tavern and the Club; as well as the art schools that fostered modernism: Hofmann's school, Amédée Ozenfant's school, the Subjects of the Artist School, the Department of Art Education of New York University, and Stanley William Hayter's Atelier 17.

Geographic proximity gave rise to the constant exchange of studio visits, and these constituted the underlying network that wove together the artists' community and encouraged further meeting in public places. First-generation artists had begun the process, and they soon involved their students and young artists in their activities. In the fall of 1948, Motherwell, Baziotes, Rothko, and David Hare (joined somewhat later by Newman) established the Subjects of the Artist School in a loft at 35 East Eighth Street. To broaden the experience of their students, other artists were invited to speak on Friday evenings. The sessions were open to the public and were attended by all interested in advanced art (some 150 persons an evening). The school closed in May 1949, and the space was taken over by three professors in New York University's Department of Art

Education—Robert Iglehart, Hale Woodruff, and Tony Smith—to provide additional studio space for their students, among whom were Goodnough, Leslie, and Rivers. Of the professors, Smith was the most active on the New York art scene and the closest to the artists, notably Pollock, Newman, Rothko, and Still. His insights into Abstract Expressionism inspired many young artists. With the help of a few students, notably Goodnough, Smith continued the Friday evening lectures at the loft, which was renamed Studio 35.

Among the speakers at the Subjects of the Artist School and Studio 35 were Jean Arp, Baziotes, Cage, Joseph Cornell (who showed his films), Herbert Ferber, Fritz Glarner, Gottlieb, Harry Holtzman, Richard Huelsenbeck, de Kooning, Motherwell, Newman, Reinhardt, Harold Rosenberg, and Rothko. The final activity of Studio 35 was a three-day closed conference in April 1950, whose proceedings were stenographically recorded, edited by Motherwell, Reinhardt, and Goodnough, and published in *Modern Artists in America.*[5]

In the late fall of 1949, de Kooning, Kline, Reinhardt, Tworkov, and their friends downtown, including the somewhat younger Resnick, organized a club (dubbed simply the Club but sometimes called the Eighth Street Club or the Artists Club) and rented a meeting place at 39 East Eighth Street (two doors away from Studio 35).[6] It was to be the focal point of New York School activities for more than a decade. The main activity was weekly panel discussions held on Friday nights, and up to 1954, free-wheeling round table discussions on Wednesday nights. Young artists were soon invited into membership, for example, Rauschenberg and Frankenthaler at the end of 1951, and in the following year, Leslie, Larry Rivers, Joan Mitchell, Paul Brach, Raymond Parker, Grace Hartigan, Louis Finkelstein, Nell Blaine, and Goldberg. As early as 1952, members of the early wave were asked to participate in the Friday night panels; e.g., a panel on Abstract Expressionism was composed of Freilicher, Hartigan, Leslie, Mitchell, O'Hara, and Rivers, and moderated by John B. Myers.[7] Every conceivable aesthetic issue was a topic for discussion at the Club; however, there were recurring themes, the most debated of which was the basis of group identity and what changes had occurred in the New York School as the fifties progressed—and it is noteworthy that the matter of their growing and changing community should have preoccupied both the first and second generations. The information imparted to the newcomers at the Club was useful to them, but of greater importance was the opportunity to meet and befriend their elders, the pioneers of Abstract Expressionism, and artists of their own generation. The most numerous and active artists in the Club were in the circle around de Kooning. Thus gestural styles received the most attention, although Club membership was too varied to embrace any one aesthetic position.

By the end of 1952, the first generation began to attend the Club with decreasing regularity. But increasing numbers of young artists were voted into membership (after having attended as guests for a period of time). By 1955, second-generation artists such as Brach, Stefanelli, and Finkelstein were appointed to the voting committee, the governing body of the Club. Also in that year, Phillip Pavia, who had been the Club's prime mover, ceased to be active, and young artists, in the main identified with Tenth Street, assumed more and more of the leadership of the Club and made it their forum, particularly after I was made responsible for the Friday night programs in 1956.

In 1951, several charter members of the Club decided to present the painting and sculpture of the New York School to the public. They invited each of sixty-one artists to submit one work and installed them in an empty store on East Ninth Street. This "salon," dubbed the Ninth Street Show, included at least thirteen young artists—Dzubas, Frankenthaler, Goodnough, Hartigan, Harry Jackson, Elaine de Kooning, Leslie, Mitchell, Robert de Niro, Fairfield Porter, Resnick, Stefanelli, and Goldberg (exhibiting under the name of Stuart)—indicating that at an early date, second-generation artists were invited by their elders to join more or less as equals in communal activities. The artists considered the Ninth Street Show sufficiently successful to warrant another, and in 1953 organized a sequel at the Stable Gallery; the shows then turned into yearly affairs called the Stable Annuals. These shows were selected by committees of artists elected by those who had participated in the last one. In 1956, the second generation, especially the part associated with Tenth Street, began to dominate the committees of selection, just as they did the leadership of the Club.

More than the Club, the Cedar Street Tavern, close by on University Place off Eighth Street, was the spot for informal talk. The artists and their friends, particularly those who lived downtown, found the Cedar's decor comfortable; its drabness and anonymity typified their public stance and even the life-style of many. (It is noteworthy that the artist clientele once convinced the owners to cancel their plans for renovation.) Colorlessness was taken as a sign of seriousness, conforming to a self-image of the artist as "creator" rather than as "creative liver," either in the style of Bohemia or the world of fashion. As an additional increment, the drabness of the Cedar's decor discouraged Greenwich Village Bohemians and slumming Madison Avenue types from frequenting the bar. But the Tavern was not so ordinary that it had a television set to attract neighborhood folk. Intent on conversation, the artists did not want a TV to distract them (except around World Series time when one was rented), and the owners acquiesced. Young artists also met their elders and peers at openings of shows at the Fifty-seventh Street galleries of Betty Parsons, Samuel Kootz, Charles Egan, and Sidney Janis, which represented the first generation and would in time offer shows to members of the second.

The second-generation's sense of "family" was even stronger than that of the first, partly because its members at the beginning of their careers could congregate in the meeting places established by their elders.[8] But many young artists had met while students and had formed groups of their own prior to entering the milieu of the New York School. Most attended schools in the downtown area, notably the Hans Hofmann School of Fine Arts. Out of town, young artists met primarily at the California School of Fine Arts in San Francisco; Black Mountain College in North Carolina; and various schools in Paris, where as Americans (many of them ex-servicemen), they naturally banded together.

Most of the early wave had studied with Hofmann, for example, Frankenthaler, Goodnough, Kaprow, Rivers, and Stankiewicz.[9] Meeting day after day in a small school, it was natural for Hofmann's students to develop close associations (and many remained lifelong).[10] But Hofmann himself fostered their communal inclinations. As one student recalled: "Through force of personality he transformed his classes into energy situations within which students were able to learn more from each other rather than from himself."[11] The sense of community was carried outside the school. Indeed, it was so intense that two groups, composed largely of Hofmann's ex-students, formed new galleries: the Hansa, named after Hofmann, and later the James.

Several members of the second generation such as John Chamberlain, Kenneth Noland, and Rauschenberg met while students at Black Mountain College in North Carolina. This experimental "communal" school was "dedicated to two enterprises—establishing a community in which people shared common purposes and responsibilities, and creating a climate in which art of the highest excellence might flourish."[12] Black Mountain's program was so innovative and its leadership so inspired that it attracted the most avant-garde artists of the forties and fifties (until its closing in 1956). On the faculty at different times were composers Cage and Stefan Wolpe; choreographer-dancer Merce Cunningham; translator Mary Caroline Richards; designer-engineer Buckminster Fuller; critics Eric Bentley and Paul Goodman; poets Edward Dahlberg, Olson, Creeley, and Robert Duncan; photographers Harry Callahan and Aaron Siskind; and architect Walter Gropius. In the visual arts, the leading spirit was Josef Albers, but the college was visited by a steady stream of artists and an occasional critic, mainly from New York and particularly during the summer sessions; including Motherwell (1945); Willem and Elaine de Kooning (1948); Theodoros Stamos and Clement Greenberg (1950); Motherwell (1951); Kline and Tworkov (1952); and Vicente (1953).[13]

The Black Mountain graduates who came to New York formed two loose groups: one frequented the Cedar Street Tavern, often in the company of Kline; the other gravitated toward Cage (and Cunningham, whose musical director he has been since 1943), meeting frequently at musical evenings at his apartment. Kline's role deserves special mention, for many young artists were influenced by his life-style. As Harry F. Gaugh described him:

> He liked beer at the Cedar Bar and English tea in the studio. He could play the dandy or the clown, act like Ted Lewis, Wallace Beery, or Mae West, talk about rugs, vintage cars. Géricault's horses, baseball, and Baron Gros. He loved jazz and Wagner. He was a confirmed New Yorker, but had roots that he never forgot in the gritty coal country of eastern Pennsylvania. . . . He could juggle life until it came up fun. But he believed all artists are lonely.
>
> Kline had an inclusive knowledge of art and could talk eruditely about it at length if he wished.[14]

The Black Mountain ex-students, inspired by Kline and other first-generation artists, were disposed to paint in gestural styles; those attracted to Cage, such as Rauschenberg, were inspired by Cage's aesthetic, which was to grow in influence as the decade

10   Franz Kline, *Mahoning,* 1956.
80″ x 100″. Whitney Museum of American Art, New York.

progressed. In 1955, Rauschenberg met Johns, who had a studio in the same building, and soon introduced him to Cage. So close did their friendship become that in 1958, the two young artists put up their own money to present a retrospective of Cage's music.

The year before the concert, Cage taught a class in music composition at the New School for Social Research which included Kaprow and somewhat later George Brecht, Al Hansen, Dick Higgins, and Jackson MacLow. Cage encouraged his students to experiment with intermedia theater events. Other young artists soon joined Cage's students in their activities. Friends, among them George Segal, Jim Dine, and Larry Poons, visited some of his classes.[15] Dine, who moved to New York in 1959, became friendly with Kaprow, Whitman (who had been a student of Kaprow's at Rutgers University), Oldenburg, and later Johns and Rauschenberg. Oldenburg was impressed by a talk given by Kaprow at the Club in 1958; by his tar-coated figurative sculptures; and by his essay on Pollock.[16] The two met in that year, and Kaprow introduced Oldenburg to his associates. Oldenburg also became friendly with Grooms, who in 1958 exhibited Oldenburg's work for the first time in New York in his studio which he turned into a gallery.[17] A group of artists stimulated by Cage's teaching organized themselves into the New York City Audio-Visual Group which, as Hansen recalled, "met on Sunday mornings at a Bleecker Street coffee shop called the Epitome where we performed and taped experimental notations."[18] This group at one time or another included Hansen, Higgins, Poons, MacLow, La Monte Young, and Ray Johnson.

Another group of second-generation artists met while students at the California School of Fine Arts in San Francisco. Under the guidance of Douglas MacAgy, this art school from 1946 to 1950 had become one of the liveliest and most forward-looking in America. MacAgy brought together a group of remarkable teachers, including Still (from 1946 to 1950), Rothko (in the summers of 1947 and 1949), and Reinhardt (in the summer of 1950). Still was the major influence.[19] He did not teach about the mechanics of painting but tried to liberate his students from "banality," tradition, and convention. "I do not want other artists to imitate my work—they do even when I tell them not to—but only my example for freedom and independence from all external, decadent and corrupting influences."[20] Jon Schueler remarked that Still conveyed "the idea that an artist is nothing unless he accepts the total responsibility for everything that he does. . . . It is . . . by making a responsible move that he makes a statement." He maintained: " 'You can make a picture out of the truth,' rather than you can make a picture and here's how," and that changed Schueler's life.[21] Two of Still's most devoted disciples, Ernest Briggs and Edward Dugmore, were among the Californians who moved to New York. Both artists injected Still's demands for a visionary art and his moralist and iconoclastic stance into the thinking of the second generation. Others who had attended the school were also active in New York, notably Hultberg, Schueler, and Grillo, who was close to the Hansa, de Nagy, and Tanager gallery groups. Many artists who settled in New York met while students in Paris in the late forties and early fifties, among them Norman Bluhm, Al Held, Paul Jenkins, Ellsworth Kelly, Mitchell, Noland, Stankiewicz, and Jack Youngerman.

Contributing to the organization of a New York School community were art critics Greenberg, Hess, and Harold Rosenberg, and art historian Schapiro, all of whom made a practice of visiting studios and of bringing together kindred artists. Schapiro's frequent lectures were attended by nearly all vanguard artists. His role as mentor in the development of two generations of the New York School was nothing short of inspirational. Kaprow wrote of how thrilling it was to hear him give a critique whether it was of one's own work or anyone else's. And he was a very great champion of young artists as well as being an extraordinary historian.[22] Freilicher agreed, remarking on Schapiro's incredible erudition and more important, his loss of himself in art, his egoless and almost saintly dedication.[23]

Greenberg had been a discoverer of Pollock and an early champion of Abstract Expressionism. His art criticism in the *Nation* and *Partisan Review* was more closely read and respected than that of any other critic. Hess was closer in age to the artists of the early wave. He had written the first book featuring the first generation.[24] During the fifties, he was executive editor of *Art News*, then America's leading art magazine, and was largely responsible for turning it into the "family journal" of the New York School in general, and in particular, of de Kooning and his circle downtown. Rosenberg rarely wrote about individual artists, but his general essays, notably "The American Action

Painters," published in 1952, focused attention on Abstract Expressionism and provoked interest in the controversy about its aesthetic premises.[25]

The early wave of the second generation tended to exhibit in three galleries: two co-operatives, the Jane Street and the Hansa; and one commercial gallery, the Tibor de Nagy. During its existence from 1944 to 1949, the Jane Street Gallery numbered among its members mostly ex-Hofmann students, such as Blaine and Rivers. They followed no single aesthetic, but Blaine was the prime mover. In the late forties, the artists in her circle were influenced by Mondrian, Arp, and Léger. During the following decade, she and other Jane Street artists turned from abstract to figurative painting, influenced mainly by Bonnard, Soutine, Cézanne, and de Kooning.[26]

At the end of 1951, a group of Hofmann's students arranged a show of their own work in the loft of Wolf Kahn and Felix Pasilis at 813 Broadway, the address providing the name for the show. It included works by Miles Forst, Grillo, Pasilis, Kahn, Müller, and Lester Johnson (who had not studied with Hofmann). Forst, Kahn, Müller, and Pasilis were so excited by the show that they decided to organize a cooperative gallery and invited other artists to join them, including fellow students Jean Follett, Kaprow, and Stankiewicz. In 1952, they rented a space for a gallery on East Twelfth Street and called it the Hansa after their teacher. In 1954, they moved the gallery uptown to Central Park South. At any time, there were from ten to fifteen members of the Hansa, each contributing dues which fluctuated from ten to thirty dollars a month to its upkeep. In 1955, Richard Bellamy and, somewhat later, Ivan Karp were hired as the directors.

The members of the Hansa Gallery were not committed to any aesthetic program as a group. Indeed, their work ranged from purist abstraction to realism. However, there were two general tendencies. Several of the members were disposed toward painterly realism with an Expressionist cast, for example, Müller, the acknowledged spiritual leader of a group including Kahn, Pasilis, and Kaprow. The other group constructed their work largely from found materials, for example, Stankiewicz and Follett, and after 1957, Kaprow and Whitman, who had been inspired by Cage. Other Hansa artists whose work was verging in this direction were Chamberlain, Lucas Samaras, and George Segal. The Hansa was generally in financial difficulty, as were most cooperatives. But its basic problem was to find agreement on whom to exhibit. The gallery began to decline in 1958 when Müller died and Stankiewicz moved to the Stable Gallery, and it closed the following year.

The Tibor de Nagy Gallery, which opened in December 1950, represented most of the early-wave painters who made the first strong impression on the New York School's audience (including critics and curators). Responsible in large part for its success was its director John B. Myers, who had been an editor of the Surrealist magazine *View*; had run a puppet theater; and was an enthusiast about everything avant-garde, indeed becoming a kind of impresario of the avant-garde, running a gallery, publishing poetry, arranging theatrical productions. He was "a sort of young American Diaghilev."[27]

In the summer of 1949, Myers became converted from French to American art, and moved to do something about it, decided to open a gallery. He was advised by Lee Krasner Pollock to represent unknowns, since the major figures of the New York School were already taken by the Parsons, Kootz, and Egan galleries. Greenberg, whom Myers met at the Pollocks', recommended Rivers, Hartigan, Leslie, Frankenthaler, de Niro, Goodnough, and Leatrice Rose. Myers also turned to Tony Smith for advice, and he approved the artists chosen by Greenberg, three of whom (Rivers, Leslie, and Goodnough) had been Smith's students. With the exception of Rose, all were given shows at the de Nagy Gallery. Other artists that Myers was to exhibit during the fifties were Blaine, Goldberg, Freilicher, Porter, Elaine de Kooning, Dzubas, Grillo, and Noland.

The Tibor de Nagy Gallery did not have an aesthetic bias. However, most of the painters who showed there had studied with Hofmann and looked for inspiration to de Kooning. Therefore, the de Nagy group was more in the mainstream of fifties painting than the members of the Jane Street and Hansa galleries. When the de Nagy artists were caught in the rivalry between de Kooning and Pollock and were pressured to choose between joining de Kooning's camp or staying on the outside, most chose to join, with the notable exception of Frankenthaler.[28]

De Kooning was greatly admired and influential as an artist. But he offered even more to young artists. He made himself available in a way that Pollock, who lived in East Hampton, could not. And he was the exemplar of a way of life which centered in the studios on and around East Tenth Street, the Cedar Street Tavern, and the Club. Young artists were very much attracted to this life, and it is not surprising, for it was elating to find oneself in the company not only of de Kooning but of Kline, Guston, and many other respected artists, and also such critics as Hess and Rosenberg; such artists who wrote criticism for *Art News* as Elaine de Kooning, Porter, Goodnough; the dance critic Edwin Denby; the film maker-photographer-painter Rudolph Burckhardt; such gallery dealers as Egan and Leo Castelli; and such poets as O'Hara, Ashbery, Schuyler, Guest, and Koch. These poets, whose writing was first published by Myers, collaborated on poem-paintings with second-generation artists, and, with the exception of Koch, wrote criticism for *Art News*. There was a pervading feeling of work, great work, being done that communal esprit was furthering.

Aside from de Kooning himself, the pivotal figures in the coterie were O'Hara and Elaine de Kooning. Elaine de Kooning was, aside from Willem's wife, a respected painter and writer on art. She was, in O'Hara's words, "The White Goddess: she knew everything, told little of it though she talked a lot, and we all adored (and adore) her."[29] O'Hara was not only esteemed as a poet and critic but as an organizer of many fine exhibitions for the Museum of Modern Art. He achieved the position of curator in 1966 shortly before his death. Of greater importance, O'Hara was a friend of the early-wave artists; indeed, as Freilicher remarked: "It was inspiring to have his support. He was interesting and amusing as well as a wonderful poet. He had an infinite capacity for attachments to people; everybody was his best friend."[30] Morton Feldman was even more positive than Freilicher about O'Hara's contribution: "What really matters is to have someone like Frank standing behind you. That's what keeps you going. Without that your life in art is not worth a damn."[31]

The Tibor de Nagy Gallery was soon joined by other private galleries featuring the second generation of the New York School. The most important were the Stable and the Martha Jackson galleries, beginning in 1953; the Poindexter, which opened in the fall of 1955; and the Leo Castelli, which opened in 1957. The Stable Gallery provided space for the so-called Stable Annuals and gave one-man shows to Dugmore, Mitchell, Rauschenberg, Schueler, Elaine de Kooning, Briggs, Ortman, Stankiewicz, and Alex Katz. The Martha Jackson Gallery showed Sam Francis, Goldberg, Paul Jenkins, Alfred Jensen, Leslie, and Morris Louis. Exhibiting at the Poindexter Gallery were Blaine, Richard Diebenkorn, de Niro, Goldberg, Al Held, and Resnick. Among the second-generation artists given one-person shows at the Castelli Gallery in the fifties were Schueler, Brach, Johns, Dzubas, Rauschenberg, and Gabriel Kohn.

As the fifties progressed, newcomers in ever-growing numbers moved to downtown New York. They entered into the existing community and around the middle of the decade began to dominate it, for example, assuming leadership of the Club. The newcomers added to the scene a number of cooperative galleries on and in the vicinity of Tenth Street between Third and Fourth avenues. These galleries—organized, financed, and managed by the artists themselves—were initiated because the prestigious uptown galleries were uninterested in exhibiting the work of unknown artists. But the cooperatives also became focal points of communal activities, places where artists could always find fellow artists to talk to, and on the joint Friday night openings of all the galleries, where they could participate in festivities that resembled big block parties. Members of the early wave took part in this Tenth Street scene, but many were somewhat removed from it, having established their primary social relationships earlier, in the milieu of Hofmann's school and the Tibor de Nagy Gallery.

The first of the Tenth Street cooperatives was the Tanager Gallery, which opened in 1952 in a former storefront on East Fourth Street and moved in the following year to Tenth Street. The gallery, organized by Charles Cajori, Lois Dodd, Angelo Ippolito, William King, and Fred Mitchell, numbered among its later members Sally Hazelet (Drummond), Ben Isquith, Katz, Philip Pearlstein, Johnson, and Ortman. Prior to 1960, the Tanager showed more than 130 artists, half for the first time in New York, and gave 21 non-members their first New York shows, including Grillo, Alfred Jensen, and Gabriel Kohn.

The members of the Tanager were varied in their aesthetic predilections, but most shared a bias (rarely articulated) against the "school" of de Kooning, much as they admired de Kooning himself. For example, Katz's flat portraits, Ben Isquith's and Sally Hazelet's monotone field paintings—greatly influenced by Reinhardt—Angelo Ippolito's abstractions inspired by de Stael, or George Ortman's abstract Surrealist boxes, were not closely related to the prevailing manner of the fifties. And yet, despite the diverse styles of its members, the Tanager Gallery had a collective mission, shared to some extent by

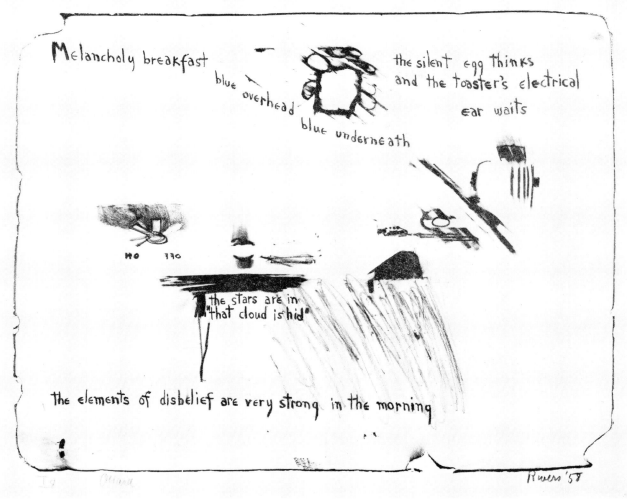

11  Larry Rivers and Frank O'Hara, *Stones:* Plate 8: "Melancholy Breakfast," 1957–60.
15″ x 19¹/₈″. The Museum of Modern Art, New York.

12 Grace Hartigan and Frank O'Hara, *What Fire Murmurs Its Seditions Beneath the Oaks,* 1953.
48¹/₂″ x 38¹/₂″. Collection, Gertrude Kasle, Detroit, Michigan.

13 Norman Bluhm and Frank O'Hara, *Noel,* 1960.
19¹/₄″ x 14″. New York University Art Collection, Grey Art Gallery and Study Center.

the other downtown cooperatives: to show art that artists deemed worthy and that was overlooked by the commercial galleries, to a public composed largely of other artists who were "simultaneously participants and spectators." The Tanager was considered by its members as a "public extension of the artist's studio" and as a "barometer of the New York art scene" whose shows reflected the diverse aesthetic issues that artists themselves believed were of consequence.[32]

The Tanager and Hansa galleries showed the way to others, who soon organized artists' cooperatives and private galleries that were semi-cooperative in the area. Among them were the James Gallery, formed in 1954; the Camino and the Fleischman galleries, in 1956; and in the next year, the March, Brata, Nonagon, Phoenix, and Great Jones galleries; in 1958, the Area Gallery; and in 1959, the Reuben Gallery. The downtown galleries were independent of each other, but occasionally would cooperate to the limited extent of opening on the same Friday nights and organizing a few collective Christmas shows, as in 1957, each gallery retaining the responsibility of who would be shown.

Apart from the Tanager Gallery, the most important of the Tenth Street galleries were the Brata and the Reuben. The leading Brata artists were painters Held, Ronald Bladen, and Nicholas Krushenick, and sculptor George Sugarman. They worked in a gestural manner during the fifties but by the end of the decade, they had begun to react against the spatial ambiguity of gestural art and instead, to clarify their forms and colors.

The Reuben Gallery, which opened in the fall of 1959, stood aloof from the other downtown galleries. In a way, it was an outgrowth of the Hansa Gallery, some of the members, e.g., Kaprow, Segal, Samaras, and Whitman, having shown there first. Other members were Brecht; Grooms, who had turned his successive studios into the City Gallery (1958–59) and the Delancey Street Museum (1959–60); and Dine and Oldenburg, who exhibited at the Judson Gallery in 1959–60. The Reuben Gallery was identified with the aesthetic position of Cage and his ex-student Kaprow. Its members assembled pieces from urban substances, mainly junk, whose subject was the city and its inhabitants and whose content was the artist's response to his found materials and urban themes. The exhibiting artists also were disposed to create environmental works and introduce theatrical actions into them. Among the makers of such events from October 1959 to April 1961 (when the gallery closed) were Kaprow, Grooms, Whitman, Dine, George Brecht, Simone Morris (Forti), and Oldenburg.

The bases of the overlapping and shifting associations of second-generation artists were social, aesthetic, the carryover of student days, a matter of gallery affiliation, or geographic proximity, or a combination of two or more of these. For example, Held, Bladen, and Sugarman were friends, interested in similar aesthetic issues, and members of the Brata Gallery. At times, aesthetic considerations predominated. For example, in April 1957, a group of artists including Follett, Hultberg, Alfred Jensen, Ortman, and Stankiewicz met twice to discuss forming a group that might exhibit together. These artists were inclined to Surrealism (although they decided against using the label because of its associations to past, "dead" styles) and believed that Surrealist-inspired tendencies had been neglected for being eccentric or outside the "mainstream." The group disbanded when it quickly became clear that it could reach no consensus as to what its specific organizing ideas should be and which artists might be included in the group.

Frequently, association depended mainly on who one's immediate neighbors chanced to be. For example, a lively community developed on Coenties Slip on the southern tip of Manhattan. Among its members were Fred Mitchell, Kelly, Robert Indiana, Youngerman, Agnes Martin, and James Rosenquist. It may be that geographic separation from Tenth Street encouraged the artists on the slip to develop styles different from the prevailing gestural ones, even though Tenth Street was a relatively short walk away.

In the history of Western art, artists have generally congregated in certain cities and frequently formed groups, but rarely on the scale and with the intensity of the New York School during the fifties. But then, seldom were so many conditions that fostered artists' association present. Numbering from two hundred to three hundred painters and sculptors, the avant-garde community was large enough to offer a variety of personality and opinion, and small enough for artists to get to know well most of their fellows. Moreover, the artists on the whole lived within strolling distance of each other and of the places they established or designated to meet in, such as the Cedar Street Tavern, the Club, and the Tenth Street galleries. And most important, feeling alienated from and rejected by society at large, avant-garde artists banded together for mutual support and with a sense of aesthetic mission: to maintain the standards of high art while venturing into the new—in the face of an omnipresent pseudo- or mass culture.

However, toward the end of the decade, the sense of community lessened. Generally responsible was the decline of Abstract Expressionism and the emergence of competing styles whose initiators found Tenth Street hostile and avoided it. More specifically accountable was the success of a significant number of Tenth Street artists generally considered the best—success in that they were asked to join prestigious commercial galleries uptown. Moreover, many of these artists were the initiators and activists in the downtown galleries. They came more and more to feel that they had put in their time on Tenth Street and lost their enthusiasm and interest.[33]

As the best artists began to exhibit away from Tenth Street, what remained to be seen there was of decreasing interest. Aggravating this situation was the increase of mediocre, derivative, and eclectic work produced by the influx of newcomers who could show with greater ease—and did. This glut of inferior art drove away the audience and discouraged lively and ambitious young artists from exhibiting downtown. To state it bluntly, it was no longer *important* to show on Tenth Street—or to be there—and when this occurred, the scene declined.

# Notes

1. Renato Poggioli, in *The Theory of the Avant-Garde*, p. 91, observed that in general: "The formation of groups friendly and hostile to avant-garde art takes place by sympathy and antipathy. . . . 'those who understand it and those who do not' . . . . almost by spontaneous generation, by means of single and independent joinings of isolated individuals, a group emerges . . . individuals who end up finding, in the object of their own enthusiasm, reasons for community as well as for separation [from other publics]." The fortuitous character of individual encounters should be stressed. For example, in the case of Rivers, in the summer of 1945, while playing the saxophone at a Maine resort, he became friendly with the wife of a fellow musician, Jane Freilicher, a painter who knew many artists in the New York School. Encouraged by the Freilichers, he began to paint. A year later, Rivers met Nell Blaine, who was living near him in New York City. At her suggestion he enrolled in Hofmann's school in January 1947 and studied there until the summer of 1948. He also attended New York University, where Tony Smith and Baziotes taught, earning his degree in 1951. Fellow students at New York University were Goodnough and Leslie.

2. Kozloff, "An Interview with Friedel Dzubas," p. 49.

3. Ibid.

4. In 1956, the Tanager Gallery organized a show titled *Painters and Sculptors on Tenth Street*, composed of the works of twenty-five artists living on the street. The artists were George Spaventa, Gabriel Kohn, Angelo Ippolito, Saul Leiter, Charles Cajori, Michael Goldberg, Martin Craig, Steve Wheeler, Al Kotin, William King, Albert Swinden, James Rosati, Pat Passloff, Howard Petersen, Vita Petersen, Philip Guston, Robert Bek-Gran, Ruth Abrams, Alfred Jensen, George Cavallon, Linda Lindeberg, Esteban Vicente, Ludwig Sander, Milton Resnick, and Willem de Kooning.

5. Robert Motherwell and Ad Reinhardt, eds., *Modern Artists in America* (New York: Wittenborn, Schultz, 1952).

6. For a discussion of the history of the Club in its early years, see Irving Sandler, "The Club," *Artforum*, September 1965, pp. 27–31.

7. Club panel, "A Group of Younger Artists," 7 March 1952.

8. Many art students in the late forties were veterans of World War II and were more mature and certain of their vocation than the ordinary student. The veterans found it easy to communicate with recognized artists older less in age than in experience as artists.

9. A list of fifty artists who studied with Hofmann appears in Sandler, "Hans Hofmann: The Pedagogical Master," p. 54. Among the ex-students in the second generation were Nell Blaine, Jean Follett, Miles Forst, Mary Frank, Jane Freilicher, Paul Georges, Michael Goldberg, John Grillo, Wolf Kahn, Jan Müller, Robert de Niro, George Ortman, Felix Pasilis, Milton Resnick, Joseph Stefanelli, and Myron Stout.

10. Hofmann's summer school was in Provincetown, Massachusetts, a resort whose size made it possible for all the artists there to get to know each other. Hofmann's students were at the center of activities and attracted artists unaffiliated with the school.

11. Robert Richenberg, *Hofmann Students Dossier*.

12. Duberman, *Black Mountain*, p. 246.

13. For a fuller list of full-time and part-time faculty, see Duberman, *Black Mountain*, chaps. 12–14 passim.

14. Harry F. Gaugh, "Franz Kline's Romantic Abstraction," *Artforum*, Summer 1975, p. 28.

15. Al Hansen, *A Primer of Happenings & Time/Space Art* (New York: Something Else Press, 1965), pp. 94–5. Kaprow wrote of the role played by Rutgers University in bringing artists

together: "Watts originally came to teach engineering; I teach art history. Segal was a chicken farmer nearby; and Brecht in his inimitable way of seeming anonymous, chose to live in a split-level while working as a scientist for Johnson and Johnson Company." (Lawrence Alloway, *American Pop Art*, exhibition catalogue [New York: Collier Macmillan Publishers, 1974], p. 20). Lichtenstein joined the faculty in 1960. Among the students were Lucas Samaras and Robert Whitman.

16. Allan Kaprow, "The Legacy of Jackson Pollock," *Art News*, October 1958, pp. 24–26, 55–57.

17. See Barbara Rose, *Claes Oldenburg*, exhibition catalogue (New York: Museum of Modern Art, 1970), pp. 25–26.

18. Hansen, *A Primer*, p. 103.

19. There was an anti-Still faction at the California School of Fine Arts composed of David Park, Elmer Bischoff, Richard Diebenkorn, and like-thinking associates and students.

20. McChesney, *A Period of Exploration*, p. 37.

21. Ibid., p. 46.

22. Seckler, interview with Allan Kaprow, p. 17.

23. Conversation with Jane Freilicher, New York, 3 January 1974.

24. Thomas B. Hess, *Abstract Painting: Background and American Phase* (New York: Viking Press, 1951).

25. Harold Rosenberg, "The American Action Painters," *Art News*, December 1952, pp. 22–23, 48–50.

26. Lawrence Campbell, "Blaine Paints a Picture," *Art News*, May 1959, p. 62.

27. Barbara Guest and B. H. Friedman, *Goodnough* (Paris: Pocket Museum, Editions Georges Fall, 1962), p. 24.

28. In an interview with Friedel Dzubas, New York, 26 April 1957, he said that de Kooning managed to create a claque around himself, unlike Pollock, and the claque did not like Pollock or Greenberg, who they felt thought Pollock was a greater painter than de Kooning. Greenberg was close to de Kooning up to around 1950 or 1951, and then the relationship deteriorated. De Kooning's partisans also pushed Still, Newman, and Rothko aside. During the forties, the Abstract Expressionists were like conspirators banded together because of their own loneliness. Only when a public was slowly created did they indulge in the luxury of splitting up, going out for votes to be on top with the public.

B. H. Friedman also commented on the rivalry between Pollock and de Kooning, that "as Pollock's work moved out into the larger world, de Kooning watched along with everyone else goading him on in the role of the competitor, not always the friendly competitor. The promoters of this championship fight were the critics. Greenberg was deeply committed to Pollock. . . . On the one side, Rosenberg, . . . was becoming more and more interested in Willem de Kooning. . . . Alongside, or ahead of Rosenberg in this view was Tom Hess."

According to Friedman, Hess considered the rivalry " 'as between two guys on the same team going after a home-run record.' That may be part of the truth. But if, on one level, Pollock and de Kooning were playing on the same team, on another, they were playing for themselves" (B. H. Friedman, *Jackson Pollock: Energy Made Visible* [New York: McGraw-Hill Book Company, 1972], pp. 146–48).

The rivalry between Pollock and de Kooning continued after Pollock's death. For example, on 30 November 1956, not long after Pollock's death, there took place a Club panel, "An Evening for Jackson Pollock," with Brooks, Willem de Kooning, Greenberg, Reuben Kadish, Frederick Kiesler, Kline, Newman, and Rosenberg (moderator). The evening was meant to be a memorial for Pollock, but not all that was said was favorable. At one point, Newman remarked: "Jackson lives" (meaning his spirit, of course). De Kooning turned on him: "What do you mean 'lives?' They dug a hole and they buried him. I was there." Later in the evening, de Kooning called Pollock an "ice-breaker." This angered Greenberg, who thought that the implication was that Pollock was merely a transitional figure who showed the way to artists better than he. In my opinion, the entire session was hardly an homage to Pollock. B. H. Friedman viewed it differently: "In short, throughout the evening two opposing feelings were expressed strongly: first, that this should be a proper memorial, and second, that there should be neither sloppy sentimentalizing nor premature mythmaking" (Friedman, *Jackson Pollock*, p. 254).

29. O'Hara, "A Memoir," in Hunter, *Larry Rivers*, p. 52.

30. Interview with Jane Freilicher. O'Hara wrote poems or short prose introductions for artists' gallery catalogues, including Norman Bluhm, Frankenthaler, Freilicher, Goldberg, Hartigan, and Rivers. He wrote major pieces on Porter and Rivers. See Frank O'Hara, *Art Chronicles: 1954–1966* (New York: George Braziller, 1975) and *Standing Still and Walking in New York* (Bolinas, Calif.: Grey Fox Press, 1975).

31. Morton Feldman, "Frank O'Hara: Lost Times and Future Hopes," *Art in America*, March–April 1972, p. 55.

32. Irving Sandler, Introduction, *Tanager Gallery*, exhibition catalogue (New York: Tanager Gallery, 1959), unpaginated.

33. Young artists judged success primarily in terms of their peers' opinion, but they hoped that a positive consensus would encourage private dealers to represent them. The artists complained frequently about the commercial galleries, but accepted and joined them nonetheless. A few artists talked of Tenth Street as a potential competitor to the existing support system, but most considered their downtown affiliations only temporary.

# 3
# The Colonization
# of Gesture Painting

THE EARLY WAVE of the second generation inherited from the first a new territory in art open for colonization. But as far as many young painters, among them Frankenthaler, Mitchell, Hartigan, Goldberg, and Leslie, were concerned, the terrain was so vast that the pioneering seemed far from over. Besides, the idea of being the first to enter was not deemed too important. The ambition was to realize a genuine image of self, which, if genuine, would be original—and the worth of the gesture painting of their elders was not so much its newness or radicality, although that was valued, as the method it provided for self-exploration.

Such was the existential rhetoric of gesture painting, and very convincing it was.[1] As early as 1950, Motherwell had written that the

> . . . process of painting . . . is conceived of as an adventure, without preconceived ideas on the part of persons of intelligence, sensibility, and passion. Fidelity to what occurs between oneself and the canvas, no matter how unexpected, becomes central. . . . The major decisions in the process of painting are on the grounds of truth, not taste. . . .
>
> . . . no true artist ends with the style that he expected to have when he began, . . . it is only by giving oneself up completely to the painting medium that one finds oneself and one's own style.[2]

Similar ideas were advanced by Rosenberg in 1952, in a widely read and debated article entitled "The American Action Painters": "The painter no longer approached his easel with an image in his mind; he went up to it with material in his hand to do something to that other piece of material in front of him. The image would be the result of this encounter. . . . A painting that is an act is inseparable from the biography of the artist. The painting itself is a 'moment' in the adulterated mixture of his life—. . . The act-painting is of the same metaphysical substance as the artist's existence."[3] According to Rosenberg, the action painter confronted his canvas without preconceptions, and in the process of adding "right" gesture to gesture arrived at an image of his individual identity. Painting was conceived of as a continual struggle for self-definition in pursuit of self-transformation. The appeal was not to art, the creation of art objects, but to the "real-life" experience of self-change.

Uneasy perhaps with Rosenberg's stress on the act of painting as an extra-aesthetic rather than an art-concerned event, yet partaking of the same mood, Schapiro wrote in 1957:

> The consciousness of the personal and spontaneous [which above all motivates the gesture painter] . . . stimulates the artist to invent devices of handling, processing, surfacing, which confer to the utmost degree the aspect of the freely made. Hence the great importance of the mark, the stroke, the brush, the drip, the quality of the substance of the paint itself, and the surface of the canvas as a texture and field of operation—all signs of the artist's active presence. . . .
>
> The impulse . . . becomes tangible and definite on the surface of a canvas through the painted mark. We see, as it were, the track of emotion, its obstruction, persistence or extinction.[4]

But the spontaneous is not all, for, as Schapiro continued:

> . . . all these elements of impulse which seem at first so aimless on the canvas are built up into a whole . . .
>
> . . . The artist today creates an order out of unordered variable elements to a greater degree than the artist of the past. . . .
>
> . . . The order is created before your eyes and its law is nowhere explicit. . . .
>
> . . . This power of the artist's hand to deliver constantly elements of so-called chance or accident, which nevertheless belong to a well defined, personal class of forms and groupings, is submitted to critical control by the artist who is alert to the rightness or wrongness of the elements delivered spontaneously, and accepts or rejects them.[5]

In a similar vein, Parker, an artist of the second generation, characterized what he called "direct painting."

> The process of painting is improvisational—excluding set method, plan, sketch as study, drawing as preliminary to coloring, or relative stages of finish. It may be fast or slow in tempo, impulsive or thoughtful in character. Changes are made in-process; nothing can be fixed up, no additions or corrections made. . . .
>
> The painting is both a thing and an event. . . . an "esthetic" object, . . . [and] behavior in the form of a significant record. While the painter's subject is the painting, the painting's subject is the artist himself as his experience is consummated in the making.[6]

Parker also wrote: "The working attitude of the painter is critical. He is suspicious of anything appearing in the painting that he recognizes; he questions the already-known.

This is antistylistic in bias and bars quotes or allusions. . . . He must learn—and relearn for each painting—the creative leap to accept that which is seen for the first time: the painting is completed in the moment of his realization."[7]

There is a pronounced disposition toward Existentialist philosophy in the thinking of Motherwell, Rosenberg, Schapiro, and Parker. In fact, Existentialism was very much in the air during the late forties and well into the fifties, and artists and critics often borrowed from its terminology, speaking of painting as an unpremeditated "situation" in which a creatively "committed" artist "encountered" images of "authentic being." The process of self-creation was a solitary one of "struggle," fraught with "anxiety," even "anguish." More than all other commentators, Rosenberg considered existential experience to be the mainspring of action painting, elevated above picture-making, aesthetic performance, or any received ideas imposed from without. Indeed, the "genuine" action of self-definition and transformation was so vital as to render picture-making trivial, and the aestheticist, beautifully crafted painting associated with contemporary Parisian abstraction beneath contempt. Moreover, action painting was an ethical process, aiming at self-knowledge, at truth to experience, no matter how raw and unseemly, uncompromisingly yielding nothing to the exercise of artistic taste or notions of style. Indeed, the cultivation of style, that is, *making* a picture in a known or definable style, was a betrayal of radical art whose purpose was to venture into the unknown, to risk painting the as yet undefinable.

De Kooning was generally considered the exemplary gesture painter, above all by Rosenberg. Indeed, de Kooning's pictures, in which open areas composed of raw, "unfinished" brushstrokes are ceaselessly shifting, suggest a perpetual state of becoming. It seemed as if his aim was to avoid the ruts of habit—in a word, stylization—in order to convey more nakedly than ever before in art a sense of his passionate creative struggle. His images look as if they are found in that direct and improvisational striving, done without precalculation and cleaning up. The painterly marks convey the burden of "felt" content. Kline said that "if you meant it enough when you did it, it will mean that much."[8]

Yet de Kooning and gesture painters on the whole had reservations about Rosenberg's conception of action painting. They thought that he had misunderstood their intention. To be sure, they believed that what a picture meant depended substantially on how it was painted. An artist's immersion in the unpremeditated process of painting, responding at once to the flow of consciousness and to the immediacies of painting, would yield a picture different from that based on preconception, a picture more likely to express feeling honestly. This process was valued, but so was the quality of the resulting picture—and Rosenberg neglected this *object*, by focusing almost exclusively on action painting as an *event* and failing to specify how its aims were realized in actual pictures.

Early-wave artists went even further than their elders, questioning the very relevance of heavy existential and ethical rhetoric (but not of honest feeling). Most continued to pay lip service to the moralizing of the first generation, but halfheartedly, a few poking fun at it, as Rivers did when he called it *"ich-schmerz."* [9] Why did artists need to struggle, to make anguished leaps into the unknown or stabs in the dark? Would a picture look or even feel the less for it if artists while working improvisationally nonetheless stressed the role of consciousness, of thoughtful picture-building, and of cultivation of a style? Besides, could style be avoided, even if an artist intended to? Tworkov said no, and he spoke for his younger contemporaries:

> To approach the canvas without any pre-conceptions is in a sense impossible. Many painters approach their canvas without any preliminary drawing, or any preliminary image. Yet they each end up with a characteristic work that cannot be mistaken for anyone else's, because they are, however freely they approach their work, already committed to certain forms, to certain colors, materials, and to certain manners of manipulation. Klines always come out Klines, and Pollocks always come out Pollocks. [10]

This being so, could not artists be somewhat more deliberate in developing both their imagery and painterly qualities—even in a "professional" manner?

Indeed, could not artists introduce pictorial ideas—culled from art history or contemporary art, from nature or other external sources—that were not necessarily the issue of their struggles for images of self, and still remain true to their felt experience? After all, such choices could be private, determined by an individual's feelings, dispositions, appetites, and tastes. Could not an artist *consolidate* accumulated knowledge and awareness? Rosenberg denied this possibility in action painting, but Tworkov thought that an artist could, in fact, should: "No artist is an artist all by himself. He is an artist only by virtue of the fact that he voluntarily permits other artists to act on him, and that he has the capacity to react in turn." Instead of spurning "the ideas of others in order to be more himself," [11] the artist ought to accept them: "Thus he becomes free to use whatever he can in whatever way he can. By releasing himself from the struggles of what he considers not himself, he becomes richer at once. More possibilities loom up for him. Instead of being in a constant state of anxiety, he can be in a constant state of absorption." [12]

In my opinion Tworkov came closer to the true intention of gesture painting than did Rosenberg, whose simplistic approach did not take into account the *complexity* of the art. Finkelstein, more than any other critic, focused on this issue. What impressed him as most significant and radically new about gesture painting was its "polyreferentialness," achieved when an artist rendered a true account of his multilayered living experience in all of its openness, transience, disorderliness, and ambiguity. Using Mitchell's work as an example, he wrote:

> Virtually all of her paintings are in some sense landscapes. Yet in what sense? Are they organizations of spatial relations such as are found in landscape, a set of symbols of landscape elements and of themes associated with landscape, a recall of retinal impressions derived from landscape, the species of distribution of focus and unfocus, of closed and opened, of weighted and unweighted, or in and out; are they the rhythms of landscape or of body and eye movements while in landscape;

14   Joan Mitchell, *George Went Swimming at Barnes Hole, but It Got Too Cold*, 1957.
85¹/₂″ x 78¹/₂″. Albright–Knox Art Gallery, Buffalo, New York.

are they calligraphic play involving an analogy of brushstrokes to natural forms;
are they the recall of specific landscape or of the modes of transformation of landscape into art; or are they indeed all of these and perhaps more?

In each and every Abstract-Expressionist work such issues of transformation
are up for grabs. Moreover it seems of particular importance that the categories of
interpretation seem to shift in the course of our looking at the picture, so that we
are never left with the clear support for just one reading. Thus we can never see it
as an esthetic whole, never the patent form . . . but rather the sum of possible
suggestions. [13]

It was the potential of polyreferentialness, a concept that owes more to John Dewey
than to Sartre, that appealed to and challenged fifties gesture painters. Thus they
shrugged off the stern existentialist claims of Abstract Expressionism. There was great
resistance to this shift in thinking, for if gesture painting was not to be "ethical," would
it not become "beautiful" or decorative, a quality to be spurned. It was widely accepted,
as Elaine de Kooning remarked: " 'Beautiful' is a term that rarely can be applied to
painting any more. The struggle with oneself that now produces art is more likely to
leave harsh, even ugly tracks."[14] But less often than was believed. To be sure, much of
fifties gesture painting, e.g., some of that by de Kooning, Resnick, Goldberg, Leslie,
and Hartigan, looked raw, even violent. But the greater part of it is primarily hedonistic,
tending toward a cool, light lyricism, as is evident in the works of such younger artists as
Mitchell, Frankenthaler, and Resnick (in works executed toward the end of the decade),
and of highly regarded artists of de Kooning's generation, many influenced by him and
available to their juniors, such as Brooks, Bradley Walker Tomlin, Tworkov, Vicente,
George Cavallon, and most of all, Guston.

Many artists proclaimed that avant-garde art could give pleasure, and they gave
freer rein to sensuous inclinations. However, they believed that yielding to the pleasure
principle would not necessarily make their pictures any less honest or difficult, if the
bent toward hedonism was genuine, that is, lacking in artifice. Moreover, during much
of the decade, when gesture painting was not well *known* or easily imitated, artists had
to strive to find forms that embodied the complexity of their true experience—of inner
life and the outer world, of art, and of the "life" of the unfolding picture. Their pictures
did not divulge their content "easily" even when openly lyrical; viewers had to work
hard to *see* it. The difficulty in making and responding to fifties gesture painting pre-
vented the best of it from deteriorating into parody or the merely pretty, decorative, or
artificial. Rather, the delight in bold and skillful painterly activity enabled the early
wave and a number of their elders to put gesture painting on a different tack.

Hess recognized this as early as 1950, when he wrote that the painting of the young
was distinguished by sensibility, skill, cultivation, enthusiasm, and painterliness. "A
sense of pleasure in the creative act is felt throughout."[15] Goldwater's response was similar, but he applied Hess's adjectives to most of the gesture painting of the first as well as
the second generation: "With certain exceptions (of whom De Kooning is the most obvious) this is a lyric, not an epic, art. . . . Judged by their finished works, . . . here are
artists who like the materials of their art: the texture of paint and the sweep of the brush,

the contrast of color and its nuance, the plain fact of the harmonious concatenation of so much of art's underlying physical basis to be enjoyed as such."[16]

Goldwater went on to say:

> Robustiousness is the typical tone of the New York paintings. . . . But whether it is the dripping paint can, the loaded brush, or the slashing palette knife that is thus consciously brought to mind in the observation of the finished work, this remains an art of harmonies as well as of contrasts. The over-all effects may be large and strong, but details are subtle and soft; . . . the tiny area must be noted within the sweeping line and the frequently immense size. . . . It is an art which is as often delicate as it is powerful, and indeed in the best work is both at once.[17]

Goldwater's observations indicate that with the passage of time, the *angst* and violence that seemed to pervade most Abstract Expressionist work dissipated. For example, Pollock's "drip" painting looked more and more beautiful, prompting many to wonder if it was ever as anxious, angry, and full of suffering as much that was written about it claimed. Like Goldwater, gesture painters of a lyrical or hedonist bent not only experienced the pictures of the first generation as pleasurable and aesthetic, but they responded favorably to the open hedonism and well-painted qualities of French modernists such as Bonnard and Matisse. Moreover, both in feeling and "look," much of second-generation gesture painting resembled Impressionism more than Expressionism. It is noteworthy that as the fifties unfolded, there was a growing interest in historic Impressionism. Laying the groundwork was the publication in 1946 of John Rewald's lavishly documented and illustrated *The History of Impressionism*.[18] Following in 1948 was a major Bonnard retrospective at the Museum of Modern Art. It was this show that stunned early-wave artists such as Rivers, Kahn, Blaine, and Freilicher, and revealed to them pictorial possibilities for their own work. The art-conscious public was repeatedly stimulated during the next half-dozen years by shows of Pissarro, Monet, and Renoir, and their successors Bonnard and Vuillard in museums and galleries; by books and articles in art magazines; by a boom in the international art market; and, perhaps most of all, by museum acquisitions, the most prestigious of which was the purchase in 1955 of one of Monet's large *Nymphéas* by the Museum of Modern Art.[19] Indeed, in the fifties, there occurred a convergence in the opinion of artists, critics, curators, dealers, collectors, and gallerygoers concerning the worth of Impressionist paintings that reveals a taste or sensibility of that decade far different from that of the forties.

Given this focus of attention on Impressionism, it is not surprising that critics saw affinities between it and first-generation Abstract Expressionism.[20] It was also natural for them to assume that the earlier movement, because it came first in time, had influenced the pioneers of the later tendency.[21] But this was not the case. The first generation during its germinal period was indifferent or antipathetic to Impressionism. Greenberg recalled in 1955 that Monet "was pointed to as a warning . . . Bonnard's and Vuillard's art . . . [was] deprecated by the avant-garde."[22] Besides, Monet's late *Nymphéas*, which had the closest stylistic affinities to the abstractions of Pollock, Still, Newman,

15

16, 17

18

15 Pierre Bonnard,
*The Breakfast Room,* 1930–31.
62$^7/_8$″ x 44$^7/_8$″.
The Museum of Modern Art, New York.

16 Wolf Kahn, *Arnold's Place,* 1954.
28″ x 36″. Courtesy Grace Borgenicht
Gallery, New York.

17  Nell Blaine, *Harbor and Green Cloth, II,* 1958.
50″ x 65″. Whitney Museum of American Art, New York.

18  Claude Monet, *Water Lilies,* c. 1920.
78¹/₂″ x 235¹/₂″. The Museum of Modern Art, New York.

and Rothko, had not been seen by these artists, since none had been exhibited in America until the fifties.[23] In looking for inspiration to the pictorial ideas of the Impressionists, the early wave took few if any cues from its elders. Indeed, it is the Impressionist component in the gesture painting of the second generation that more than anything else distinguishes it from that of the first (or at least from that which achieved the greatest notoriety), so much so that it is fitting to label the later phase Abstract Impressionism in contrast to the Abstract Expressionism of the earlier period.

Elaine de Kooning saw this in 1955, observing that, "Abstract-Impressionists (who outnumber Abstract-Expressionists two to one, but, curiously, are seldom mentioned). . . . [retain] the quiet, uniform pattern of strokes that spread over the canvas without climax or emphasis."[24] De Kooning recognized that Abstract Impressionism was qualitatively different from its nineteenth-century predecessor. The New York painters "keep the Impressionist manner of looking at a scene but leave out the scene. . . . As the Impressionists attempted to deal with the optical effects of nature, . . . [they] are interested in the optical effects of spiritual states, thereby giving an old style a new subject."[25] To put it somewhat differently, where a Monet began by observing lily pads and ended up with a near-abstract art of subjective sensation, a Guston (who came to be considered the exemplar of Abstract Impressionism) started with the more or less unpremeditated process of painting and arrived at allusions to landscape.

The profile of Abstract Impressionism changed from low to high in 1956 with the emergence of Guston. Even though he was not the first to venture in the direction of Abstract Impressionism, having been preceded by Reinhardt and Tomlin, Guston took the limelight with a show at the Janis Gallery at the start of 1956. Later that year, his reputation was further enhanced by his inclusion in the 12 Americans exhibition at the Museum of Modern Art.[26] Guston's nuanced and spacious painting in the middle and late fifties was hailed both as a novel *extension* of Abstract Expressionism in the direction of Impressionism, and as a lyrical *alternative* to the aggressive, occasionally violent painting of his better-known colleagues. Because of this, Guston began to rival de Kooning as an influence.[27]

What interested the gestural Abstract Impressionists in the pictures of their nineteenth-century predecessors was that each was an allover field, more or less, of hand-painted marks, creating an illusion of light, space, and air which opened up fresh possibilities in painterly painting. It should be noted that this tendency in Abstract Expressionism had ceased to interest Greenberg, who was the first to systematically relate Impressionism to Abstract Expressionism, or more accurately, to the abstraction of Still, Rothko, and Newman. Greenberg focused on a conception of an abstract painting as a holistic or unbroken color field, a conception which was not given widespread consideration until late in the fifties. At the time, the Abstract Impressionists were taken generally to be gesture painters who stressed painterly activity as well as allover composition.

The fullest exposition of the "New Look: Abstract-Impressionism," was an article of that title written by Finkelstein in the spring of 1956. He remarked that the *Nymphéas*

19  Philip Guston, *Dial,* 1956.
72″ x 76″. Whitney Museum of American Art, New York.

by Monet, recently acquired by the Museum of Modern Art, "gives us the opportunity
to re-examine . . . the work of a number of painters who, having grown up in the environment of Abstract-Expressionism, have assumed a direction more closely related to
the specifically visual character of Impressionism."[28] These artists, among whom were
Blaine, Goodnough, Mitchell, Müller, and Parker, were intent on the "discovery of nature in the course of painting, on painting a "field of luminous atmosphere
suggestive of nature," but not from nature. To achieve the desired "continuity of space,"
they disintegrated forms and constructions of forms, that is, the relational design associated with Cubism. Thus, they took their cues from the coloristic and improvisational Fauvism of Matisse and Vlaminck, and the latter-day Impressionism of Bonnard.
"The role of color has become more important whereas drawing, which denotes conceptual control [as against the sensuousness of color], is not very evident. The brokenness of
color—perhaps the most obvious point of similarity [between historic and Abstract Impressionist pictures]—works to produce an over-all activity."[29]

The Abstract Impressionists, even more than the Abstract Expressionists who preceded them, rejected Cubism's rational, deliberately knit together scheme of interrela-
tionships as "too expectable and predetermined to deal with the contemporary artist's
experience," that experience felt to be fluid, transitory, and conditional. Instead of the

"accumulation of parts," the Abstract Impressionists attempted to create a total or mass or single image whose final form would be determined by "some interior means of recognition."[30] Finkelstein concluded that Abstract Impressionist pictures possess a "sense of contemplativeness, as opposed to the athleticism of Expressionism, . . . which brings us back to the waters of the *Nymphéas*."[31]

# Notes

1.  For an extensive analysis of the premises of gesture painting, see Sandler, *The Triumph of American Painting*, chap. VII ("The Gesture Painters").

2.  Robert Motherwell, Introduction, *The School of New York*, exhibition catalogue (Beverly Hills, Calif.: Perls Gallery, 1951), unpaginated.

3.  Rosenberg, "The American Action Painters," pp. 22–23.

4.  Schapiro, "The Liberating Quality of Avant-Garde Art," pp. 38–39.

5.  Ibid., pp. 39–40.

6.  Ray Parker, "A Cahier Leaf: Direct Painting," *It Is* 1 (Spring 1958): 20.

7.  Ibid.

8.  Frank O'Hara, "Franz Kline Talking," *Evergreen Review* 2 (Autumn 1958): 63.

9.  Hess, "U.S. Painting: Some Recent Directions," p. 196.

10.  Jack Tworkov, "A Cahier Leaf: Journal," *It Is* 1 (Spring 1958): 25.

11.  Ibid.

12.  Ibid.

13.  Louis Finkelstein, "Gotham News, 1945–60," *Art News Annual* 34 (1969): 116.

14.  Elaine de Kooning, "Kline and Rothko: Two Americans in Action," *Art News Annual* 27 (1958): 177.

15.  Thomas B. Hess, "Seeing the Young New Yorkers," *Art News*, May 1950, p. 23.

16.  Robert Goldwater, "Reflections on the New York School," *Quadrum* 8 (1960): 30.

17.  Ibid., pp. 33–34.

18.  John Rewald, *The History of Impressionism* (New York: Museum of Modern Art, 1946).

19.  So widespread and intense was the interest in Impressionism by 1956 that Thomas B. Hess reported that Monet's *Nymphéas* "have become a fad, as Clement Greenberg notes in his perceptive essay on the artist in the forthcoming *Art News Annual*, and, as he adds, one's instinct is to back away" (Thomas B. Hess, "Monet: Tithonus at Giverny," *Art News*, October 1956, p. 42). The following month, Hilton Kramer observed that Monet's name "has now replaced that of Cézanne on the lips of many painters . . . the process of reconstructing Monet into an *avant-garde* master of heroic dimensions is now in full swing" (Hilton Kramer, "Month in Review," *Arts*, November 1956, p. 52).

20.  See Sam Hunter, "Guggenheim Sampler," *Art Digest*, 15 May 1954, pp. 8–9, 31; Robert Rosenblum, "Varieties of Impressionism," *Art Digest*, 1 October 1954, p. 7; Greenberg, " 'American-Type' Painting," pp. 179–96; and Louis Finkelstein, "New Look: Abstract-Impressionism," *Art News*, March 1956, pp. 36–39, 66–68. For example, Rosenblum "was surprised at Impressionism's . . . unexpected analogies to recent developments. . . . [e.g.,] the pictorial explorations of a Rothko, a Pollock, a Guston. Like Monet, these new artists challenge traditional (here *cubist*) conventions of formal structure, daring to make a cohesive work of art from unbounded color areas, from the immediate excitement of the paint surface itself" (p. 7).

21.  William Seitz, "The Relevance of Impressionism," *Art News*, January 1969, p. 58, summed up the dilemma: "Aside from its powerfully original components, it is now recognized

that Abstract-Expressionism was more than anything else a meeting of Surrealist imagery and automatism with Cubist form. This view must be augmented in retrospect to recognize the Impressionist component of the mixed currents to which the New York School painters responded, either in sympathy or self-defense." However, Seitz went on to ask: "How is Monet's relevance to Pollock . . . best explained? So far as I know, Pollock showed no special concern for Monet or Impressionism." And to my knowledge, neither did Still, Rothko, Newman, or the other first-generation Abstract Expressionists (with the possible exception of Reinhardt) during the forties.

22. Greenberg, " 'American-Type' Painting," p. 190. In this article, Greenberg was the first to fully develop the idea that Monet's late *Nymphéas* had stylistic affinities to (though not necessarily an influence on) the color-field abstractions of Still, Rothko, and Newman, but Greenberg's essay was written long after the three artists had achieved their mature styles. Greenberg did not think that Pollock was related to Impressionism, but William Rubin did much later, in "Jackson Pollock and the Modern Tradition, Part II," *Artforum*, March 1967, pp. 28–37.

23. My research indicates that Impressionism was not an important force in shaping Abstract Expressionism during its genesis, most likely not until after 1948, that is, after Pollock and Still had achieved their mature styles. According to William Rubin it was Newman who was "the first of the New York painters to speak of rejecting Cézanne as 'my father,' insisting on Monet and Pissarro as 'the true revolutionaries' in whom he had more interest. While not arguing his own direct descent from Impressionism (or that of any of his contemporaries), Newman's emphasis on Monet was important in generating the Monet revival" (Rubin, "Jackson Pollock . . . Part II," p. 37).

Yet, as late as the end of 1948, Newman's attitude to Impressionism was ambivalent. In an article entitled "The Sublime is Now," *Tiger's Eye*, December 1948, pp. 51–53, Newman opposed "notions of beauty" with a "desire for sublimity." In his opinion, the urge for absolute beauty shaped European art and was responsible for its decline, while a yearning for the sublime was accountable for the vitality of the painting of a few New York artists. The ancient Greeks had invented beauty; in their art and that of their successors to the present, e.g., Mondrian, "the sense of exaltation is to be found in perfect form." In contrast to the Greek ideal was "the Gothic or Baroque, in which the sublime consists of a desire to destroy form; where form can be formless." Although his disposition to form as formless may have indicated a leaning toward Impressionism, Newman did not mention it in that context. He did introduce it later in his essay when he remarked that the Impressionists had become disgusted with "the established rhetoric of beauty" in Western art and began to destroy it by insisting on "a surface of ugly strokes." This was Impressionism's revolutionary role as Newman saw it then, but he disparaged its lack of "an adequate substitute for a sublime message," and its inability to evoke "a new way of experiencing life."

24. Elaine de Kooning, "Subject: What, How or Who?" *Art News*, April 1955, p. 62.

25. Ibid.

26. See Kenneth Sawyer, "Art Chronicle," *Hudson Review* 5 (Spring 1957): pp. 111–16; Dore Ashton, "Art," *Arts and Architecture*, March 1956, pp. 14–15, 43–44; and Leo Steinberg, "Month in Review," *Arts*, June 1956, pp. 42–45.

27. Guston had begun to achieve a reputation among artists before 1956. For example, in 1955 Thomas B. Hess wrote: "In America, the new impulse in abstract painting developed in two (not opposite) directions among its originators and the younger painters who emerged on the scene after them: . . . De Kooning's magisterial *Woman* dominates . . . [one direction] . . . Guston's seismographic recordings of sensations of light and touch, are at the other extreme, which tends away from but could still be classified as landscape." (Thomas B. Hess, "Trying Abstraction on Pittsburgh," *Art News*, November 1955, p. 42).

28. Finkelstein, "New Look: Abstract-Impressionism," p. 36.

29. Ibid., p. 67.

30. Ibid., p. 66.

31. Ibid., p. 68.

# 4

# Frankenthaler, Mitchell, Leslie, Resnick, Francis, and Other Gesture Painters

HELEN FRANKENTHALER was among the first of her generation to turn from Cubist design and designing (the kind of picture-making taught in the more "advanced" art schools during the late forties) to a freer construction. After 1949, she took her cues first from Miró and the early Kandinsky, and then from Gorky, whose painting was more fluid and flatter than Kandinsky's and thus more to her liking. In 1950, Greenberg, who had become a close friend, directed her attention to Abstract Expressionism. At the time, de Kooning's gesture painting interested her most.

In her first show in 1951, Frankenthaler exhibited pictures in which she loosened Synthetic Cubist composition by drawing and painting impulsively and by introducing a variety of biomorphic shapes. These works, e.g., *Abstract Landscape*, are clearly eclectic, yet they possess a certain openness, a lightness of touch, a translucency of color (and this despite the frequent use of heavy textures)—all of which anticipate her later, more individual work. In the following year, Frankenthaler completed an ambitious sixteen-foot-long canvas titled *Ed Winston's Tropical Gardens* (1951–52). In it she dissolved Cubist design even more than in *Abstract Landscape*. Line does verge toward rectilinearity, but it is also freewheeling, suggesting rather than defining shapes. The painting is loose like the drawing but dissociated from it.

Frankenthaler would soon achieve a more unified design and even greater spontaneity and fluidity by looking for inspiration to Pollock. His show of black-and-white pictures in 1951 stunned her; as she later wrote: "It was as if I suddenly went to a foreign country but didn't know the language, but had read enough and had a passionate inter-

20, 21
22, 23
24, 25
26, 27
28, 29
206
Pl. I


20



22

20   Helen Frankenthaler, *Abstract Landscape*, 1951.
69″ x 71⁷/₈″. Collection, the artist.

est, and was eager to live there . . . and master the language."[1] Frankenthaler quickly
recognized that she "could stretch more in the Pollock framework," take off from him.[2]
In this she differed from most of her contemporaries, e.g., Mitchell or Leslie, who
thought of Pollock as a dead end.

Later, Frankenthaler visited Pollock in his studio and learned at first hand of his
method of laying a canvas on the floor and applying pigment by "dripping" from all four
sides—letting a picture *happen* rather than *making* it.[3] Her "breakthrough" to an independent style occurred in the fall of 1952, when, in a picture later titled *Mountains
and Sea*, she poured thinned pigment from used coffee cans onto unsized cotton duck,
creating what can be called an art of stain-gesture. Of the change in her work she wrote:
"Before, I had always painted on sized and primed canvas—but my paint was becoming
thinner and more fluid and cried out to be soaked, not resting. In 'Mountains and Sea',
I put in the charcoal line gestures first, because I wanted to *draw* in with color and

21   Helen Frankenthaler, *Mountains and Sea,* 1952.
86$^7/_8$″ x 117$^1/_4$″. Collection, the artist.

22  Jackson Pollock *Echo,* 1951.
91⁷/₈″ x 86″. The Museum of Modern Art, New York.

shape the totally abstract memory of the landscape. I spilled on the drawing in paint from the coffee cans. The charcoal lines were original guideposts that eventually became unnecessary."[4] Dzubas and Greenberg, who saw the picture the day it was made, "agreed it was 'finished' and shouldn't be touched; that is, complete and shouldn't be added to . . . Clem encouraged me to go ahead and make more. I did. In all kinds of combinations and possibilities; I couldn't try them out fast enough."[5]

The spilled area of color became the basis of Frankenthaler's painting. As she said, she used "line, fluid line, . . . not as line, but as . . . color shape acting as the line."[6] This flooded calligraphy enabled her "to push the development of Cubism so that line *per se* disappeared, but . . . the memory or function of it remained."[7] The vestiges of Cubist design—the vertical and horizontal accents that echo the picture edges—continued to be a force as well as a foil in her work as a whole.

However, Frankenthaler came to rely less on drawing and more on relating discrete areas of color. In this she differed from Pollock, who preferred to compose with skeins of paint. He rarely used planar elements, except in his black paintings (1951–52), and it is noteworthy that in them, he eliminated color. His best pictures convey a sensation of an allover tonality, of one "color" and not of the interaction of colors. Pollock and Frankenthaler also differed in their facture. Pollock's paint is generally thick; it sits on the surface as a tactile substance. Frankenthaler's diluted pigment is soaked into the canvas,

23   Helen Frankenthaler, *Round Trip,* 1957.
70¼″ x 70¼″. Albright–Knox Art Gallery, Buffalo, New York.

24   Helen Frankenthaler, *Open Wall,* 1952–53.
53³/₄″ x 131¹/₈″. Collection, the artist.

25   Helen Frankenthaler,
*Blue Territory,* 1955.
113″ x 58″.
Whitney Museum of American Art, New York.

26   Helen Frankenthaler, *Trojan Gates,* 1955.
72″ x 48⁷/₈″. The Museum of Modern Art, New York.

27 Helen Frankenthaler, *Mountain Storm,* 1955.
72″ x 48″. Andre Emmerich Gallery, New York.

making it more optical and less tactile than Pollock's. Indeed, staining enabled Frankenthaler to create colors that were more disembodied, immediate, and open than those of any of her contemporaries, and this even in pictures executed in 1955 and 1956 which were more heavily pigmented in an ostensible gestural manner, perhaps in response to prevailing New York School styles. Not until 1959 did Morris Louis exhibit pictures which surpassed Frankenthaler's in opticality.

Unlike Pollock and Louis, Frankenthaler rarely allowed her poured areas to stand untouched. She "drew" in color by puddling, rubbing, blotting, and brushing, and by introducing linear elements reminiscent of Gorky's and de Kooning's. By manipulating liquid pigment, Frankenthaler produced a variety of textures, slight to be sure but textures nonetheless, ranging from the turpentine spread at the edges of shapes to luminous washes to denser areas where pools of paint had dried—all of which contrasted with expanses of cotton duck left bare.

28  Helen Frankenthaler, *Eden,* 1957.
103″ x 117″. Collection, the artist.

The modulation of thinned pigment added substance to the forms and, at the same time, generated illusionistic space, "false space," as she called it. The suggestion of a third dimension was of great importance to Frankenthaler, probably a carry-over of Hofmann's teaching. As she wrote: "The 'why' of how a picture works best for me involves how much working false space it has in depth. . . . It's a play of ambiguities."[8] One of the ambiguities was that her pictures were at once atmospheric and flat. Staining allowed Frankenthaler to have it both ways since an image was optical on the one hand, and on the other hand, was neither on top of nor behind the picture plane but physically fused with the fabric ground.

The unprimed canvas whose weave was visible in the thinly painted and bare areas alike not only countered the sense of depth and of paint substance but, as the entire surface, acted as a *field*, contributing a quality of openness, of expansiveness. The canvas also constituted a source of light beneath the washes of color that made them luminous; an arena of color events; and, when left untouched, a color in itself.

After 1957, Frankenthaler cultivated a more open style, diluting her pigment and leaving expanses of canvas unpainted, as in *Eden*, a major work of that year. In other pictures, she suppressed intricate linear patterns and splashed details in favor of the large stained color area, this tendency anticipated by *Open Wall* (1952–53). Frankenthaler did not limit herself to a single manner of working for long. Throughout her career, she frequently circled back to earlier ideas, developing them in new ways or integrating them with more recent ideas. Her work not only fluctuated between an emphasis on line as against soft-edged color film; but on the painterly as against the volatile, stained effect; on the spare as against the complicated; on the open field as against the contained, massed image.

By working into spilled paint, Frankenthaler also made her abstractions gestural—controlling accidents, making them *hers*, and exposing her personal touch. She was as concerned with gesture as any other member of the early wave. When asked what it meant to her, she replied: "When I say gesture, my gesture, I mean what my mark is. . . . It is a struggle for me to both discard and retain what is gestural and personal, 'Signature.' . . . 'Gesture' must appear out of necessity not habit."[9] Unlike most of her contemporaries, Frankenthaler dissociated gestural qualities from the loaded brush. Lacking the muscularity of heavy paint marks, her touch is light, more often than not, delicate.

Perhaps as important to Frankenthaler as painterly gesture was nature. Landscapes—actual, recalled, or imagined—were essential catalysts of feeling. It is noteworthy that her move to the medium of staining was preceded by a series of watercolors she had painted from nature the summer before. The openness of landscape possibly contributed to her desire for a more open medium, leading to her staining. And staining can also be viewed as a translation of watercolor technique into oil painting.

The combination of Frankenthaler's personal gesture and conception of internalized landscape yielded abstractions that are lyrical, in the sense that they are primarily impulsive, sensuous, and hedonistic. Barbara Rose situated them in the tradition of "the *fête champêtre*, or lovers' picnic, with its erotic overtones and allusions to a paradise of youth, beauty, joy, and sensual delectation. . . . [yet possessed of] ephemeralness and . . . fugitiveness."[10] This kind of content was more acceptable in the fifties than in the forties, but Frankenthaler carried it to an extreme which prompted frequent criticism—and occasional praise. In 1960, Schuyler singled her out from her contemporaries, remarking that her "special courage was in going against the think-tough and paint-tough grain of New York School abstract painting. Often pale (not weak), soaked in (only sometimes), quickly dwelt upon—she . . . chanced beauty in the simplest and most forthright way."[11]

29   Helen Frankenthaler, *Basque Beach,* 1958.
58¹/₂″ x 69¹/₂″. Hirshhorn Museum and Sculpture Garden, Smithsonian Institution, Washington, D.C.

30   Joan Mitchell, *14th of July,* c. 1956.
60″ x 108″. Collection, Mr. and Mrs. Gifford Phillips, New York.

The early development of Joan Mitchell paralleled that of Frankenthaler. She too was schooled in Cubism and around 1950 reacted against it because of a need to paint more freely. Mitchell unlocked her shapes and set them into motion, but without relinquishing (then or later) the stabilizing orthogonal infrastructure of Cubism. Like Frankenthaler, Mitchell was traditionalist in her outlook, that is, in large measure she derived her art from art. As she said: "I've tried to take from everybody. . . . I can't close my eyes or limit my experiences. . . . Because I live now, I am more interested in art now. It's different as any art is different from period to period. But, it's no better or worse."[12]

Mitchell looked for guidance first to Kandinsky's improvisations (1910–19) and the lines of force in Duchamp's "futurist" pictures (1911–13), and then to Gorky's fluid calligraphy, and de Kooning's and Kline's energetic painterly drawing. She was also influenced by the linear configurations in Mondrian's Analytic Cubist trees and (more than has been acknowledged) Pollock's "drip" paintings. In a sense, she subjected ideas that interested her in the works of Kandinsky, Duchamp, Gorky, Mondrian, and Pollock to a gestural approach inspired by de Kooning and, to a lesser degree, Kline. By choosing de Kooning as her exemplar rather than Pollock, Mitchell parted aesthetic paths with Frankenthaler.

The abstractions that Mitchell exhibited in her first show at the start of 1952 are thinly painted, predominantly white fields traversed by interlacing, arm-long, curving, sketchy brushmarks. Later in the fifties, her pictures became denser, composed of fleshier, more assertive strokes of full-bodied color which interact with each other rather than with the white. But even in these more recent canvases, the gestures are markedly linear, this distinguishing them from the broader swaths favored by de Kooning and Kline. Indeed, what Mitchell borrowed, she transformed; her painterly networks are unmistakably hers.

The prevalence of swift, arcing lines makes Mitchell's pictures appear lyrical in a way that de Kooning's, especially, and Kline's do not, although like theirs, hers were often characterized as aggressive, even violent.[13] Augmenting the lyrical quality of Mitchell's painting is her imagery. Unlike de Kooning's city-inspired canvases of the early fifties, e.g., *Excavation*, and Kline's abstractions of bridges and half-constructed or demolished skyscrapers (all of which strongly impressed her), Mitchell's painting had its origins in nature, in recollected landscapes and waterscapes, e.g., the Chicago lakefront where she lived as a child. She appears to have been driven to recapture in her abstractions the intensity of emotions associated with certain scenes in the past. As she once said about a work: "I'm trying to remember what I felt about a certain cyprus tree."[14] She used the direct process of painting not to describe the scene literally but to re-create the sentiment that the initial experience of it gave rise to. And it is the painting as painting that is the primary conveyer of feeling.

Although there are sometimes frightening intimations, e.g., of lake storms, in her work, it is on the whole pleasurable, often joyful. In *George Swimming at Barnes Hole, but It Got Too Cold* (1957), the image of shimmering water and sunstreaked atmos-

14, 30
31, 32
33, 207
Pl. II

14

31   Joan Mitchell, *Hemlock,* 1956. 91″ x 80″.
Whitney Museum of American Art, New York.

32   Joan Mitchell, *Mont St. Hilaire,* 1957.
80″ x 76″. The Lannan Foundation, Palm Beach, Florida.

33 Joan Mitchell, *City Landscape,* 1955.
80″ x 80″.
The Art Institute of Chicago.

phere is interspersed with bleak whites, which were prompted by memories of a hurri-
cane that struck Long Island in 1954.[15] But the stronger feeling is one of delight.
Indeed, the empathetic viewer is involuntarily caught up in the exuberant and graceful
sweep of Mitchell's painterly drawing, marveling at her ability to give rein to impulse
while remaining in control, and to paint boldly and subtly at one and the same time.

Alfred Leslie, Michael Goldberg, Grace Hartigan, and Milton Resnick (in the
early and middle fifties), in contrast to Frankenthaler and Mitchell, represented the anti-
lyrical side of gesture painting. Porter characterized the work in Leslie's first show in
1952 as a "reckless expressionism— . . . his paintings seem violently revealed."[16] The
"make-it-tough-even-ugly" approach had its attractions. It showed that an artist was too
"serious" to contrive decorative and easy art, the kind of art that appealed to middle-
class taste. Indeed, the aim was to challenge conventional taste. Adjectives such as elegant, handsome, and beautiful were considered insulting by gesture painters on the
whole, even by those whose art could be called elegant, etc.

The model for the more violence-bent of younger artists was de Kooning. His pictures seemed the rawest and most dynamic of any painted by his contemporaries. They
looked "unfinished" because he allowed the signs of his creative struggle to remain. This
direct gestural action implied emotional honesty—carrying a painting only as far as passion would allow and stopping, refusing to revise or touch up, no matter how seemingly
anarchic and shocking the resulting work. Parker recalled that "painters were dedicated

34, 35
36, 37

34 Alfred Leslie, *The Minx,* 1955.
56³/₄″ x 40¹/₂″. Collection, Mr. and Mrs. Sidney Kohl, Milwaukee, Wisconsin.

35 Alfred Leslie, *Collage with Stripes,* 1956.
24¹/₂″ x 18¹/₂″. Whitney Museum of American Art, New York.

to the idea that they could surprise themselves." Pictures which were an outpouring often ended up looking ugly or bizarre, and that came to be valued. "Often painters talked about disliking canvases that looked too correct or too finished or too beautiful so the rawness or horror of the painting was more important, more highly praised than any kind of painting that looked like it had a history or like it belonged somewhere or looked calculated in any way at all."[17] This attitude was encouraged by Existentialist thinking. Artists felt called upon to risk all by submitting to the dictates of their immediate experience and to express every facet of that experience, no matter how unseemly, in the cause of "authenticity." More than that, leading Existentialists focused on the squalid side of life, e.g., Sartre in *Nausea*.

Painting that was raw, particularly on a large scale, was often considered a metaphor for urban (New York) living or for Americanness. The new American painting in its roughness was thought to challenge French taste, that is, the tradition of the beautifully painted picture associated with the School of Paris. There was implicit in this notion an avant-garde stance. In a statement of 1953 proclaiming the superiority of American over French versions of Abstract Expressionism, Greenberg wrote: "Every

36   Alfred Leslie, *Abstraction,* 1956. 48″ x 48″. Neuberger Museum, State University of New York at Purchase.

74

37   Alfred Leslie, *Soldier's Medal,* 1959.
92″ x 119″. Albright–Knox Gallery, Buffalo, New York.

fresh and productive impulse in painting since Manet, and perhaps before, has repudiated received notions of finish and unity, and manhandled into art what until then seemed too intractable, too raw and accidental, to be brought within the scope of esthetic purpose."[18]

There was another aim of many of the ruder and wilder gesture painters: the ambition to paint big-time pictures, pictures that would jar the art-conscious audience into paying attention. This led to the painting of huge and aggressive canvases. Some of these were truly powerful and dramatic; most lapsed into a socko-whammo parody, shock-for-shock's-sake, appealing to a taste for the "ugly" which could be just as banal as the taste for "beauty."

The clumsiness of artists who were obviously virtuoso was early and often questioned. Were the impetuous, slashed gestures on huge canvases truly felt or contrived for theatrical effect? Were they genuine communication or inflated rhetoric? Did they issue from a painter's own artistic identity or were they slapdash manneristic rehashes of de Kooning and others of his generation? Critics who responded favorably to the work of a Leslie or a Goldberg acknowledged the undeniable influence of de Kooning, "the rare painter whose following includes artists of high capacity,"[19] and went on to acclaim their headlong energy and muscularity, and their daring "directness that makes much vanguard painting seem tight and prim by comparison," as Porter wrote of Leslie's work in 1952.[20] These critics did not consider wildness only "ugly," "harsh," or "fierce" (frequent adjectives), but elegant and exuberant as well, even exhilarating, as Steinberg wrote of Goldberg's "undoctored splashings of thick paint . . . Pigment is smeared and knifed, scratched away and masked out by paper diapers and canvas strips. But it works, and works joyously."[21] Yet in the same review, Steinberg had reservations: "The raw, rash, rapid handling of paint is the Hofmannerism of our day; . . . Surely the right to these sweeping streaks must be earned by the grace of some fugitive or feverish vision and the discovery of some equally sudden design. Expressionism is . . . a passionate involvement in the moment of crisis, . . . [without which] you get a *Dies Irae* arranged by George Melachrino."[22]

Milton Resnick was one of the more aggressive of the painters working in the vein of de Kooning. However, around 1958, he began to change from a raw Abstract Expressionism to a lyrical Abstract Impressionism, soon becoming the most extreme and consummate gesture painter identified with that tendency. Inspired by the late Monet, Resnick softened his former packed, slashing brushmarks, turning them into loose dabs of pigment varied with calligraphic strokes, all of which were improvised into atmospheric, open, often wallsize fields. Despite their lack of clear focal points, these allover abstractions tense and relax as do live organisms. Resnick's touches of paint do not simulate the movement of light in nature, as do Monet's, but "look the way Monet might have painted if he had never gone outdoors."[23] However, like the Impressionist master's gestures, Resnick's convey sensations of calm and sensuousness.

Clyfford Still did not exert as strong an influence on the second generation as de Kooning, Hofmann, Pollock, and Guston, but his ideas were proselytized by ex-

38  Michael Goldberg, *At Patsy's,* 1958.
59″ x 54″. Collection, Mr. and Mrs. Sidney Kohl, Milwaukee, Wisconsin.

39  Michael Goldberg, *Summer House,* 1958.
89″ x 86″. Albright–Knox Art Gallery, Buffalo, New York.

40 Milton Resnick, *RR*, 1957.
36″ x 38″. New York University Art Collection, Grey Art Gallery and Study Center.

41 Milton Resnick, *Low Gate*, 1957.
76″ x 68½″. Whitney Museum of American Art, New York.

students, such as Ernest Briggs, Edward Dugmore, and Jon Schueler, who had moved from San Francisco to New York in the early fifties, began to exhibit there, and achieved growing recognition. These artists had studied with Still at the California School of Fine Arts during the brief period from 1946 to 1950 when "a free and inspired spirit was born—tonic for any painter with a desire for discovery," as Hubert Crehan wrote. "There was a search afoot for a new idea, a way out of the impasse bequeathed by Cubism."[24] Not only Still's teaching, but his painting, which became known in 1947, pointed the way for many students. "It overlapt the Cubist impasse entirely; it was not just a work in progress, experimental, but a fully mature and new expression. Thereafter, for many artists in San Francisco the sense of discovery and investigation of the possibilities of free-form painting was quickened; any fears that there was no way out of the dilemma—that simple geometric abstraction or representational Expressionism were the only alternatives to Cubism—were exploded."[25]

In 1950, Crehan had written "that Still's forms are *open to refinement and extension.*"[26] The styles of Briggs, Dugmore, and Schueler in the fifties do bear a family resemblance to Still's while differing substantially because of their more explicit references to nature, their greater lyricism, and their stress on painterly finesse.

The pictures of the three young artists are strongly evocative of natural processes or images. Briggs's landslides of patches of pigment are metaphors for nature as a cataclysmic force. Schueler's earlier abstractions envisage nature's actions in a gentler way; later pictures are more suggestive of landscape, a landscape whose source was in Schueler's psychic world. Believing that art ought to change life, he began to search for his inner landscape in the outer world. He found it on the northwest coast of Scotland and, moving there in 1957, painted his emotional response to water and particularly sky—to actual scenes he had first imagined. These luminous, atmospheric seascapes, composed primarily of simple, horizontal rectangles, are related more to Rothko's abstractions than to Still's.

Still's canvases, while elating in their expansiveness, are on the whole stark and forbidding. The pictures of Briggs, Dugmore, and Schueler are comparatively sensuous, refined, and inviting. Critics were quick to perceive their graceful and relaxed lyrical qualities. In an early review of Dugmore's works, Crehan wrote that they are for the most part painted with a knife but contain thinly brushed "misty, gentle passages [which] give them a fullness and richness."[27] Sawin remarked of Schueler that he "handles paint in a way that . . . combines abstract-expressionist vigor with . . . finesse and nuanced rendering."[28] Although Briggs, Dugmore, and Schueler did not fully abandon Still's visionary aspirations and, particularly, his non-Cubist space, their concern with painterly quality and celebration of nature separated them from their teacher and brought them close to their East Coast contemporaries. This provided the three West Coast painters with relatively easy access into the New York School (although they sometimes resented such identification).[29]

The most original of the young San Francisco abstract painters was Sam Francis, who was not enrolled at the California School of Fine Arts but nearby at the University

44, 45
48, 49

46, 47

50, 51
52, 53

42   Milton Resnick, *Genie,* 1959.
     104″ x 70″. Whitney Museum of
     American Art, New York.

43   Clyfford  Still,  *Untitled*, 1957.
112″ x 154″. Whitney Museum of
American Art, New York.

44  Ernest Briggs, *Untitled,* 1953.
66″ x 37¹/₂″. Collection, the artist.

45  Ernest Briggs, *Untitled,* 1955.
57″ x 127″. Collection, the artist.

46 Edward Dugmore, *Untitled, 1951—Red,* 1951. 69¹/₂″ x 52″. The Maurice E. Odoroff Family Collection, Alexandria, Virginia.

47 Edward Dugmore, *Untitled, 1959—J,* 1959. 77¹/₂″ x 59″. Collection, the artist.

54   of California at Berkeley. Francis studied, speedily assimilated, and used authoritatively the pictorial ideas of Still and, even more, Rothko, who was the primary influence on the young painter. After receiving an MA degree, Francis moved to Paris and made it his home. Thus he did not participate in the New York art scene except for a period from the end of 1958 to the beginning of 1960. However, his paintings were well known in New York; in 1955 and 1958 respectively, the Museum of Modern Art acquired two

51   large works, both of 1953, *Big Red* and *Black in Red*, and included him in its *12 Americans*, 1956, and *The New American Painting* show, which circulated throughout Europe and ended up in New York, 1958–59. He was also given shows in 1956, 1957, and 1959. Moreover, what was exhibited was closely scrutinized because of the enormous reputation Francis had achieved in Europe after 1952.[30]

The two pictures acquired by the Modern are composed of almost allover fields of thinly painted, trickling cell-like areas of more or less the same color, size, and shape among which are visible bits of cells of other colors, e.g., in *Big Red*, details of blue and orange show beneath the scarlet screen. Although there was no mistaking Francis's style, his painting owed much to others: its fluidity to Gorky and Rothko; its airiness and luminosity to Rothko; and its alloverness and unbounded expansion to Still, Monet, and to a lesser degree Pollock and Tobey.[31] Francis and Frankenthaler did not know each other's work, but both favored washes of pigment. However, unlike her, he did not stain into unsized cotton duck, preferring to paint his canvas white before using color, thus creating a more opaque, less open surface. Like Frankenthaler's work, that of Francis is essentially lyrical in "the Watteau to Matisse tradition of French hedonism."[32] But the cellular abstractions, despite the beauty of their soaring, incorporeal, glowing colors, are

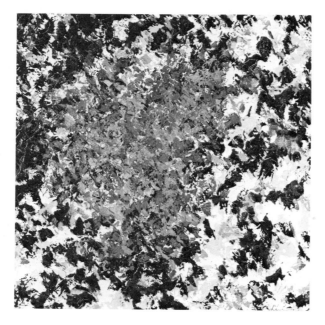

48   Jon Schueler, *Counterpoint,* 1953.
50″ x 48″. Collection, Rosemary Franck.

49   Jon Schueler, *Snow Cloud and Blue Sky,* 1958.
80″ x 71″. Whitney Museum of American Art, New York.

50   Sam Francis, *Blue-Black,* 1952.
117″ x 76¼″. Albright–Knox Art Gallery,
Buffalo, New York.

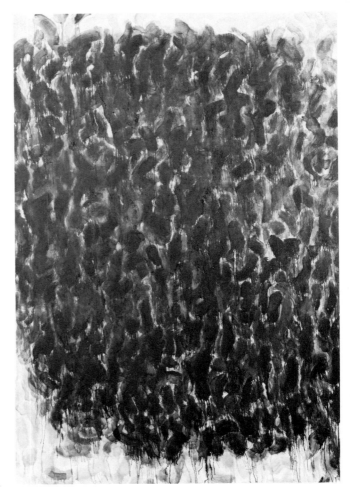

51   Sam Francis, *Big Red,* 1953.
120″ x 76¼″. The Museum of Modern Art, New York.

52  Sam Francis, *Red and Black,* 1954.
76³/₄″ x 38¹/₈″.
The Solomon R. Guggenheim Museum, New York.

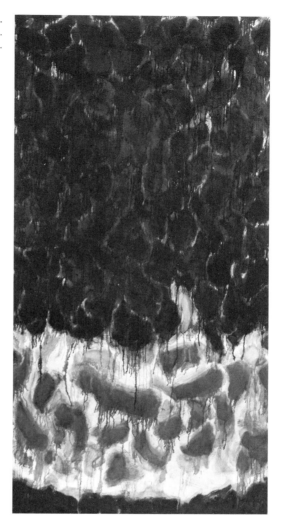

also unnerving, calling to mind magnified human corpuscles, and in the red pictures particularly, bleeding tissue—an expression perhaps of the prolonged illnesses from which Francis suffered during much of his adult life.

In 1956, Francis turned from painting limitless fields of color-drenched cellular units to improvising clusters of cells which are more varied in shape and size and which throw off spatters and runs of pigment. These clusters of mostly red, blue, and yellow are spotted on a field of primed and/or painted white—suggesting richly colored islands floating in a limitless sea of white, as in *The Whiteness of the Whale* (1957), a germinal work. The new emphasis on white was prompted by trips in 1957 and 1958 to Japan, where Francis was strongly affected by Oriental calligraphy. However, unlike ink drawing, he began to paint in a heavier, more painterly fashion, making the white active and assertive, more like Kline's surfaces. At roughly the same time that Francis embraced ideas in Eastern art, he responded to gesture painting in New York, particularly after

53

53  Sam Francis, *The Whiteness of the Whale,* 1957.
104$^{1}/_{2}''$ x 85$^{1}/_{2}''$. Albright–Knox Art Gallery, Buffalo, New York.

54  Sam Francis, *Shining Back,* 1958.
79³/₈″ x 53¹/₈″. The Solomon R. Guggenheim Museum, New York.

55  Sam Francis, *Abstraction, 1959.*
84″ x 50″.
Whitney Museum of American Art, New York.

moving there in 1958. And yet, despite the physicality of his pictures at the end of the fifties, they remain disembodied and spacious, even in the denser, more corporeal ones, e.g., *Emblem* (1959).

The archipelago images that Francis executed on a mural scale from 1957 to 1960 are his best known. Toward the end of this period, he tended to paint more and more of the surface white, often in the centers, like a vertical channel bordered by high-keyed clusters. These immense abstractions are reminiscent of all-white pictures Francis made in Paris from 1950 to 1952 which were unknown in New York, and they also anticipate subsequent vast pictures in which the white covers all but a multicolored strip along the canvas edges, suggesting "the void." In his work generally, Francis appeared to seek to escape gravity,[33] which weighs down finite bodies, and to attain a state of levitation in an infinite and ethereal, iridescent space.

# Notes

1. Barbara Rose, *Helen Frankenthaler* (New York: Harry N. Abrams, 1971), p. 29.

2. Henry Geldzahler, "An Interview with Helen Frankenthaler," *Artforum*, October 1965, p. 37.

3. Frank O'Hara, *Helen Frankenthaler*, exhibition catalogue (New York: Jewish Museum, 1960), p. 6. Frankenthaler's facture was anticipated by James Brooks, who had been a fellow student in the classes of Wallace Harrison in 1949. At that time, taking his cues from Pollock, Brooks poured diluted paint onto the backs of raw canvas, using the suggestions of the forms that soaked through as the points of departure for his painting. Until around 1954, he painted thinly and preferred fluid-looking shapes.

4. Gene Baro, "The Achievement of Helen Frankenthaler," *Art International*, 20 September 1967, p. 36.

5. Ibid.

6. Ibid., p. 34.

7. Ibid.

8. Ibid.

9. Geldzahler, "An Interview with Helen Frankenthaler," p. 38. Frankenthaler went on to say: "I don't start with a color order, but find the color as I go."

10. Rose, *Helen Frankenthaler*, p. 50.

11. J[ames] S[chuyler], "Reviews and Previews: Helen Frankenthaler," *Art News*, May 1960, p. 13.

12. "Is Today's Artist With or Against the Past? Part 2," *Art News*, September 1958, p. 41.

13. See B[etty] H[olliday], "Reviews and Previews: Joan Mitchall," *Art News*, January 1952, p. 46; and D[orothy] G[ees] S[eckler], "Reviews and Previews: Joan Mitchell," *Art News*, March 1955, p. 51.

14. John Ashbery, "An Expressionist in Paris," *Art News*, April 1965, p. 63. See also Irving Sandler, "Mitchell Paints a Picture," *Art News*, October 1957, pp. 44–47, 69–70, and Marcia Tucker, *Joan Mitchell*, exhibition catalogue (New York: Whitney Museum of American Art, 1974).

15. Sandler, "Mitchell Paints a Picture," p. 70.

16. F[airfield] P[orter], "Reviews and Previews: Alfred Leslie," *Art News*, February 1952, p. 39.

17. Mary Fuller, "Was There a San Francisco School?" *Artforum*, January 1971, p. 53.

18. "Is the French Avant-Garde Overrated?" *Art Digest*, September 1953, p. 12.

19. Leo Steinberg, "Month in Review," *Arts*, January 1956, p. 46.

20. P[orter], "Reviews and Previews: Alfred Leslie," p. 39.

21. Steinberg, "Month in Review," p. 46.

22. Ibid., pp. 47–48.

23. J[ames] S[chuyler], "Six Highlights This Winter: Milton Resnick," *Art News*, February 1960, p. 43.

24. Hubert Crehan, "Is There a California School?" *Art News*, January 1956, pp. 34, 35.

25. Ibid., p. 64.

26. Ibid., p. 65.

27. H[ubert] C[rehan], "Edward Dugmore: A Second One-Man Show by One of the Younger Romantic Painters," *Arts Digest*, 15 October 1954, p. 9.

28. M[artica] S[awin], "Jon Schueler," *Arts*, March 1957, p. 55.

29. Fuller, "Was There a San Francisco School?" pp. 47–48.

30. There were developments parallel to American gesture painting in Europe known in

New York. One in Paris was called Informal Art, Lyrical Abstraction or Tachism. Aside from Sam Francis, the best of the young artists working in this vein was Jean-Paul Riopelle. Outside of France, the most important tendency was Cobra (named from the first letters of Copenhagen, Brussels, and Amsterdam) formed by Karel Appel, Corneille, Asgar Jorn, Pierre Alechinsky, and others devoted to an extreme Abstract Expressionism. In England too, there was a related development, exemplified by the painting of Patrick Heron, Peter Lanyon, and Alan Davie. Another consequential movement in Europe was Art Brut initiated by Jean Dubuffet, but much as his "matter painting" and that of his leading follower, Tapies, was admired in New York, it did not exert much influence here.

31. For a detailed analysis of Francis's artistic development, see Robert T. Buck, Jr., "The Paintings of Sam Francis," in *Sam Francis: Paintings 1947–1972.* exhibition catalogue (Buffalo, N.Y.: Albright-Knox Art Gallery, 1972), pp. 14–24.

32. Priscilla Colt, "The Painting of Sam Francis," *Art Journal*, Fall 1962, p. 1.

33. Katherine Kline, Chronology, in *Sam Francis: Paintings 1947–1972*, p. 134.

# 5
# Gestural Realism

FOLLOWING THEIR OWN inclinations and their sense of what might be a fresh direction in Abstract Expressionism, many early-wave artists turned toward "realism" while painting in a gestural manner. Hess noted in 1954 that for those artists whose work has a " 'New York look' . . . with descending age comes an increasing interest in figurative elements."[1] The poles within realist painting, as early-wave artists saw them, were near-literal representation and gestural near-abstraction. On the one hand, an artist could paint "things like an old woman's legs, as in a Rivers painting."[2] On the other hand, the process of painting could take precedence and be used to impose style on subject matter, or to find both subject matter and style. Freilicher remarked that the choices depended on an emphasis on "image" or "process." "In the old masters, the image is so strong that the process seems to be magic. With Cézanne [as with the later gesture painters] you can see where he started and where he finished." An unfinished "look" gives rise to "a nervous quickening which is exciting. It makes you think of the artist." Painters of the fifties naturally looked for "the how of it [in Hess's words]—the speed, rise and fall of the pigment and so on." Concerning her own work, Freilicher professed "a desire to cover all traces, but then you give up freshness and looseness and a certain charm that comes from being able to see the process."[3]

Like Freilicher, such artists as Porter and Katz were intent on the scrutiny of the subject. Others, including Hartigan and Elaine de Kooning, took the other tack, displaying gestural manners of approaching the subject.[4] Another group, among them Blaine and Kahn, worked in between the two positions. The versatile Rivers painted on all sides of the image-process dialectic. Instead of observed subject matter, a number of other artists substituted an invented, symbolic figuration, emphasizing either imagery, as Jan Müller did, or the process of painting, as Lester Johnson did.

The painterly "look" was important to early-wave realists, since like that of gesture painting, it conveyed the impression of directness and of honesty. Moreoover, the rela-

56   Larry Rivers, *Double Portrait of Frank O'Hara,* 1955.
15¹/₄" x 19¹/₈". The Museum of Modern Art, New York.

57  Larry Rivers, *Molly and Breakfast,* 1956.
47³/₄″ x 71³/₄″. Hirshhorn Museum and Sculpture Garden, Smithsonian Institution, Washington, D.C.

58  Jane Freilicher,
*Portrait of John Ashbery,* 1954.
Approx. 42″ x 55″.
Whereabouts unknown.

59  Jane Freilicher, *The Mallow-Gatherers,* 1958. 72″ x 72″. Collection, the artist.

60  Nell Blaine, *Autumn Studio II,* 1957–8. 45″ x 38″. Courtesy of the Fischbach Gallery, New York.

tion to abstract gesture painting guaranteed the contemporaneity of their kind of realism and separated it from tendencies taken to be retrogressive and provincial, such as Social Realism, Regionalism, and Magic Realism, which had had their heyday in the thirties.[5] Still, many artists old and young continued working in these manners, and in 1953, a number of them as well as modernist figurative artists generally admired by the New York School, among them Milton Avery, published a magazine titled *Reality*, which was militantly opposed to Abstract Expressionism for being concerned only with "mere textural novelty" for its own sake and not as "the means to a larger end, which is the depiction of man and his world." Cliché-ridden manifestos dedicated to "a respect and love for the human qualities in painting" had little if any meaning to early-wave realists.[6] Indeed, they were so persuaded by abstract gesture painting and its justifications that they could not help but cultivate its pictorial innovations while striving to achieve individual styles.

Because of their sympathy to abstraction, young realists were troubled by the objections of doctrinaire abstractionists, the most vociferous of whom were geometric and color-field painters. The older abstract artists recounted their earlier struggles against academic social and regionalist realists and reviled any move *back* to the figure as a betrayal of modernism at worst, and at best, a cowardly loss of nerve. They advanced the doctrine that the flatness of the picture plane was a *sine qua non* of modernist painting. Suspicious of the shallow depth in gesture painting, they had only contempt for early-wave painting in which solid, recognizable images were placed in recessive space. Reinhardt, who was identified with both the geometric and the color-field vanguards, was the strongest propagandist for this modernist position, which he carried to a purist art-for-art's-sake extreme. He contended that the true goal of contemporary art was to distill the artness of art and that painting was diminished if impure elements such as representational imagery and illusionistic space were permitted.

It should be noted that there was aesthetic enmity between the geometric abstractionists who had constituted the avant-garde in the thirties and the Abstract Expressionists, color-field and gestural, who had supplanted them. Yet the dogmas of the earlier vanguard still carried weight. However, the early wave was concerned more with the criticism of those within its immediate circle, for example, Crehan's, which struck not only at the younger realists but at their mentor, de Kooning. Crehan asked:

> Does de Kooning, or any painter today, especially an artist who has previously jettisoned so many of the banalities and the associative encumbrances of the subject, does such an artist need an image to express an emotion in his work, even an emotion about Woman? Are we on the scene of a reaction? Is our revolution in painting imperiled so soon? . . .
>
> Great creative expression in the arts is always an exploration into the unknown, and the artist in the vanguard, way out in front, can get lonely or hysterical; the inclemencies of the experience may drive him back to snug and familiar surroundings.
>
> De Kooning was out there in the unknown not so long ago, connecting with

61  Willem de Kooning, *Marilyn Monroe,* 1954.
50″ x 30″. Neuberger Museum, State University of New York at Purchase.

something new, something wonderful; but now he's back home again, reworking the image—and he hasn't connected.[7]

Even more worrisome than Crehan's thrust at the very heart of gestural realism was the attack of Greenberg, since he was the most respected of modernist critics in America and an early champion of the second generation. In 1954, Greenberg turned against representation, asserting that it could yield only minor art since "the best art of our day tends, increasingly, to be abstract. And most attempts to reverse this tendency seem to result in second-hand, second-rate painting . . . In fact, it seems as though, today, the image and object can be put back into art only by *pastiche* or parody—as though anything the artist attempts in the way of such a restoration results inevitably in the second-hand."[8]

The arguments against realism as a potentially major modernist tendency were vigorously rebutted by spokesmen for the early wave. The polemicists for abstract art—branded the "avant-garde," in a sarcastic tone, of course—were scoffed at for being too "narrow" and idea-ridden. Porter turned a favorite avant-garde weapon—iconoclasm—against the "avant-garde": "I want to do everything that avant-garde theoreticians say you can't do. When someone [e.g., Reinhardt] says you can't disregard the past fifty years of art history, it makes me want to prove you can—the avant-garde implies a protocol which is more a challenge than a guide. Not that the Academicians aren't even more ignorant!"[9] The early-wave realists vehemently rejected any aesthetic dogma. Abstract Expressionism, as they conceived it, had no program. Therefore, a turn to representation could not constitute a turn away (retreat or counterrevolutionary cop-out) from first-generation abstraction. There was much in the painting of their elders which they found inspirational and useful.

The most wide-ranging and persuasive defense of "the painter *in the avant-garde* who takes any visual aspect of nature as a subject" was written by Elaine de Kooning in 1955. She strongly denied Greenberg's claim that "any painter today not working abstractedly is working in a minor mode." Challenging the belief that abstract art is revolutionary and that representational art is reactionary, de Kooning remarked: "Docile art students can take up Non-Objective art in as conventional a spirit as their predecessors turned to Realism."[10] There was no significant difference in this regard between subject matter *put in* or *left out* of art. If the one could result in *pastiche* or parody, so could the other, and both, of course, could yield much more.

De Kooning also repudiated Reinhardt's purist position, whose battle cry was *"Enter nature, exit art."*[11] Her attack was two-pronged. On the one hand, she argued with those who insisted that the "physical presence of the painting . . . is its only end," and thus that the " 'artist must respect the integrity of the picture plane' (integrity here is a synonym for flatness in this doctrine)." De Kooning countered: "In art, flatness is just as much an illusion as three-dimensional space. Anyone who says 'the painting is flat' is saying the least interesting and least true thing about it."[12] On the other hand, she defined nature as anything which presents itself as visual fact, including all of art. Art no matter how non-objective could not help but call nature to mind.

Just as subject matter could not be avoided, so "in art there is no getting away from a look. . . . another name for style."[13] Every variety of style could be found in both objective and non-objective art. "You can be influenced by the style of Géricault and paint an abstraction. You can be influenced by the style of Kandinsky and paint a landscape. Influence alway rides on style, never on subject. . . . But a dead style can be brought to life—sometimes a larger life than it had originally—by a living subject."[14]

62  Fairfield Porter, *Katie and Anne,* 1955.
80¹/₄″ x 62¹/₈″. Hirshhorn Museum and Sculpture Garden, Smithsonian Institution, Washington, D.C.

63   Elaine de Kooning, *Scrimmage,* 1953.
25" x 36". Albright–Knox Art Gallery, Buffalo, New York.

Elaine de Kooning's emphasis on style was appropriate, for the early wave deliberately cultivated style. In this, it differed from earlier realists, beginning with Courbet, who in the name of political or moral causes tried to record truthfully what they saw and thus were anti-stylistic in bias. For example, Rivers's portraits of his naked, flesh-sagging mother-in-law might be considered in the lineage of Courbet. But unlike the nineteenth-century realist, who accepted ugliness and awkwardness because he desired to be true to life, Rivers seemed more intent on artistic style as the reflection of life-style, of the image of himself as outrageous and perverse.

The gestural realists' concern with "style-as-the-subject" distinguished them from earlier representational artists, as de Kooning saw it: "Today, for the artist with a signature, there is no simple *what*—no reality, no subject, that does not include *who* he is and *how* he perceives it."[15] Moreover, contemporary artists could not avoid the "*When* and *Where* and *Why*," since no artist painting in the fifties in New York "can possibly have the same motives as the artist of thirty, forty, or even ten years ago."[16]

Of greater importance to de Kooning than the degree of representation and of illusion in painting was the *openness* in attitude and process, an openness that had its primary source in first-generation gesture painting. As early as 1952, she rejected the "avant-garde's" narrow aesthetic preconceptions in favor of an unpremeditated approach to painting, that is, in favor of an artist putting himself "in the position of following, not leading his painting." This allows him to "be surprised by the development of . . . his own paintings in a way that avant-garde artists . . . knowing beforehand what they are trying to do—can never be surprised."[17]

Older gesture painters also encouraged younger artists to employ representation. Willem de Kooning's greatly admired *Woman* series provoked a "widespread urge to re-make figure-painting into a new grand style," as Hess observed.[18] Rivers remarked that de Kooning's painting "from a distance seemed to touch on objects and landscapes, but as you drew closer everything disappeared and you saw a dipsy-doodle energy that kept pestering you long after looking."[19] And there was Hofmann's insistence that his students draw from nature or at least with nature in mind, prompting the simple move to a more literal treatment of subject matter. Additional confirmation came from Pollock's "return to the figure" in his black-and-white paintings of 1951.

However, the early wave was equivocal in its acceptance of first-generation gesture painting, particularly abstract. As O'Hara remarked, "the impact of THE NEW AMERICAN PAINTING . . . was being avoided rather self-consciously rather than exploited. . . . If you drink with Kline, you tend to do your black-and-whites in pencil on paper."[20] The young artists were attracted by representation because it was different—and thought to be fresher—than the prevalent abstraction. Indeed, the turn away from abstraction was taken by some to be audacious—a kind of kicking up one's heels at one's (newly) established elders. Tworkov noted in a review of a show of flower pictures that such subject matter was so taboo "that the young painters who attempt it get credit for bravado."[21]

Partly because of their reluctance to be too closely identified with the first generation, early-wave realists were less equivocal about Impressionism than Expressionism.

The Bonnard retrospective of 1948 revealed the possibilities of representation as well as of Impressionism. The two tended to be linked together, for Abstract Impressionists generally were inclined to an imagery evocative of nature. But the issue was a complex one, and a variety of positions were taken, as is clear in the following fragment of discussion at the Artists Club in 1956 (and typical of art talk at the time). The question which prompted the exchange was whether a form could ever be non-objective or "un-natural":

Angelo Ippolito: What is an unnatural form? I have never seen one.

Elaine de Kooning: Mondrian said that the meeting of two straight lines in a right angle—the interaction—is unnatural.

Ippolito: Not to me. I've seen it. [He crosses his fingers.]

Al Newbill: We may arrive at the lily pond but in a different way than Monet did.

Kyle Morris: Many painters are working in such a way as not to end up in the lily pond.

Newbill: We all end up with nature.

Unidentified voice: By intent or by accident?

Newbill: By every unconscious and conscious intent.

William Kienbusch: In the nineteenth century, painters painted outside, using umbrellas as shields from the sun. Today, Americans don't use umbrellas.

Morris: What about Rauschenberg [who had affixed a real umbrella to the surface of one of his "combine-paintings"]?

Unidentified voice: Gorky worked right from nature. The straight observation of nature may be very important to paint inner reality.

Ippolito: You don't need to get sunstroke to know about the power of the sun.

Kienbusch: You have to see the lily pond.

Ippolito: Or jump into one.

John Ferren: I watched Monet paint the lily pond. He never even looked at it when he painted, and besides, he was half blind.

Ippolito: There are many ways of struggling with nature.

Newbill: Abstract painting put the painter into nature. He is no longer an isolated observing entity but is in nature and in the painting.[22]

The early wave was interested not only in Bonnard but also in Vuillard, Renoir, Soutine, Matisse, and the Fauves (most of whom were given major shows in 1950 and 1951). Indeed, the second generation was inspired by these and other modern masters, figurative and non-figurative, as much as by nature. To a greater or lesser degree, art history became a substitute for nature, a kind of "second nature," parallel to but independent of the real world.[23]

In their preoccupation with nature, art history, and self-conscious conceptions of style, gestural realists rejected the dogmatic demands of some of their contemporaries who held that gesture painting to be genuine had to be based exclusively on what Kandinsky called "inner necessity," and thus had to exclude stimuli from sources external to self. And yet, maintaining an attitude somewhat similar to their elders, early-wave realists scrutinized nature, foraged in the art of the past, and weighed stylistic possibilities in search of catalysts to induce fresh subjective or internalized responses. Indeed, the young artists were open to what they saw in nature and in the museums in much the same spirit as they reacted to their own painterly gestures. Every kind of stimulus was permissible, subject to personal choice or taste—in pursuit of felt, individual style.

# Notes

1. Hess, "The New York Salon," p. 57.

2. Wolf Kahn, in remarks from the floor, at a Club panel, "Nature and New Painting III," 11 February 1955 (notes taken by me). The participants were Thomas Hess, Harry Holtzman (moderator), Franz Kline, Willem de Kooning, and Ad Reinhardt.

3. Fairfield Porter, "Jane Freilicher Paints a Picture," *Art News*, September 1956, p. 66. Freilicher restated a centuries-old aesthetic issue—the contradictions that exist between painting what one sees, requiring a certain objective scrutiny and controlled execution, and painting under the influence of inspiration or indulging in the delights of the hand, or of virtuosity, all of which entailed speed of execution. See Ernst H. Gombrich, *Art and Illusion* (New York: Pantheon Books, 1961), passim.

4. See Frank O'Hara, "Nature and New Painting," *Folder* 3 (1954–55): unpaginated.

5. In an interview, Freilicher recalled that there was a bias against too factual representation. This she attributed to a general admiration of energy and power which painterly painting appeared to suggest.

There was a fear, however, of exploiting the up-to-date look of gesture painting for corrupt purposes. Thomas B. Hess, "At the Whitney: Cinemiconology and Realstraction," *Art News*, December 1952, p. 67, defined "realstraction" as painting in which the "dominant influence is abstract painting" turned into a

> . . . formula which will enable the artist to (1) set a stage for his display, (2) suggest a mood-background for the object displayed. A carefully duplicated element of reality—a fish, flower, little man, big woman, star, streetlight—is inserted into the abstract setting, much as a piece of merchandise is inserted into an *haute couture* window display; . . . So the pigment is applied in what (one fears) they call "the modern way," and then the image turns around and says "look, goldfish" or "how small, indeed, is man."

6. "Statement," *Reality* 1 (Spring 1953): 1.

7. Hubert Crehan, "A See Change," *Art Digest*, 15 April 1953, p. 5.

8. Clement Greenberg, "Abstract and Representational," *Arts Digest*, 1 November 1954, p. 7. On page 6, Greenberg insisted that his only criterion for judgment was quality. "No one has yet been able to show that the representational as such either adds or takes away anything from the aesthetic value of a picture or a statue." His estimate, he insisted, was based on his "experience" of art. Greenberg's change in attitude was rather sudden. At the beginning of 1954, he was not yet anti-figurative. In the *Emerging Talent* show he selected for the Kootz Gallery in January, he included Paul Georges, Philip Pearlstein, and Theophil Repke.

9. Frank O'Hara, "Porter Paints a Picture," *Art News*, January 1955, p. 39.

10. De Kooning, "Subject: What, How or Who?" p. 26.

11. Ibid., p. 27.

12. Ibid., p. 29.

13. Ibid., p. 61.

14. Ibid., pp. 61–62.

15. Ibid., p. 62.

16. Ibid.

17. Elaine de Kooning, "The Modern Museum's Fifteen: Dickinson and Kiesler," *Art News*, April 1952, pp. 66–67. Finkelstein also extolled painterly painting for its responsiveness to an open-ended variety of feelings, motives, purposes, structural and rendering ideas, reminiscences, and ways of mediating experience. In *Painterly Representation*, an exhibition catalogue for a show at the Ingber Gallery in 1975, he wrote:

That kind of representation we call painterly comes into being precisely because of this process sense of things. The time which is transfixed is . . . the flowing of consciousness in interaction with first the resistances and challenges which the world of appearances presents to our grasp, and secondly with the ways pictorial language itself generates metaphors of the meanings of things and of states of mind. Rather than a one-to-one correspondence with things which retain their meaning in some normative standard way, for painterly vision everything is always up for grabs: the style, the space, the structure, the attitude, affect the way we are touched by the world.

18. Hess, "Trying Abstraction on Pittsburgh," p. 42.

19. Larry Rivers, "A Discussion of the Work of Larry Rivers," *Art News*, March 1961, pp. 53–54.

20. O'Hara, "A Memoir," in Hunter, *Larry Rivers*, p. 18.

21. Jack Tworkov, "Flowers and Realism," *Art News*, May 1954, p. 56.

22. Club panel, "Valid Motivations for the Artist Today."

23. Hilton Kramer, "Art Chronicle," *Hudson Review* 16 (Spring 1963): 97.

# 6

# Rivers, Hartigan, Goodnough, Müller, Johnson, Porter, Katz, Pearlstein, and Other Gestural Realists

MORE THAN ANY other second-generation figurative artist, Larry Rivers focused on the relationship between image and process. He wanted both to render his subjects literally and to reveal the act of painting. At different times in his career, he carried each approach to as much of an extreme as he could without completely sacrificing the demands of the other.

But before facing these challenges, Rivers felt compelled to convince himself (and the art world) of his "genius," to prove that he could draw and paint in a virtuoso fashion.[1] In 1948, excited by the Bonnard retrospective at the Museum of Modern Art, he began to work in the manner of the late Impressionist, trying to outdo him. In Greenberg's opinion, Rivers succeeded in part,[2] and that judgment was very gratifying to the young beginner. In 1951, under the influence of Soutine, who had been given a retrospective at the Museum of Modern Art the year before, Rivers painted a major work titled *The Burial*. It was obviously based on Courbet's *Burial at Ornans* but also on recollections of the funeral of his own grandmother. In the future, Rivers would often paint subjects chosen from the history of art and from his autobiography. He extended his Expressionist style by taking cues from de Kooning (himself inspired by Soutine), as in *Portrait of Frank O'Hara* (1951), *Football Players* (1951) and other pictures of figures painted in 1951 and 1952.

Rivers was now ready to confront a primary problem faced by contemporary figura-

56, 57
64, 65
66, 67
68, 69
70, 71
208
Pl. III

64

65

64　Larry Rivers,
*The Burial,* 1951.
60″ x 108″. Fort
Wayne Museum of Art,
permanent collection.

65　Larry Rivers, *Portrait of Frank
O'Hara,* 1952.
30¹/₂″ x 26″. Whitney Museum of American
Art, New York.

tive artists: the "avant-gardist" dismissal of realism as old hat and boring. He solved the problem by painting pictures that were at once sufficiently virtuoso and ironic to entice and shock his audience (primarily the New York School), compelling its attention. De Kooning had shown the way, but Rivers was more of a grandstander. In 1953, he painted *Washington Crossing the Delaware*, based on a popular picture by Emanuel Leutze. Rivers's intention was to outrage. He said:

> I was energetic and ego-maniacal and, what is even more important, cocky and angry enough at the time to want to do something no one in the New York art world doubted was disgusting, dead and absurd, rearrange the elements, and throw it at them with great confusion. Nothing could be dopier than a painting dedicated to a national cliché. . . .
>
> In relation to the immediate situation in New York . . . [it] was another toilet seat—not for the general public as it was in the Dada show, but for the painters. [3]

66   Larry Rivers, *Washington Crossing the Delaware*, 1953.
83⅝" x 111⅝". The Museum of Modern Art, New York.

Rivers's mixture of academicism and modernism was confusing at the time. The subject matter of his literary "machine" is associated with academic art but not the "unfinished" facture, which calls to mind Gorky's late improvisations and gesture painting. For a painter identified with the New York School to choose for a model an old master was in itself perverse, a kind of anti-avant-garde avant-gardism. But to choose a rhetorical, patriotic Salon picture, considered (if it was considered at all) so debased as to be on a par with calendar art, compounded perversity. As a pop-old-masterpiece, it parodied both the great art of the past and the serious gesture painting of the present.[4] It was not that Rivers's *Washington* was representational; de Kooning, Hofmann, and Pollock had worked and/or were working in gestural figurative veins—but not with subjects the likes of Leutze's "corny" narrative. And perhaps most subversive of all, Rivers, like his mentors de Kooning and Hofmann, seemed ambitious for a masterly synthesis of tradition and modernism but, unlike them, he ended up by poking fun at that ambition.[5]

And yet, Rivers's dopiness had a serious side: the implication that an artist to be contemporary or even modern had to assume an ironic stance. Could Rivers affirm believably about Washington or anybody, particularly himself, what Delacroix had proclaimed about Napoleon, that his life "is the epic theme of our century in all of the arts"? It is noteworthy that Napoleon fascinated Rivers, who painted his portrait after David's and titled it *The Greatest Homosexual* (1964). In my opinion, Rivers's perversity was genuinely rooted in his being, and moreover, it exemplified a feeling of alienation in postwar America, indeed in modernism. His aesthetic aim was not to trivialize the serious (camping it, as it were), but its opposite, to try to be serious in the face of a perpetually defeating sense of absurdity that led him invariably to self-mockery. In this sense, his stance was existential, but he ridiculed public professions of *angst*. Rivers no doubt wanted to be a great artist but he also believed his aspiration was pretentious. Therefore, he transformed "any concept of the artist-as-hero into one of the hero-as-clown."[6] Besides, as he said, he was easily bored, and boredom was as profound an artistic stimulus as anything else.[7] (It is boredom in part that prompted Rivers to ask: What was so *interesting* about modernist aims, really?) Rivers also appeared to believe that his irony could be masterfully embodied in his art, and that he might achieve success—as the King of Parody[8]—and why not even "greatness."

In the *Washington*, Rivers announced what would become his essential style. As Porter described it at the time: "Drawing dominates painting, . . . As a whole, the painting looks like an enormous page from a sketch book: there are different positions for the arms, and the head on the depicted paintings is like another try at the head. . . . The paint is thin: almost like stains."[9]

However, before Rivers continued his stylistic development in this direction, he painted a series of portraits of stark naked figures of friends and relatives in which he suppressed loose brushwork and probed toward a factual extreme. These pictures, particularly *Double Portrait of Berdie* (1955), Rivers's mother-in-law, struck most of his contemporaries as outrageous as the *Washington*. What other aim than shock could Rivers have had for venturing into portraiture, long considered moribund by the avant-garde,

67

and moreover, in rendering Berdie not only once but twice "with so clinical an eye for obnoxious detail."[10] However, Rivers's literal portraiture also prompted strong positive responses. Campbell wrote: "Its unabashed, unidealized nakedness, its bulk, its realism strike an entirely fresh note. . . . It sounds a call for an appraisal . . . of all kinds of discredited subject paintings—flowers, historical genre, portraits."[11]

A new note was also struck by Rivers's suppression of gesture in order to render details accurately. But painterly facture was not completely abandoned; rather, it was relegated to the images of inanimate objects surrounding the figures. O'Hara remarked on the "divorce" between figure and background, asserting that Rivers "felt that it satisfied the requirements of what he saw in nature and what he sought in painting, without recourse to stylistic overstroking, slashing or obtrusive drawing."[12] Other critics disagreed with O'Hara, chiding Rivers for failing to integrate his uningratiating "finished" figures with their seductive "unfinished" settings.[13]

67   Larry Rivers, *Double Portrait of Berdie,* 1955.
70³/₄″ x 82¹/₂″. Whitney Museum of American Art, New York.

Rivers himself appears to have recognized the conflict between a desire for natural- istic treatment, in which details (a finger) had to be fused smoothly into larger images (a hand, an arm, the body), the parts subordinate to the whole, and his desire for a more disjunctive painterly handling in which painterly and poetic impulses would be given freer rein. A move away from tight realism toward looser abstraction seemed called for, and Rivers took it in late 1955. In the process, he resumed the kind of sketchy drawing and painting found in the *Washington*.

Rivers continued to render details in sharp focus—any bit of experience that inter- ested him—but interspersed them with bare areas, often thin washes, painted in an improvisational (or seemingly improvisational) manner associated with gesture painting. Paradoxically, although the new style of painting yielded a more unified picture, it also spotlighted the realistic details more than in the earlier work. The disconnected, isolated detail had long fascinated Rivers. As a student, he "recalled challenging Hofmann, . . . [asking] him how we can enjoy the surviving 'fragments' of partially destroyed old mas- ters, in view of Hofmann's insistence that a work of art can only be experienced aestheti- cally as a totality, . . . He won from Hofmann the concession that the artist's 'psychological insight' did after all count, and revealed itself in fragments as well as wholes."[14] Rivers himself "thought of a picture as a surface the eye travels over in order to find delicacies to munch on; . . . A smorgasbord of the recognizable, and if being a chef is no particular thrill, it was as much as I could cook up."[15] This cookery is ex- emplified in *The Studio* (1956), like Courbet's picture of the same title, a large (6'10" x 16'1"), stagy, and major work. A kind of diaristic billboard, it contains sketchy, double or triple portraits of O'Hara, Berdie, and the artist's two sons, and a variety of images from the artist's life, the components overlapped and interpenetrated in a kind of ges- tural, stroboscopic, and double exposure, seemingly random in spatial and temporal relationships—but not in design, since the motifs are organized along vertical and hori- zontal axes whose source is in Cubism. There are also elements that might be mistakes, erasures and/or corrections, which are allowed to stand.[16] It all adds up to a scene whose point of view is roving, multiple, and episodic. The emphasis seems not so much on the subject matter as on "the various manners of approaching the subject."[17]

Rivers's "smorgasbord" was related to the poetry of O'Hara, who with Ashbery and Koch were his close friends. The major influence on New York School poets, O'Hara conceived of a poem as a series of poetic fragments—moments of his experience—not necessarily connected in any obvious way. His writing was like his conversation, "self- propelling and one idea, or anecdote, or *bon mot* was fuel to its own fire, inspiring him verbally to blaze ahead."[18] About O'Hara's content, Ashbery wrote: "The nightmares, delights and paradoxes of life in this city went into Frank's style, as did many of the pas- sionate friendships he kept going."[19]

Around 1958, Rivers began to integrate the separable details, aiming for a unified picture. In the process, he verged toward gesture painting. Instead of assuming, he said, "that if each part that I do interests me and it sort of has something, then it should add up to a great painting," he came to believe that "there is such a thing as a whole thing, not just parts."[20] This led Rivers to emphasize the abstract or formal qualities of his art,

68   Larry Rivers, *The Studio,* 1956.
82¹/₂″ x 193¹/₂″. Minneapolis Institute of Arts.

69   Larry Rivers, *Berdie with the American Flag,* 1957.
20″ x 25⁷/₈″. Nelson Gallery Atkins Museum, Kansas City, Missouri.

particularly color applied in thinly painted areas whose role grew in importance as drawn imagery was simplified into rough sketching in keeping with the "unfinished" facture. He remarked in 1961 that not subject matter but "the color you are going to choose and where you are going to put it on the surface and the way you put it there is what has meaning and you don't even have to love it: what you choose and where you put it and how."[21]

It is significant that at the moment that Rivers's imagery became more abstract and painterly, a new realist tendency in contemporary art, exemplified by Jasper Johns, emerged and immediately received recognition. Rivers found himself in the middle, seemingly related to both gestural abstraction and its competitor, the new realism, yet not really sympathetic to either.[22] Rivers rejected the literalism of the new realism and instead proclaimed that the source of his painting was "Life," defined as "everything but everything as it moves through the individual depositing mountainous amounts of material, adding and destroying and organizing on new bases as it passes through, creating associations, memory and passion."[23] The gesture painters also believed that art was shaped by "Life," but by that they meant art dictated by inner necessity. For example, when de Kooning made a gesture, he hoped, or so it was believed, that it would sum up his total experience, an heroic ambition. When it (invariably) did not, he was compelled to change it, leaving the traces of his anxious and passionate process. Rivers knew beforehand that he would change whatever he first painted. The revisions and erasures of "mistakes" were the evidence of what he found "thrilling" (a favorite word). This implied a search for self, but not in the Expressionist sense. Rather, as he put it: "When I say myself, I mean what interests me, what irritates me, what bores me, what bothers me, what can never satisfy me . . . my immediate responses, some reflective ones, my history, etc."[24] Rivers stood back from his experience. In 1959, he painted *ME*, in which he intended to include "glimpses of everything that's happened to me from birth to the present. I expect it to go down in history as the most egomaniacal painting ever."[25] But the information was provided by photographs, removed from self, as it were.

Rivers's "mistakes" can also be considered signs of a display of picture-making and aesthetic performance—the young master at work. In the context of the art of the late fifties, Rivers is most aptly characterized as a gestural realist who wanted to show off his drawing, and perhaps in response to the emerging new realism (which he anticipated) was prompted to enlarge his repertory of forms and approaches, his "bag of tricks," as he called it, by introducing motifs from popular culture, such as lettering and imagery taken from commercial art, signs, brand labels, magazine photographs. These he juggled like an assortment of type, which they resemble and which were a source, e.g., *Cedar Bar Menu* (1959). Rivers's intention was not the new realist one of copying the surface of the world as it actually was. Instead, as he remarked: "I'm quite a one-eyed face maker and probably think my drawing is greater than anyone's around. Letters of the alphabet & home-made stencils . . . because of their manufactured look, set off the artiness of my rendering. There are smudges. The right amount of laziness, etc."[26]

70   Larry Rivers, *ME*, 1959.
114¼" x 177½". Chrysler Museum at Norfolk, Virginia.

But Rivers could not escape seriousness so easily, and much as he mocked it, his subjects occasionally refer to political events of consequence—happenings at the U.N., race relations—and are treated with sentiment as well as with irony. But news was also the occasion for a perverse self-mockery. *The Last Civil War Veteran* (1959), which depicts the death of the last Confederate soldier, is "the spectacle of a non-hero who had become a hero by the simple fact of having outlived the others and . . . had managed to die on schedule to accommodate *Life* magazine which covered both the dying and death with appropriate journalistic ceremony." [27] Rivers must have been attracted by a real event turned into a mass media "event," since it touched on his role as an artist.

71

Summing up what motivated him, Rivers said: "Embarrassment with seriousness, quote 'straight painting.' Perhaps accident, innocence and of course fun & the various reliefs experienced in the presence of absurdity. It is these things I think which account for much more in my choosing portions of Mass Culture than the obvious everyday humanistic or politically responsible overtones." [28]

Grace Hartigan did not venture into gestural realism until late in 1952, some time after Rivers did, but her reputation soon rivaled his. The pictures exhibited in her first

72, 73
74, 75

71  Larry Rivers, *The Last Civil War Veteran,* 1959.
82¹/₂" x 64¹/₈". The Museum of Modern Art, New York.

72  Grace Hartigan,
*"Rough Ain't It!,"* 1949–50.
40" x 53". Whereabouts unknown.

73  Grace Hartigan, *The Persian Jacket,* 1952.
57¹/₂" x 48". The Museum of Modern Art, New York.

76, 209

Pl. IV

two shows in 1951 and 1952 were abstract. She had seen Pollock's early "drip" paintings in 1948 and had been stunned by their energy and freedom.[29] They revealed to her a new conception of a painting: an allover labyrinthine image with no beginning and no end that seemed to thrust out at the spectator. But at the same time that she sought to achieve this effect, she felt that she could not adopt the "drip" technique without lapsing into imitation.

Hartigan soon met Pollock, who advised her to see de Kooning. His work revealed to her the kind of facture that she wanted: energy-packed, calligraphic brushwork. Moreover, she learned from de Kooning how to "put in more, do more, [but] without violating what . . . [she] had come to accept as a new way of making a picture." Toward the end of her abstract period, Hartigan increasingly differentiated and varied the areas in her painting, as de Kooning had in *Excavation* or *Attic.* One critic wrote that they remained "nonfigurative—as before . . . [but] seem to reflect the shapes and rhythms of human and vegetable life."[30]

Hartigan's imagery was verging toward the recognizable, but her move to realism had another, more urgent stimulus: the problem of meaning. She said: "I began to get guilty for walking in and freely taking their [Pollock's and de Kooning's] form . . . [without] having gone through their struggle for content, or having any context except an understanding of formal qualities. . . . I decided I had no right to the form—I hadn't found it myself—and that I had to paint my way through art history. . . . I started to paint from the masters, from reproductions, in a very free way." Hartigan became preoccupied with Rubens, Velázquez, Goya, Zurbarán, Tiepolo, and Dürer, more than with gesture painting, or so she thought. However, most critics did not see her work in quite the way she did. They called attention to the directness with which it conveyed feeling. One wrote that her subject was an "image-in-the-making," an image

74  Grace Hartigan, *Grand Street Brides,* 1954.
72″ x 102¹/₂″. Whitney Museum of American Art, New York.

in constant flux "that breaks through seething brushwork and overlaid color . . . The weight of a seated figure . . . makes itself felt just . . . [as] it is swept into a maelstrom of turbulent strokes (that are somehow independent and yet dependent upon the subject)."[31] Later, Hartigan herself thought of her painting as "not 'abstract' and not 'realistic.' "[32]

Hartigan drew not only on past masterworks but on live models, such as O'Hara and Ashbery. In one picture, she painted a friend dressed as a bullfighter after Goya. She also began in 1954 to look at the urban environment for subject matter, e.g., mannequins of brides in Grand Street store windows or loaded pushcarts on the Lower East Side. Of these pictures, for which she was best known in the fifties, she wrote: "I have found my 'subject,' it concerns that which is vulgar and vital in American modern life, . . . [The] rawness must be resolved into form and unity; without the 'rage for order' how can there be art?"[33] And yet, much as Hartigan was inspired by the city and desired for her painting to convey some of its impact, she continued to think of past art while painting, of Goya in the *Grand Street Brides* and of Matisse in the *River Bathers*.

74, Pl. IV

Toward the end of 1957, Hartigan moved to Long Island, where she lived for a year. There her imagery changed from figuration to gestural abstraction. The new work was composed of energetically brushed areas of color set off by heavy calligraphic lines, at once awkward and virtuoso. Although her work was somewhat reminiscent of landscape, Hartigan was more intent on painting as an existential action, shaped by a "vision of self as inviolable, powerful and nervy—self as the only real thing in an unreal environment."[34]

75  Grace Hartigan, *New England, October*, 1957. 68¼" x 83". Albright–Knox Art Gallery, Buffalo, New York.

77, 78
79, 80
81
Pl. V

Robert Goodnough was one of the more abstract of gestural realists. He was also the one who looked most to Cubist design for inspiration. Indeed the work painted after 1956, for which he is best known, is marked by a synthesis of Cubist quasi-geometric composition and gestural feature. Following the examples of de Kooning and, to a lesser degree, Pollock, Goodnough took as his points of departure the painterly, open scaffolds of Analytic Cubism and the tight compositions of cleanly edged flat forms of the Synthetic phase which he loosened and opened up. Goodnough appeared to believe, as Greenberg later remarked, that the great achievement of the first generation was the "grafting of painterliness on a Cubist infra-structure."[35] His aim was to further that achievement.

There is in this enterprise a strong tradition-mindedness. Goodnough himself remarked: "I feel there is a continuity between the past and the present; it isn't only a matter of what you want to do yourself, but what you *must* do because that's what painting has become."[36] As if to underline his concern with art history, Goodnough went so far as to quote Picasso's drawing and treatment of subject matter. But as his statement reveals, he was more intent on bringing art history up-to-date. For example, in *Rearing Horses* (1959), he redid Rubens's copy of Leonardo's *Battle of Anghiari* with one eye on the early Cubism of Picasso and Mondrian, and the other on gesture painting.

Goodnough's art training contributed to his bent for traditionalism *and* contemporaneity (as well as for control *and* spontaneity). In 1946, he began to study with Ozenfant, a founder of Purism, whose emphasis was on the classicizing tradition in modern art, on "discipline, precision and care. . . . We were always painting to a fine edge—and painting with three coats, at that."[37] At the same time, Goodnough visited the Hofmann School, enrolling there in the summer of 1947. This prompted him to "free-up," as he put it.

The earliest pictures that Goodnough exhibited, e.g., *Abstraction* (1951) or *Pegasus* (1952), are abstract mazes of curvilinear brushstrokes that look almost completely impulsive. The calligraphy is also dynamic, uncoiling or snaking out of the centers of the pictures into fields of bare canvas. After 1955, the design became grid-like, often allover, and the imagery, figurative. As Goodnough wrote: "My great problem remains subject matter. . . . I have to paint *something*, start with some theme, some object to 'transpose.' "[38]

By "transpose," Goodnough meant to reshape a subject according to the pressures of feeling and of formal demands, the latter mostly derived from Hofmann's teaching. As Goodnough remarked:

> My own interest is in solving the conflict between the painting's two-dimensional plane and the effect of depth: the illusory third dimension. I always start with the figure in the round and flatten it instead of going into the distance beyond it; I try, you might say, to "uncube the cube." . . . [Then] I want to achieve a sense of body and volume. . . . The whole surface comes to have the same kind of body as the object; the "figure" does not exist independently but as part of the whole surface.[39]

76  Grace Hartigan, *Sweden,* 1959.
83³/₄″ x 87¹/₂″. Whitney Museum of
American Art, New York.

77  Robert Goodnough, *The
Struggle,* 1957.
44″ x 60″. Albright–Knox Art Gallery,
Buffalo, New York.

78  Robert Goodnough, *The Frontiersman*, 1958.
67″ x 60″. Collection, Larry Aldrich,
Ridgefield, Connecticut.

79  Robert Goodnough, *Battle Landscape,* 1958.
65″ x 85″. New York University Art
Collection, Grey Art Gallery and
Study Center.

Although Goodnough thought "in terms of objects and figures,"[40] he did not preconceive them. "Each picture I do is started in a somewhat different way and usually without a clear idea at the outset—perhaps only a vague feeling. Gradually as something gets down on the canvas, it does not matter too much what to begin with, ideas form. I like to keep colors and shapes very flexible. . . . The image gradually becomes more or less clear . . . At some point the painting begins to set its own direction . . . and the flexibility diminishes. At the end there is none at all. The idea becomes concrete."[41] Goodnough's interest in improvisation prompted him to "reverse" Cubist design. Instead of first sectioning the entire picture plane, he started in the center of his canvases and worked out toward the edges, as in the series begun in 1955 and culminating in 1960 with *Carnival II*.

During the fifties, Goodnough's figurative painting ranged from the open linear grids spotted with color, e.g., *The Frontiersman* (1958), to compositions of more or less defined flat areas, e.g., *Laocoön* (1958). The one is reminiscent of Analytic Cubism, e.g., Picasso's *Ma Jolie* (1911–12) but more rectilinear, like Mondrian's façades of 1913–14. The other calls to mind Synthetic Cubism, but it is more profuse and brushy. Goodnough's work throughout the decade (and well into the sixties) is enormously varied. For example, *Cha-Cha-Cha* (1956) has no linear tracery, whereas *The Chair*

78

Pl. V

80  Robert Goodnough, *Pink Reclining Nude*, 1959. 53¼″ x 70″. Whitney Museum of American Art, New York.

81   Robert Goodnough, *Standing Figure,* 1960.
64″ x 63⁷/₈″. Brandeis University Art Collection, Waltham, Massachusetts.

(1957) is primarily a pattern of lines. *The Bathers* (1960) are clearly recognizable but not the "figures" in *Laocoön*. The taut, quasi-geometric grid of *Carnival II* is poles apart from the washy, wriggling *Abduction* of the same year.

Goodnough gave many of his pictures mythic titles: *Pegasus, The Frontiersman, Calamity Jane* (1958)—subjects, often American, suggesting energy. He also desired his painting in itself to convey a similar quality. As he remarked: "The feeling of activity and energy through the use of shapes of color or brush movements is an underlying subject of my recent paintings. Sometimes this is worked out abstractly, at other times suggested by the activity of running horses or figures in conflict."[42] Goodnough's predilection for dynamism attracted him to Abstract Expressionism. As he wrote: "There is a feeling in the best work of American painters of the 'wild' which has been the heritage of this country. The covered wagons, the Indians, the rolling prairies, the immense forests and mountains are part of one's memory. Thoreau's belief that dullness and tameness are the same, that it is the wild that attracts us in literature, seems also to apply to painting."[43]

To sum up, Goodnough's gesture painting was motivated by a wish for flexibility; by art history—what appealed to him in the past and the next move in painting, as he saw it; by his need to "transpose" a subject according to the dictates of feeling and form; and by his desire for energy and surprise which symbolized the American myth.

Jan Müller opened up new possibilities in gesture painting by shaping it into explicit mythic and religious symbols, both abstract and figurative, and often literary in origin. In 1952, two years after he finished studying with Hofmann, he painted his first major picture, an abstraction titled *The Robe* in which multihued, short brushstrokes of roughly the same size are arranged more or less vertically in a mosaic pattern which calls to mind a symbolic content—the robe of Christ, Byzantine mosaics—heavy in feeling despite the variety of colors.

In 1953, Müller turned the brushstrokes into mythological figures, e.g., jousting knights in *The Heraldic Ground.* In 1955, he started a series of imaginary landscapes whose prominent features are paths. These sunlit works are Müller's most serene, and yet the paths (leading where?) are disquieting symbols and, though more cryptic, so is an underlying geometry, formed by the paths, tree trunks, and areas of grass and foliage.

In the summer of 1956, Müller began to populate the "path" pictures with witches, devils, angels, and other apparitional figures in what would constitute his body of major works, including *Of This Time–Of That Place, Hamlet and Horatio,* and two versions of *Walpurgisnacht–Faust,* all of 1956, and in the next year, *The Temptation of St. Anthony, The Search for the Unicorn,* and lastly *Jacob's Ladder–of Hell and Conformity,* which remained unfinished at his death at the age of thirty-six early in 1958.

Müller's demons, often masked or chalky-faced like ghosts or corpses, are grimacing or staring fixedly at the spectator, engaging in bestial rites, thrusting into the picture plane at odd—and unnerving—angles, or constituting parts of arcane geometric configurations. The subjects were inspired by medieval sculpture; by myths—of the Creation and Paradise, of bacchanals, of the quests and torments of heroes, of death, hell, and

82, 83
84, 85
86

82

84

86

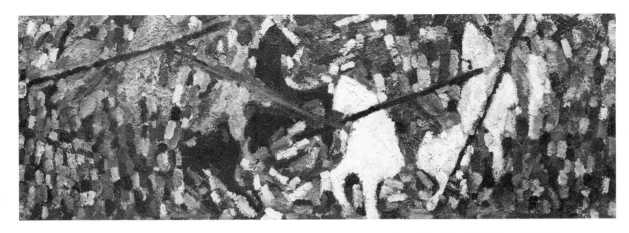

82   Jan Müller, *The Heraldic Ground*, 1953.
14¹/₂″ x 41″. Estate of Jan Müller.

83   Jan Müller, *Double Circle Path #1*, 1956.
38″ x 42″. Estate of Jan Müller.

84   Jan Müller, *The Temptation of St. Anthony,* 1957.
79″ x 120³/₄″. Whitney Museum of American Art, New York.

85   Jan Müller, *Faust, 1,* 1956.
68¹/₈″ x 120″. The Museum of Modern Art, New York.

86　Jan Müller, *Jacob's Ladder,* 1958.
83¹/₂″ x 115″. The Solomon R. Guggenheim Museum, New York.

resurrection;[44] by the folklore of Germany where he was born and lived until the age of nine; by the Bible and the writings of Goethe, Cervantes, and Shakespeare; and by the tormented religious paintings of Nolde and Ensor. The conviction and urgency with which Müller painted his grotesques—making the other-worldly feel real—probably issued from his poor health, aggravated by an unsuccessful heart operation in 1956, which made death a constant concern.

It was the seriousness of Müller's pictures that made them acceptable at the least to the New York School, and this despite their explicit, literary themes (anathema to "modernists"); their utter lack of irony, though not of touches of grim humor; and their relationship to German Expressionism, which was belittled as outworn and lacking in pictorial values. But it was clear that Müller's archetypal vision was his own and that it did not rely only on subject matter but was realized in the painting and design.

Like Müller, Lester Johnson searched for images that symbolized the human condition, but he depended more on the improvisational process of painting than on literary themes. And like Müller, he commanded the attention of the avant-garde while puzzling it, since as Schuyler wrote in some wonderment, Johnson's picture was "unequivocally both New York School and rare bird, Action Painting with nameable subject matter."[45]

87, 88

89

87    Lester Johnson, *Mother and Children,* 1959.
34″ x 22″. Courtesy the artist.

It took a half-dozen years for Johnson to achieve this kind of imagery. In his first show in 1951, he exhibited geometric abstractions with an Expressionist cast, both in color and painterly facture. A number of these pictures were allover, anticipating his later gestural work. Configurations of circles in *The Hero* seemed to continue beyond the picture frame which cut them, and in *My Love*, they were submerged beneath a field of yellow. Around 1953, Johnson turned the circles into heads, and in the following year, began to paint more freely and heavily. Porter remarked in 1955: "Now he is more direct: the inch-wide line around the face is not so tight, . . . He uses few colors, two shades of almost black; . . . or green, olive and black. . . . He can be truly called an Expressionist."[46]

The "breakthrough" in Johnson's painting occurred in 1956. It was then that he became, as he said, an "action painter" but with "content."[47] Sawin described his process: "In the course of a painting's evolution . . . [a] head is painted in and painted out countless times in different sections of the canvas, and eventually there results a heavy ground of many layers whose scars and markings bear witness to the brush's countless path across its surface."[48]

The palpable signs of process in Johnson's painting call to mind the flow of time, which symbolizes the process of life. The images themselves contribute to this content.

88    Lester Johnson, *Profile with Tree,* c. 1959.
26" x 40". Courtesy Zabriskie Gallery, New York.

Off-centered, silhouetted figures or fragments of figures, still lifes or landscapes and the continuous substance through which they appear to travel are homogeneous, all composed of viscous yet vigorous painterly drawing, generally brackish earth-green or brown. "My painting doesn't start or stop," Johnson said, "It just moves across—like time."[49] Despite the importance of "the process of 'finding through painting,' " he had an idea, visionary to be sure, of man passing through, which he felt impelled to paint repeatedly for more than six years. This separated Johnson from the "pure" gesture painter, because his "concern is with an idea and the embodiment of that idea in a given image, and his sights are set on an ultimate product."[50]

On one extreme of the image and process dialectic were Fairfield Porter and Alex Katz. They were "realists," meaning, as Porter wrote of Katz, "that you recognize every detail in his painting, and the whole too, though the whole takes precedence and the detail may be only an area of color, in short, abstract."[51] Their intention was to articulate the appearance of things—and to help them in this, they chose as subjects familiar people and light-filled places—while allowing the medium to make itself felt on its own terms. As Schuyler wrote of a Porter landscape: "The paint has its own movement, as brushed, stirred and rippled as the windy grass, trees and water it describes."[52]    91

"Composition, for Porter, is a conscious procedure, an advance of decisions which become more and more irrevocable as the work goes on," O'Hara remarked. There is "little or no element of 'painting as discovery' or of subconscious revelation as we know it in 'Action-Painting' or Expressionism."[53] At the same time, Porter distrusted ideas, indeed painting from nature to begin without them. Katz was more open to ideas, e.g., flattening images or looking for geometric design in nature, but he recognized that painting directly from what was in front of him—and he could conceive of no other way—loosened concepts.    90    92

Porter and Katz diverged in certain significant ways. Where Porter looked to Bonnard and Vuillard, Katz looked to Matisse and Mondrian. Katz more than Porter suppressed descriptive and painterly detail to achieve flatness and thus a more modern look—and a more impersonal one. Katz also, as Schuyler remarked, "risks banality: the prettiness of a pretty woman is as factual, and as simply achieved as an ad."[54] Like billboards and advertisements and Abstract Expressionist paintings, notably Rothko's, Katz enlarged the size of his pictures. His scale after 1957 (even in his small pictures) is more monumental, less intimate and genre than Porter's, and it is the difference in scale that most distinguishes them.    93

Like Porter and Katz, Philip Pearlstein was a realist at heart, but more than they, he submitted to the influence of gesture painting. The pictures in his first show at the beginning of 1955 were of imagined scenes, generally rocky mountains near the sea. They were influenced by Soutine, de Kooning, and Kline, whose painting he perceived as a "choreography of movements across the picture surface."[55] Pearlstein was drawn to gestural abstraction, but he read imagery into it all. Moreover, he saw atmosphere in all paintings, even those that made a shibboleth of flatness, and atmosphere suggested nature to him.    94, 95

This way of seeing led Pearlstein in the summer of 1956 to begin working directly

89  Lester Johnson,
*Three Men,* 1960.
53″ x 68″. Courtesy Zabriskie
Gallery, New York.

90  Fairfield Porter,
*Jimmy and John,* 1957–58.
36″ x 45¹/₂″. Courtesy
Hirschl and Adler Galleries,
Inc., New York.

91 Fairfield Porter, *Red Wheel Barrow*, 1959.
40⁷/₈″ x 38¹/₂″. Courtesy Hirschl
and Adler Galleries, Inc., New York.

92 Alex Katz, *Luna Park*, 1960.
40″ x 30″. Collection, the artist.

93   Alex Katz, *Ada Ada,* 1959.
50″ x 50″. New York University Art Collection, Grey Art Gallery and Study Center.

from nature, the Maine landscape. He said of that experience: "Faced with the over-whelming abundance of interesting detail, I wished I could develop the kind of symbolic writing that Marin had used in dealing with the same landscape. But after a few abortive attempts, I decided to record in drawing as much detail as I could . . . as realistically and accurately as possible."[56] Pearlstein feared being old-fashioned. "Then I had a dream in which Landis Lewitin appeared and told me that it was time somebody discovered that you can't draw a forest without putting in all the trees."

Pearlstein approached nature in a traditional manner, rendering every detail in three-dimensional space and using a single, strong light source. But the painting remained Expressionist in look, partly because of a conception of a picture he desired, and partly because of the "struggle I have with paint." Such critics as O'Hara, Rosenblum, Otis Gage, and Kramer, all of whom responded positively to Pearlstein's early land-scapes, called attention to their strong sense of design but were taken even more by their romantic treatment of subject—"a generalized, primeval face-of-the-earth image"[57]—and of painting—its "sensuousness and frenzy, . . . high-keyed emotion and dazzlement of surface."[58]

94  Philip Pearlstein, *Rock Mound*, 1958.
44″ x 52″. Whitney Museum of American Art, New York.

However, Pearlstein himself denied "any profound philosophical or mystical involvement with nature." Nor was he "consciously concerned with expressing moods," although "feelings must find their way into my paintings." Instead:

> I use nature in a calculated way as a source of ideas . . . At the moment I like to work with landscape ideas just because they allow me to remain uninvolved. I can look at them abstractly . . . and just concentrate on painting. I choose a subject not because I like the view as such, but because I feel its potential of giving me a structure on which to build an interesting picture. I turned to rocks, pebbles, etc., because I find in them a more interesting variety of ideas than I can dream up by myself. But I look for ideas in nature that already conform with painting ideas I have.

Toward the end of the fifties, a conflict developed between Pearlstein's desire for an empirical realism and his painting ideas. More and more he began to strip away the painterly overlay which struck him as increasingly decorative, to reveal an underlying, precisely drawn, literal realism that, much as it seemed well-known, pointed to one of the uncharted paths realism could take—and did in the sixties.

In 1957, a school of San Francisco figurative artists began to achieve national recognition. The most eminent were David Park, who in 1950 was the first to change from abstraction to figuration, and Elmer Bischoff and Richard Diebenkorn, who followed in 1953 and 1955 respectively. (All three artists had been on the faculty of the California School of Fine Arts when Still taught there, adding to the aesthetic ferment.) Paul

95   Philip Pearlstein,
*Positano I,* 1960.
66″ x 96″. Collection,
Dorothy Pearlstein, New York.

Mills, who organized the first show of the group in 1957, wrote that their painting was part of a new direction in figurative art because it continued "the bold methods of handling paint which are a mark of abstract expressionism."[59] However, gestural realism in San Francisco differed from that in New York in that it tended to look slapdash and open, suggestive of vast Western spaces and not of the city.

Although Diebenkorn turned to realism later than Park (a teacher of his) and Bischoff, he quickly took the limelight, winning recognition as the strongest painter of the group. In the early fifties, he painted gestural abstractions influenced by de Kooning but evocative of the spare, dry landscape, often as seen from the air, of Northern California and New Mexico. After 1955, he introduced into this vast, abstract out-of-doors recognizable figures, often in room- and patio-like enclosures. But the painting remained gestural, as Herschel B. Chipp observed, suggesting "a prolonged struggle with the various images that are produced. . . . [which are] expanded, contracted, reversed, . . . into altogether different forms, meanings and contexts. . . . through various stages which may be or may not be related."[60] The mood generated by solitary figures in yawning inside-outside spaces is lonely, akin to that of Hopper, who was an early and continuing inspiration to Diebenkorn. Even more crucial as an influence—and a growing one—was Matisse, whose works Diebenkorn first saw in 1944.

Word of a new figurative movement in Chicago began to reach New York in 1955—through articles and occasional shows, e.g., of the works of Leon Golub and George Cohen. But it was not until 1959 that the leading artists of what came to be called the Chicago Monster Roster were exhibited together in New York—in the *New*

96, 97

98, 99

96  Richard Diebenkorn,
*Berkeley No. 37,* 1955.
70″ x 70″. Museum of Art,
Carnegie Institute,
Pittsburgh, Pennsylvania.

97   Richard Diebenkorn, *Girl on a Terrace*, 1956.
71″ x 66″. Neuberger Museum, State University of New York at Purchase.

*Images of Man* show organized by Peter Selz at the Museum of Modern Art. The Chicagoans emerged around 1950,[61] roughly the same time as the San Franciscans. Unlike the West Coast painters, they had little sympathy for Abstract Expressionism which meant only "self-disclosure . . . the recording of the artist's process of working. . . . ineffable sensations,"[62] and they aimed for "more," that is, for symbols of primal emotion. In order for these symbols to be potent, they had to refer to recognizable images, and because they reflected the age of World War II, Buchenwald and Hiroshima, they were irrational and violent, monstrous and demonic.

The Chicagoans looked for inspiration to Dubuffet, Giacometti, and Bacon; and further back in time to Munch, Ensor, Soutine, Nolde, and other Expressionists; to Grünewald, Bosch, and Goya; and to primitive art of every variety and period. They also read studies of primitive cultures and psychology; and the darker and more deviant of modern novels, e.g., those of Kafka, Céline, Nathanael West, and Djuna Barnes.[63] Because of the diversity of sources, the Chicagoans—unlike the San Franciscans—tended to stylistic heterogeneity.

The monster-maker who commanded the most art-world attention was Golub. In the early fifties, his imagery was based primarily on primitive art and mythology. As the decade progressed, he looked for inspiration increasingly to Roman colossal statues. But

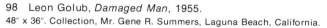

98   Leon Golub, *Damaged Man,* 1955.
48″ x 36″. Collection, Mr. Gene R. Summers, Laguna Beach, California.

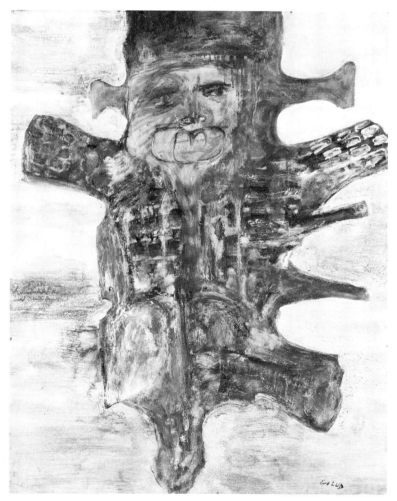

99 Leon Golub, *Colossal Heads (I)*, 1959.
81″ x 131″. Collection, Mr. Ulrich E. Meyer, Chicago, Illinois.

he mutilated these late-classical images, brutalizing the paint to create a sense of cor-roded flesh or stone, of the scarred and lacerated, the burnt, the diseased, and the decaying. In Golub's pictures, Humanist man survived, but barely, the ravages of twentieth-century experience. And yet, his debased figures are imposing, even grand, suggesting that it was his ambition to revive the monumental figure in contemporary art and communicate a social message about the surviving victim as hero to the public.

Bay Area figurative painting was better received by the New York School than monster painting, because it was gestural and well-painted on the whole. The Chicagoans' approach was alien to most New Yorkers, and so was their indifference to aesthetic quality. Even their strongest champion, Franz Schultze, admitted that they were "more doggedly infatuated with symbol, image, dream and pungent anecdote than they are concerned with the need to give these elements articulate form."[64]

# Notes

1. Frank O'Hara, "An Interview with Larry Rivers," *Horizon*, September 1959, p. 97.

2. Clement Greenberg, "Art," *Nation*, 26 April 1949, p. 454.

3. Rivers, "A Discussion of the Work of Larry Rivers," p. 54.

4. Rivers was ambivalent about the old masters, frequently submitting to their influence, e.g., Courbet's *Burial at Ornans* in *The Burial*; Géricault's nude study at the Metropolitan Museum in *O'Hara* (1954); and a study of a nude by Delacroix in *Augusta* (1954).

5. Rivers was ambivalent in his attitude to tradition. On the one hand, he wrote of creating "toilet seats." On the other hand, he remarked, "Not only did I want to be a great painter in modern times, I really felt as if I had . . . to make a figure . . . just as great as anybody in the past" (Larry Rivers, interviewed on Voice of America, March 1960).

6. W[illiam] W[ilson], "Larry Rivers," *Artforum*, October 1965, p. 11.

7. See Rivers, "A Discussion of the Work of Larry Rivers," p. 53.

8. See de Kooning, "Subject: What, How or Who?" p. 28.

9. F[airfield] P[orter], "Reviews and Previews: Larry Rivers," *Art News*, December 1953, p. 43.

10. Leo Steinberg, "Month in Review," *Arts*, January 1956, p. 48.

11. Lawrence Campbell, "New Figures at the Uptown Whitney," *Art News*, February 1955, pp. 34–35. Campbell went on to say that "abstraction has cleaned house," and a vacuum exists which Rivers has filled in a way that figurative artists generally who have absorbed abstraction have not.

12. O'Hara, "Nature and New Painting," unpaginated.

13. See [H]ilton [K]ramer, "Fortnight in Review: Larry Rivers," *Arts Digest*, 15 December 1954, p. 22; and Steinberg, "Month in Review," p. 48.

14. Hunter, *Larry Rivers*, p. 18.

15. Rivers, "A Discussion of the Work of Larry Rivers," p. 54.

16. Rivers's device of allowing erasures to stand as part of the image has its source in Matisse. So does the one-eyed image often seen in his work, in the *Piano Lesson* (1916).

17. O'Hara, "Nature and New Painting," unpaginated.

18. James Schuyler, "Frank O'Hara: Poet Among Painters," *Art News*, May 1974, p. 44.

19. John Ashbery, Introduction in *The Collected Poems of Frank O'Hara* (New York: Alfred A. Knopf, 1971).

20. Larry Rivers, interviewed on Voice of America, 1960.

21. Rivers, "A Discussion of the Work of Larry Rivers," p. 45. In 1965, Rivers wrote a letter to David Hockney: "The place you choose for the pigment and the physical relationship between the various parts seemed like a sensitive digestion of certain abstract paintings but brought to a halt by the limits of your interest in the commonly experienced subject." This applies equally well to Rivers's own work. (Larry Rivers and David Hockney, "Beautiful or Interesting," *Art and Literature* 5 [Summer 1965]: 96.)

22. Rivers anticipated the new realism of Jasper Johns and Pop Art. He painted his *Washington* in 1953 and *Berdie with the American Flag* in 1955. However, he was not an important influence on subsequent realist styles.

23. Rivers, "A Discussion of the Work of Larry Rivers," p. 45.

24. Ibid., p. 44.

25. O'Hara, "An Interview with Larry Rivers," p. 102.

26. Larry Rivers, statement read to the International Association of Plastic Arts, New York, Museum of Modern Art, 8 October 1963, reprinted in John Russell and Suzi Gablik, *Pop Art Redefined* (London: Thames and Hudson, 1969).

27. Sydney Simon, "Larry Rivers," *Art International,* 20 November 1966, p. 20.

28. Rivers, statement read to the International Association of Plastic Arts.

29. The information in this section, unless otherwise indicated, was taken from an interview with Grace Hartigan, Baltimore, Maryland, 14 January 1974.

30. J[ames] F[itzsimmons], "In the Galleries: Grace Hartigan," *Art Digest,* 1 April 1952, p. 23.

31. B[etty] H[olliday], "Reviews and Previews: George [Grace] Hartigan," *Art News,* April 1953, p. 39.

32. Dorothy C. Miller, ed., *12 Americans,* exhibition catalogue (New York: Museum of Modern Art, 1956), p. 53.

33. Ibid.

34. Seminar at the University of Minnesota, typescript.

35. Clement Greenberg, "The 'Crisis' of Abstract Art," *Arts Yearbook: New York: The Art World* 7 (1964): 91.

36. "Is Today's Artist With or Against the Past?" *Art News,* Summer 1958, p. 42.

37. Guest and Friedman, *Goodnough,* pp. 14–15.

38. "Is Today's Artist With or Against the Past?" p. 42.

39. Ibid.

40. Robert Goodnough, Statement, *Robert Goodnough,* exhibition catalogue (Fort Worth, Tex.: Ellison Gallery, 1960), unpaginated.

41. Ibid.

42. Robert Goodnough, Statement in Lee Nordness, ed., *Art USA Now* (New York: Studio Books, Viking Press, 1963), vol. 11, p. 318.

43. Robert Goodnough, "Statement," *It Is* 1 (Spring 1958): 46.

44. See Martica Sawin, "Jan Müller: 1922–1958," *Arts,* February 1959, pp. 44–45.

45. J[ames] S[chuyler], "Five Shows: Lester Johnson," *Art News,* March 1958, p. 40.

46. F[airfield] P[orter], "Reviews and Previews: Lester Johnson," *Art News,* November 1955, p. 65.

47. Club panel, 24 January 1958.

48. Martica Sawin, "Month in Review," *Arts,* March 1959, p. 47.

49. Club panel.

50. Sawin, "Month in Review," p. 47.

51. Fairfield Porter, "Art," *Nation,* 1 October 1960, p. 216.

52. James Schuyler, "Immediacy Is the Message," *Art News,* March 1967, p. 69.

53. O'Hara, "Porter Paints a Picture," pp. 40–41.

54. J[ames] S[chuyler], "Reviews and Previews: Alex Katz," *Art News,* January 1959, p. 15.

55. Philip Pearlstein, notes of a lecture at New York University, 2 August 1970.

56. Philip Pearlstein, notes of a statement made at a Club panel, "The Artist's Inolvement with Nature," 15 March 1957. Unless otherwise cited, the information in this section is taken from these notes.

57. F[rank] O'H[ara], "Reviews and Previews: Philip Pearlstein," *Art News,* February 1955, p. 56.

58. Hilton Kramer, "Month in Review," *Arts,* March 1957, p. 48. See also Robert Rosenblum, "In the Galleries, Philip Pearlstein," *Art Digest,* 1 February 1955, p. 23, and Otis Gage, "Art," *Arts and Architecture,* March 1955, pp. 9, 37, 39.

59. Paul Mills, *Contemporary Bay Area Figurative Painting,* exhibition catalogue (Oakland, Calif.: Oakland Art Museum, 1957), p. 5.

60. Herschel B. Chipp, "Diebenkorn Paints a Picture," *Art News,* May 1957, p. 45.

61. The initiators of the Chicago School—Cosmo Campoli, George Cohen, Ray Fink, Leon Golub, and Joseph Goto—were all veterans of World War II who attended the Art Institute

of Chicago and took part in *Exhibition Momentum*, 1950, which can be considered the starting point of the movement, since it "brought them into close contact and enabled them to clarify their ideas" (Patrick T. Malone and Peter Selz, "Is There a New Chicago School?" *Art News*, October 1955, p. 36).

62. Ibid., p. 59.

63. Franz Schultze, *Fantastic Images: Chicago Art Since 1945* (Chicago, Ill.: Follett Publishing Company, 1972), p. 14.

64. Ibid., p. 5.

# 7

# Assemblage: Stankiewicz, Chamberlain, di Suvero, and Other Junk Sculptors

AMONG THE aesthetic options that the early wave believed open to it were first, to extend gesture painting in the direction of Impressionism, abstract but nonetheless evocative of nature, and second, to turn toward explicit representation in a more or less painterly manner. A third possibility, related to the other two, was to assemble works from junk materials of city origin, which retained references to their sources in reality, and which, in their rawness, called to mind the appearance and spirit of gesture painting. This course was taken by such artists as Stankiewicz, in his rusty found-metal sculptures;[1] Follett, in her black reliefs; Rauschenberg, in his "combines" of detritus; Chamberlain, in his crushed automobile assemblies; Oldenburg, in his painted, corrugated cardboard reliefs; and di Suvero, in his constructions of weathered timbers, chain, rope, tires, and pipe. All three options led young artists toward visual reality or "life" and away from the generally abstract art of their elders, while retaining the gestural "look" of a part of it, so much so that the choice between reality and abstraction may be considered a generational one, marking off the art that emerged in the fifties from that of the forties.

Although assemblage, as constructions of junk materials came to be called,[2] tended to relief and sculpture, de Kooning's paintings—and to a lesser degree, Kline's black-and-white abstractions—were just as strong an influence on it as on second-generation gestural abstraction and representation. Rauschenberg, di Suvero, and Chamberlain were so taken with the pictures of de Kooning and Kline that they even aped their "look." However, paradoxically, these artists seem to have chosen junk as their medium

100
102

103

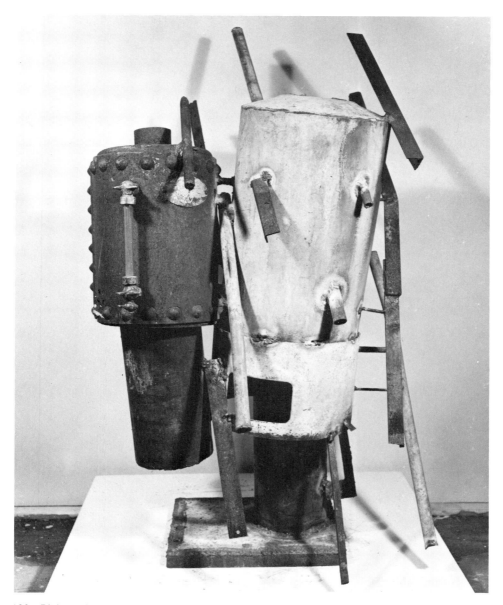

100   Richard Stankiewicz, *Untitled,* c. 1959.
c. 48″ high. Courtesy Zabriskie Gallery, New York.

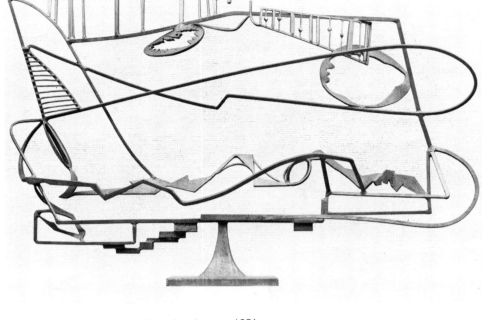

101　David Smith, *Hudson River Landscape*, 1951.
49¹/₂″ x 75″ x 16³/₄″. Whitney Museum of American Art, New York.

in order to avoid mannerizing the older painters they admired, and because they recognized that the unorthodox materials disclosed new possibilities for form and meaning. Cast-off objects were also attractive because they were readily available and generally free.

101　　　David Smith played an influential role in the evolution of junk sculpture. His metal constructions, widely esteemed for their formal qualities, occasionally incorporated discarded machine parts. However, the use of detritus enabled young junk sculptors to take a different tack from that of other established avant-garde sculptors of the fifties, such metal welders who spurned found materials as Herbert Ferber, David Hare, Ibram Lassaw, Seymour Lipton, and Theodore Roszak.

These older artists looked inward—to psychic sources—rather than outward—toward their urban environment. Using the oxyacetylene torch somewhat like a brush, they welded complicated, biomorphic structures whose space was in restless, ambiguous flux and whose surfaces were bubbled, pitted, fretted, and tattered. The structure, space, and textures often were fanciful metaphors for natural processes, such as germination and growth, decay and death.[3] Frequently the forms referred to viscera, bones, jaws, teeth, thorns, petals, and claws, combined into violent or erotic hybrid inventions whose antecedents were in Surrealism.

The older welders had early in the fifties achieved the styles for which they were recognized and did not change them much. Moreover, by 1956 or 1957, they had spawned so many followers that virtuoso construction in metal of intricate, bizarre creatures became a kind of vogue.[4] The glut of such cliché-ridden, precious fabrications was responsible in part for the growing interest in assemblage. It also most likely prompted Chamberlain and di Suvero to turn to simpler structures whose formal qualities were clear, like David Smith's. Furthermore, it accounted in part for the avoidance of Surrealist-related imagery by Rauschenberg, Chamberlain, Oldenburg, and di Suvero, although not by Stankiewicz and Follett.

It was not only the direct, improvisational, energetic appearance of gesture painting that impressed young assemblage-makers. They were also inspired by its references to urban experience. In particular, de Kooning's painting was considered "an incarnation of the city."[5] Moreover, in 1952, he had pasted mouths cut from "pop" posters and advertisements on the early stages of *Woman 1*. This fact was well known, for Hess had reported it in an article on the artist.[6]

There were other precedents for assemblage, notably the collages and constructions of the Dadaists, particularly Kurt Schwitters, and of the Cubists and Futurists in general, and of such Surrealists as Joseph Cornell.[7] However, assemblage was markedly different from past and contemporary styles because the urban refuse from which it was pieced together was often unchanged and looked so unseemly that it appeared initially to be utterly lacking in aesthetic qualities. Indeed, Crehan called Stankiewicz's junk constructions "*almost* ready-mades."[8] More than any of their predecessors—certainly David Smith and even Schwitters—assemblage-makers used "the mud of this civilization. . . . to create new and unexpected meanings," as Porter wrote of Stankiewicz.[9] Assemblage-makers were indifferent to the clean "modern" design, for example, of International Style architecture. Instead, they preferred "what is broken, cast off, rubbishy, awkward, ugly and rusty. . . . [putting] least things first."[10]

Indeed, the throwaway junk of city life was the substance of assemblage. As I remarked in the first general article on this tendency, published in 1960, found material "suggests urban forms and images, metaphors for both the poverty and the richness of city life, its terror and anxiety as well as its particular spectacle and rhythm. There is poignancy in this rejected matter—the expendable detritus of a concrete, steel and glass leviathan—that evokes the tragic vulnerability of the city dweller, his progressive insignificance."[11] Seitz also believed that both the ugly and potentially beautiful attributes of the city were a source of inspiration and meaning for fifties assemblage-makers: "This 'rurban' environment is truly a collage landscape: an unplanned assemblage of animated gasoline displays, screaming billboards, . . . graveyards of twisted and rusting scrap, lots strewn with bed springs and cracked toilet bowls."[12]

So strong was the impact of city life, particularly in New York, on American assemblage-makers that I maintained that a distinction had to be made between them and their European counterparts. The New Yorkers

> . . . have evolved a variant of American-scene art without having been influenced in any specific way by past realist styles. The resemblances of certain

102   John Chamberlain, *Essex*, 1960.
108″ x 80″ x 43″. The Museum of Modern Art, New York.

103   Mark di Suvero, *Barrell,* 1959.
96″ high. Now destroyed.

. . . attitudes [of assemblage-makers] to those of the Ash Can School (even the
name is appropriate) around the turn of the century must be more than accidental. "The Ash Can School stood for 'truth' as against 'beauty,' for 'life' as against
'art,' for the 'real' as against the 'artificial.' They accepted Henri's advice: 'Be
willing to paint a picture that does not look like a picture.' The realists defended
crudity and ugliness because such things were true . . . . They refused to dodge
the philistinism, the gaucheness of American life; on the contrary, they sought to
live and picture that life in its common aspects."[13]

Much as I stressed the urban realism of assemblage, I pointed to a subjective or
psychological dimension, quoting Henry Miller: "Only the object haunted me, the separate, detached, insignificant thing. It might be . . . a staircase in a vaudeville house;
. . . a smokestack or a button I had found in the gutter. Whatever it was enabled me to
open up, to surrender, to attach my signature . . . I was filled with a perverse love of
the thing-in-itself—. . . as if in the discarded, worthless thing which everybody ignored
there was contained the secret of my own regeneration."[14] Thus, the assemblage-
maker's special way of seeing diverse urban materials and their juxtapositions entered
into the content of his or her works.

Despite its roots in established past and contemporary styles, assemblage was not
readily accepted by the New York School as a whole, which dismissed it as an anti-art
joke at best. In fact, the label "Neo-Dada," because of its derogatory connotation, was
the one commonly applied as late as 1961, when it was supplanted by "assemblage."
This negative reception by the New York School suggests a growing conservatism, at
least in the refusal to consider work not executed in traditional and permanent media. It
also indicates a fixation on existentialist rhetoric in a good part of "vanguard" thinking
in the fifties. One would have expected advanced artists to have been open-minded
enough to have taken assemblage *seriously*, whether or not they agreed with its aesthetic
intentions. After all, it did reveal fresh expressive possibilities; but even if these were un-
acceptable, its creators were *bona fide* members of the second generation, who did not
consider themselves radical and whose work was clearly influenced by and related to the
prevalent gesture painting. Besides, the use of "non-art" materials was hardly new;
Picasso and Braque had made the first collages more than four decades earlier.

Among the harsher critics of assemblage within the New York School was Crehan,
whose entire review of Rauschenberg's show in 1954–1955 read: "Since he is determined to avoid the responsibility of an artist, it is better that he should show blank
canvases rather than the contraptions that he has hung in this side show."[15] Leo Steinberg was as unsympathetic; at the beginning of 1956, he wrote: "On the merry work
of Robert Rauschenberg the kindest comment I can make is that some of my friends,
whose (other) judgments I respect, think it is not out of place in an art exhibition."[16]
And in the spring, he asked of Jean Follett's work: "But is it art?" and answered:
"Really, I haven't the faintest idea."[17]

Even the little written about assemblage that was favorable was more often than not
patronizing, treating the work as amusing—and trifling. For example, in 1955, Crehan

104   Richard Stankiewicz, *Natural History,* 1959.
14³/₄″ x 34¹/₄″ x 19¹/₄″. The Museum of Modern Art, New York.

called the sculpture of Stankiewicz "minor but delightful,"[18] and Ferren wrote about
one of his more humorous pieces: "I abjure all my firm opinions about *objets trouvés,*
realize how silly it sounds, forget about art, and recommend that it be mass-produced
and placed in every New York apartment from Park Avenue to the Bronx as a contribution to the gaiety of nations."[19]

Of course, not all artists and critics shared the hostility. Porter had written very
early that Stankiewicz "makes objects that touch one's emotions most deeply. He is
more than clever, he creates on several levels of significance."[20] When, at a Club panel
in 1955, Stankiewicz was attacked for using junk and thus for being Dadaist, Ibram Lassaw and Sidney Geist jumped to his defense, asserting that he liberated undignified
things to make art. Stankiewicz himself, who was present, insisted: "I am not Dada. I
don't want to shock anyone. It is natural for me to do and use what I do, just as natural
as a South Sea islander uses shells. Maybe you are disturbed that my work is too accidental. I find most of the materials that I use, but I throw most of these away, even
after keeping them a long time. I select very carefully. Nothing happens that I don't
want to happen."[21] The same applied to Chamberlain, who more often than not cut his
forms from wrecked automobiles to his specification, and to di Suvero, who shaped his
found forms, and to most other assemblage-makers.

After 1955, assemblage was taken more and more seriously. In the fall of that year,

Porter wrote a major article on Stankiewicz's work in *Art News*,[22] and the following January, poet-critic Barbara Guest remarked in a review accompanied by a full-page reproduction: "This is work that . . . the dadaists, with their regard for the 'found object,' would have liked. But it is not something we have seen before; it is totally sculpture and among the most original on the contemporary scene."[23] On the whole, Stankiewicz's work was better received than Rauschenberg's, but as early as 1955 O'Hara had written that the latter's combines were "brilliant"; some were "wildly ingenious . . . ecstatic"; others "have a gentle and just passion for moving people. . . . [revealing] a serious lyrical talent."[24] Hess included him among the twenty-one artists he selected for a show at the Stable Gallery in 1955 and in a major article titled "U.S. Painting: Some Recent Directions," published the following year.[25]

By the end of the fifties, the distinctions between Dada constructions and New York School assemblage had become clear to most of the audience for advanced art. It was evident that Dada gave fifties junk artists certain permissions—to use non-art materials in incongruous and seemingly random juxtapositions—but that its iconoclastic intentions were poles apart from theirs. At the time, I (using the term "Neo-Dada" to apply to assemblage) wrote that

> . . . unlike the Dadas who carried on an organized insulting of modern civilization and who used art as part of their "shock treatment," the Neo-Dadas are accepting of their condition and are primarily interested in expressing a heightened sensitivity to it. Their work, in a word, is art, and they mean it as such regardless of how it may appear to others. . . . This does not mean that Neo-Dada objects are "esthetic"; they are seamy, crude and unnerving, but they draw their vigor from the streets, not from the barricades.[26]

Although assemblage-makers used detritus to escape the conventional criteria associated with traditional paintings and sculpture, they were very much occupied with formal matters.[27] However, the aesthetic quality of assemblage at its best was difficult for many viewers to perceive, because the found objects, often little if at all transformed, called attention to their prior "real" roles so strongly that their function as components of "abstract" design was neglected or even overlooked entirely. The overwhelming impact made by the "realism" of assemblage, by the explicit references to the "ugly," indeed "brutish," city environment was so immediate and unpalatable that even sensitive viewers initially could not achieve the mixture of distance and familiarity generally needed for the contemplation of aesthetic values. But that was only the initial response; the formal qualities of the best of assemblage provided its sustaining interest.[28]

Stankiewicz ventured into junk sculpture in the winter of 1951–52 after he had decided to dig a garden in the courtyard of the loft building in which he had a studio. "The spade began hitting old hunks of metal which I tossed against the building. . . . I sat down to catch my breath and my glance happened to fall on the rusty iron things . . . Their sense of presence, of life, was almost overpowering. I knew instantly what I had to do. I bought a welding outfit, mask and gloves, and a do-it-yourself

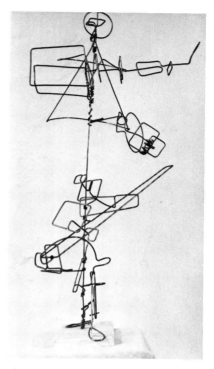

105  Richard Stankiewicz, *Kabuki Dancer,* 1956.
84″ x 24″ x 26″. Whitney Museum of American Art, New York.

106  Richard Stankiewicz,
*Figure,* 1952.
31″ x 14″ x 15″. Courtesy Zabriskie Gallery,
New York.

book—How to Become a Welder in Your Spare Time. My first sculpture was finished in a day."[29]

Stankiewicz's inspiration was sudden, but he had had considerable training as an artist which prepared him for it. From 1948 to 1950, he studied with Hofmann, and then in Paris, with Zadkine and Léger, the first modern master to choose as his subjects the artifacts of industrial civilization. At the time, Stankiewicz began to make abstract terra-cotta sculptures whose images were quasi-geometric labyrinths. He made the elements increasingly thinner and in the process changed to a lighter medium: plaster (at times embedded with shredded rope, buttons, and the like) over bent wire. These works suggested insects with long threadlike legs and small bodies, which he treated loosely so that he could make distortions for abstract reasons.[30]

Stankiewicz returned to New York late in 1951, and the following year he exhibited the linear sculpture in two shows. The second of these was titled *Fantastic Creatures and Satiric Poses,* pointing to the kind of content that would occupy him in his junk constructions first shown in 1953. Sympathetic critics were quick to see, as one

107 Richard Stankiewicz, *Our Lady of All Protections*, 1958.
51″ x 31″ x 32″. Albright–Knox Art Gallery, Buffalo, New York.

108 Richard Stankiewicz, *The Candidate*, 1960.
37″ high. Collection, Mr. and Mrs. Gifford Phillips, New York.

wrote, "the witty relationship between the mechanical and the human."[31] To another, the work came close to a child's game of monster building in a vacant lot.[32] These comments are exemplified in his most notorious piece, *Secretary* (1955), which is composed of a wrecked typewriter embedded in the belly of a cast-off boiler painted blue whose arms are pipes; legs, sharp-angled metal rods; and hair, a wire fan.

Stankiewicz's creatures are the kin of Smith's, Picasso's and Gonzalez's, but on the whole more Surrealist in their bizarreness. He called them: "Ghoulish buggy creepers, erect starers, careening exerters, floating fliers, squatting blocky ones."[33] But Stankiewicz breathed fresh life into old subjects which many in the New York School thought moribund by re-creating them in new materials in an improvisational manner. His process was akin to gesture painting; as he said in 1955: "I follow the sculpture, I don't boss it around too much, . . . There is a dialogue between myself and the work."[34]

Although Stankiewicz's sculptures retained references, often humorous, to people, animals, and insects, e.g., birds in 1957, double heads in 1960, it became increasingly abstract toward the end of the decade, as if to focus attention on formal values. Shaped forms and their structuring took precedence over psychologically charged recognizable images and rusty metal and its tendency to assert its former function as boilers, pipes,

109   Richard Stankiewicz, *Untitled,* 1960.
50″ x 17″ x 19″. Collection, Hanford Yang, New York.

faucets, etc.[35] Indeed, as Hilton Kramer observed as early as 1956, Stankiewicz's "sculptural vision . . . addresses itself to fundamental problems, whatever jokes it may choose to make in the process," and to "the sculptural possibilities still to be uncovered in . . . direct-metal sculpture whose short history is so disproportionate to its impact on our artistic culture."[36]

110, 111    Stankiewicz's development of junk sculpture was considerably influenced by a constant exchange of ideas with Follett, a fellow student at the Hofmann School and a close friend until late in the fifties. Before he ventured into assemblage, she was applying paint so thickly that her pictures look three-dimensional, and she had also taken the short step of embedding found materials in the impasto. Throughout the fifties, Follett assembled black-and-white bas-reliefs from paint, plaster, pieces of wood, metal, horsehair, string, nails, and heavier substances. These *objets trouvés* were formed into figures and faces, the fetishes of a private order.

Although Stankiewicz's sculpture had affinities with gesture painting, as did Rauschenberg's assemblages which will be dealt with in another context, a truly gestural junk construction emerged only at the end of the decade, the creation of Chamberlain

110   Jean Follett, *Lady with the Open Door Stomach*, 1956. 46³/₄″ x 48″ x 3″. Whitney Museum of American Art, New York.

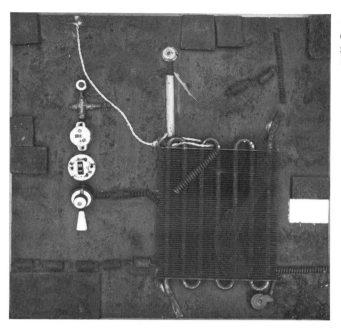

111   Jean Follett, *Many Headed Creature,* 1958.
24″ x 24″. The Museum of Modern Art, New York.

112   John Chamberlain, *Wildroot,* 1959.
66″ x 65″. Sammlung Karl Stroher im Hessischen Landesmuseum Darmstadt.

and di Suvero. Indeed, the two young artists were influenced by the improvisational process of de Kooning and Kline and by the look of their pictures, de Kooning's, in the case of Chamberlain (although he claimed to owe more to Kline), and Kline's, in the case of di Suvero. Chamberlain translated de Kooning's rough painterly lines and overlapping and interpenetrating planes that give the illusion of slicing swiftly in and out of shallow depth into autobody parts and thrust them in real space.[37] His crumpled and scarred found-metal constructions also emulated the rawness and violence of de Kooning's canvases.

It was natural for Chamberlain to conceive of de Kooning's and Kline's canvases in three dimensions, since he thought like a gesture painter. He called his works "self-portraits. . . . [They] have certain kinds of balance and rhythm that are characteristic of myself."[38] Moreover, he denied that he intended any social reference, but the extraordinary economic, recreational, status, symbolic, and other roles that the automobile plays in American life are so omnipresent that it is difficult not to think of them while experiencing his sculpture.

The works that Chamberlain first showed were welded from iron planes and rods in the David Smith manner. He grew dissatisfied with the pictorial emphasis; his urge for the physicality of volume led him in 1957 to piece together space-enclosing car fenders. He was so taken with this medium that he worked exclusively with it from 1959 to 1963. Chamberlain's sculptural aim was to discover in his response to his materials and in the unpremeditated action of assembling the "fit" of wrecked auto parts, the "squeeze and the compression"[39] of their hugging together, and his pieces often look bear-hugged, conveying the force needed to crumple forms and couple them. He was also concerned with the interaction of ready-made colors. These inhered in his material; they were not added, enabling Chamberlain to orchestrate them from the inception of a work. Not since the Middle Ages had color been used so organically and freely in sculpture, and that was but part of Chamberlain's contribution; his "found" enamel and lacquer palette was new and daring in art.

What interested Chamberlain most was the relationship of the forms he found and shaped and their battered colors. "I wanted the sculpture to exist on its own terms coming through the process of myself."[40] Although some critics saw Chamberlain's work on its own terms, that is, as formal and abstract, others were struck by the human metaphors evoked by cast-off, bruised autobodies. In an early review, I dealt with both aspects, on the one hand: "Mangled body parts, heaped on each other, might be witty or mordant comments on the wreckage of industrial civilization, metaphoric mechanical demons, or possibly monuments to highway speeders. . . . The constructions are elegant, but they have a painful quality. They barely survived the crash—metal entrails wind in and out—and yet they strut."[41] On the other hand, I stressed that "Chamberlain does not seem interested in such allusions. His primary concern is with formal relations. . . . Yet his pieces retain the look of junk. The haphazard enhances the formal."[42] Donald Judd was interested only in the abstract aspect of Chamberlain's construction, primarily its "voluminousness." "The sculpture seems open which in the

113   John Chamberlain, *Cord,* 1957.
16″ x 12″ x 10″. Courtesy Allan Stone Gallery, New York.

114   John Chamberlain, *Nutcracker,* 1958.
50″ x 50″ x 30″. Courtesy Allan Stone Gallery,
New York.

usual sense, it is not, since it is massed. . . . . its involutions enclose so much space."[43]

Indeed, the viewer's eye is led into the shadowy interior spaces of a piece and made aware that each bent and twisted plane encloses a hollow of air whether it can be seen or not. The complex flow of space, masses of space, in and around the painted forms is reminiscent of Baroque illusionism, auto-metal drapery substituted for cloth.

Like Chamberlain's assemblage, di Suvero's is gestural both in its improvisational process and appearance. The works that he exhibited in 1960 are composed of massive, roughly splintered and hacked wooden beams and planks and other rugged found materials that jut and tilt powerfully into space, at once volumetric and muscular drawing in the round on a gigantic scale. Three pieces, at nine, twelve, and sixteen feet, were particularly huge for that time. The heavy timbers sprawl and are frequently precariously balanced, but they are also tied into stable-looking structures. Disequilibrium is strongly felt at first, but it ends up calling attention to the firm design which overcomes it. The composition is novel, since it tends not to be organized centripetally around a single axis—as sculpture traditionally has been—but around several foci from which the components branch out—they seem flung out—at various angles and interlock, often supporting one another.

103, 117
118, 119
120, 121

115 John Chamberlain, *Hudson,* 1960.
27″ x 27″ x 12″. Courtesy Allan Stone Gallery,
New York.

116 John Chamberlain,
*Swannanoa,* 1959.
45¹/₄″ x 64¹/₂″ x 35″;
base: 20″ x 3¹/₂″ x 3¹/₂″.
Courtesy The Mayor
Gallery, London.

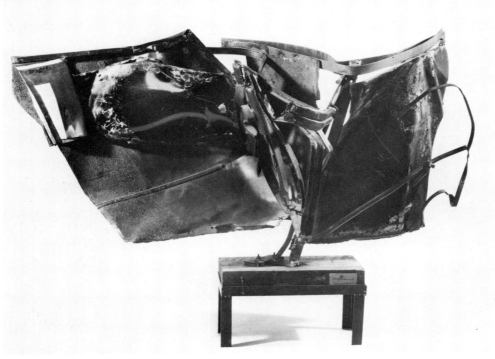

117 Mark di Suvero,
*Che Faro Senza
Eurydice,* 1959.
84″ x 104″ x 91″.
Private collection,
New York.

118 Mark di Suvero, *For Sabater,* 1959.
Approx. 96″ high. Now destroyed.

The two primary impulses (often considered contradictory) in di Suvero's work are Constructivism generally and Abstract Expressionism, notably Kline's because it was starker and less ambiguous than any of his fellow gesture painters. Di Suvero once said: "My sculpture is painting in three dimensions."[44] Geist, in the first article on the artist, wrote of a development in modern sculpture he called "Constructive Expressionism, . . . whose latest point is di Suvero." "While preserving the original Constructivist vision of an imageless sculpture of relatively slender elements arranged in an open style, the modular, machine-like, predictable quality of the pioneer work (with its concomitant ideas of social order) has given way in recent years to an irregular, temperamental, unpredictable quality (with its overtones of *Existenz*)."[45]

The organization of hulking, raw elements on a heroic scale reveals a tension—indeed, a stress—to say nothing of drama that is Expressionist in spirit. It is noteworthy that Rodinesque sculptures of hands that di Suvero modeled before turning to assemblage were marked by strain. And at the same time, the clearly articulated form of the constructions can be appreciated for its "purity." Like Chamberlain's work, di Suvero's cannot help but evoke the American scene, in his case, the raw guts of demolished buildings (from which many of his materials are salvaged). But it also suggests di Suvero's robust, enthusiastic, and generous nature. At the same time, it calls attention to its self-referential formal qualities: the adjustment of a piece's physical components on a grand scale, the balance of massive lines and the voids they delineate, of stresses and counterstresses, of clenching and unclenching spaces.

120

119   Mark di Suvero, *Hankchampion*, 1960.
77½" x 149" x 150". Whitney Museum of American Art, New York.

120  Mark di Suvero, *Hand Pierced*, 1959.
60¹/₂″ high. Private Collection, New York.

121  Mark di Suvero, *Ladder piece*, 1961–62.
75″ high. Private collection.

# Notes

1. Stankiewicz was the first of his generation to exhibit assemblages, in 1953.

2. The term was coined by William C. Seitz and popularized at the time of *The Art of Assemblage* exhibition he organized at the Museum of Modern Art in 1961. Seitz defined assemblages as collages, objects, and constructions which "are predominantly *assembled* rather than painted, drawn, modeled, or carved," and whose constituent elements, entirely or in part, "are preformed natural or manufactured materials, objects, or fragments not intended as art materials." William C. Seitz, *The Art of Assemblage*, exhibition catalogue (New York: Museum of Modern Art, 1961), p. 6.

3. See Irving Sandler, "American Construction Sculpture," *Evergreen Review*, 8 (Spring 1959): 139.

4. In 1959, I had noted: "Among the diverse tendencies in advanced American sculpture, metal construction claims a proportionately large number of devotees. So many of them are imitators or taste merchants that metal work in itself can no longer be considered the emblem of the avant-garde" ("American Construction Sculpture," p. 136).

5. Seitz, *The Art of Assemblage*, p. 74. Seitz remarked: "For a new generation and in another spirit, de Kooning's adulterative gesture may have had an effect not unlike Picasso's in 1912."

6. Thomas B. Hess, "De Kooning Paints a Picture," *Art News*, March 1953, pp. 32–33.

7. Taking his cue from Cubist collages, Apollinaire wrote in 1913 (Seitz, *The Art of Assemblage*, p. 14): "You may paint with whatever material you please, with pipes, postage stamps, postcards, playing cards, candelabra, pieces of oil cloth, collars, painted paper, newspapers." Around the same time, the Futurists began to employ the materials of modern society to symbolize its dynamism. In the *Technical Manifesto of Futurist Sculpture*, 1912, Umberto Boccioni wrote (Seitz, *The Art of Assemblage*, p. 25): "Even twenty different materials can compete in a single work to effect plastic emotion. Let us enumerate some: glass, wood, cardboard, iron, cement, horsehair, leather, cloth, mirrors, electric lights, etc., etc." The Dadaists used junk to subvert all social and aesthetic conventions; the Surrealists used incongruous juxtapositions to create psychic and poetic shock.

8. H[ubert] C[rehan], "Fortnight in Review: Stankiewicz," *Arts Digest*, 1 January 1955, p. 22.

9. F[airfield] P[orter], "Reviews and Previews: Richard Stankiewicz," *Art News*, December 1954, p. 55.

10. Fairfield Porter, "Stankiewicz Makes a Sculpture," *Art News*, September 1955, p. 63.

11. Irving Sandler, "Ash Can Revisited, A New York Letter," *Art International*, 25 October 1960, p. 28.

12. Seitz, *The Art of Assemblage*, p. 76.

13. Sandler, "Ash Can Revisited," p. 28. The reference to the Ash Can School is from Milton Brown, *American Painting from the Armory Show to the Depression* (Princeton, N.J.: Princeton University Press, 1955), pp. 12–13.

14. Ibid.

15. H[ubert] C[rehan], "Fortnight in Review: Rauschenberg," *Arts Digest*, 1 January 1955, p. 30.

16. Leo Steinberg, "Month in Review," *Arts*, January 1956, p. 46. Two years later, Steinberg publicly "regretted" this earlier review. Leo Steinberg, "Letters," *Arts*, May 1958, p. 9.

17. Leo Steinberg, "Month in Review," *Arts*, April 1956, p. 45.

18. C[rehan], "Fortnight in Review: Stankiewicz," p. 22.

19. Ferren, "Stable State of Mind," p. 64. The sculpture was *Secretary* (1955).

20. P[orter], "Reviews and Previews: Richard Stankiewicz," p. 55.

21. Club panel, "Sculptural Influences on Sculpture," 25 March 1955 (notes taken by me). The participants were Sidney Geist (moderator), Ibram Lassaw, Day Schnabel, Richard Stankiewicz, and Albert Terris. Three years later, at a Club panel, "Patriotism in the American Home," 28 March 1958 (notes taken by me), in which Allan Kaprow, Frederick Kiesler (moderator), George Ortman, Robert Rauschenberg, and Richard Stankiewicz participated, Stankiewicz reiterated this point: "I am not interested in revolution against the old ways. I have an intention and whatever material lends itself, I use. It is just dropping the limits on materials."

22. Porter, "Stankiewicz Makes a Sculpture," pp. 36–39, 62–63.

23. B[arbara] G[uest], "A Season for Sculpture: 'Gross Sitter' by Richard Stankiewicz," *Arts*, January 1956, p. 19.

24. F[rank] O'H[ara], "Reviews and Previews: Bob Rauschenberg," *Art News*, January 1955, p. 47.

25. Hess, "U.S. Painting: Some Recent Directions."

26. Sandler, "Ash Can Revisited," p. 29. Thomas B. Hess, in "Mixed Mediums for a Soft Revolution," *Art News*, Summer 1960, pp. 62, 68, maintained that junk assemblage was a protest not against the values of middle-class society as was Dada, but against the values of high (or what later came to be called "elitist") art. Thus asemblage aimed to please the public. Alloway agreed with Hess that junk culture was sympathetic to society, but questioned whether Dada was only nihilistic, since it established "a new relation between pop art and art. . . . [bringing] expendable and repeatable objects into the timeless and unique field of art" (Lawrence Alloway, "Junk Culture as a Tradition," in *New Forms–New Media I*, exhibition catalogue [New York: Martha Jackson Gallery, 1960], unpaginated).

27. See Sandler, "Ash Can Revisited," p. 30.

28. Robert Goldwater, in "Art Chronicle: A Surfeit of the New," *Partisan Review* 29 (Winter 1962): 120, supported this view. "It has taken only a few years for cast off machine and boiler parts to become so traditional that we examine them largely for their aesthetic qualities."

29. Harriet Janis and Rudi Blesh, *Collage: Personalities, Concepts, Techniques* (Philadelphia and New York: Chilton Book Company, 1962), p. 234.

30. Richard Brown Baker, interview with Richard Stankiewicz, New York, 20 August 1963, reel 7, p. 28. Transcript in the Archives of American Art.

31. G[uest], "A Season for Sculpture: 'Gross Sitter' by Richard Stankiewicz," p. 19. See also F[airfield] P[orter], "Reviews and Previews: Richard Stankiewicz," *Art News*, December 1953, p. 44; and Hilton Kramer, "Month in Review," *Arts*, December 1956, p. 47.

Richard Stankiewicz, in "New Talent in the U.S.A.," *Art in America*, February 1956, p. 46, remarked that "scruffy surfaces have a strong appeal to me and . . . the postures and attitudes to be seen in sundry accidental objects are extremely exciting. They are suggestive of the human. Then, too, there are sometimes analogies to be found between the functions of mechanical devices and those of organic creatures—which in fact I sometimes use."

32. Brown, interview with Stankiewicz, February 1963, reel 1, p. 2.

33. Philip Pearlstein, "The Private Myth," *Art News*, Sept. 1961, pp. 44, 61.

34. Porter, "Stankiewicz Makes a Sculpture," p. 36.

35. From his student days, Stankiewicz believed in first achieving a strong structure since that would release for all sorts of freedom in the treatment of materials and all the rest that goes into a painting or sculpture. (Brown, interview with Stankiewicz, February 1963, reel 6, p. 20.)

36. Hilton Kramer, "Month in Review," *Arts*, December 1956, p. 47.

37. Elizabeth C. Baker, in "The Chamberlain Crunch," *Art News*, February 1972, p. 27, stresses that "the physical assertion of volume" in Chamberlain's sculpture makes it substantially

different from Abstract Expressionist painting, whose heart "lies in conflicting surface-depth cues, whose ambiguity is made more ambiguous, rather than clarified, through color."

38. Phyllis Tuchman, "An Interview with John Chamberlain," *Artforum*, February 1972, p. 39.

39. Ibid.

40. Diane Waldman, *John Chamberlain*, exhibition catalogue (New York: Solomon R. Guggenheim Museum, 1971), p. 17. Chamberlain also remarked that he learned this attitude at Black Mountain College: "I mean it's like how Pound talks and how Williams talked and how Olson talked. They all had different estimates about how form was built."

41. I[rving] H. S[andler], in "Reviews and Previews: New Names This Month: John Chamberlain," *Art News*, January 1960, p. 18.

42. Ibid.

43. Donald Judd, in "Chamberlain: Another View," *Art International*, 16 January 1964, p. 39.

44. James K. Monte, *Mark di Suvero*, exhibition catalogue (New York: Whitney Museum of American Art, 1975–76), p. 12. Di Suvero's remark was made to Barbara Rose.

45. Sidney Geist, "A New Sculptor: Mark di Suvero," *Arts*, December 1960, p. 43.

# 8

# The Duchamp-Cage Aesthetic

ON THE WHOLE, the artists of the second generation adopted their predecessors' existentialist outlook, but in most cases only the rhetoric, and a few began to respond ironically or negatively to professions of *angst*. It was John Cage who launched a major assault on the existentialist influence on the visual arts—major, because of its direct influence on gifted young artists such as Rauschenberg, Johns, and Kaprow.

122, 123

Cage met Duchamp in 1941 and was so strongly affected by him that it is fitting to link their names. As Duchamp said: "If people choose to associate us, it's because we have a spiritual empathy and a similar way of looking at things."[1] A third name belongs with Cage and Duchamp, that of dancer and choreographer Merce Cunningham, a close collaborator of Cage's since 1943.[2]

Cage's impact on Rauschenberg, Kaprow, and others of their generation, such as George Brecht, Al Hansen, and Dick Higgins, was stronger than Duchamp's, since all had studied with the composer and knew him personally. Duchamp was older, a historical eminence, and more aloof. Moreover, the full range of his work and ideas was not made known until 1959, when Robert Lebel's comprehensive and lavishly illustrated study of the artist was published.[3]

Duchamp believed that the primary concern of the New York School was the manipulation of paint as an end in itself, that is, for purely visual or, as he put it, "retinal" purposes. Since he considered art that appealed solely to the eye a thing of the past, he had little regard for Abstract Expressionism, which he denigrated as the epitome of this optical approach.[4] Duchamp began to turn against easel painting as early as 1913 (the year that his *Nude Descending the Staircase*, exhibited at the Armory Show, made him a household name in America). He then chose to work increasingly with glass "to get away from all traditional oil mediums."[5]

Cage was more favorably inclined toward painting than Duchamp and admired the pictures of a few Abstract Expressionists, because each was "a surface which in no sense has a center of interest, so that it is truly distinguished from most art, Occidental and

Oriental, that we know of. The individual is able to look at first one part and then another, and in so far as he can, to experience the whole. But the whole is such a whole that it doesn't look as if the frame frames it. It looks as if [it] . . . could continue beyond the frame."[6]

However, Cage had no sympathy for the Abstract Expressionist belief that the true sources of art were in the artist's psychology, subjective expression, and creative process. He challenged the value of an artist forging his or her own identity in the act of creation, and the anguish and struggle that ought to entail.

Duchamp too loved to poke fun at the high aspirations of artists, their seriousness and obsession with self, the "stink of artists' egos," as Johns remarked.[7] In his own work, Duchamp aimed for indifference. He insisted that in selecting his Readymades, which were mass-produced commercial artifacts, "the thing was to choose one that you were not attracted to . . . and that was difficult because anything becomes beautiful if you look at it long enough. . . . [My intention was to] completely eliminate the existence of taste, bad or good or indifferent."[8]

Cage's antipathy toward the Abstract Expressionist's "elitist" image of himself as a special being, a combination of existential hero or shaman and master painter, is exemplified in the following two anecdotes. One: Cage told of a conversation with de Kooning, who said: "We are different. . . . You don't want to be an artist, whereas I want to be a great artist." Cage commented: "Now it was this aspect of wanting to be an artist . . . who had something to say, who wanted through his work to appear really great . . . which I could not accept."[9] Two: recalled by Feldman, a visitor to Cage's home in Stony Point was praising the contribution made by the composer to music. Walking over to the window and looking out into the woods, Cage said: "I just can't believe I am better than anything out there."[10]

Just as Duchamp and Cage repudiated the role of the artist as master, so they rejected the conception of the work of art as masterpiece-for-the-ages, or even an object of special interest. Duchamp showed the way in his Readymades, which were factory-made and not transformed by the artist, and in his works in glass, a medium so fragile that chances were it would not last for long. Cage's attitude was revealed in a lecture entitled "Sand Painting," delivered in 1949 at the Subjects of the Artist School to an audience composed largely of Abstract Expressionists. He said: "I was promoting the notion of impermanent art. . . . something that, no sooner had it been used, was so to speak discarded. I was fighting at that point the notion of art itself as something which we preserve."[11]

Duchamp's search for an alternative to a "retinal" art led him to elevate the intellectual component of art above all. Taking a somewhat different tack, Cage focused on the everyday physical environment as the primary source for his art, the vein opened up by the Readymades, an approach that was of lesser interest to Duchamp himself.[12] Uninterested in the confession of an artist's inner life and of its emotional qualities, Cage instead looked out at the world, at what was experienced through the senses. The "use" of art was to "change ways of seeing [and hearing], to open up one's eyes to just seeing

122   Robert Rauschenberg, *Canyon*. 1959.
86¹/₂″ x 70″ x 23″. Private Collection, New York.

what there was to see,"[13] and one's ears to just attending the activity of sounds.[14] Art's ability to do so was confirmed by E. H. Gombrich: "Contemporary artists such as Rauschenberg have become fascinated by the patterns and textures of decaying walls with their torn posters and patches of damp. Though I happen to dislike Rauschenberg, I notice to my chagrin that I cannot help being aware of such sights in a different way since seeing his paintings."[15]

In order to simulate what existed in one's surroundings, Cage rejected any hierarchy of sounds in music, and of materials, forms, and colors in the visual arts. Each element as it occurred was to exist only for itself, allowed to come into its own "rather than being exploited to express sentiments or ideas of order."[16] To put it positively, any sound or material by itself or in any combination, whether intended or not, *is* art.[17] Noise is music—and so is silence, which Cage denied could even exist, since in nature there is always to be found a continuum of sound.

Thinking in a similar vein, Cunningham insisted that any movement, no matter how natural or eccentric, including ordinary walking, falling, and running, could be dance, greatly enlarging the potential range of movements definable as "dance." Moreover, none of the actions in a dance has any significance beyond itself. Movement was

123 Jasper Johns, *Painted Bronze,* 1960.
13½″ x 8″ diameter. Collection, the artist.

not intended to tell a story, be symbolic, or convey a message, mood, emotion, or idea, but was made for its own sake. As Cage remarked, it was meant to engage the viewer's "faculty of kinesthetic sympathy. It is this faculty we employ when, seeing the flight of birds, we ourselves, by identification, fly up, glide and soar."[18] Moreover, Cunningham asked each dancer to move in conformity with his or her particular physical constitution. Such individualization constituted a rejection of the hierarchical leader and chorus relationship found in most of dance.

Cage summed up his outlook: "I want to change my way of seeing, not my way of feeling. I was perfectly happy about my feelings."[19] Elsewhere he said: "I would like to think that the sounds people do hear in a concert could make them more aware of the sounds they hear in the street, or out in the country, or anywhere they may be."[20] Becoming alive to one's actual environment would lead to happiness. "I prefer laughter to tears [of Abstract Expressionism] . . . If art was going to be of any use, it was . . . not with reference to itself but . . . to the people who used it, and they would use it not in relation to art but . . . to their daily lives . . . [which] would be better if they were concerned with enjoyment rather than misery."[21]

The purpose of art then, as Cage saw it, was "a purposeless play. . . . [which]

however, is an affirmation of life—not an attempt to bring order out of chaos nor to suggest improvements in creation, but simply a way of waking up to the very life we're living, which is so excellent once one gets one's mind and one's desires out of its way and lets it act of its own accord."[22] But there was more to it than that. As Tomkins remarked, Cage insisted that the true function of art in our time was to reveal to people the immensities of the changes taking place in their lives so that they could be "free to enter into the miraculous new field of human awareness that is opening up."[23]

Cage's passive acceptance of society was the very opposite of the subversive social activism generally identified with Dadaism. But he chose to focus on the potentially positive thrust of Duchamp's thinking, as he said, "this concern which interests us more than anything else: the blurring of the distinction between art and life," a blurring exemplified by the Readymades.[24]

Cage was also able to turn Dadaism's essentially negative attitude toward society into a positive one, accepting of what is, by introducing into his thinking ideas culled from Zen Buddhism, which did not much interest Duchamp. (Cage began to study Oriental philosophy in 1945, during a crisis in his life, at which time he looked to Zen rather than to psychoanalysis for the solution of personal problems.) In Cage's eyes, Dada and Zen were akin, despite divergent aims, because they related art to everyday life in an unsentimental, shocking, and humorous fashion. Moreover, both repudiated willful and rational creation, and encouraged the use of accident and discontinuity to an extreme unprecedented in Western art.[25]

The Zen doctrine of greatest use to Cage was articulated by Dr. Daisetz T. Suzuki in his lectures at Columbia University that Cage attended in the late forties. As he recalled it: "Everything and everybody . . . is the Buddha. These Buddhas are all, every single one of them, at the center of the Universe. And they are all in interpenetration, and they are not obstructing one another."[26] Cage took this Zen doctrine to mean that every material or sound here and now is valid in itself. It also led him to the belief that he should not impose his feelings on other people. "Therefore [beginning in 1950] the use of chance operation, indeterminacy . . . . the non-erection of patterns of either ideas or feelings on my part in order to leave those other centers free to be the centers."[27]

Cage's antipathy toward the establishment of willful patterns and obstructing relationships was evident in the now legendary event that he organized at Black Mountain College in 1952. As he recalls, it involved Rauschenberg's painting, Cunningham's dancing, Olson's and Richards's poetry recited from ladders, Tudor's piano playing, films, slides, phonograph records, and a lecture by Cage which ends: "A piece of string, a sunset, each acts."[28] The participants were free to do whatever they wished or nothing at certain predetermined periods of time arrived at through chance operations by Cage, in this case tossing I Ching coins, his favorite method of composing. As he said: "I had no knowledge of what they were going to do. I had a vague notion of where they were going to do it. . . . The thing had not been rehearsed." In the Black Mountain event, Cage desired to create a situation in which simultaneous actions could not have been foreseen or preconceived. "If we did bring about patterns, they were patterns which we had not measured; furthermore, which we didn't wish to emphasize. We simply wished to permit them to exist."[29]

Such dissociation of actions was anticipated in the early forties by Cage and Cunningham in their collaboration. Each did his part of a dance, choreography and composing, separately. Treating music and dance as two distinct entities enabled each to develop more freely, dance as dance, music as music. This also created a situation in which interactions between movement and sound could not have been predicted.[30] Like Cage, Cunningham had used the stage as a continuous field no part of which is more important than any other and in which there is no fixed center or points to which dancers relate, but rather "an all-over relatedness of shifting movement."[31] Thus, his works are intended to be seen from all sides; they are non-climactic in space and time.

Cunningham also began experimenting with chance as one method of choreographing in 1951. He drew elaborate charts of the various components of dance—number of dancers, kinds and directions of movement, tempo, spacing—and then tossed coins and dice to determine the sequence of a work. However, unlike Cage, who relied entirely on chance, Cunningham treated it as one technique among others. In this respect, he can be considered more traditional than Cage, but only in this respect, for Cunningham revolutionized modern dance.

Cage's event at Black Mountain had precedents in Dada and Surrealistic performances.[32] There were also the well-known environmental works that Duchamp created in (more accurately, of) Surrealist exhibitions, such as the one in New York, 1941, in which he crisscrossed the gallery space with sixteen miles of white string, producing a labyrinthine environment in which both works and viewers were enmeshed.[33] Perhaps most important of all was Duchamp's *The Bride Stripped Bare by Her Bachelors, Even* (1915–23), also called the *Large Glass*, the image of which was on free-standing glass through which the viewer could not help but look at his surroundings, which thus were incorporated into the work. Johns remarked that the *Large Glass* participated and, at times, got lost in its environment. "The walls of the Philadelphia Museum show through it, attack it, are absorbed or reflected by it. . . . [It allows] the changing focus of the eye, of the mind, to place the viewer where he is, not elsewhere."[34]

Cage's reliance on chance operations in itself was not radical, since it had been employed earlier by the Dadaists and the Surrealists,[35] even though he used it as his exclusive method of composing. However, Cage, like Duchamp, rejected the Surrealist use of automatism to suspend conscious behavior in order to reveal deeper, preconscious truths. Instead, Cage used chance to avoid psychological interpretation, literally to achieve self-abnegation in order to create "a music free from one's memory and imagination,"[36] unconscious and conscious tastes, desires, inspiration. (Cage has not succeeded in eliminating his self from his art. All his compositions have been unmistakably his. Paradoxically, the chance operations that he favored are somehow dominated by his artistic personality.[37])

But the suppression of self was a means to a greater artistic end: to ape nature's manner of operation (more important than recording the appearance of things).[38] Ac-

124  Marcel Duchamp, *The Bride Stripped Bare by Her Bachelors, Even* (large glass), 1915–23. 109¼" x 69¼". Philadelphia Museum of Art.

cording to Cage, chance was nature's forming principle, something to be valued because it was, a turn of thinking different from Duchamp's. Cage understood that relinquishing the control of sound "seems at first to be a giving up of everything that belongs to humanity—for the musician, the giving up of music." However, he hastened to assert that using chance as the mainspring of art "leads to the world of nature, where gradually or suddenly, one sees that humanity and nature, not separate, are in this world together; that nothing was lost when everything was given away. In fact, everything is gained. In musical terms, any sounds may occur in any combination and in any continuity."[39]

Cage's own accident-determined art, which aspires to the annihilation of the artist's self and of every distinction between art and everyday experience, "life," reality, or nature, is unprecedented in the history of art. Feldman believed that this quest was religious in character: "Cage stepped aside to such a degree that we really see the end of the world, the end of art. That is the paradox. That this very self-abolishment mirrors its opposite— . . . art's final revelation."[40] Commenting on Cage's influence, Feldman summed up: "He does not give the young people of this generation an ideal. He does not cry, like Mayakowski, 'Down with your art, down with your love, down with your society, down with your God.' The revolution is over. Mayakowski's and ours. What Cage has to offer is almost a type of resignation. What he has to teach is that just as there is no way to arrive at art, there is no way not to." [41]

Hess came to a similar conclusion about Cage-inspired art, although his response to it was negative, reflecting the attitude (without the outrage) of the New York School as a whole. In a review of assemblage, he wrote that

> . . . a great many artists today seem dissatisfied with the basic limits of Art, . . . There is a kind of protest . . . not against the values of middle-class society as were Dada manifestations. . . . [but] in favor of society—or for People in general—and against the invisible, crystal-hard barriers that an oil-on-canvas or a sculptured-sculpture place between the witness and the finished object. It is as if many of these artists were trying to reach out from their works to give the specta-tor's hand a good shake or nudge him in the ribs. You are invited to . . . be a participant . . . in a game with art. [42]

Hess went on to say that much of assemblage was "an attack on the aristocracy of art by and with art," and that was the extent of its revolution. [43]

Cage's primary influence on such artists as Rauschenberg, Johns, and Kaprow was in directing their attention to the American scene and in convincing them to accept it as it was, in a Zen-like spirit of "joy and revolution." [44] Their artistic discovery of everyday images, artifacts, and events constituted a kind of Americanization of Zen or a spiritual-ization of the American environment, for its familiar components became objects of contemplation or of faith, like secular icons. And all of this was done in the name of the avant-garde.

Cage's interest in Duchamp prompted young artists in his circle to take the older artist very seriously. Although Cage was not particularly drawn to the conceptual side of Duchamp's thinking, Johns was and moved, as he said Duchamp had, "through the retinal boundaries which had been established with Impressionism into a field where language, thought and vision act upon one another," [45] even though his work possessed an anti-Duchampian painterly dimension and finesse.

Thus, Duchamp's thinking led in two interconnected directions, both providing al-ternatives to the gestural aesthetics that dominated fifties painting. Via Cage, Du-champ's example led artists to try to fuse art and life in events that resembled theater more than painting and sculpture, for instance, by using aesthetically disreputable mate-rials found in "life," or to work in the gap between the two, as Rauschenberg did, the direction that was of lesser interest to Duchamp himself. [46] Or, it led, as in the case of Johns, in the direction of a Neo-Duchampian art in the service of the mind, an art based on conceptions about what art could be, on visual and verbal mixtures, paradoxes, ambiguities, and games.

# Notes

1. Otto Hahn, "Passport No. G255300: United States of America," *Art and Artists*, July 1966, p. 7.

2. Cunningham identified Cage as the greatest single influence on his work. See Richard Kostelanetz, "Profile of Merce Cunningham," *Michigan Quarterly Review* 14 (Fall 1975): 373. Cage has served as the musical director of the Cunningham Dance Company from 1943 to the present. Rauschenberg designed the costumes and sets for most of Cunningham's dances for a decade beginning in 1954. See Calvin Tomkins, *The Bride and the Bachelors* (New York: Viking Press, 1968), p. 265.

3. Robert Lebel, *Marcel Duchamp* (New York: Grove Press, 1959).

4. Katharine Kuh, *The Artist's Voice* (New York: Harper & Row, 1962), p. 89.

5. Ibid., p. 88.

6. Interview with John Cage, New York, 6 May 1966. Cage's favorite older artist was Mark Tobey. He admired him for the craft and complexity of his painting and the subtlety of his color, qualities he found lacking in Pollock's "drip" pictures.

7. Jasper Johns, "Marcel Duchamp [1887–1968]," *Artforum*, November 1968, p. 6.

8. "Some Late Thoughts of Marcel Duchamp: From an Interview with Jeanne Siegel," *Arts Magazine*, December 1968–January 1969, p. 21.

9. Interview with Cage.

10. Morton Feldman, "The Anxiety of Art," *Art in America*, September–October 1973, p. 92.

11. Interview with Cage.

12. Ibid. Duchamp considered the Readymade as essentially an idea. "He [Duchamp writing of himself in the third person] CHOSE it. He took an ordinary article of life, placed it so that its useful significance disappeared under the new title and point of view—created a new thought for that object" (Tomkins, *The Bride and the Bachelors*, p. 41).

Cage later remarked on the difference between his and Duchamp's conception of Readymades: "He didn't do what we have since done—extend the notion of the Readymades to everything. He was very precise, very disciplined. It must have been a very difficult thing for him to make a Readymade, to come to that decision" (Moira and William Roth, "John Cage on Marcel Duchamp: An Interview," *Art in America*, November–December 1973, p. 75).

13. Interview with Cage.

14. John Cage, *Silence: Lectures and Writings* (Cambridge, Mass.: M.I.T. Press, 1967) p. 10.

15. E. H. Gombrich, "Visual Discovery Through Art," *Arts Magazine*, November 1965, p. 25.

16. Cage, *Silence*, p. 69.

17. As early as 1937, Cage wrote: "I BELIEVE THAT THE USE OF NOISE . . . TO MAKE MUSIC . . . WILL CONTINUE AND INCREASE UNTIL WE REACH A MUSIC . . . WHICH WILL MAKE AVAILABLE . . . ANY AND ALL SOUNDS THAT CAN BE HEARD" (Cage, *Silence*, pp. 3–4).

In 1952, Cage performed 4′33″, a composition consisting of four minutes and thirty-three seconds of "silence," or rather of the sounds that happened to be in the environment.

18. Kostelanetz, "Profile of Merce Cunningham," p. 368.

19. Interview with Cage.

20. Tomkins, *The Bride and the Bachelors*, p. 101.

21. Interview with Cage.

22. Cage, *Silence*, p. 12.

23. Tomkins, *The Bride and the Bachelors*, p. 75.

24. Roth, "John Cage on Marcel Duchamp: An Interview," p. 78. This attitude would lead Cage to experiment with computer technology and to embrace the theories of Buckminster Fuller.

25. See Seitz, *The Art of Assemblage*, p. 37.

26. Interview with Cage. Cage, in *Silence*, pp. 46, 47, elaborated:

SUZUKI SAID THAT THERE WAS A DIFFERENCE BETWEEN ORIENTAL THINKING AND EUROPEAN THINKING, THAT IN EUROPEAN THINKING THINGS ARE SEEN AS CAUSING ONE ANOTHER AND HAVING EFFECTS, WHEREAS IN ORIENTAL THINKING . . . THERE ARE AN INCALCULABLE INFINITY OF CAUSES AND EFFECTS, THAT IN FACT EACH AND EVERY THING IN ALL OF TIME AND SPACE IS RELATED . . . BEING SO THERE IS NO NEED TO CAUTIOUSLY PROCEED IN DUALISTIC TERMS OF SUCCESS AND FAILURE OR THE BEAUTIFUL AND THE UGLY OR GOOD AND EVIL BUT RATHER SIMPLY TO WALK ON "NOT WONDERING," TO QUOTE MEISTER ECKHART, "AM I RIGHT OR DOING SOMETHING WRONG."

27. Interview with Cage. The use of chance operations is different from the use of indeterminacy. The first is a method of composition whose results, once determined, are not changed; the second allows performers a certain freedom of choice, so that each performance cannot be predicted.

28. Cage, *Silence*, p. x.

29. Interview with Cage. For a full description of Cage's event at Black Mountain College, see Duberman, *Black Mountain*, pp. 348–58.

30. It is noteworthy that this kind of relationship between dance and music outraged the audience for dance perhaps more than any other of Cunningham's innovations.

31. Tomkins, *The Bride and the Bachelors*, p. 265.

32. Information about Dada events was published the year before Cage's event in Robert Motherwell, ed., *The Dada Painters and Poets* (New York: Wittenborn, Schultz, 1951). There was also the influence of Antonin Artaud's writings on Cage. Cage visited Paris for three months in 1949. Duberman, in *Black Mountain*, p. 350, reported that "among the new contacts he made was with Pierre Boulez, who brought Artaud's work to Cage's attention. He, in turn, passed Artaud on to David Tudor and Mary Caroline Richards, and at Black Mountain, the three of them often read Artaud together, M. C. [Richards] later becoming one of Artaud's first English translators."

33. Duchamp transformed the main gallery of the International Surrealist show in Paris in 1938 by hanging twelve hundred coal sacks from the ceiling and covering the floor with dead leaves.

34. Jasper Johns, "The Green Box," *Scrap* 2 (23 December 1960): 4.

35. In 1913, Duchamp composed a piece of music entitled "Musical Erratum," by putting notes in a hat and pulling them out.

36. Cage, *Silence*, pp. 10–11.

37. Tomkins, in *The Bride and the Bachelors*, p. 112, taking his cue from Virgil Thomson, asked: "If Cage selects the materials he will use, and makes all the decisions necessary to set up the mechanism of chance, is the result really controlled by chance at all?"

38. John Cage, in *A Year From Monday* (Middletown, Conn.: Wesleyan University Press, 1969), p. 31, wrote that he found the doctrine in Ananda K. Coomaraswamy's book, *The Transformation of Nature in Art*.

39. Cage, *Silence*, p. 8.

40. Feldman, "The Anxiety of Art," p. 92.

41. Ibid.

42. Hess, "Mixed Mediums for a Soft Revolution," p. 45.

43. Ibid., p. 62.

44. Tomkins, *The Bride and the Bachelors*, p. 137.

45. Johns, "Marcel Duchamp," p. 6.

46. Occasionally, Robert Rauschenberg made a Duchampian gesture more intellectual than in keeping with his art-life strategy, as when in 1953, he erased a drawing by de Kooning, a gesture calling to mind Duchamp's penciling a moustache on a reproduction of the *Mona Lisa*. In another Duchampian gesture, when Rauschenberg was asked to do a portrait of Iris Clert, he sent her a telegram that read: "This is a portrait of Iris Clert if I say so." Cage in "26 Statements re Duchamp," *A Year From Monday*, p. 71, summed it up: "Duchamp showed the usefulness of addition (mustache). Rauschenberg showed the function of subtraction (De Kooning). Well, we look forward to multiplication and division. It is safe to assume that someone will learn trigonometry, Johns."

Cage recognized that Jasper Johns, because of his interest in ideas, was probably closer to Duchamp than himself or Rauschenberg. See Roth, "John Cage on Marcel Duchamp: An Interview," p. 78.

# 9
# Rauschenberg and Johns

122, 125
126, 127
128, 129
131, 132
133, 134
135, 211
Pl. VI

IN 1953, ROBERT RAUSCHENBERG exhibited canvases painted flat white, the first of a succession of works that scandalized the New York School. These pictures, made in the summer of 1952, were conceived prior to Cage's composition of four minutes and thirty-three seconds of silence, as the composer himself acknowledged.[1] This admission, however, should not divert attention from the enormous influence of Cage's thinking on Rauschenberg. The two had become friends by 1951 when Cage purchased one of the young artist's pictures. In the following year, Rauschenberg was the only student invited to participate in Cage's theatrical event at Black Mountain.

Certainly, Cage's insistence that there could be no void in hearing or in vision inspired Rauschenberg. But the all-white pictures were also anticipated by paintings he began in 1949 and showed in 1951. The earlier works are composed of white grounds inscribed with spare abstract configurations, at once quasi-geometric and calligraphic, sometimes forming abstract symbols—arrows, circles, numbers. Rauschenberg thought

126

of these abstractions as symbolic, for he gave them such titles as *Crucifixion and Reflexion, The Man with Two Souls,* and *Trinity.* The geometric component in them reveals the influence of Albers, with whom Rauschenberg had studied; the allover quality, the

125

prompting of Cage. The subsequent all-white canvases can still be read as geometric, since they often contain a number of panels placed close together, suggesting ensembles of rectangles. However, each canvas constitutes an entire picture or a picture *field.* A further influence of both Albers and Cage was in the impersonality and self-effacement of bare paintings that lacked touch and color.[2]

However, the all-white canvases are not without "color," for they possess a "self-color," which constantly changes as the light changes, or as shadows are cast on it, as Cage remarked. They are "airports for the lights, shadows and particles."[3] At the time the pictures were produced, Rauschenberg wrote of the appeal of nothingness, of silence, and of absence.[4] Later, he said that it is hard to paint nothing. A picture is an object, a whole, that isn't just waiting for someone to express anything. It is finished before

125   Robert Rauschenberg, *White Painting* (Seven Panels), 1951.
72″ x 128″. Collection, the artist.

126   Robert Rauschenberg,
*Crucifixion and Reflexion,* 1950.
51″ x 47¹/₂″. Andrew J. Crispo
Collection, New York.

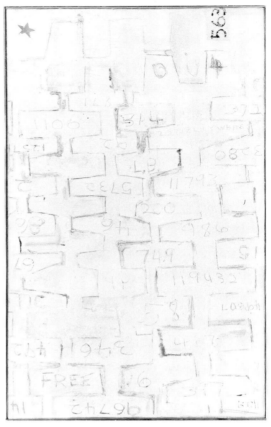

127 Robert Rauschenberg, *The Lily White* (formerly known as *White Painting with Numbers,* 1949), ca. 1950. 39½″ x 23½″. Collection, Mr. and Mrs. Victor W. Ganz, New York.

it is painted. He concluded that the white paintings were probably more beautiful than anything else he had done.[5]

Rauschenberg stated his essential artistic intention as follows: "Painting relates to both art and life. Neither can be made. (I try to act in that gap between the two.)"[6] The all-white canvases are close to "life," for their image is "life's" action *on* them. In 1952, perhaps wanting to be less passive, and in order to express "life's" action *in* paintings, or to venture in that direction, he assembled more or less all-black collages from torn and crumpled, mostly rectangular pieces of newsprint dipped into or coated with black enamel and oil paint. Rauschenberg said of them that he "was interested in getting complexity without their revealing much,"[7] presumably of his personality, feelings, and concepts.

The following year was for Rauschenberg a period of intense experimentation on the edge between "life" and "art." In the one direction—toward "life"—he made *Dirt Painting: For John Cage,* which sprouted real plants and had to be watered periodically. This was in keeping with Cage's belief that art should emulate or demonstrate nature's processes. But unlike the composer's events, Rauschenberg's work resembled a conventional picture, raising questions of whether the painting was functioning as a picture; or as though it was nature; or whether nature was functioning as though it was a painting.

In the other direction—toward "art"—he adopted ideas culled from gesture painting, in which he was well-versed, for at Black Mountain he had studied with Motherwell, Tworkov, and Kline, and in New York with Vaclav Vytlacil.

The painter who influenced Rauschenberg most was de Kooning, but the young artist's feelings were ambivalent. In 1953, he asked de Kooning for a drawing which he proposed to erase, and the older artist obliged. Rauschenberg's activity was not wholly destructive, for the ghost of the drawing remained visible, yet it was generally considered to be an act of Dadaist nihilism, akin to Duchamp's defacing of the *Mona Lisa* (except that Rauschenberg subtracted instead of added), or if not nihilism then iconoclasm, a kind of wiping the slate clean of Abstract Expressionism.[8] Yet Rauschenberg's gesture can also be considered a positive one, as the transformation of de Kooning's pictorial ideas (subtracting anxiety from them) by Cage's aesthetics (adding artistry to them)—and this was to be his basic artistic strategy well into the sixties.[9] Rauschenberg's erasure carried de Kooning's drawing close to the state of the "silent" all-white canvases, with the difference that instead of beginning with "nothing," Rauschenberg began with something, and a masterpiece at that. On another level, the rubbing can be seen as an enigmatic "ghost" image which had a private meaning for Rauschenberg, for throughout his career he had been fascinated by the obscure or obliterated presence of an image or an object, as in the erased imagery of the Dante drawings (1960).

The partly visible image was also a sign of Rauschenberg's inability to escape de Kooning, even if he wanted to, which he certainly did not in the works which developed from the all-black collages, the so-called combine-paintings, these constituting the main body of his work from 1953 to 1962. No matter how far Rauschenberg veered toward "life" or "reality," he retained the structure and facture that he derived from de Kooning. Rauschenberg's method of improvisation was closer to de Kooning's than Cage's. To be sure, he found many of his materials by accident, but he did not use chance to compose. Still, Rauschenberg ventured toward "life" in a way that no gesture painter had, interspersing his painterly areas with a multiplicity of found objects and materials, in *Canyon* (1959), for example, torn paper, corrugated tin, a baby photograph, a frayed shirt cuff, a stuffed eagle perched on an empty carton, and a puffed-out pillow.[10]

122

Cage's theorizing about commonplace objects, images, and events was a stimulus in the creation of the combine-paintings. Rauschenberg once said: "There are very few things that happen in my daily life that have to do with turpentine, oil, and pigments."[11] In his eyes, found objects were lost sculptures or sculptures waiting to be found. Furthermore, he treated all materials as equivalent; as he said: "Paint itself is an object, and canvas also."[12] But more important, the profuse "junk" in Rauschenberg's combine-paintings can be thought of as "noise," at an opposite pole from "silence" but a part of a single vision. Earlier, Cage had predicted that "noise" would be a major ingredient in the music of the future.[13] He also observed that Rauschenberg's works remind "us of a multiplicity of events in time and space."[14]

This multiplicity can be considered the essential content of the combine-paintings, and they provide viewers with ways of perceiving and experiencing their environment.

128   Robert Rauschenberg, *Charlene,* 1954.
89″ x 112″. Stedelijk Museum, Amsterdam, The Netherlands.

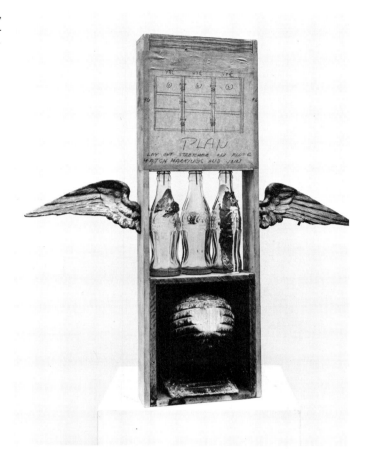

129  Robert Rauschenberg,
*Coca-Cola Plan,* 1958.
27" x 26" x 6".
Collection, Panza, Milan, Italy.

As Brian O'Doherty saw it, Rauschenberg's work could help people cope with "informational overload," which was unavoidable in daily life, by tolerating discontinuities. Finding out exactly what the images meant was not relevant. Nor were attempts to relate them.

> The images were chosen not for the content they could unload on each other through juxtaposition, but for their nonspecificity. . . .
>
> Their description of reality, at the time they were made, depended on this dissociative rather than associative effect. His art encouraged what could be called the city dweller's rapid scan, rather than the art audience's stare. . . .
>
> Rauschenberg had introduced into the museum and its high-art ambience not just the vernacular object but something much more important, the *vernacular glance.*[15]

O'Doherty went on to say:

> The vernacular glance is what carries us through the city every day, a mode of almost unconscious, or at least divided, attention. . . . [It] tags the unexpected and quickly makes it the familiar . . . The vernacular glance doesn't recognize cat-

egories of the beautiful and ugly. It's just interested in what's there. . . . It dispenses with hierarchies of importance, since they are constantly changing according to where you are and what you need. . . . The vernacular glance is . . . extraordinarily versatile in dealing with experience that would be totally confusing otherwise.[16]

It is important to stress, as O'Doherty did, that Rauschenberg attempted to portray reality as it was, literally. He was not interested in symbol and metaphor, as were the Surrealists.

Not only did the "vernacular glance" work against the "museum stare," but it acted against the tradition-oriented, Cubist-inspired design of de Kooning that Rauschenberg borrowed to structure his art, that is, his objects and images refused to be absorbed into a picture design. Rauschenberg allowed his materials to be themselves, each to assert the physical identity it once had in "life" at the threat to the coherence of pictorial order.[17]

130    In this respect, he differed from the Cubists or Schwitters (a favorite of his), who integrated found objects into a total design, subordinating them to the work as an entity.

Inspired by Cage, Rauschenberg ventured not only toward "life" but theater, particularly in his combine-paintings, which invited the spectators to participate as well as to

128    observe. *Charlene* (1954) is as much a multimedia environment as an object. Almost room-size, it contains blinking lights and their cast shadows, a sheet-metal mirror in which to look by lifting the gauze covering it, a hole through which to see the wall. As O'Hara wrote: "He provides a means by which you, as well as he, can get 'in' the painting."[18] Later, in *Broadcast* (1959), which incorporates three radios that viewers can play, he mixed the aural with the visual. Rauschenberg's art has been inclusive, verging not only toward theater and music but at times toward literature, as in the case of his illus-

132    trations of Dante's *Inferno* (1960). Indeed when these thirty-four works were first shown, each was accompanied by a written text to help viewers decipher the montages of blurred images which were transfers from magazines and newspapers.

In another vein, Rauschenberg made works in which a single object is more or less the entire work, presented rather than represented, actual rather than illusionistic—acting in the gap between reality and art, between what is real and what is depicted. In his

133    notorious *Bed* (1955),[19] the identification of the thing and the work of art is so total that one might sleep on the bed-picture, if placed on the floor and unless one is put off by the fact that the real quilt and pillow are clotted with real paint and pencil scrawls.[20]

By insistently documenting his environment, Rauschenberg diverged from the primary intention of gesture painting. More than that, his work constituted a challenge to the moral stance of the Asbtract Expressionists, to their insistence that in order to be worthwhile a picture had to be found in the struggle of painting. They deemed without value a picture that was not a unique event evolving from anxious existential action but was a matter of aesthetic performance. To undermine this notion, Rauschenberg in

134, 135    1957 made a gestural combine-painting titled *Factum 1* and then executed a near-duplicate of it. This raised the upsetting question of whether the "found" picture was any more valuable than its "made" near-copy, and how could one tell. Critics were

130  Kurt Schwitters, *V-2,* 1928.
5¹/₈″ x 3¹/₂″. The Sidney and Harriet Janis Collection.

131  Robert Rauschenberg, *Monogram,* 1955–59.
48″ x 72″ x 72″. National Museum, Stockholm, Sweden.

132  Robert Rauschenberg, Illustrations for Dante's *Inferno: Canto XXXI: The Giants,* 1959–60.
14$\frac{1}{2}$″ x 11$\frac{1}{2}$″. The Museum of Modern Art, New York.

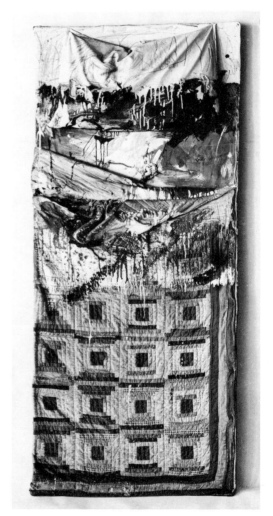

133  Robert Rauschenberg, *Bed,* 1955.
74″ x 31″. Collection, Mr. and Mrs. Leo Castelli, New York.

quick to grasp the issue; one wrote that when one discovers that *Factum 1* has a twin, "with its patient, scrupulous duplication of every dribble and tatter, one is forced to admit that the same combination of impulse and discipline that produces more conventional pictures is also operating here."[21] In time, the subtle differences in the two versions became more pronounced to viewers, and indeed of greater interest than the similarities, complicating the issues raised.

Rauschenberg shocked the Abstract Expressionists who denigrated his work as anti-art, but it never was.[22] In his best combine-paintings he succeeded in balancing the often contradictory demands of "life" and "art," sensitive to random found objects and easel painting. His intention was to provoke people into seeing both their actual environment and art. Much as he believed that "a picture is more like the real world when it's made out of the real world," he said: "I don't want a picture to look like something it isn't. I want it to look like something it is."[23] Rauschenberg's devotion to pictorial conventions inhibited moves toward environments and theatrical events (or Happenings, as they are commonly called). It prompted him to favor such objects as photographs, handkerchiefs, street signs, ladders, and postcards not only because they were real, but because they conformed to the rectangular, flat shape of the picture plane and lent themselves to composition within it.[24] But the viewers' consciousness of pure aesthetic qualities, e.g., the finesse with which objects of diverse textures are placed and related to the painting, is perpetually disrupted by the impure materials that suggest an unselected inventory of contemporary American life, forcing the viewers' attention to, and heightening their consciousness of, it.

Even more than Rauschenberg, Jasper Johns chose as the subjects of his paintings everyday objects and images: the American flag, targets, lowercase letters, and printed numbers. The pictures of flags and targets, begun around 1955 and shown in 1958, were so close to the real things that the one could be taken (or mistaken) for the other, thus breaking down distinctions between "art" and "life."[25] When Leo Steinberg asked Johns whether he painted letter types because he liked them or because that was how they came, he replied: "But that's what I like about them, that they come that way."[26]

123, 136
137, 138
141, 142
143, 213
Pl. VII

Because Johns's pictures are so factual, they call to mind Duchamp's Readymades, and in fact, Johns was powerfully attracted to the Dadaist's "art" and thought, about which he had learned from Cage and from Motherwell's anthology, *The Dada Painters and Poets* (1951).[27] Johns recognized the artistic potential of Duchamp's Readymades, but probably of greater importance, he was fascinated by the elaborate, sly games Duchamp played with incompatible aesthetic *ideas*—with the definition of art and non-art; "real" objects and "art" objects; with the connection of verbal and visual images, of the optical and tactile, of the literal and the illusionistic, of the two- and three-dimensional, of what is conceptualized and what is seen, that is, with the complex and ambiguous process of experiencing art. Moreover, Johns in his work has engaged in a continuing dialogue with the Dada *par excellence*.

Duchamp's aim was primarily anti-artistic, but his Readymades can be viewed as art, if only because they have been put on pedestals and proclaimed "sculpture." Plac-

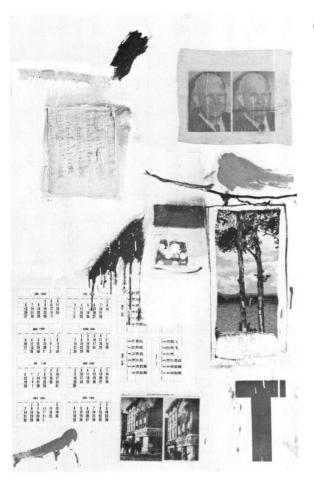

134   Robert Rauschenberg, *Factum I,* 1957.
62″ x 35½″. Collection, Panza, Milan, Italy.

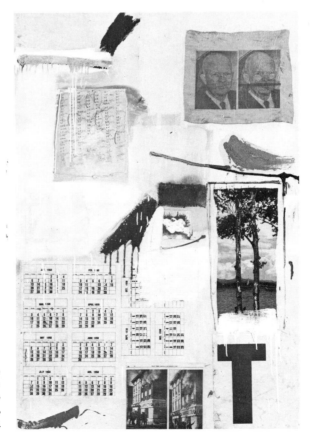

135   Robert Rauschenberg,
*Factum II,* 1957.
62″ x 35½″. Collection,
Mr. and Mrs. Morton Neumann,
Chicago, Illinois.

136 Jasper Johns, *Target with Four Faces,* 1955. 25" x 26". The Museum of Modern Art, New York.

ing, or more accurately, displacing, them in an art context conferred on them the status of art. Unlike Duchamp's objects, Johns's works are made like "art" and are not real artifacts, although they look as if they could function as such in "life." Therefore, they provoke the question of whether they are real or art, the things themselves or representations or re-creations, objects or subjects, or perhaps, signs or symbols. For example, can a painted copy of a flag which could pass for a flag point to a flag as a sign or be its symbol? What is the difference between *presenting* a flag *as* a work of art and *representing* it *in* the work? Moreover, does re-creation result in "transformation"? Johns denied that it does in his case. Taking his cue from Cage, he remarked: "If you have one thing and make another thing, there is no transformation, but there are two things. I don't

137

137  Jasper Johns, *Flag,* 1958.
42″ x 60″. Collection, Mr. and Mrs. Leo Castelli, New York.

think you would mistake one for the other."[28] This conception also has a source in Magritte's picture of a pipe and accompanying statement: "This is not a pipe."

Another question that Johns poses is: If a picture of a flag is not a representation, is it non-representational? Greenberg puzzled over the ambiguity between abstraction and representation in Johns's pictures. This is surprising since Greenberg generally avoided dealing with art other than that which he championed. Apparently he could not resist the kind of games Johns proposed. Greenberg wrote:

> The original flatness of the canvas, with a few outlines stenciled on it, . . . [represents] all that a picture by Johns really does represent. The paint surface itself, with its de Kooning-esque play of lights and darks, is . . . completely superfluous to this end. Everything that usually serves representation and illusion is left to serve nothing but itself, that is, abstraction; while everything that usually serves the abstract or decorative—flatness, bare outlines, all-over or symmetrical design—is put to the service of representation.[29]

Greenberg's remarks pointed to the stunning originality of Johns's painting. Indeed, he created a realist art that does not resemble any other. His artistic strategy was to be more literal than past figurative artists while introducing pictorial ideas associated with modernist abstract painting, such as extreme flatness, achieved by the elimination of conventional figure-ground relationships and the sense of depth they suggest; by choosing flat objects as subjects and making the image and the picture plane contiguous, the flatness of each augmenting the other; and by painting the entire surface with a uniform density. Johns did not achieve two-dimensionality at the expense of a suggestion of depth or pictorial space, for having employed design to establish flatness, he used painterly means to create a shallow illusionism. This ambiguity between two- and three-dimensionality enabled Johns to fuse in startling ways pictorial elements from past styles commonly considered antithetical: gesture painting superimposed on a ruled design associated with geometric abstraction but put in the service of representational description.

As important to Johns as Cage's aim to disclose the familiar world—to see *what* in nature there is to see—was *how* it is perceived, that is, to investigate and reveal the equivocal nature of vision, and to instruct viewers on how to cope with it. As he said, choosing to paint rudimentary flags or targets, "things the mind already knows. . . . gave me room to work on other levels."[30] And on one of these levels, Johns dealt with how art is perceived and experienced. For example, in *Three Flags* (1958), three flags of decreasing size, each a separate canvas, are stacked on top of each other. The perceived image is confusing, since the canvases are physical objects projected in the room—like a relief sculpture composed of plank-like elements—while pictorially, the flags appear to be receding along perspectival lines. Also, in *Painting with Two Balls* (1960), composed of two canvases physically wedged apart by two small balls, Johns examines the ambiguity and the tension between a painting as a painted surface and as an object. Moreover, illusionistic atmosphere is contrasted with real space introduced in the wedge. In *Coat Hanger* (1959), an actual hanger hangs on a knob that projects from the canvas. In *Shade* (1959), a window shade that conceals the canvas becomes another kind of surface. In other pictures, beginning with *False Start* (1959), in which the impersonally stenciled names of colors are superimposed on handpainted colors, e.g., a printed RED painted blue placed on a green area, there is a contradiction between the verbal images and the colored areas, between the flat stenciled labels and the space-generating painterly marks. The viewer wonders whether in this context the given information can be considered true or false, or whether such matters are beside the point. In a grisaille *Jubilee* (1959), do the names of colors call the colors to mind? **138**

Such issues of perception and conception are also raised by Johns's sculpture, begun in 1958. One work, *Painted Bronze* (1960), is composed of two plaster cylinders cast into bronze on which are painted *trompe l'oeil* Ballantine ale labels so that the work replicates ale cans. What is seen: ale cans or Johns's sculpture? Non-art and/or art? Reality and/or sculpture? Multiple readings are possible. Max Kozloff wondered whether Johns's ale cans were to be thought of "as objects aspiring to be sculpture . . . as tin cans. . . . [or] as sculptures trying to be the objects they already are."[31] And Andrew Forge remarked: "We don't see real beer cans 'through' the sculpture. . . . Nor do we see an organization of cylinders and cubes. What we see is precisely the thing in front of us, an object which appears incredibly to resemble a beer can, and offers us all sorts of ways of reflecting on how it might be related to a beer can, but which is ultimately itself. It is an absurd object."[32] **123, 139 140**

138   Jasper Johns, *False Start,* 1959.
67¹/₄″ x 54″. Private Collection, New York.

139  Jasper Johns, *Painted Bronze (ale cans)*, 1960.
5¹/₂″ x 8″ x 4³/₄″. Kunstmuseum Basel, Collection Ludwig.

On close examination, the viewer does not confuse Johns's work with the object it duplicates. Although a "subject" strongly asserts its original identity, the manner in which it is painted transforms it or reveals the process of being transformed. And this painterly activity of Johns is masterly. Unlike Duchamp, who influenced our response to a ready-made object by changing its context—essentially a cool intellectual operation—Johns acts on the materials of art—warming up his concepts—to re-create a commonplace object, a second object, as it were, in the process making it extraordinary by adding the sensuous patina of art in a virtuoso fashion.[33] Such transformation enabled Johns to avoid repeating Duchamp's work and to call attention away from its subversive political and aesthetic rationale in which he had little interest, in part because anti-art and anarchic activity seemed unbelievable in the fifties. Once Duchamp presented his Readymades, that gesture constituted his individual "style." Moreover, that "style" encompassed all artifacts—literally everything—when considered in the context of art, for Duchamp's gesture was immediately and involuntarily called to mind; as Dali once announced: " 'Ready-mades' cover the globe."[34]

Johns's painterly performance served to rehabilitate visually exhausted things in "life," things that are seen "and not looked at, not examined," as Johns said.[35] His

140 Jasper Johns,
*Lightbulb II,* 1958.
3¹/₈″ x 8″ x 5″. Collection, the artist.

141 Jasper Johns, *Numbers in Color,* 1959.
66¹/₂″ x 49¹/₂″. Albright–Knox Art Gallery,
Buffalo, New York.

lavishing of craft and artistry in the re-creation of lowly objects led to an emphasis on the objects' potential as art. The way they were made by hand transformed them. Thus Johns opened up the possibility of a viable Neo-Duchampian *art*, which is different from Dada, which indeed subverts (ironically) the iconoclastic anti-art impulse of Dada.[36]

Johns also used seductive brushwork to subvert and transform the ethic of gesture painting. His facture partook of and resembled that of Guston and others, but because it was beautifully *made*, it challenged their notion that a picture had to be *found* in the unpremeditated and passionate action of painting. Indeed, Johns revealed his absorption with deliberate and dispassionate craft by working in encaustic, building up finely nuanced surfaces slowly and neatly by layering pieces of newsprint dipped in and coated with wax. Making a picture of gesture painting upset his New York School contemporaries more than his choice of ordinary and banal subjects and preconceived ideas of image and design. Paradoxically, his obvious masterliness, because it was presumed immoral, added to the notion that Johns was Neo-Dada.

Johns's pictures were not only a gloss on gesture painting but on Cubist-inspired abstraction and Impressionism. His design was geometric, a throwback to the Cubist abstraction of the thirties which Abstract Expressionism had supplanted. However, in contrast to Cubist pictures, Johns's were flatter since their schematic subjects were two-dimensional to begin with, and paradoxically, more illusionistic, since atmosphere was generated by articulated brushwork that the Cubists generally avoided. Moreover, Johns's paintings were non-relational, since the relations were given, intrinsic to the subjects, e.g., the stripes and stars of the flags, and not invented by the artist. As Barbara Rose put it, Johns's

> . . . single images did not depend on Cubist "rhyming" for their structure, nor could they be read as having discrete parts, because they were understood first as holistic *gestalts*, recognizable by identification. Nor did they have any fixed visual focuses, for this same reason. Moreover the rich [more or less similar, small] brushstrokes making up their surfaces were . . . methodically applied with equal pressure over the entire canvas surface. . . . [and thus were] reminiscent of mature Impressionism.[37]

Moreover, the sensuous impasto can be appreciated for its poetic appeal, for example, the funereal gray in *Tennyson* (1958), and the overlay of white brushstrokes in *White Flag* (1955) which so bleaches the image as to suggest that Johns wanted it to hover between appearance and disappearance. Furthermore, the obscuring white serves as a haunting shroud. Adding to the poetry is the isolation of insignificant objects which makes them extraordinary. Finally, the revelation of the problems of perception, of reality and illusion, is poetic precisely because it is enigmatic.

Johns's facture after 1960 often looks genuinely "Expressionist," and this counter to his stated intention: "I have attempted to develop my thinking in such a way that the work I've done is not me—not to confuse my feelings with what I produced."[38] Not only did Johns's rendering and "colors," mostly poignant grays, suggest a private rumi-

143

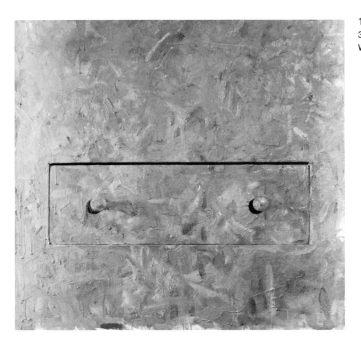

142  Jasper Johns, *Drawer,* 1957.
30³/₄″ x 30³/₄″. Brandeis University Art Collection,
Waltham, Massachusetts.

143  Jasper Johns, *Tennyson,* 1958.
73¹/₂″ x 48¹/₄″. Des Moines Art Center.

nation and reverie, even melancholy, but many of his common subjects, e.g., kitchen utensils, books, coat hangers, are the intimate objects of his experience, ostensibly chosen because they were. However, despite the growing Expressionist aspect in Johns's work, it remained essentially an intellectual art about art, about the "language" of art, about what a picture is, or might be, or has been said to be.[39]

# Notes

1. See Cage, *Silence*, p. 98.

2. Like Cage, Albers distrusted individualistic self-expression. Both believed in trying to see directly what there was to see, the particular as against the abstract.

Duberman, in *Black Mountain*, p. 71, wrote that Rauschenberg said: " 'I consider Albers the most important teacher I've ever had,' . . . citing especially the sense of discipline that Albers communicated, his insistence on each student developing a 'personal sense of looking,' and his attention to (and respect for) the specific properties of the materials being used."

Albers also focused on the properties of commonplace objects and materials. On p. 68, Duberman remarked that "Albers felt this Dadaist playing with surfaces was for some of his students—and especially for Robert Rauschenberg—the most exciting and durable feature of their Black Mountain experience."

3. John Cage, "On Robert Rauschenberg, Artist, and His Work," *Metro* 2 (1961): 43.

4. See letter from Robert Rauschenberg to Betty Parsons, no place or date, probably early fall, 1951, in Archives of American Art.

5. Club panel, "Patriotism in the American Home."

6. Robert Rauschenberg, Statement, in Dorothy C. Miller, ed., *Sixteen Americans*, exhibition catalogue (New York: Museum of Modern Art, 1959), p. 58.

7. Andrew Forge, *Rauschenberg* (New York: Harry N. Abrams, 1968), p. 37. In 1953, Rauschenberg made a series of all-red paintings in a manner similar to the all-black ones.

8. Rauschenberg liked to parody Abstract Expressionism. *Winter Pool* (1959), which contains a ladder presumably inviting viewers to get into the picture, pokes fun at Pollock's famous statement which had become a cliché.

9. Cage, in Duberman, *Black Mountain*, p. 358, said Rauschenberg differed from him in that "he makes a mystery of being an artist."

10. Earlier combine-paintings invite the viewer close-up so that details can be "read." Later works tend to be sparer and more unified, holding the viewer at a distance.

11. Club panel, "Patriotism in the American Home."

12. Seitz, *The Art of Assemblage*, p. 25.

13. See Cage, *Silence*, pp. 3–4. Cage's statement was made in 1937.

14. Forge, *Rauschenberg*, p. 2.

15. Brian O'Doherty, *American Masters: The Voice and the Myth* (New York: Ridge Press, Random House, 1973), pp. 197–98.

16. Ibid., p. 201.

17. Rauschenberg once said: "I would like my pictures to be able to be taken apart as easily as they're put together—so you can recognize an object when you're looking at it." (Gene Swensen, "Rauschenberg Paints a Picture," *Art News*, April 1963, p. 46.)

18. O'H[ara], "Reviews and Previews: Bob Rauschenberg," p. 47.

19. In 1959, *Bed* was censored out of an international festival in Spoleto, Italy.

20. Of his motivation in making *Bed*, Rauschenberg said: "I didn't have any money to buy canvas, and I wanted to paint. I was looking around for something to paint on. I wasn't using the quilt, so I put it on a stretcher. It looked strange without a pillow, so I added the pillow. It wasn't a preconceived idea." (Swensen, "Rauschenberg Paints a Picture," pp. 44–45.)

21. R[obert] R[osenblum], "In the Galleries: Robert Rauschenberg, *Arts*, March 1958, p. 61.

22. Tomkins, *The Bride and the Bachelors*, pp. 103–4.

23. Rauschenberg, at a panel discussion, "Art 1960," at New York University, New York, 21 April 1960, denied being a Dadaist. He said that Dada was exciting and that one could feel a hunger for its excitement, "but we don't really hold their kind of chips. Things are easier now."

24. Rauschenberg claimed to be anti-Expressionist, and yet he could not avoid personal attachments, particularly in the earlier combine-paintings. Forge, in *Rauschenberg*, p. 18, remarked that "there are preferences, favorite preoccupations, both formal and iconographic. The trailing horizontal line that wanders across so many canvases, a certain crispness around the edges of things, dearly held icons—birds, umbrellas, the Statue of Liberty." On pp. 20, 25, Forge went further, maintaining that in the two versions of *Rebus* (1955), images suggesting physical prowess, sex, childhood, and natural history have a strong autobiographical flavor and are "a meditation on his own youth, his family past, his sense of identity."

25. Rauschenberg and Johns were close friends. Both artists had studios in the same loft building from 1955 to 1960. Johns's early work, e.g., *Construction with a Piano* (1954), exhibited at the Tanager Gallery in 1955, is clearly in debt to Rauschenberg. See F[airfield] P[orter] on Tanager show in *Art News*, January 1955, p. 48.

26. Leo Steinberg, "Jasper Johns," *Metro* 4–5 (May 1962): 94.

27. Johns met Duchamp in 1959. See Max Kozloff, *Jasper Johns* (New York: Harry N. Abrams, 1967), p. 44.

28. G. R. Swensen, "What is Pop Art: Interview with Jasper Johns," *Art News*, February 1964, p. 67. On p. 43, Johns said: "I am concerned with a thing's not being what it was, with its becoming something other than what it is, with any moment in which one identifies a thing precisely and with the slipping away of that moment." In Walter Hopps, "An Interview with Jasper Johns," *Artforum*, March 1965, pp. 35–36, Johns said "that if a painting is an object, then the object can be a painting."

29. Clement Greenberg, "After Abstract Expressionism," *Art International*, 25 October 1962, pp. 26–27.

30. Leo Steinberg, *Jasper Johns* (New York: George Wittenborn, 1963), p. 15.

31. Kozloff, *Jasper Johns*, p. 31.

32. Andrew Forge, "The Emperor's Flag," *The New Statesman*, 11 December 1964, p. 938.

33. Johns denied an interest in sensuousness. "I've never wanted a seductive quality. I've always considered myself a very literal artist." (Joseph E. Young, "Jasper Johns: An Appraisal," *Art International*, September 1969, p. 52.) Duchamp refused to acknowledge that Jasper Johns had been a masterly painter "because his applying paint to it [the sculpture of two ale cans] was absolutely mechanical or, at least, as close to the printed thing as possible. It was not an act of painting, actually, the printing was just like printing except it was made by hand by him. That doesn't add a thing to it—it's just the idea of imitating the beer can that is important." ("Some Late Thoughts of Marcel Duchamp: From an Interview with Jeanne Siegel," p. 21.)

34. Salvador Dali, Preface, in Pierre Cabanne, *Dialogues with Marcel Duchamp* (New York: Viking Press, 1971), p. 13.

35. Hopps, "An Interview with Jasper Johns," p. 34.

36. Johns said: "The Dadaists were Dadaists by agreeing to be; it was political rather than stylistic. I am identified with Dada . . . [because I] use 'ready-mades,' but aside from this, I have little to do with Dada." (Panel, "Art 1960" at NYU.)

37. Barbara Rose, "The Graphic Work of Jasper Johns: Part 1," *Artforum*, March 1970, p. 39.

38. Vivien Raynor, "Jasper Johns: 'I have attempted to develop my thinking in such a way that the work I've done is not me,' " *Art News*, March 1973, p. 22.

39. Andrew Forge, "An American Note Book," *Art and Literature* 2 (1964): 46.

# 10
# Environments and Happenings: Kaprow, Grooms, Oldenburg, Dine, and Whitman

CAGE'S SINGLE EVENT at Black Mountain College in 1952 did not immediately inspire young artists to experiment with the fusion of the arts. It was not until after 1958 that Allan Kaprow, who had studied with Cage at the New School for Social Research the year before, and George Brecht, Al Hansen, Dick Higgins, and Jackson MacLow, who enrolled in the class somewhat later, and other young artists such as Jim Dine, Red Grooms, Claes Oldenburg, and Robert Whitman, took up the composer's challenge: "Where do we go from here? Towards theater. That art more than music resembles nature. We have eyes as well as ears, and it is our business while we are alive to use them." [1]

Cage introduced his students to the thinking of Duchamp, Zen Buddhism, Artaud, and Satie. They read Suzuki's books; Motherwell's *The Dada Painters and Poets*, in which Dada assemblages, environments, and performances were described; [2] and Artaud's *The Theatre and Its Double*, newly translated by M. C. Richards, which called for a total theater not confined to speech but embracing gesture and mime, in brief, everything "specifically theatrical in the theatre," that is, the *mise en scène*, considered as a drama of movement in space, in which the audience would take an active part. [3]

As important as Cage's thinking in guiding young artists toward a new, synaesthetic art was Abstract Expressionism and junk assemblage. Indeed, it was the contribution of vanguard painting and construction that made Cage-like events viable in 1958 in a way that they had not been a half-dozen years earlier. [4] Moreover, it was the artists who

144 Allan Kaprow, *An Apple Shrine*, 1960.

began as painters and sculptors, notably Kaprow, Dine, Grooms, Oldenburg, and Whitman, who made the major contributions to a new form of theater whose primary sources were visual, given the names "happening," the "painter's theater," the "action theater," and the "theater of mixed means."

Kaprow, initially the leader of the Cage-inspired artists, suggested how both the Duchamp-Cage aesthetic and the various tendencies within the New York School, despite their opposing aims, together played a role in his thinking. Cage prompted Kaprow to repudiate all received aesthetic ideas, standards, and categories—to the extreme of obliterating every line demarcating art from non-art. As Kaprow put it, he wanted to "get rid of all the conditions of the conventional arts, or at very best to arrive at another kind of condition . . . which always was uncertain of its condition as art." Kaprow came to think that "the best way to achieve a quasi-art . . . [or] non-art, is to operate on the margins of what happens to be the latest acquisition of the [New York] art world." He had to be acutely aware of whatever "entered into our cultural world as accepted options for the creative person . . . [in order to] operate outside . . . [and] avoid the contexts of art."[5] But there was also a positive influence: the idea of "action" in Harold Rosenberg's notion of "action painting," which Kaprow came to think could be separated from "painting," or, as he put it, lead "not to more painting, but to more action."[6] Ironically, Rosenberg's idea applied more to Happenings than to the gesture painting to which it was meant to apply and which Kaprow came to reject. Kaprow was the first of his generation to move from within gestural painting to assemblage, which he then enlarged into room-size Environments, and by introducing theatrical actions, amplified into Happenings (the name invented by Kaprow).[7]

144, 145    An ex-student of Hofmann's, Kaprow was given his first show in 1953 at the Hansa
146, 147    Gallery. In it, he exhibited two kinds of work: in one vein, high-keyed abstractions of
148, 149    petal-like clusters, and abstract, paint-tangled woodland scenes with figures, influenced by Jan Müller, the Fauvist Matisse, and Vlaminck; and in the other vein, Cubist-inspired paintings arranged at angles to each other so that they looked like constructions. These assemblages of canvases anticipated the Environments that Kaprow was to piece together some six years later. But at the time, they struck him as too conventionally
145    Cubist, so he abandoned that direction, concentrating instead on his Fauvist and Expressionist painting—until around 1956.

146    In his show that year, however, Kaprow exhibited several sculptures—plaster figures coated with roofing tar—that in their use of unconventional materials and gro-

145    Allan Kaprow, *George Washington Bridge (with Cars)*, 1955.
41½″ x 49¼″. Collection, Mrs. and Mrs. Michael M. Peters, Stamford, Connecticut.

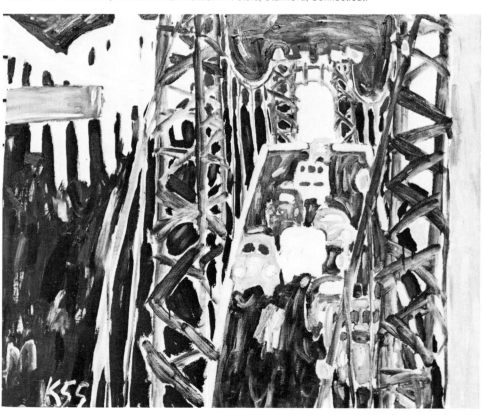

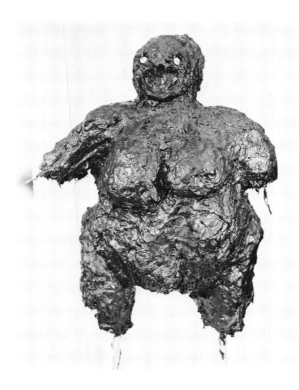

146 Allan Kaprow, *Woman Out of Fire,* 1956.
Approx. 36″ x 24″. Collection, the artist.

tesqueness were different from his earlier work. During 1957, he carried over the fierce mood of these urban totems into a series of wall-size, allover collage paintings, composed of muslin, silver foil, newsprint, rough scrawls, and marks, suggestive of figures, animals, and words (one picture was covered with "HaHa"). These works were influenced by Pollock's "drip" paintings and Rauschenberg's combines but were more jangled, frenetic, the "chaos of fragments" suggesting the rawness and violence of the city,[8] or in Kaprow's words, "the nameless sludge and whirl of urban events."[9] The environmental scale of the collages prompted Kaprow to extend his work into the actual environment by building in from the walls and ceiling. He also took his cues from the junk assemblages of Stankiewicz and Follett (fellow members of the Hansa Gallery), and Rauschenberg. Indeed detritus itself, because it was once part of the viewers' "life," pointed the way to Environments by reducing the aesthetic distance that usually separates a work of art from its audience.[10] It is for such reasons too that many environmental artists favored unaesthetic and perishable materials.[11]

Near the end of 1957, Kaprow ventured away from the assembled object and toward environmental art. In a transitional work of that year, he coated a large canvas with tar, wrapping paper, and bushels of autumn leaves. This was meant to be a "fragment of a much larger work which when completed will have a recorded accompaniment of leaf sounds, collage sounds, tar sounds, and electric-light sounds."[12] A reviewer for *Art News* found the work "sensational" but was bothered by the "division of the surface into four neat rectangles, each in a different medium [which] seems at odds with

147  Allan Kaprow, *Hysteria,* 1956.
72¹/₂″ x 67¹/₄″. Collection, Dr. Hubert Peeters,
Bruges, Belgium.

148  Allan Kaprow, *Grandma's Boy,* 1957.
Right Panel: 18¹/₂″ x 15³/₄″ x ¹³/₁₆″, left panel: 16⁷/₁₆″
x 12³/₈″ x 1⁷/₈″. Collection,
Rhett and Robert Delford Brown, New York.

the raucousness of the materials employed."[13] Kaprow also considered this a contradiction and soon resolved it.

In 1958, Kaprow exhibited his first Environment. The entire gallery was divided into aisles whose walls were strips of plastic and cloth of varying widths, hung with some variation in length from ceiling to floor. The transparent and opaque material was splashed with paint in spots and dressed with tinfoil, crumpled cellophane, and Christmas tree lights. As the viewer walked up and down the aisles, he or she caught glimpses of other viewers who became part of the work, like actors in a stage set. Kaprow also transformed his Environment into a quasi-Happening by performing in the gallery each afternoon, introducing a theatrical element in time.

In 1959, Kaprow presented his first full-blown Happening entitled "18 Happenings in 6 Parts," at the Reuben Gallery, which, along with the Judson Gallery, became the primary showplace for Happenings.[14] He described the event as follows:

> There are three rooms for this work, each different in size and feeling. The rooms are nearly transparent. No matter where a person is, he is aware of something happening in another room. One room has red and white lights in rows along its top, like a used car lot at night. The other has blue and white lights. The

149  Allan Kaprow, *Interchangeable Panels,* 1957–59. 96″ x 204″. Collection, Dr. Hubert Peeters, Bruges, Belgium.

third has a blue globe hanging in its center. There are two large wall collages, some colored Christmas bulbs seen from behind a wall and two rows of spot lights. Purple scrolls are dropped at a certain time. Five longish mirrors are placed around. These are looked into also at a certain time. Chairs—perhaps seventy-five to one hundred—are arranged throughout where guests are to be seated. The guests will change seats according to numbered cards. Each guest will sit once in a different room. Some guests will also act. Slides will be shown. Tape recorded sounds, produced electronically, will come from four loudspeakers. From these there will be heard as well a collage of voices. There will be live sounds produced. Words will be spoken. Human actions will occur of different but simple kinds. In addition there will be non-human actors. They will be a dancing toy and two constructions on wheels. The same action will never happen twice. The actions will mean nothing formulable so far as the artist is concerned. It is intended, however, that the whole work is to be intimate, austere, and of somewhat brief duration.[15]

150     Kaprow considered assemblages, Environments, and Happenings to be similar in essence: "An Environment is an extension of assemblage, which is in turn a three dimensional extension of collage. That is, an Environment is a surrounding, of any material whatever, involving the sense of touch, sound and even smell, composed into either a room or rooms, or out-of-doors. The visitor is literally *in* the art, . . . A

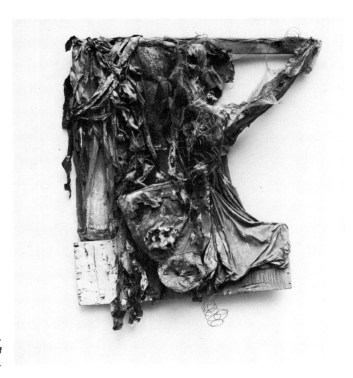

150   Jim Dine, *Household Piece,* 1959.
54¼" x 44¼" x 9¼". The Museum of
Modern Art, New York.

Happening is a stepped-up environment, where movement and activity are intensified within a compressed time—say, a half-hour—and where people usually assemble at a given moment for a performance."[16] It must be stressed that a Happening is designed to take place in an Environment. This distinguishes it from other types of theatrical events and other events to which the label has been vulgarly applied. But there are clear differences among the three forms. An assemblage differs from an Environment because it is an object, too small in scale to be physically entered and thus incapable of immediately engaging the viewer in actual space and turning him or her into "a real part of the whole."[17] An Environment is unlike a Happening because it is more "visual, tactile, and manipulative," calling attention to actual space and tangible objects rather than to events in time, sound, and the presence of people.[18]

Kaprow's step-by-step progression from painting to Happenings was accompanied by a series of public statements, letters to art magazines, and articles which provide a clear justification for Environments and Happenings. First in a kind of ritual of a new avant-garde dethroning the old, Kaprow began a campaign against Abstract Expressionism. Early in 1958 at the Club, he announced that painting had gone as far as it could and had no future. Furthermore, it had become a bore. He demanded the destruction of discipline not only in painting but in all of the arts, calling for moving arms instead of a brush, for making noise instead of music, for doing everything and anything.[19] The old avant-garde counterattacked by accusing Kaprow of being anti-art and giving up art. But he denied both. During a later session at the Club, Kaprow claimed to be wounded by remarks that he was a Neo-Dada, insisting that he was moved by what was vital to him, and that it was his intention to make works of art.[20]

In the fall of 1958, Kaprow published in *Art News* a major article entitled "The Legacy of Jackson Pollock." He wrote that Pollock's death in 1956 made it clear that modernist art in general was slipping, becoming dull and repetitious or retrogressive. "Thus, we reasoned, Pollock was the center in a great failure: the New Art."[21] However, there was much that was viable to be learned from Pollock, from his trying to physically enter his work, to be "in" it, and from his diaristic act (his "dance") of painting. Moreover, Pollock's allover image gave rise to "an experience of a continuum going in all directions simultaneously, *beyond* the literal dimensions of any work"; his canvases were so enormous in size that "they ceased to become paintings and became *environments*"; and finally, "the *entire* painting comes out at the participant (I shall call him that, rather than observer) right into the room."[22] Kaprow summed up Pollock's "drip" paintings as "a type of art which . . . tends to fill our world with itself, an art which, in meaning, looks, impulse, seems to break fairly sharply with the traditions of painters back to at least the Greeks. Pollock's near destruction of this tradition may well be a return to the point where art was more actively involved in ritual, magic and life than we have known it in our recent past."[23]

Concerning the future of art, Kaprow saw two alternatives. One was to continue in Pollock's vein, varying his aesthetic "without departing from it or going further." The other alternative was to give up painting pictures and to

. . . become preoccupied with and even dazzled by the space and objects of our everyday life, . . . Not satisfied with the *suggestion* through paint of our other senses, we shall utilize the specific substances of sight, sound, movements, people, odors, touch. Objects of every sort are materials for the new art: paint, chairs, food, electric and neon-lights, smoke, water, old socks, a dog, movies, a thousand

other things . . . [We will show] as if for the first time, the world we have always had about us, but ignored, . . . [and will] disclose entirely unheard of happenings and events found in garbage cans, police files, hotel lobbies, seen in store windows and on the streets, and sensed in dreams and horrible accidents. . . . all will become materials for this new concrete art.[24]

Or, as Oldenburg summed it up: "The canvas on which I now (a post-Pollock painter) am standing on not only stretches as far as I can see or hear, but has layers, roofs, floors, basements, etc. Seeing gold frames around Pollocks now is funny and also hurts."[25]

The following month, in the announcement of his first Environment, Kaprow wrote a statement, "Notes on the Creation of a Total Art." His aim was to achieve "an all-encompassing artistic experience." But this could not be created by mixing existing

151    Claes Oldenburg, *Snapshots from the City,* 1960.

art forms "which have been developed over a long period of a high degree of articulation," since they were self-sufficient. The alternative via Cage was to begin with "the totality of nature itself as a model or point of departure" and juxtapose elements "known or invented, 'concrete' or 'abstract,'" for example, "a literal space with a painted space."[26]

Kaprow also saw a new role for the viewers of Environments, as components whose shapes, colors, and movements were unpredictable: "There is, therefore, a never-ending play of changing conditions between the relatively fixed or 'scored' parts of my work and the 'unexpected' or undetermined parts."[27] Because of the changeable activity of the viewers, Environments constantly offset "any desire to see them in the light of the traditional, closed, clear forms of art as we have known them." Instead, what is experienced "is a form which is as open and fluid as the shapes of our everyday experience, without simply imitating some part of it."[28]

The following autumn, Kaprow proposed that the Happening is a "separate kind of art . . . which is not to be confused with the others, nor is it in competition with them. Neither is it a combination of already existing disciplines. It is an art which happens in time and it must be performed. Its nature is 'abstract' in the sense that there is no plot or story as in the theater. Nor is there a stage for this art. The visitor to a performance finds himself in the same space as the events occurring and thus becomes willy-nilly a part of them."[29]

Thus Kaprow and his colleagues did not set Happenings *against* conventional theater, as did Ionesco and other avant-garde playwrights in the Theater of the Absurd, but *apart* from it. Increasingly, Kaprow began to think of Happenings as "theater pieces," but possessing

> . . . some crucial qualities which distinguish them from the usual theatrical works, even the experimental ones of today. First, there is the *context*, the place of conception and enactment. The most intense and essential happenings have been spawned in old lofts, basements, vacant stores, in natural surroundings and in the street, . . . [There is] no separation of audience and play (as there is even in round or pit theatres), the elevated picture-window view of most playhouses, is gone, as are the expectations of curtain openings and *tableaux-vivants* and curtain-closing. . . . The sheer rawness of the out-of-doors or the closeness of dingy city quarters, in which the radical Happenings flourish, are more appropriate, I believe, in temperament and unartiness, to the materials and directness of these works. . . . Thus a Happening [which consists of chunks of the city] is rough and sudden and it often feels "dirty."[30]

The second difference is the replacement of a plot by theatrical units, each more or less self-contained, and juxtaposed as the elements in a combine by Rauschenberg, a dance by Cunningham, or a three-ring circus. A conventional play is based on a verbal story line that unfolds in a connected series of events and builds up to a climax. The drama occurs in a single matrix of time and place on a proscenium stage with a single focus. In contrast, a Happening tends to be non-verbal, discontinuous, and non-sequen-

152   Robert Whitman, *E. G.,* 1960.

153   Claes Oldenburg, *Shirt,* 1960.
29$^{1}/_{8}$″ x 25$^{1}/_{4}$″ x 5″. Whitney Museum
of American Art, New York.

154   Jim Dine, *The Valiant Red Car,* 1960.
54″ x 123″. Collection, The Martha Jackson Gallery, New York.

tial, non-matrixed, multifocused, and open-ended.[31] Nor is there the conventional development of the characters as believable people. The participants in a Happening are given tasks to do that they do being who they are. They are not asked to "play roles." Often, in Happenings, those involved are treated no differently than props. In fact, Oldenburg imagined a "theater of action or of things (people too regarded as things)."[32] It is noteworthy that the works created by Kaprow, Oldenburg, and Dine prior to their Environments and Happenings were figurative. Oldenburg and Dine in particular had been interested in evolving a new realism different from gestural figuration. In 1959, they invited Kaprow and Lester Johnson to participate with them in a panel titled "New Uses of the Human Image in Painting."[33] This concern encouraged them to use real people and objects in their later events and to treat the two as equivalent, that is, as equally alive and dramatic.

The most radical intention of Happening makers was their attempt to turn the members of the audience into active participants in the dramatic action rather than passive spectators. This separated Happenings from other existing avant-garde theaters, e.g., the Theater of the Absurd, in which the actors played roles and the stage represented a place other than what it was.[34] In comparing Happenings to conventional theater, Kaprow stressed their dependence on improvisation, unpremeditation, and chance, relating them to jazz and gesture painting. "A Happening is *generated in action* by a headful of ideas or a flimsily-jotted-down score of 'root' directions."[35] After 1961, when Kaprow wrote these remarks, many Happenings, including his own, ceased to be as spontaneous or accidental as he claimed. There was generally a script, but because it was mostly of activities and sounds, it did not resemble the text of a traditional play. Moreover, the kind of planned events Happening-makers generally preferred possessed a great potential for unpredictable and thus surprising results, and something unforeseen was even more likely to happen because the materials were often fragile. As Kirby remarked: "The action in Happenings is often *indeterminate* but not improvised."[36]

Despite the fact that the Happenings by Kaprow, Dine, Grooms, Oldenburg, and Whitman were relatively plotless and unrehearsed, each was shaped by the maker's desires and appetites and tried to realize an intention and convey a message, an approach that diverged sharply from Cage's, creating two tendencies in the theater of mixed means.[37] As Kaprow wrote in 1965, and he spoke for his associates: "My works are conceived on, generally, four levels. One is the direct 'suchness' of every action, . . . with no more meaning than the sheer immediacy of what is going on. . . . The second is that they are performed fantasies not exactly like life, though derived from it. The third is that they are an organized structure of events. And the fourth level, no less important, is their 'meaning' in a symbolical or suggestive sense."[38]

Kaprow tended to use mythic symbols and rituals more than the other Happening-makers. For example, in *Courtyard* (1962), there was a

> . . . dream girl . . . [who is] the embodiment of a number of old, archetypal symbols. She is the nature goddess (Mother Nature). She is either benign, yielding nature or devouring, cruel nature (she usually has those two sides to her) . . . When the girl in *Courtyard* walked amongst the people, lost in herself, she was Aphrodite (Miss America) as well—a goddess of Beauty, which is another subdivision of the large, benign nature image: . . .
>
> It is not that such symbols are esoteric: they are not. They are so general and so archetypical that actually almost everyone knows vaguely about these things. . . . In my case I try to keep the symbols universal, simple, and basic.[39]

155    Dine's content was the struggle—and often, the inability—to communicate the disasters of everyday living. In his first Happening, *The Smiling Workman* (1960), he "acted" an artist. With a spotlight on him, he approached an empty canvas and a table with three jars of paint and two brushes on it. As he recalled: "I was all in red with a big, black mouth: all my face and head were red, and I had a red smock on, down to the floor. I painted 'I love what I'm doing' in orange and blue. When I got to 'what I'm doing,' it was going very fast, and I picked up one of the jars and drank the paint, and then I poured the other two jars of paint over my head, quickly, and dove, physically, through the canvas. The light went off. It was like a thirty-second moment of intensity."[40] Dine forgot to mention the unearthly sound he hummed throughout the performance, and as I remember it, the last word he painted was "Help."[41] In *Car Crash* (1960), Dine "seemed to be choking. He was trying to tell us something; then he tried to write with fat chalk on a blackboard. The chalk kept breaking; he was trying too hard . . . . . as he gurgled, trying so hard to communicate."[42]

151    The content of Oldenburg's early Happenings is suggested by the title of one, *Snapshots from the City* (1960). They deal with the dirt, the violence, the spectacle, the nightmares, and accidental possibilities of the city. Other influences on Oldenburg were Hollywood movies, which led him to remark: "I mix realistic and fantastic events, as the

155  Jim Dine, *The Smiling Workman*, 1960.

imagination does, and I consider the imaginary event as real as the 'real' one."[43]

156         Grooms's events were also extravagant, as is clear from his remarks about *The Burning Building* (1959). "When I was a kid, the big influence on me was Ringling Brothers, Barnum & Bailey, and the Cavalcade of Amusement which would roll in every year for the Tennessee State Fair. . . . *The Burning Building* . . . was an extension of my backyard theatre. I wanted to have some of the dusty danger of a big traveling show. And the chicken-coop creakiness of a backyard extravaganza. And the mysteries of the operations behind the proscenium. . . . firemen and their apparatus offered a good

152    vehicle for my medieval melodrama."[44] Whitman's performances were as exuberant as Grooms's, but they were more Happenings than theater pieces, fantastic spaces and objects acted in and upon by the participants.

The New York School's response to Happenings was not as negative as it was to junk assemblage. Certainly the early audiences, small to be sure, were composed primarily of artists, and enthusiastic ones at that. The familiarity with junk assemblage,

156   Red Grooms, *The Burning Building*, 1959.

Plate I    Helen, Frankenthaler, *Jacob's Ladder*, 1957.
113⅜″ x 69⅞″. The Museum of Modern Art, New York.

Plate II  Joan Mitchell, *Ladybug*, 1957.
77⅝″ x 108″. The Museum of Modern Art, New York.

Plate III   Larry Rivers, *The Pool*, 1956.
103⅜″ x 92⅝″. The Museum of Modern Art, New York.

Plate IV    Grace Hartigan, *River Bathers*, 1953.
69⅜″ x 88¾″. The Museum of Modern Art, New York.

Plate V    Robert Goodnough, *Laocoön*, 1958.
66⅜″ x 54⅛″. The Museum of Modern Art, New York.

Plate VI    Robert Rauschenberg, *Rebus*, 1955.
94″ x 144″. Collection, Mr. and Mrs. Victor Ganz, New York.

Plate VII   Jasper Johns, *Painting with Two Balls*, 1960.
65″ x 54″. Collection, the artist.

**Plate VIII** Ellsworth Kelly, *Rogue*, 1956.
34″ x 38″. Anonymous collection.

then some half-dozen years old, probably eased the way to acceptance of Happenings. Also accountable was the strong case Kaprow made for them, and it is noteworthy that he was permitted to present it in *Art News* and *It Is*, magazines favorably disposed to the New York School. However, much as Kaprow tried to make it seem as if Happenings were a threat to existing painting and sculpture, there were few rebuttals. Artists evidently thought of Happenings as theater, too removed from what they were doing to be considered competition. Kaprow himself wrote of Happenings as a new kind of theater and desired recognition from the theater world, but to his disappointment that was not forthcoming until well into the sixties.

# Notes

1. Cage, *Silence*, p. 12. Allan Kaprow, in *Assemblage, Environments & Happenings* (New York: Harry N. Abrams, 1966), p. 212, wrote: "Since my own first efforts, in 1957, were done in Cage's composition class, where he described this event [at Black Mountain], I should mention it as an important catalyst."

2. Robert Motherwell, ed., *The Dada Painters and Poets* (New York: Wittenborn, Schultz, 1951).

3. Antonin Artaud, *The Theatre and Its Double* (New York: Grove Press, 1958), translated from the French by M[ary] C[aroline] Richards, p. 40.

4. Artists verging toward a synaesthetic art were influenced not only by Abstract Expressionist painting and assemblage but had seen or knew of Frederick Kiesler's *Galaxies*, environmental "clusters" of painting and sculpture, the first of which was shown at the Museum of Modern Art in 1952. Kiesler remarked, in Elaine de Kooning, "The Modern Museum's Fifteen: Dickinson and Kiesler," p. 22: "To separate sculpture and painting from the flow of our daily environment is to put them on pedestals, to shut them up in frames, thus destroying their integrative potentialities and arresting their continuity with our total mode of life."

The Gutai Group of Osaka, Japan, anticipated moves in New York toward a theater by painters. Its activities were reported in an article entitled "Japanese Innovators" by Ray Falk (*New York Times*, 8 December 1957, sec. 2, p. 24) which described how the Gutai artists added action to their art, turning it into theater. Eighteen of its members exhibited twenty-eight paintings (one, a poured tar surface embedded with coarse sand; another, of crumpled paper applied to canvas and covered with paint and lacquer) at the Martha Jackson Gallery in the fall of 1958. See T[homas] B. H[ess], "Reviews and Previews: New Names this Month: Gutai," *Art News*, November 1958, p. 17, and Dore Ashton, "Art: Japanese Avantgardism," *Arts and Architecture*, November 1958, pp. 4–5, 34. Allan Kaprow in *Assemblage, Environments & Happenings*, p. 212, wrote that he did not know of Gutai activities until 1959 and did not see photographs of their events until 1963. However, Oldenburg did. See Rose, *Claes Oldenburg*, p. 25.

Other antecedents of Happenings, according to Kaprow, were "Mime, the circus, carnivals, the traveling saltimbanques, all the way to medieval mystery plays and processions" (Allan Kaprow, " 'Happenings' in the New York Scene," *Art News*, May 1961, p. 39). There was also interest in the Futurist theater, in which everyday sounds and noise were used. See Hansen, *A Primer*, pp. 5–7, and Dick Higgins, *Postface* (New York: Something Else Press, 1964), pp. 18–23, part of which is a translation of Martinetti's "Manifesto," 1924, calling for an anti-psychological theater of mixed means.

5. Dorothy Seckler, interview with Allan Kaprow. See Allan Kaprow, "The Demiurge," *Anthologist* 30 (Winter 1959): 4 (a publication of Rutgers State University).

6. Michael Benedikt, *Theatre Experiments* (New York: Doubleday & Company, 1967), p. 355.

7. See Kaprow, "The Demiurge" (including "Something to Take Place: A Happening"), p. 5.

8. I[rving] S[andler], "Reviews and Previews: Allan Kaprow," *Art News*, February 1957, p. 10.

9. Kaprow, *Assemblage, Environments & Happenings*, p. 164.

10. See Alloway, "Junk Culture as a Tradition."

11. See Kaprow, *Assemblage, Environments & Happenings*, pp. 166–69. Kaprow also preferred impermanent materials because they forced artists to work on the outer edge of accepted art and challenged many of its conventions, for example, that a work of art be an enduring, fixed object.

12. J[ohn] A[shbery], "Reviews and Previews: Six Exemplary Paintings and One Sculpture," *Art News*, November 1957, p. 12.

13. Ibid., pp. 12–13.

14. Kaprow helped Anita Reuben arrange shows and events at the Reuben Gallery. The art program at the Judson Church on Washington Square South in 1959–60 was planned by Oldenburg and assistant minister Bud Scott.

15. Allan Kaprow, Statement, *18 Happenings in 6 Parts*, exhibition catalogue (New York: Reuben Gallery, 1959). For a chronology of Environments, Happenings, and related intermedia events, see Hans Sohm, ed., *Happenings & Fluxus*, exhibition catalogue (Cologne, Germany: Kölnischer Kunstverein, 1970), and Jürgen Becker and Wolf Vostell, eds., *Happenings: Fluxus: Pop Art: Nouveau Realisme* (Renbek near Hamburg: Rowohlt Verlag, 1965). Both of these books are documentation. Selections of the scenarios of Happenings and notes on performances appear in Michael Kirby, *Happenings* (New York: E. P. Dutton & Co., 1965); Sohm, ed., *Happenings & Fluxus*; Becker and Vostell, eds., *Happenings*; Hansen, A *Primer of Happening & Time/Space Art*; and Benedikt, *Theatre Experiments*.

16. Allan Kaprow, in "In the Art Galleries" by Irving Sandler, *New York Post*, 16 June 1963, magazine section, p. 14.

17. Kaprow, *Assemblage, Environments & Happenings*, p. 165.

18. Ibid., p. 184.

19. Allan Kaprow, statement from the floor at a Club panel, "Has the Situation Changed?" 17 January 1958, in which Alfred H. Barr, Jr., Thomas B. Hess, and Harold Rosenberg participated.

20. Club panel, "Patriotism in the American Home." Kaprow was interested in Dada. He liked the polemics in Motherwell, ed., *The Dada Poets and Painters*, particularly the "paradox of denying art while producing it" (Seckler, interview with Kaprow, p. 36). He thought that in a general way Dada's "contribution was extremely important, for rather than being simply anarchistic, it was, at heart, liberating. I see its 'anti-art' position as nothing more than a healthy hatred for clichés and smug aesthetics. . . . Yet, specifically, I cannot count it as a major influence on my art, either in attitude, subject matter or method" (Sandler, "In the Art Galleries," p. 14).

21. Kaprow, "The Legacy of Jackson Pollock," p. 25. Kaprow continued his attack on Abstract Expressionist painting in "Letters," *Arts*, December 1958, pp. 7, 9, and "Editor's letters," *Art News*, February 1959, p. 6.

22. Kaprow, "The Legacy of Jackson Pollock," pp. 26, 56.

23. Ibid., p. 56.

24. Ibid., pp. 56–57. For an elaboration of these ideas, see Allan Kaprow, "The Principles of Modern Art." *It Is* 4 (Autumn 1959): 51.

25. Claes Oldenburg, statement in "Jackson Pollock: An Artists' Symposium, Part 2," *Art News*, May 1967, p. 66.

26. Allan Kaprow, "Notes on the Creation of a Total Art," in *Allan Kaprow*, exhibition announcement (New York: Hansa Gallery, 1958). Kaprow also wrote that the idea of a total art grew from collage, which, though it was a form of painting, led to the rejection of traditional painting but not of the use of paint.

27. Ibid.

28. Ibid.

29. Kaprow, "The Principles of Modern Art," p. 52.

30. Kaprow, " 'Happenings' in the New York Scene," pp. 58–59.

31. For a discussion of Happenings as "compartmented" and "non-matrixed," see Kirby, *Happenings*, pp. 13–14. Kaprow remarked in " 'Happenings' in the New York Scene," p. 59: "A play assumes words to be the almost absolute medium. A Happening will frequently have words, but they may or may not make literal sense. . . . Words, however, need not be used at all." Unlike text-bound plays, there was generally no dialogue in Happenings.

32. Claes Oldenburg, *Store Days* (New York: Something Else Press, 1967), p. 80.

33. Rose, *Claes Oldenburg*, p. 200. The panel took place at the Judson Gallery.

34. See Richard Schechner, "Is It What's Happening, Baby?" *New York Times*, 12 June 1966, sec. 2, p. 3.

35. Kaprow, " 'Happenings' in the New York Scene," p. 59.

36. Kirby, *Happenings*, p. 19. On p. 47, Allan Kaprow wrote in a statement: "I really direct a Happening inside out, as most of us do."

37. Cage, in Michael Kirby and Richard Schechner, "An Interview with John Cage," *Tulane Drama Review* 10 (Winter 1965): 69, objected strongly to the course Happenings had taken: "The only way you're going to get a good performance of an intentional piece, that furthermore involves symbols and other relationships which the artist has drawn in his mind, is to have lots of rehearsals, and you're going to have to do it as well as you can; . . . You're involved in a whole thing that we have been familiar with since the Renaissance and before."

On p. 55, Cage said that he was involved with something else. "The structure we should think about is that of each person in the audience. . . . [whose] consciousness is structuring the experience differently from anybody else's . . . So the less we structure the theatrical occasion and the more it is like unstructured daily life, the greater will be the stimulus to the structuring faculty of each person in the audience. If we have done nothing he then will have everything to do."

38. Kaprow, "A Statement," in Kirby, *Happenings*, p. 49.

39. Ibid., pp. 49–50.

40. Jim Dine, "A Statement," in Kirby, *Happenings*, p. 185.

41. My recollection is corroborated by Higgins, *Postface*, pp. 39–40.

42. Hansen, *A Primer*, p. 30.

43. Kirby, *Happenings*, p. 202.

44. Ibid., p. 118.

# 11

# Hard-Edge and Stained Color-Field Abstraction, and other Non-gestural Styles: Kelly, Smith, Louis, Noland, Parker, Held, and Others

THE MAKERS of Happenings transformed the painterly "action" of gesture painting into bodily gestures in actual space, carrying the visual arts outside of themselves into theater. Thus Happenings can be viewed as a reaction against gesture painting as well as an extension of it. There was another kind of reaction that remained within the area of abstract art. As gesture painting became the established vanguard manner of the fifties, growing numbers of painters turned against its spontaneity, ambiguity, and complexity and adopted instead preconception, relative clarity of design and color, and simplicity. In time, new non- and anti-painterly styles would develop from within the milieu of gesture painting, notably those of Raymond Parker and Al Held, but first, they emerged from outside the New York School: the hard-edge abstraction of Ellsworth Kelly, Leon Polk Smith, and Myron Stout; and the stained color-field abstraction of Morris Louis, Kenneth Noland, and Jules Olitski.[1]

The early hard-edge painters were aware of but relatively unconcerned with Abstract Expressionism, intent neither on extending it nor rejecting it. And yet the impact of "hard-edge" on the New York School was a strong one. Responsible was the recogni-

157  Ellsworth Kelly,
*Black Ripe,* 1956.
63″ x 59″.
Private Collection.

tion that Kelly, Stout, and Smith were developing a fresh manner of geometric abstraction which could not be subsumed under existing geometric styles and so dismissed as backward looking.[2] But more important, hard-edge abstraction opened up fresh possibilities in a direction away from gesture painting, whose claims to avant-garde status were losing believability. Kelly's work, in particular, beginning with his show in 1956, forced                157
itself into the discourse, the polemics, of the New York School. Its entry was timed at the right historical moment, although that was unintentional.

More important in the development of hard-edge abstraction than Abstract Expressionism were works of earlier twentieth-century masters, notably Matisse, Miró, Jean                158
Arp, Sophie Taeuber-Arp, and Brancusi. The hard-edge painters owed more to these artists than to Cubist-inspired geometricists, such as Mondrian in Europe and most                159
American abstract artists in the thirties.[3] But Cubist and hard-edge painters shared an urge for classical values and for a certain cleanliness of edge and surface. Moreover, all spurned the extravagance and phantasmagoria of Surrealism. Yet the divergencies in their styles were so pronounced that to differentiate the new from the old, the label "hard-edge" came into common use.[4]

One difference between the abstraction of a Kelly or a Smith and a Mondrian is                160, 161
that the Mondrian is based on rectangular shapes and appears non-objective, even when it purports to refer to nature, whereas the Kelly or Smith tends to be based on free forms, generally the silhouettes of phenomena seen and sketched and sometimes photo-

158 Henri Matisse, *Bather,* 1909.
36¹/₂″ x 29¹/₈″. The Museum of Modern Art, New York.

159 Piet Mondrian, *Composition
in Red, Blue and Yellow,* 1937–42.
23³/₄″ x 21⁷/₈″. The Sidney and Harriet
Janis Collection.

160  Leon Polk Smith, *May
Twenty,* 1959.
68″ x 68″. Collection, the artist.

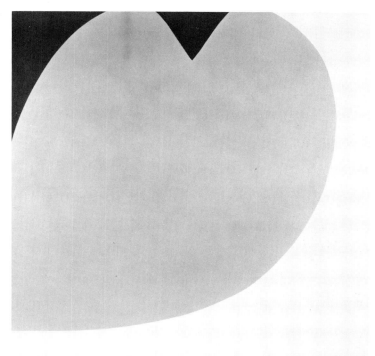

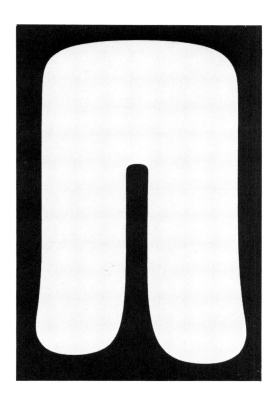

161  Myron Stout, *No. 3, 1957,* 1957.
26″ x 18″. Museum of Art, Carnegie Institute, Pittsburgh,
Pennsylvania.

graphed.[5] The model here was Matisse, who reduced his subjects to large planes of color, rather than Miró and Arp, who used Surrealist automatism to arrive at imaginary images. But hard-edge painters ventured further toward abstraction than Matisse did. Indeed, their subjects are often unrecognizable. For example, Kelly frequently chose to depict ephemeral shadows or the "negative" space between objects. But he also secreted nature to draw attention to the painting as painting. Visualizing objects in silhouette facilitated the translation from the three-dimensionality of nature to the two-dimensionality of the picture surface. Still, the signs of nature or nature as a sign were rarely lost.[6] Thus, in their reliance on direct observation, hard-edge painters revealed a different outlook from, and perhaps a distaste for, Mondrian's Neo-Platonic vision of the underlying laws governing the universe. Where the one tended to be perceptual and specific, the other was conceptual and generalized.

It was not only attitude that separated a Kelly or a Smith from a Mondrian. Their conceptions of a picture differed sharply. The hard-edge painters rejected the relational design of Cubism, a design that had come to seem outworn. Indeed, they represented visual phenomena to avoid Cubist-inspired composing. They simplified their formats, often to two planes of a different color each or of black and white, abutted in clear juxtapositions rather than interwoven in intricate patterns. As Kelly remarked, his purpose was to *divide* the whole space of a picture and not to *arrange* forms.[7] The focus in hard-edge abstraction, then, was not on the *relationship* of shapes but on the color-shape as *color-shape*. At the same time, shapes often do not appear to be contained within the picture limits, as in Cubist design, but continue beyond the picture limits, seemingly "cut-off" fragments of still larger areas. The expansiveness and openness of hard-edge painting were most likely influenced by Matisse and the older Abstract Expressionists, notably the color-field wing. The pictures of Kelly and Smith (but not Stout) also differ from earlier geometric styles in that they are often very large, again taking after Matisse and the first generation.[8] Simplified design on a large scale makes an immediate impact, like that of an abstraction by Newman, very different from the slow part-to-part-to-whole reading required by the complex designs on a small scale in Mondrian's abstraction.

As the work of Matisse shows, the reduction of drawing leads to a greater awareness of color. And paradoxically, it makes line more important since any lapse in simplified drawing is readily apparent. Certainly the expressiveness of a picture by Kelly depends on color (even when black and white) as Cubist-inspired geometric abstractions do not. Yet, after the vivid hues and black and white make their immediate impact, it is the refinement of the contour drawing and the subtle relation of color to shape that long engages the viewer. This is fitting since Kelly began his painting with drawing, with the shape of color, signifying its primacy. As he said: "I work from drawings . . . [which] always comes first . . . Sometimes I stay with the sketch, . . . But most of the time there have to be adjustments during the painting. Through the painting of it I find the color and I work the form and play with it and it adjusts itself."[9]

Despite the clarity of the color-shapes in hard-edge abstraction, there is considerable ambiguity. In many of Kelly's works particularly, the spare forms on a single plane are so abutted that the sharp edges unsnap them, creating an optical oscillation that

162  Ellsworth Kelly, *Atlantic,* 1956.
80″ x 114″. Whitney Museum of American Art,
New York.

163  Ellsworth Kelly, *Aubade,* 1957.
80″ x 80″. Museum of Art, Carnegie Institute,
Pittsburgh, Pennsylvania.

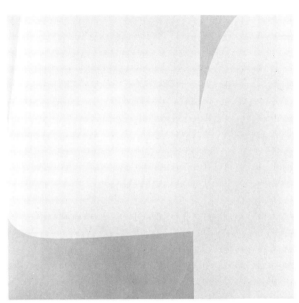

164  Ellsworth Kelly, *New York, N.Y., 1957.*
73¼″ x 91″. Albright–Knox Art Gallery, Buffalo,
New York.

165  Ellsworth Kelly, *Bay*, 1959.
70″ x 50″. Collection, Joseph A. Helman, New York.

makes it difficult to focus on a form and to determine whether it is figure or ground. As the eye skims over the surface—a reason for uniformly uninflected surfaces—all of the shapes are perceived at different moments as positive, or more accurately in figure-ground reversals. This obliteration of a conventional foreground-image-on-background relationship was rare in modern art, indeed, unprecedented before Matisse experimented with it in his late cutouts.

Because of the precise drawing and unmodulated painting, hard-edge abstraction was seen by critics to be a classical revival, and with justification. However, the indeterminate, restless fluctuation of the forms was visually unsettling, and when coupled with the dramatic impact of large, seemingly expansive shapes appeared to be a violation of classical containment and balance.[10] Yet Kelly's concern with clarity of shape was so strong that as early as 1955, he ventured into sculpture, motivated by the idea that "a shape can stand alone."[11]

Despite the elimination of gesture, there was an Expressionist (for want of a better word) aspect in hard-edge painting that made it look different from the geometric abstraction of an earlier period, whose emphasis was didactically idealistic and universalist. It may be that the Expressionist component is brought to mind by the frequency of curved forms suggestive of natural, often anthropomorphic sources, and a certain voluptuousness (and this despite the starkness of hard-edges, unmodulated surfaces, and frequent austere colors). But more important, hard-edge was rooted in private sensibility;

166   Ellsworth Kelly, *Green White,* 1959.
46″ x 60″. Private Collection.

167   Ellsworth Kelly, *Running White,* 1959.
88″ x 68″. The Museum of Modern Art, New York.

the contour, color, and placement of shapes appeared to be determined by feeling.

157, 162
163, 164
165, 166
167, 168
169, 170
Pl. VIII

Kelly was attracted to flat forms in nature, often so insubstantial that people neglected to see them, as I remarked. As he said: "I like to work from things that I see whether they're manmade or natural or a combination of the two. . . . like a window, or a fragment of a piece of architecture, or someone's legs; or sometimes the space between things, or just how the shadows of an object would look. . . . I'm not interested in the texture of the rock, or that it is a rock but in the mass of it, and its shadow."[12] Kelly's way of seeing was a personal one.[13] But as Goossen believed, it may also have been influenced by his work in military camouflage during World War II which made him sensitive to an object's "telling shape."[14] This may moreover have disposed him to art in which images are clearly profiled, beginning with Byzantine paintings and mosaics, and art in which nature is distilled, such as Brancusi's.

After his return to New York in the summer of 1954, and throughout the fifties, Kelly painted hard-edge abstractions based mostly on two-color combinations, from 1954 to 1957, predominantly black and white, after which time he often converted the black into color, e.g., *Green White* (1959). Kelly favored two kinds of imagery. One was a large, single, complete shape barely contained within the canvas limits, biomorphic, e.g., *Black Ripe* (1956), or angular, e.g., *Cowboy* (1958). The other was a cut-off plane that seemed to sweep off or into the picture surface, a fragment of a larger image which the viewer could imagine existed beyond the framing edges, again curved, e.g., *Atlantic* (1956), or geometric, e.g., *Bar* (1956).

166

157

162

Taking his cue from the sense of volume imparted by his flat shapes of color, Kelly ventured into wall reliefs and segmented pictures. In *Yellow Relief* (1955), the left-hand panel is raised an inch or so higher than the one on the right, the change in volume and the cast of a shadow varying the tone of a uniform yellow. In *Painting in Five Panels* (1956), each canvas is separated by an interval of space and is perceived as a thing. In 1959, Kelly began to make free-standing, polychromed sculpture, often sculptural translations of paintings. For example, in *Gate*, a bent X-like plane quotes the pictorial image in *South Ferry* (1956).[15]

As I have remarked, Kelly's imagery is neither classical nor purist, although it strives for clarity in form and color. Nor is it realistic, although it is based on phenomena observed in nature, nor Expressionistic, although it is shaped by feeling and intuition. And yet, it partakes of all three contradictory strategies. By mixing them, Kelly achieved an original and major style. But the appeal of Kelly's painting, aside from its quality, depends as much on his artistic temperament as on his originality, that is, on a quality of moderation, maintaining a balance between the ascetic and the sensual, the controlled and the free, the clear and the ambiguous, the restrained and the dramatic. Kelly favored expanses of intense color, but he rarely allowed them to become emotive or sensuous, restraining them within rigid contours and distancing them through impersonal, immaculate facture. Moreover, to keep his color cool, he confined his palette in most works to black and one ordinary color—red, yellow, blue, or green—generally bright but blandly unpsychological.

168   Ellsworth Kelly, *Pony,* 1959.
31″ x 78″ x 64″. Collection, Mr. and Mrs. Miles Q. Fiterman, Minneapolis, Minnesota.

169 Ellsworth Kelly, *Charter*, 1959.
95¹/₂″ x 60″. Yale University Art Gallery, New Haven, Connecticut.

170 Ellsworth Kelly, *Blue White*, 1960.
85″ x 68″. Art Gallery of Ontario, Toronto.

160, 171
172, 173

Like Kelly, Smith was tied to visual reality, as is clear from the following recollection. "I discovered, in 1954, the particular space concept which I have been working
with since, it was in a circle. I was looking at an athletic catalogue . . . [at drawings] of
the tennis ball, football, baseball and basketball. They were just line circles with a drawing of the seams on the covering of the balls. I was fascinated by the space that was between these lines . . . and started immediately drawing some of my own."[16]

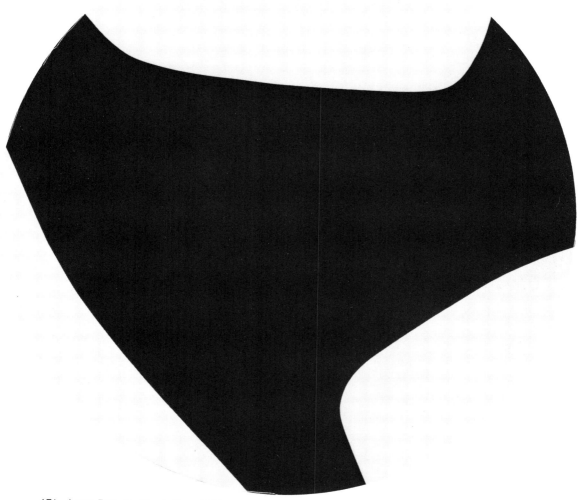

171   Leon Polk Smith, *Anitou,* 1958.
56⁵/₈″ diameter. The Museum of Modern Art, New York.

172  Leon Polk Smith, *Expanse,* 1959. 68¹/₂″ x 74″. Whereabouts unknown.

Smith also employed two-color combinations to make the surface continuous. Thus, he minimized the interaction of discrete forms associated with geometric styles he had earlier worked in, notably Neo-Plasticism. "Mondrian's discovery of the interchangeability of form and space" influenced Smith as early as 1945, but the American soon "set out from Mondrian to find a way of freeing this concept so that it could be expressed with the use of the curved line as well as the straight."[17] The drawings of stitched seams on balls showed him the way.

Unlike Kelly, Smith avoided figure-ground reversals and curbed opticality by manifesting tactile traces of his brushwork. He made the colors on both sides of a dividing line equivalent. "I . . . draw this one line through the canvas which creates two forms, one on either side of the line, . . . I am having to think of both sides of the line, feel both sides, know both sides, and one side is no more important to me than the other."[18] Feeling then determined the choice of the two colors, but color equivalence also had a metaphysical meaning in that it created "two worlds, in direct opposition to each other and yet so well related that they fit into each other as a jigsaw puzzle must."[19]

Stout began to paint the hard-edge canvases for which he is best known in 1954. They are small, generally under two feet, black and white, heavily painted yet matte, and each is composed of a single rounded form contained within the picture frame. These shapes, though organic, do not call to mind visual phenomena, and indeed are not based on things observed, as are Kelly's and Smith's works. Stout frequently titled

161, 174
175

173   Leon Polk Smith, *Correspondence:
Red Black,* 1960.
33″ x 27″. Whereabouts unknown.

174   Myron Stout, *Number 3,* 1954.
20¹/₈″ x 16″. The Museum of Modern Art, New York.

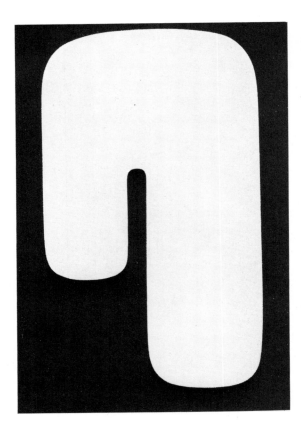

175   Myron Stout, *Untitled*, 1954–55.
20″ x 14″. Collection, Mr. and Mrs. Charles
H. Carpenter, Jr.. New Caanan. Connecticut.
Photo: Rudolph Burckhardt.

his pictures after Greek gods and legends, if he felt that the form had some "metaphoric resonance."[20] Thus, his abstractions can be viewed as emblems, but perhaps less of mythology than of classic art—in their emphasis on drawing, restraint of "color," clarity, wholeness, containedness, stability, and finish. But the quality they convey most strongly is one of the obsessive building of a form, minutely shaped and reshaped, until its contour and scale—the relation of black form to white field—fulfill some private expectation or ideal of perfection.

Hard-edge painting, in its simplicity, lack of surface modulation, clarity and openness of design, and generally large scale, has affinities to stained color-field abstraction. But the differences are more significant, primarily that between an emphasis on the *tactile*, monolithic, self-contained *shape* of color as against the *optical field* of stained areas of color, that is, of color-form as against color-field.

176   Stained color-field painting was also different from hard-edge abstraction because it was more directly an outgrowth of Abstract Expressionism. Although the artists who initiated it, Louis, and soon after, Noland, lived in Washington, D.C., at a distance from the New York School, they accepted Greenberg as their aesthetic advisor. Greenberg first met Noland at Black Mountain College in the summer of 1950. They resumed their acquaintance in 1953 at which time Noland, who acted as go-between New York and Washington, introduced Greenberg to Louis.[21] During that visit, Greenberg took

176   Morris Louis, *Point of Tranquility*, 1958.
101³/₈″ x 135″. Hirshhorn Museum and Sculpture Garden,
Smithsonian Institution, Washington, D.C.

Louis and Noland to Frankenthaler's studio. In the following year, Greenberg included both Washingtonians in a new talent show at the Kootz Gallery. In 1959, he arranged one-person shows for the two artists at the French and Company Gallery, and in 1960, wrote a major article on their stained painting and its justifications.[22] However, well before this article, in 1955, Greenberg had published another essay presenting the premises of the color-field abstraction of Still, Rothko, and Newman, which strongly influenced the younger artists.[23]

Underlying Greenberg's aesthetic was the conviction that "modernist" painting aspires to be "pure," that is, occupied exclusively with what is unique and irreducible in the medium, notably the two-dimensional picture plane. He rejected what he called "painterly painting" (his name for gesture painting) because it is based on the contrast of light and dark values which create illusionistic space and destroy pictorial flatness.[24] As he saw it, value contrast was the "chief agent of structure and unity" in Western painting.[25]

However, a revolutionary assault on this fundamental convention had been made by the Impressionists, who muffled values "in response to the effect of the glare of the sky." This caused their pictures to be criticized for a "lack of 'form' and 'structure.' " In reaction against Impressionist "formlessness," Cézanne introduced "contrasts of warm and cool color," which remained nonetheless contrasts of dark and light. In Greenberg's opinion, this was from the start a conservative move, and that art begat by Cézanne, e.g., Cubist and painterly painting, remained retrogressive.[26]

Greenberg went on to say that Cézanne had been venerated by the avant-garde, while Monet had been deprecated. But a change in ways of seeing was taking place, and it coincided with the emergence of Still, Rothko, and Newman, all of whom looked to Impressionism and rejected Cubism.[27] They were developing the most important and original styles of the time and showing abstract painting a way out of academicism by venturing toward chromatic abstraction. Greenberg insisted that American color-field painting was "the most radical of all developments in the painting of the last two decades, and has no counterpart in Paris . . . as so many other things in American abstract expressionism have had since 1944."[28]

It is noteworthy that Greenberg viewed "impressionist" abstraction from the vantage point of color-field painting, and *not* gesture painting, as Finkelstein had when he used the term "Abstract Impressionism." Finkelstein welcomed pictorial illusion, atmosphere evocative of nature and produced by overlapping and scumbling handpainted marks. Conversely, Greenberg renounced painterly effects and their suggestion of nature and of depth in abstract painting.[29] To put it another way, historical Impressionism's suppression of light and dark contrasts inspired Greenberg, but not its gestural component, which denied his vision of painting based primarily on sheer color. He wrote: "Because it is not broken by sharp differences of value or by more than a few incidents of drawing or design, color breathes from the canvas with an enveloping effect, which is intensified by the largeness itself of the picture."[30]

The artists featured by Greenberg in his 1955 article were all of the first generation. No younger artists were mentioned, probably because he thought it necessary first to rehabilitate certain older artists, notably Newman, who was the most extreme of the color-field painters. One problem, apparently, for Greenberg was to get the work of artists that interested him exhibited or, more accurately, exhibited under conditions that he deemed advantageous. This was solved when he was engaged as the consultant for the French and Company Gallery which opened at the beginning of 1959, a position he held until the summer of 1960.

177　　Newman, who had not exhibited his work in New York since 1951, was given the inaugural show at French and Company.[31] Kramer reported: "The sense of timing could not be better, for Newman's work will never have a more sympathetic audience than it has right now."[32] Although Kramer disliked Newman's painting and was wrong in his prediction of its future success, he must be considered sympathetic, if only because he took the pictures *seriously*, a rare response in the fifties. "I don't find this work either fraudulent or offensive, but I do find it a bore."[33] Even Newman's few admirers, with one or two exceptions,[34] tended to be ambivalent, unable to overcome in themselves the pressures of prevailing art-world opinion. Shortly after Newman's 1959 show, Jerrold Lanes wrote an article lauding the artist's work. And yet, he considered Newman's aesthetic position eccentric. On the one hand: "Newman is an exemplary painter: exemplary in the mastery and economy of his means and in the purity of his

177 Barnett Newman, *Vir Heroicus Sublimis*, 1950–51.
95³/₈″ x 213¹/₄″. The Museum of Modern Art, New York.

purpose." [35] On the other hand: "Newman is *not yet* a contemporary painter. It is a fact that no one else has gone as far, and that some of the best—De Kooning, who remains wholly within the Cubist tradition, is the least equivocal instance—do not seem *interested* in going as far. This . . . condemns him [Newman] to working in a vacuum." [36] Lanes concluded that Newman was "peripheral to the area in which other painters are working: . . . And this is why, I think, it is hard to be unreservedly enthusiastic about Newman *now*, admirable though he is in so many ways." [37]

But Newman was not peripheral to Greenberg, who urged Louis and Noland to suppress painterly details which clogged color and to treat the entire picture as an open field. But more influential than Newman and at an earlier date were Pollock and even more Frankenthaler. Indeed, Louis did not change his style until a year or so after 1953 when, accompanied by Greenberg, he saw Frankenthaler's *Mountains and Sea* (1952). Noland recalled: "We were interested in Pollock but could gain no lead from him. He was too personal. But Frankenthaler showed us a way—a way to think about, and use, color." Louis agreed. Frankenthaler "was a bridge between Pollock and what was possible." [38] As Greenberg wrote: "Abandoning [his prior Cubism] . . . he [Louis] began to feel, think, and conceive almost exclusively in terms of open color. The revelation he received became an Impressionist revelation, . . . His revulsion against Cubism was a revulsion against the sculptural. Cubism meant shapes, and shapes meant armatures of light and dark. Color meant areas and zones, and the interpenetration of these, which could be achieved better by variations of hue than by variations of value." [39] Greenberg went on to say:

21

> The crucial revelation he got from Pollock and Frankenthaler had to do with facture as much as anything else. The more closely colour could be identified with

178 Morris Louis, *Tet*, 1958.
93¹/₂″ x 115¹/₂″. Whitney Museum of American Art, New York.

its ground, the freer would it be from the interference of tactile associations; the way to achieve this closer identification was by adapting watercolour technique to oil and using thin paint on an absorbent surface. Louis spills his paint on unsized and unprimed cotton duck canvas, leaving the pigment almost everywhere thin enough . . . for the eye to sense the threadedness and wovenness of the fabric underneath. . . . The fabric, being soaked in paint rather than merely covered by it, becomes paint in itself, colour in itself, like dyed cloth.[40]

This yielded painting of unprecedented flatness, and thus "purity." At the same time, the stained color appears "somehow disembodied, and therefore more purely optical," opening and expanding the picture plane.[41] Greenberg also maintained that color-field abstraction had to be large in size, in part, to be perceived as a strictly visual entity rather than as a tactile thing,[42] in part, because more blue, for example, is simply bluer than less blue. But "the ultimate effect sought is one of more than chromatic intensity; it is rather one of almost literal openness." Allowing himself a rare statement of content, Greenberg continued: "Openness, and not only in painting, is the quality that seems most to exhilarate the attuned eyes of our time."[43]

Although the paintings of Pollock, Frankenthaler, and Louis are similar in facture, the differences are pronounced. Pollock's skeins of flung paint have substance; they sit on the surface of the canvas. But because line does not define images or outline planes—the two traditional functions of drawing—and because of its flowing quality, it trajects freely, as autonomous painterly drawing. Lashed together into an interlace, the lines constitute an expansive web of forces, and because they overlap, they seem suspended in front of the canvas, projecting out from it. At the same time, the surface, when it is bare, is not sectioned into planes but is apprehended as a field that in his best pictures appears invisible. Pollock's colors are distributed all over the surface like his configuration of lines; they do not interact as discrete colors. This suggests that Pollock was essentially a draftsman, a conception corroborated by the fact that when in 1951–52, he ventured from the flung line to the puddled area, he limited his "colors" to black on unprimed duck. Moreover, Pollock continued to cultivate textural effects contrasting thick and thin (some of which was stained).

Frankenthaler saw the possibility for a new chromatic style in these abstractions of Pollock, and she substituted colors for his black. She also thinned down the pigment to flood her line, spreading it into areas of color, and to make them more translucent, but she continued to manipulate the paint, imposing her touch. Louis diluted his pigment even more than Frankenthaler so that it was absorbed uniformly into the raw canvas. Such staining not only made his color more optical than hers by eliminating the textural quality of paint, but indicated that Louis was "at pains to avoid all suggestion of the gestural, manifestly spontaneous 'handwriting' of Abstract Expressionism."[44] Thus we find Louis fusing the techniques of Pollock and Frankenthaler with the field organization (including the vertical linear accents) of Newman and Still to achieve a new chromatic abstraction.

Louis did not receive a one-man show of his large-scale stain paintings until 1959. 176, 178 Two years earlier, in his first exhibition, he showed intricate, hectic, and dense painterly abstractions (most of which he later destroyed). These were very much in the gestural manner of the time, although most influenced by Pollock. In the painting shown subsequently, the varied textures from thin to thick are eliminated. Based exclusively on the stain, it tends toward even stronger color and simpler format while ranging between expansive color-fields in which most of the surface is dyed to almost all-white canvases in which color is compacted.

Among the series in the expansive vein are the *Veils* (1957–60), in which Louis 178 poured pigment down vertically placed canvases and with the help of gravity produced striated, diaphanous, fanned mass-images, each of a subtly blended pale color that calls to mind Art Nouveau. Also in the color-field direction are the *Florals* (1959–60), com- 176 posed of large, billowy films superimposed on each other. Unlike the near-monochrome of the *Veils*, the colors in the *Florals* are perceived as more or less discrete planes, that is, they are individuated. They are also varied, bright, particularly at the scalloped edges of the centered images, and gravity-defying, most of them floating free within a white margin at the picture edges. Although the *Florals* look expansive, the color areas are poured toward the darker centers of the canvas, palimpsests of spills, countering the emphatic flaring motion.

179   Morris Louis, *Untitled,* 1956.
83″ x 93″. Neuberger Museum, State University
of New York at Purchase.

180   Morris Louis, *Alpha,* 1960.
105¹/₂″ x 145¹/₂″. Albright–Knox Art Gallery, Buffalo,
New York.

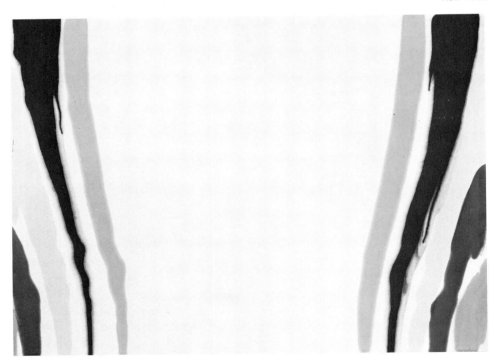

At the same time, Louis painted his most extreme open-field abstractions, the *Un-* 180
*furleds* (1960–61), in which rivulets of color—in between line and area—which rarely
overlap run downward and inward from below the upper corners of outsized, horizontal
canvases, leaving bare the unsized centers. These vast funnel-like expanses of white—at
once empty and so vibrant as to be perceived as "color"—although confined by the free-
flowing diagonals of color at the vertical limits of the canvas, seem boundless. From
1961 to 1962 (the year of his death), Louis swung from the expansiveness of the *Un-*
*furleds* to the opposite extreme. In his last series, the *Stripes,* he bundled vertical, multicolored ribbons of slightly varied thicknesses into pulsating shafts that thrust up or
down white fields from one edge almost to the other. It is as if he willfully straightened
the banked rivulets in the *Unfurleds* and made them the center of focus or abridged and
articulated the pendulous skeins that underlie the *Veils.* The *Stripes,* his best-known
works during his lifetime, convey a sense of intense color compression without sacrificing a uniform luminosity that animates colored and bare areas alike.

Noland had his first New York show in 1957, the same year that Louis did. His 181, 182
pictures then were thinly painted or stained but nonetheless gestural, composed of
complicated, overlapping areas. The canvases he exhibited the following year tended to
be even more profuse and delicate. In his show in 1959, Noland presented his "target"

181  Kenneth Noland, *Spread,* 1958.
117″ x 117″. New York University Art Collection, Grey Art Gallery and Study Center.

paintings, the style for which he first became well-known. Each of these abstractions is composed of concentric bands of color separated by white centered in a square canvas. In the earlier targets, the edges of the rings are irregular, gestural looking, but they straightened out by 1961. Noland's hard-edge stripes (in different series: circular, chevron, or horizontal) veer toward the geometric with its concern for design rather than color. But his design is symmetrical, thus neutral, unobtrusive, so as to call attention to the interaction of color (as his former teacher Albers did). Noland himself called his composition "self-cancelling" as against "self-declaring." "With structural considerations eliminated I could concentrate on color."[45]

Noland differed generally from Louis in his preference for a formal, quasi-geometric layout, softened by staining, to be sure; a controlled design; and discrete, intense colors. Noland also developed in an opposite direction from Louis, away from the color containedness in the "target" series (although the circular bands can be seen as radiating outward) to the color expansiveness in the "chevron" and "stripe" paintings, in which the color configurations do not seem confined by the picture frame.

183    Olitski did not exhibit stain paintings until 1960. His earlier pictures are composed of centered, heavily pigmented images in the manner of Fautrier. Indeed, these canvases are so impasto-laden as to approach bas-relief, and their reticent colors—grays, browns, off-whites—serve to emphasize the textures even more. The pictures in Olitski's 1960 show are composed of rounded, high-keyed planes set off against black fields. The images are reminiscent of the slabs of impasto in the earlier "pigment" pictures and of cellular organisms.

The supporters of stained-color abstraction tended to justify it on cerebral aestheticist and formalist grounds. Yet, more than any painters of the fifties—even Frankenthaler—Louis, Noland, and Olitski were hedonistic in spirit, decorously cultivating the delectability of color. They did insinuate self, nature, and other art in their choice of color, for example, a Tiffany glass palette in Louis's abstractions, targets in Noland's, and biomorphic phenomena in Olitski's, but their essential content was immediate and open, buoyant color.

Artists *within* the New York School partook of a growing urge to turn from the complexity and ambiguity of gesture painting, its exploitation of brushy facture, to simplicity and clarity, an urge so strong that it even influenced de Kooning, who, late in 1956, began to paint "landscapes," composed mainly of broad swaths of color. Younger artists went to great extremes at the end of the fifties and the beginning of the sixties. Ben Isquith (in pictures exhibited as early as 1954) and Sally Hazelet (Drummond) reduced color and gesture, ending up with near-monochromatic fields of subtly varied impasto, an original synthesis of de Kooning and Reinhardt, and it is noteworthy that both older artists had been teachers of Isquith and were friends of Hazelet. Instead of the hectic drama of gesture painting on the whole, they presented a "World of Silent Painting," as Hazelet remarked.[46] In 1956, she began to slightly deepen the color in the

184    centers of pictures square in shape. By 1960, she began to use a pointillist technique to slowly build up a vibrating, luminous, allover image and at the same time to accent

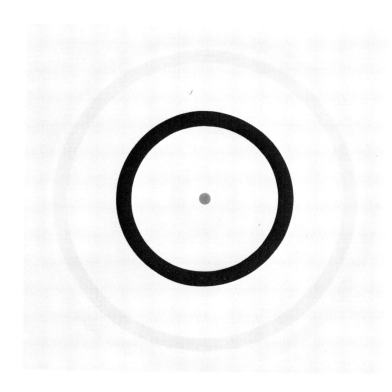

182   Kenneth Noland, *Turnsole,* 1961.
94$^{1}/_{8}$″ x 94$^{1}/_{8}$″. The Museum of Modern
Art, New York.

183   Jules Olitski, *Isis Ardor,* 1962.
80″ x 66″. Harry N. Abrams Family Collection, New York.

184 Sally Hazelet Drummond, *Hummingbird,* 1961.
12″ x 12″. The Museum of Modern Art, New York.

more than before the centrifugal radiation like an aureole, providing a focus for serene contemplation.

Parker also ventured in the direction of a new chromatic abstraction. Held, Nicholas Krushenick, and Ronald Bladen clarified or "classicized" their painterly gestures to create what I labeled a "concrete expressionism."[47] Earlier, in 1957, Alfred Jensen replaced Expressionist imagery with high-keyed checkerboard configurations, symbolic in content, which were of considerable but little-acknowledged influence. In a related vein, Brach, Miriam Schapiro, and Ortman hardened their loosely brushed areas into geometric or quasi-geometric symbols.

If color and form are considered the parameters of the post-gestural styles within New York School painting, then Parker and Held best represent each. In 1958, Parker

185
186, 187
188, 189
190
191, 192

began to paint chromatic abstractions by spreading areas of thinned pigment on un-      193
stretched primed canvas until each was fully felt visually and emotionally.[48] This approach enabled him to work directly from within color, discovering its shape and scale
without thinking of composition. The edges of his color shapes are where the spreading
colors stop; they are too uneven to be thought of as drawn line. Parker's final decision
was to determine the picture edges. This is the decision—and it is one of drawing—that
painters traditionally begin with, and it is generally their most crucial one, but it was not
Parker's—a sign of his departure from convention.

Parker reduced the number of color areas in each of his canvases generally to two,
three, or four, and made them somewhat oval or oblong in shape. Unlike Louis and
Noland, who looked to Pollock and Newman, or Kelly and Smith, who looked to Matisse and Arp, Parker was inspired by Motherwell's *Spanish Elegies* and Gottlieb's *Bursts*,
but he placed greater stress on the interaction of resonant colors than they did in their
series. Parker's shapes seem to hover between "form" and "field," too irregular to be
hard-edge and too discrete to be color-field. They are not stained but are subtly textured
so as to separate from the canvas, each taking on a character of its own.[49] They are optical enough to seem to float like giant balloons, and yet they are weighty and monumental, like a two-dimensional Stonehenge.

185  Nicholas Krushenick, *East Hampton,* 1962.
        60″ x 50″. Collection, the artist.

186   Alfred Jensen, *Family Portrait,* 1958.
75″ x 40″. Albright–Knox Art Gallery, Buffalo, New York.

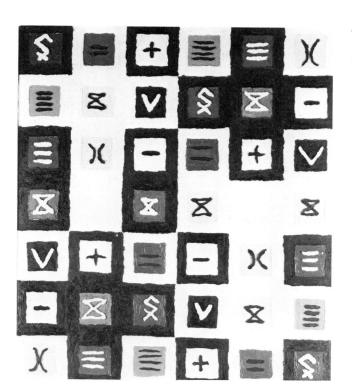

187  Alfred Jensen, *The Great Mystery II,* 1960.
50″ x 42″. Albright–Knox Art Gallery, Buffalo,
New York.

188  Paul Brach, *Merlin,* 1959.
60″ x 50″. Collection, Dr. and Mrs. Robert D.
Seely, New York.

189   Miriam Schapiro, *The Game,* 1960.
81″ x 90¹/₂″. Collection, the artist.

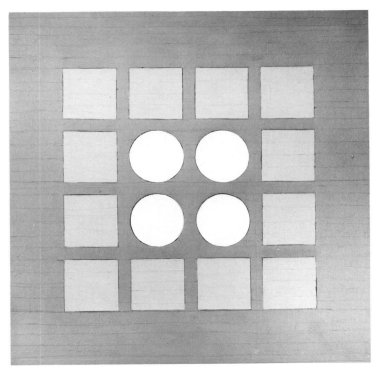

190   George Ortman, *Game of Chance,* 1959.
60″ x 60″. New York University Art Collection,
Grey Art Gallery and Study Center.

191  Raymond Parker, *Untitled,* 1956.
83″ x 49″. Whitney Museum of American Art,
New York.

192  Raymond Parker, *P. 30.*
64″ x 68″. The Art Museum, Princeton University.

193   Raymond Parker, *Untitled,* 1959.
68¹/₂″ x 69″. Albright–Knox Art Gallery, Buffalo, New York.

194, 195
196, 197   In 1959, Held created a variant of hard-edge abstraction. His classicizing impulse was also felt in his earlier gesture paintings, so-called pigment pictures because they are coated with heavy impasto. They were influenced by de Kooning and Pollock. And yet: "Held's thickly textured swaths were deliberately composed—constructed like masonry. His aim 'to give the gesture structure,' as he put it then, calls to mind Cézanne's attempt to make something solid out of Impressionism."[50] Even after Held achieved a hard-edge style, he continued to build up his surfaces, which revealed traces of innumerable revisions. This was reminiscent of the process of gesture painting, so much so that I labeled them " 'Geometric-Expressionist,' even though it seems to be a contradiction in terms."[51]

Held desired not only to clarify his forms but to dissociate them. As I remarked:

194  Al Held, *Untitled,* 1956.
66″ x 48″. Collection, the artist.

195  Al Held, *Untitled,* 1956.
108″ x 192″. Collection, Mara Held,
Santa Monica, California.

196   Al Held, *Untitled,* 1960.
50″ x 45″. Private Collection, New York.

197   Al Held, *I-Beam*, 1961.
114″ x 192″. Collection, the artist.

His huge forms do not interlock; each exists in its own isolated space.

Held is not satisfied with a painting until the forms separate—until they "leap" from what he calls the "pictorial" (i.e., relational) to the "non-pictorial" (i.e., self-contained and non-relational). That is, he strives to make each of his forms a concrete entity. "Concreteness" and "thing-ness" are the key words in Held's vocabulary.[52]

Moreover, Held attempted to thrust his object-like forms at the viewer, to make them "appear to project into the room. Held has evolved a distinctive kind of 'inverse illusionism' which resists the tendency of a picture to be a two-dimensional design,"[53] and at the same time, avoids illusionistic depth. The hardening of gestures into clear forms of clear colors in itself did not guarantee a new pictorial structure, but Held achieved that by disassociating disparate forms, placing them side by side to avoid the centripetal relational design of Cubism and the infrastructure of gesture painting.

Sharing the appetite for structural clarity were abstract sculptors Gabriel Kohn, George Sugarman and Ronald Bladen.[54] Kohn's constructions, the first of which date from 1957, are joined together from more or less evenly surfaced, quasi-geometric volumes which were first pieced together by laminating sawed planes of wood. His forms are reminiscent of Brancusi's and Arp's and of arches, buttresses, and other components

198, 199

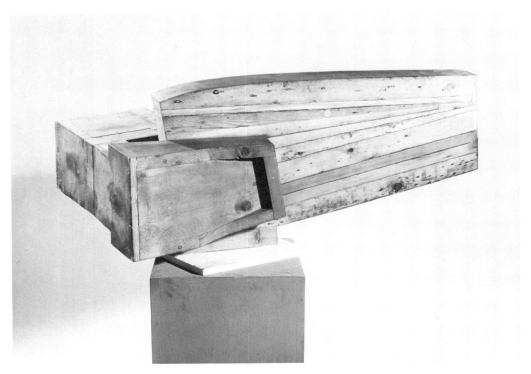

198 Gabriel Kohn, *Pitcairn,* 1958.
22⁵/₈″ x 49¹/₂″ x 24¹/₂″. Albright–Knox Art Gallery, Buffalo, New York.

199 Gabriel Kohn, *Nantucket
(Equatorial Trap*), 1960.
26″ x 35″ x 23¹/₄″. Hirshhorn Museum and Sculpture Garden, Smithsonian Institution, Washington, D.C.

of buildings, notably Le Corbusier's chapel at Ronchamp. Reducing his sculptures to a few precisely defined volumes suggestive of architecture enabled Kohn to achieve a fresh classicizing style.

Like Kohn, Sugarman assembled his constructions from laminated wood. The weighty forms in works of 1957 were organic and roughhewn. About 1960, Sugarman began to polychrome the volumes and disjoin them, somewhat as Held did. That is, Sugarman did not compose with related elements and arrange them around a central axis in what he termed "Cubist" design. Instead, he built masses disparate in shape and color and unfolded them in sequence or extended space. And like Held's paintings, Sugarman's constructions conveyed a feeling of physicality, energy, and robustness.

Bladen began as a painter. In his shows at the Brata Gallery in 1958 and 1960, he exhibited abstractions composed of cement-like slabs and mounds of pigment, suggestive of hills, foliage, and clouds. The projection of impasto into actual space prompted Bladen to venture further into the third dimension. In 1961, he began to paste up collages of rectangular paper strips whose ends are folded outward. Later that year, he constructed wood reliefs in which one or more plank-like geometric figures—an "L" or an inverted "C"—each painted a single color are suspended in front of rectangles of a

200, 201<br>202

203, 204<br>205

200   George Sugarman,
*Six Forms in Pine*, 1959.
Approx. 96″ long. Collection, the artist.

contrasting color, which are floated away from the wall. The "spread" of the work into the room pointed the way to Bladen's subsequent sculpture in the round. In the constructed reliefs, he eliminated organic forms and their associations with nature in order, as he said, to "come close to a purer kind of abstraction . . . to push abstract art a bit further."[55]

In retrospect, it is clear that by the beginning of the sixties, there had emerged a significant number of extraordinary young artists who, despite the considerable differences in their styles, had developed a manner different from gesture painting.

201  George Sugarman,
*Yellow Top,* 1960.
87¹/₂″ x 54″ x 34″, Walker Art Center, Minneapolis, Minnesota.

202   George Sugarman, *Spiral Sculpture,* 1961.
70″ x 60″ x 33″. Destroyed.

203   Ronald Bladen, *Untitled,* 1958–59.
48″ x 36″. Collection, Connie Reyes, New York.

204 Ronald Bladen, *Untitled,* 1961.
36″ x 30″. Collection, Connie Reyes, New York.

205 Ronald Bladen, *Untitled,* 1962.
96″ x 72″. Collection, Connie Reyes, New York.

# Notes

1. Kelly lived in France from 1948 to 1954; Stout lived in Provincetown, Massachusetts. He was friendly with New York artists who summered there and Hofmann's students, many of whom admired his work, but he experienced little of the aesthetic ferment in New York at first hand. Smith was a New Yorker, but as a geometric abstract painter, he stood apart from the New York School until 1956, when he showed at the Camino Gallery on Tenth Street. Louis and Noland were Washingtonians. Olitski developed color-field abstraction later under the influence of Louis and Noland.

2. Nassos Daphnis and Alexander Liberman were stylistically related to Kelly, Smith, and Stout, but their work was shown later—Daphnis in 1959, after an interval of a decade, and Liberman in 1960, in his first show. Moreover, Daphnis, in his carryovers of relational design, and Liberman, in his use of circles contained within the picture limits, call to mind earlier geometric abstract styles in a way that Kelly and Smith do not. Jack Youngerman's work is related to hard-edge abstraction, particularly Kelly's, but silhouettes in Youngerman's pictures are jagged, reminiscent of leaves and flowers, and his surfaces are thickly and unevenly painted.

3. Hard-edge painters were inspired by Cubist abstraction. Smith had been influenced by Mondrian from 1951 to 1955. In 1948, the year Kelly went to Europe, he visited Vantongerloo, a disciple of Mondrian. Kelly also met Brancusi and Arp. His *Palm* (1957) is obviously based on Brancusi's *Flying Turtle* (1940–45), as John Coplans once pointed out to me.

4. Jules Langsner, in *Four Abstract Classicists*, exhibition catalogue (Los Angeles, Calif.: Los Angeles County Museum of Art, 1959), p. 10, first used the label "hard-edge" with reference to four California artists—Karl Benjamin, Lorser Feitelson, Frederick Hammersley, and John McLaughlin, whose work did not depart from older geometric styles as radically as Kelly's or Smith's did. In New York, Langsner's label became better known than the work of these artists. It is noteworthy that Kelly rejected the label hard-edge, because he was interested more in mass and color (Henry Geldzahler, "Interview with Ellsworth Kelly," *Art International*, 15 February 1964, p. 47). Stout also disliked it.

5. Kelly rarely makes his forms rectangular when geometric (in the fifties) or biomorphic when curved, avoiding associations with Neo-Plasticism on the one hand and on the other hand, with Surrealism. Indeed, as John Coplans, in *Ellsworth Kelly* (New York: Harry N. Abrams, 1973), p. 63, suggested, the best "term for Kelly's particular mixture of the geometric and the organic would be biometric or geomorphic." (See also pp. 62, 64–65.)

6. It is also possible to view Kelly's imagery as emblematic, a kind of abstract heraldry.

7. See Coplans, *Ellsworth Kelly*, p. 25.

8. Kelly generally enlarged the scale of his paintings after his move to New York in 1954.

9. Geldzahler, "Interview with Ellsworth Kelly," p. 48.

10. See Lawrence Alloway, "Classicism or Hard-Edge," *Art International*, 4, no. 2–3 (1960): 61.

11. William Rubin, "Ellsworth Kelly: The Big Form," *Art News*, November 1963, p. 65.

12. Geldzahler, "Interview with Ellsworth Kelly," p. 48.

13. To gauge the privacy of Kelly's vision, see Phyllis Tuchman, "Ellsworth Kelly's Photographs," *Art in America*, January–February, 1974, pp. 55–61.

14. E. C. Goossen, *Ellsworth Kelly* (New York: Museum of Modern Art, 1973), p. 16. For discussions of Kelly's career prior to his moving to New York in 1954, see the above work and Coplans, *Ellsworth Kelly*, and Diane Waldman, *Ellsworth Kelly* (Greenwich, Conn.: New York Graphic Society, 1971).

15. In 1956, Kelly executed a commissioned partly painted aluminum construction, 12' x 64' x 2', for the Transportation Building, Philadelphia, Pa.

16. Leon Polk Smith and d'Arcy Hayman (a conversation), "The Paintings of Leon Polk Smith," *Art and Literature* 3 (Autumn–Winter 1964): 85.

17. Lawrence Alloway, *Leon Polk Smith's Geometric Paintings 1945–1953*, exhibition catalogue (New York: Galerie Chalette, 1970), unpaginated.

18. Smith and Hayman, "The Paintings of Leon Polk Smith," pp. 82–83.

19. Ibid., p. 83. See Lawrence Alloway, "Leon Polk Smith: Dealings in Equivalence," *Art in America*, July–August 1974, pp. 58–61.

20. Stanford Schwartz, "Myron Stout," *Artforum*, March 1975, p. 40.

21. Kenneth Noland, "Editor's Letters," *Art News*, November 1962, p. 6. Noland and Louis met in 1952.

22. Clement Greenberg, "Louis and Noland," *Art International*, 25 May 1960, pp. 26–29.

23. Greenberg, " 'American-Type' Painting," pp. 177–96.

24. Greenberg had been an early supporter of painterly painting, but he attacked it repeatedly after 1955. For example, see Greenberg, "After Abstract Expressionism," pp. 24–32. On p. 24, he defined the painterly painting of first-generation Abstract Expressionism as "loose, rapid handling, or the look of it; masses that blotted and fused instead of shapes that stayed distinct; . . . large and conspicuous rhythms; broken color; uneven saturations or densities of paint [produced by smearing, swiping, scrubbing, and scumbling], exhibited brush, knife, or finger marks— in short, a constellation of qualities like those defined by Woelfflin when he extracted his notion of the *Maelerische* from Baroque Art."

This kind of facture evoked illusionistic space and volumes, tactile-like sculpture, rather than being purely visual, as painting ought to be. On p. 25, moreover, Greenberg maintained that as the fifties progressed, painterly painting "began fairly to cry out for a more coherent illusion of three-dimensional space, and to the extent that it did this it cried out for representation." The culmination of this "impure" tendency was de Kooning's series of *Woman* pictures, 1952–55. But the representation that emerged in abstraction was "homeless," as Greenberg saw it, and by the middle fifties had hardened into mannerism and, therefore, was bad art. (At the same time, in Europe, the "furtive bas-relief," initiated by Dubuffet and Fautrier, had decayed into mannerism.)

25. Greenberg, " 'American-Type' Painting," p. 189.

26. Ibid. As Greenberg saw it, the patterns of overlapping brushwork in painterly painting partook of Cubism's relational design in shallow depth.

27. Ibid., p. 190.

28. Ibid., p. 189.

29. Later Greenberg would coin the label "post-painterly abstraction" for the art he championed.

30. Greenberg, " 'American-Type' Painting," p. 194.

31. The Newman show in 1959 consisted of twenty-nine canvases dating from 1946 to 1952. It was similar to one held at Bennington College, Vermont, in 1958.

32. Hilton Kramer, "Month in Review," *Arts*, April 1959, p. 45.

33. Ibid. In retrospect, it is astonishing that Newman's elevation to the status of serious artist should have taken as long as it did, and this despite the fact that his work was not too well known since he refused to exhibit from 1951 to 1958. Typical of the reaction to his pictures, even after the show at the French and Company Gallery, was a letter to *Arts* magazine by one Bernard Seward, which called them a "hoax [which] should have been vigorously exploded. . . . every painter knows, that Newman never had the faintest pretension to painting before 1946, that his absurd effort to get in the 'game' is the huge joke of the studios today" (Bernard Seward, "Letters," *Arts*, May 1959, p. 6).

34. See E. C. Goossen, "The Philosophic Line of Barnett Newman," *Art News*, Summer 1958, pp. 30–31, 62–63.

35. Jerrold Lanes, "Reflections on Post-Cubist Painting," *Arts*, May 1959, p. 26.

36. Ibid., p. 28.

37. Ibid.

38. John Elderfield, Introduction, *Morris Louis*, exhibition catalogue (London: Arts Council of Great Britain, 1974), pp. 8–9. Greenberg, in *Three New American Painters: Louis, Noland, Olitski*, exhibition catalogue (Regina, Canada: Norman Mackenzie Art Gallery, 1963), unpaginated, wrote that Louis, who began to stain in 1954, "had a decisive initial influence on Noland, who was a friend and neighbor of his in Washington, D.C."

39. Greenberg, "Louis and Noland," p. 28.

40. Ibid.

41. Ibid.

42. Ibid.

43. Greenberg, "After Abstract Expressionism," p. 29. On p. 28, he remarked that uneven brushwork "worked against true openness, . . . . the slapdash application of paints ends by crowding the picture plane into a compact jumble."

44. Michael Fried, "Some Notes on Morris Louis," *Arts Magazine*, November 1963, p. 25.

45. Kenworth Moffett, "Noland," *Art International*, Summer 1973, p. 26.

46. Sally Hazelet, "World of Silent Painting," leaflet, reprinted from *Arts in Louisville Magazine*, September 1957.

47. Irving Sandler, *Concrete Expressionism*, exhibition catalogue (New York: New York University, 1965). The artists included were Ronald Bladen, Al Held, Knox Martin, George Sugarman, and David Weinrib.

48. Parker began to evolve his chromatic abstractions as early as 1956. F[airfield] P[orter], "Reviews and Previews: Raymond Parker," *Art News*, November 1957, p. 13, wrote that Parker "is developing a new concept of color, where color is not equated with form (if form means an equivalent for volume) but stands instead for energy." Porter also stressed the immediacy of Parker's colors, their quickness.

49. Parker "feels that, when a painting is going well, the spots begin to acquire a certain fullness . . . [which] suggests a certain kind of presence. The white canvas becomes a spatial arena, . . . For him this [sense of presence] is the most desirable quality a form can possess." (Lawrence Campbell, "Parker Paints a Picture," *Art News*, November 1962, p. 71.)

50. Irving Sandler, "Al Held Paints a Picture," *Art News*, May 1964, p. 43.

51. Ibid., p. 44.

52. Ibid.

53. Ibid.

54. In 1960, Anthony Caro, working in England, began to make classicizing metal constructions whose influence would soon be felt in New York. He extended ideas borrowed from David Smith in a new direction by projecting his sculpture horizontally across the floor, somewhat in the manner of his teacher Henry Moore. Caro also took his cues from Clement Greenberg, who in "Sculpture in Our Time," *Arts*, June 1958, p. 23, wrote: "The new construction-sculpture points back, almost insistently, to its origins in Cubist painting: by its linearism and linear intricacies, by its openness and transparency and weightlessness, and by its preoccupation with surface as skin alone, which it expresses in blade- or sheet-like forms. Space is there to be shaped, divided, enclosed, but not to be filled or sealed in."

55. Irving Sandler, "Ronald Bladen," *Artforum*, October 1966, p. 32.

# 12

# The Recognition of the Second Generation

THE KIND of recognition New York School artists prized most was that of their peers. Their primary career goal was to have periodic one-person shows, installed with dignity by the exhibitors and their friends, in order to present a progress report to their colleagues (and to reveal to the individual artist what the work looked like in a public context outside the studio, this producing distance from the work, closing it off, so that he or she could proceed with a freer mind to new work). At best, a favorable consensus would arise in the art world. Additional increments to such a community estimate might be an unexpected sale, or an invitation by a curator to exhibit in a museum show, such as the Whitney Annual.

Artists were not nearly so pure, of course. Much as they proudly asserted their absolute prerogative in artistic matters and denied any regard for non-artist opinion, they wished for the approval of the art-conscious public, particularly "art professionals," such as curators, critics, dealers, and serious collectors. Artists also welcomed the material rewards that the "art establishment" could confer. However, there was very little kowtowing; the New York School was confident of its achievement and secure in its knowledge—of being in the know; non-artists came to the artists, not the other way around.

Material success was gratifying for making life easier and allowing an artist to concentrate on his or her work, and also for confirming in a more or less measurable way the worth of the art. "Official" acclaim could also lead to broader public notice—an artist's name might become a household word, like Pollock's. The artists were not averse to such acknowledgment, as the full-page photograph of the Eighteen Irascibles in *Life* magazine in 1951 attests, since the pioneer Abstract Expressionists not only permitted the photograph to be taken but took the time to pose.[1] Much as the artists professed to feel alienated from the public because of its taste for mass culture, they tacitly accepted the success values of American society, since few, if any, were social revolutionaries.

Hoped-for recognition was eventually forthcoming by the end of the decade for most leading Abstract Expressionists and a few young artists. By 1962 or 1963, there existed a sizable audience and market for contemporary art. Artists who just a decade earlier could not even imagine the possibility of success became culture heroes—and wealthy ones. Young students could now choose art as a career, like dentistry or accounting. I would venture too far afield to elaborate on the reasons for the sharp change in public opinion about vanguard art, a change that was a necessary precondition for its success. Briefly, a number of general social tendencies contributed, among them a slow but seemingly inexorable shift from a producer to a consumer society, in which cultural achievement assumed an ever-greater value; the growth in the number of college graduates required to pass at least one course in studio disciplines, art history, or art appreciation; the emergence largely from within this group of a sophisticated "mass" audience for art, much of it sympathetic to the avant-garde; and in response to the requirements of this audience, the proliferation of expanded art programs in colleges, and of museums and art centers whose professional personnel "educated" an ever-larger audience, making it aware of "difficult" modern and contemporary styles; and finally, America's growing affluence, which enabled this public to support the new art institutions, many of which bought recent art, and to privately purchase paintings, sculptures and, particularly, prints, which gave rise to a "renaissance" in printmaking.

However, these preconditions do not account for the particular critical and economic success of the New York School. In this chapter, I will present some of the main events occurring within the art world during the fifties which contributed to this success and cumulatively were responsible for it. I will omit most of the negative criticism of the New York School. Although hostile estimates far outnumbered positive ones, they were of little account in the long run, since they merely added quantitatively to the already prevailing opinion of advanced art. What I will try to explicate is a qualitative change in attitude and the events that generated it.

My focus will be on the second generation, but to keep its success in perspective, one should remember that the first-generation's success was even greater—and, more significantly, was substantially responsible for the recognition of the younger artists. It was difficult to document this process, since so much of it was based on word of mouth. Older, more established painters and sculptors naturally introduced and recommended their lesser-known friends to local and out-of-town curators, dealers, collectors, and other taste-makers, who, in turn, spread the word, again verbally. The greater the success of the first generation, the more its followers profited. It must also be remembered that the original Abstract Expressionists who "broke through" around 1947 were caught in a cultural lag; it took time for their work to be taken seriously, even accepted as art. Such acceptance paved the way for the quick recognition of the second generation.

Perhaps the most important contribution made by the first generation to the success of younger artists was to focus art-world attention on itself and on its scene. This enabled an artists' mechanism to influence taste-making, namely, the consensus of the artists themselves concerning the relative worth of each other's work. Dealers, curators, critics, and collectors constantly gauged artists' opinion and responded to it, so much so that it was in most cases the greatest influence on their decision-making.

Early-wave artists themselves made the first bids for recognition, individually by trying to get their work shown in commercial galleries, and collectively by organizing cooperative galleries, such as the Jane Street, Hansa, and Tanager. Older established galleries took on a few of the younger artists, but of far greater significance were newly opened galleries dealing primarily with the second generation, such as the Tibor de Nagy, Stable, Martha Jackson, Poindexter, and Leo Castelli. Indeed, the efforts of these few cooperative and commercial galleries were probably the most important single factor in the success of second-generation artists, that is, of course, of those who succeeded. This was the doing not only of dedicated dealers of remarkable taste such as John B. Myers (of the Tibor de Nagy Gallery), Eleanor Ward (of the Stable Gallery), Martha Jackson, Eleanor Poindexter, and Leo Castelli, but of the artists themselves. What prompted an artist to desire to join a certain gallery was above all respect for the high caliber of the artists already in it. In turn, dealers almost without exception consulted with their "stable" of artists before taking on anyone new. This process of mutual selection was crucial to artists' success, since it concentrated in a few galleries—known to curators, critics, and collectors—the artists generally considered the best of their generation, who, whether they were or not, had an edge over their peers in less-prestigious galleries.

Not only did artists bid for recognition by joining certain galleries, but a number also began to write criticism sympathetic to their colleagues, among them Elaine de Kooning, Goodnough, Campbell, and Porter in *Art News*; and Brach and Sidney Geist in *Art Digest*. But it was the critics whose primary enterprise was criticism who early on made the strongest impression on the art-conscious public. Foremost among these were Greenberg of the *Nation* and *Partisan Review*; Hess, executive editor of *Art News*; and Rosenberg, whose writing on art appeared mainly in *Art News*. The three men were close to the New York School, and much of their writing can be taken to reflect artists' opinion. Greenberg, Hess, and Rosenberg were in a very small minority of critics who passionately believed in the worth of American vanguard painting and sculpture.[2]

In contrast to them, senior critics on leading newspapers, e.g., the *New York Times*, and popular magazines, e.g., *Time*, paid little attention to the New York School, and were antagonistic when they did. As the fifties progressed, growing coverage was forthcoming, but it was not enough and came too late to contribute much to the public recognition of advanced American art. Howard Devree, the chief art critic of the *New York Times*, was unsympathetic to Abstract Expressionist painting, except occasionally when it had recognizable subject matter. The other *Times* critics were friendly, but it was Devree who determined art policy, and he rarely allowed a young Abstract Expressionist to be featured on the Sunday art pages, the pages that counted most nationally with respect to recognition. When New York School artists were dealt with, they were given short paragraphs without reproductions of their works. John Canaday replaced Devree in September 1959, and he changed the *New York Times* policy to open hostility to Abstract Expressionism. *Time* was also antipathetic to advanced styles. After 1958, it increased its coverage of Abstract Expressionism, but primarily as news and not as criticism, and this was relegated to a minor position in contrast to the extensive treatment of historical art first, and contemporary realist styles second.

The audience for vanguard art was indifferent to the mass media. What interested it was the opinion of such critics as Greenberg. As early as 1947, he began to call attention to the second generation. In that year, he wrote: "The more ambitious and serious of the youngest generation of American painters live south of Twenty-third Street, . . . and get almost no publicity." His review focused on the Jane Street Gallery group and singled out Blaine as "the most developed."[3] Two years later, Greenberg hailed Rivers as "this amazing beginner" and already "a better composer of pictures than was Bonnard in many instances."[4]

In 1950, a sizable number of early-wave artists received their first major recognition as a group—in a *New Talent* show selected by Greenberg and Schapiro and held at the Kootz Gallery, a prestigious uptown showplace of modern masters, including a number of pioneer Abstract Expressionists. Among the twenty-three newcomers exhibited were Elaine de Kooning, de Niro, Dzubas, Goodnough, Hartigan, Leslie, Rivers, Solomon, and Stefanelli. Hess wrote that the show "adds up to one of the most successful and provocative exhibitions of younger artists I have ever seen. And not the least part of the excitement comes from the fact that almost all the works have never been shown before and are by unrecognized talents."[5] (At the beginning of 1954, Greenberg chose an *Emerging Talent* show for the Kootz Gallery, consisting of eleven painters, among them Pearlstein, Louis, and Noland.)

From 1950 to 1952, leading artists of the first generation came to believe with growing confidence that their work was of historical consequence—and they began to assume a new stance. Motherwell and Reinhardt noted in *Modern Artists in America*, a lavish new magazine edited by them, that interest in modern art throughout America was growing at an unprecedented rate. The battle for modernism was won. Advanced art had reached such a level of sustained achievement that what was now needed was an objective rather than a polemical treatment of advanced art.[6]

The first generation's sense of its new stature had an equivocal effect on the recognition of the early wave. A number of the older artists tried to make their activities exclusive, keeping out many of their own generation and all of the newcomers. But because of the growing status of the masters of Abstract Expressionism, those activities in which younger artists were included (often projected as heirs apparent) counted for more than ever before. When in 1951, a group of first-generation artists organized a large survey of vanguard art which came to be known as the Ninth Street Show, of the sixty-one artists represented, at least thirteen were of the second generation: Dzubas, Frankenthaler, Goodnough, Hartigan, Harry Jackson, Elaine de Kooning, Leslie, Mitchell, de Niro, Porter, Resnick, Stefanelli, and Goldberg. Most of the participants did not think that the show would attract much attention, but it did beyond anyone's expectations, confirming the changed group image of the New York School.

So successful was the Ninth Street Show that in 1953, artists decided to arrange another, uptown at the Stable Gallery. This exhibition prompted others, formally called the New York Artists Annuals but dubbed the Stable Annuals, all of which were well attended and fully reported in the art media. Greenberg wrote the introduction to the 1953 show. He asserted that the more than ninety participants represented "a range of the liveliest tendencies within the mainstream of advanced painting and sculpture in New York." He went on to say that the display provided the public with

> . . . a chance to see what is going on in the studios, many blocks distant from 57th St., where the newer generation of painters and sculptors incubate what may be—in some instances—the liveliest art of the near future. This is invaluable to artists themselves, as both stimulation and information—a certain amount of rivalry is indispensable, and you have to be aware of what your rivals are doing if rivalry is to provoke self criticism . . . Exhibitions like these serve to bring art alive as a current issue, as something fluid and moving, still on the way to fulfillment and decision, not yet pinned down and fixed by the verdicts of critics or museums or "safe" collectors.[7]

Greenberg concluded with the "hope that this show, too, will find a successor, that it becomes just enough of an institution to be repeated every year, with no less a breadth of choice and no lower level of taste."[8]

The prestige of the Stable Annuals was dependent partly on the quality of the work shown, and partly on the fact that the selection was done entirely by artists, that is, by a committee chosen by all who had participated in the show the year before. The invited artists each chose a work of their own to be shown. Another committee, chosen by the first, installed the paintings and sculptures. The resulting show was the collective image of the New York School as it saw itself. As Kramer wrote: "Thus, even if one cannot claim that it is unburdened by politics, favoritism or mediocre works of art—. . . their presence in this instance more closely conforms to the natural contours of any collective social action. The exhibition is entirely lacking in the kind of bureaucratic fiddle-faddle which characterizes the official exhibitions in the museums."[9]

The Stable Annuals were repeated until 1957. After the show that year, the participating artists terminated the series in the belief that despite art-world interest, the shows had ceased to be stimulating or informative enough to warrant the effort required to organize them. Moreover, it was felt that the need was to deal less with the New York School as a whole and more with the outstanding artists in it. Some 250 different artists had shown in at least one Annual, and artists were beginning to worry about the rapid growth of the New York School and the decline in quality of the work as a whole.

Aside from the Stable Annuals, a number of group shows were consequential in the establishment of the second generation. The most important were three arranged respectively by Hess, Kyle Morris, and Schapiro. At the end of 1955, Hess organized a show of twenty-one young painters titled *U.S. Painting: Some Recent Directions*. The exhibition was held at the Stable Gallery and was followed by a lavishly illustrated, extended essay of the same name in the *Art News Annual*. The artists chosen by Hess were Bell, Blaine, Briggs, Brodie, Elaine de Kooning, de Niro, Dzubas, Forst, Frank-enthaler, Goldberg, Goodnough, Kahn, Mitchell, Stephen Pace, Pasilis, Porter, Rau-schenberg, Seymour Remenick, Resnick, Rivers, and Solomon. In his article on the painters, Hess wrote: "They have had to follow on the stage of public scrutiny the ap-plause and catcalls which have greeted Abstract-Expressionism since 1940. They have chosen to enter quietly, playing down their gifts. I feel convinced that among them are artists who will be accepted as internationally important and will rival any productions of this century." [10]

Following Hess's exhibition was another show at the Stable Gallery entitled *Vanguard 1955*, consisting of twenty painters selected by Morris at the request of the Walker Art Center in Minneapolis (where the show was first on display). A number of the artists picked by Morris were in Hess's show: Goldberg, Mitchell, Briggs, Pace, and Frankenthaler. Others were Diebenkorn, Dugmore, Grillo, Angelo Ippolito, Parker, Schueler, and Stefanelli. Morris was asked to select painters of promise whose reputa-tions were not yet securely established and was given a completely free hand. He wrote:

> Essentially this selection has been shaped by the belief I hold that the most signifi-cant painting development in recent years has been in the work called "abstract expressionism." . . . I have avoided saying "movement" because, although there may be an overlapping in a general attitude toward painting, the works of these artists reveal a personal searching, urgent and vital, and it seems to me that they fall outside of the idea of a school or movement or manifesto. [11]

On the whole, the shows organized by Hess and Morris reflect a New York School consensus as to who were the best and most provocative young painters at the mid-point of the fifties. [12] The two shows were somewhat different, partly because of differences in taste, and also because the artists Morris selected tended to have emerged somewhat later than those chosen by Hess, and several in Morris's show lived outside of New York.

In 1957, Schapiro selected a show entitled *Artists of the New York School: Second Generation*. Among those chosen were Frankenthaler and Mitchell (who were included in Hess's and Morris's shows); Brodie, Elaine de Kooning, de Niro, Forst, Goodnough, Kahn, Pasilis, Rauschenberg, Resnick, and Solomon (who were included in Hess's show); and Jean Follett, Hartigan, Johns, Johnson, Kaprow, Leslie, Müller, and Segal. It was Johns, who had not yet had a one-person show, whose work generated the greatest interest and controversy. Indeed, it was primarily because of his emergence that the show took on historic significance.

206, 207

As the fifties progressed, *Art News*, its policy increasingly influenced by Hess, be-came the "family magazine" of the New York School, and specifically of de Kooning, his followers, and friends. It is noteworthy that in 1952, when the editors of *Art News* were asked to choose their ten favorite American paintings of the twentieth century, only two were by Abstract Expressionists: Pollock and Kline. [13] Yet in the same year, Hess chided the Carnegie Institute for its neglect of the second generation generally in

206 Helen Frankenthaler, *Mount Sinai,* 1956.
30″ x 30″. Neuberger Museum, State University
of New York at Purchase.

207 Joan Mitchell, *Untitled,* 1960.
71¹/₈″ x 63″.
Philadelphia Museum of Art.

selecting its prestigious show, and specifically, for omitting Rivers, de Niro, Goodnough, and Freilicher.[14] Hess continued his support of the New York School in numerous articles throughout the fifties.

Hess also hired artists of the second generation as critics. They and others, many young poets and friends of the artists, soon began to write extended articles on painters and sculptors in the New York School. Among the younger artists featured in 1954 were Rivers (by Porter); in 1955, Porter (by O'Hara) and Stankiewicz (by Porter); in 1956, Freilicher (by Porter); in 1957, Rivers (by Parker Tyler), Mitchell (by me), and Resnick, (by Campbell); in 1958, de Niro (by Eleanor C. Munro) and Bell (by Schuyler); in 1959, Blaine (by Campbell); and in 1960, Elaine de Kooning (by Campbell).[15] Lengthy articles were also written on major tendencies in second-generation art, the most important of which were on figurative art by Elaine de Kooning and Abstract Impressionism by Finkelstein.[16] The young critics also began to weight Art News's annual lists of the "Ten Best" one-man shows in favor of their generation. Included were Rivers (1952); Mitchell (1955); Rivers and Elaine de Kooning (1956); Elaine de Kooning, Mitchell, and Resnick (1957); Porter and Goodnough (1958); Goodnough (1959); and Elaine de Kooning (1960).[17]

Art News's policy toward young artists can be deduced from an analysis of Hess's U.S. Painting: Some Recent Directions show in 1955. All but one of the twenty-one painters he selected were more or less gestural (more rather than less); ten used clearly recognizable images; twenty lived in New York City and its environs; twelve had studied with Hofmann and three more had significant contact with his ideas; fourteen were members of three galleries or had shown in them (seven in the Tibor de Nagy, four in the Hansa, and three in the Stable); six had been selected by Greenberg and Schapiro for the New Talent show at the Kootz Gallery in 1950; seven had shown in the Ninth Street Show in 1951; and three (all of whom painted representationally) were critics for Art News. Nine had major articles published about their work in the magazine during the fifties (two for Rivers). On the annual lists of ten best one-man shows (from 1952 to 1960), Elaine de Kooning appeared three times; Rivers and Mitchell, twice; Resnick, Porter and Goodnough, once.

In 1958, Art News broadened its policy to deal more fully with assemblage, or what was called Neo-Dada at the time. This move was made not out of sympathy but a fear of growing stale. Rauschenberg had been featured by Hess earlier, and Johns was given a cover of Art News in 1958.[18] Nicolas Calas's article entitled "ContiNuance" (1959), dealing with Rivers, Rauschenberg, and Johns, exemplified the shift.[19] Art News also allowed Kaprow to proselytize for Environments and Happenings.[20]

In comparison to Art News, Art Digest (whose name was changed to Arts Digest in 1954, and Arts in 1955) was broader and less focused in its recognition of the second generation.[21] That began to be forthcoming after 1951, and particularly after 1953, when articles began to appear on young artists; the first was by Geist on Stankiewicz's junk sculpture.[22] In 1954, possibly because of the influence of Crehan, recently promoted to managing editor, the magazine featured artists identified with Still: Edward Corbett,

Schueler, and Dugmore.[23] There was a lapse of some four years before another article on a second-generation artist appeared, that on Solomon (1958), followed by one on Müller (1959), and on Mark di Suvero (1960).[24] In 1955, *Arts* initiated a monthly section entitled "Month in Review," written by different critics who covered what they considered the most important shows. Most of the articles dealt with major museum and gallery shows of old and modern masters. A large proportion of the rest were devoted to the New York School. Among the younger artists singled out were Goldberg, Mitchell, Pasilis, Blaine, Goodnough, Stankiewicz, Pearlstein, Stankiewicz, again, Resnick, Johnson, Kelly, Porter, and Solomon.[25]

The aesthetic policy of *Arts* during the second half of the fifties was substantially shaped by Kramer. He was not sympathetic to Abstract Expressionism generally, but he acknowledged its energy and worldwide influence, and he tended to single out for acclaim young artists in the New York School. Within months of becoming managing editor in 1955, he wrote about the Carnegie International, that "it is the American painters who loom largest . . . the American 'look' which is everywhere visible in the abstract paintings from Europe."[26] Toward the end of the fifties, Kramer became increasingly hostile to Abstract Expressionism, condemning it for its anarchic failure of vision and abdication of craft on the one hand, and on the other, for having become the established avant-garde.[27] As he summed it up: "The entire 'school' of painting that was spawned by the immense influence and prestige that de Kooning's art wielded in New York in the fifties . . . has, less than a decade later, fallen into a complete disarray."[28] What replaced it in interest, as Kramer saw it, was an extreme reductionist abstraction, e.g., that of Kelly, and an equally extreme realism, e.g., that of Pearlstein.[29]

Of the young critics who emerged in the fifties, one of the most consistent and sympathetic on behalf of the New York School was Ashton, critic for *Art Digest* (1951 to 1956); *Arts and Architecture* (1956 to 1967); and the *New York Times* (1955 to 1960). She began to focus on the art of the second generation in 1956, favoring artists who were, in her opinion, "experimental but value-conscious," professional and craftsmanlike,[30] and above all lyrical, that is, artists who valued beauty and subtlety, like Guston,[31] and, among younger artists, Mitchell and Hartigan.[32]

In 1954, *Art in America* devoted an issue to "New Talent" in what became an annual February policy. The selection was too much of a mixed bag to count for much, but among the New York artists featured were Hartigan (1954); John Hultberg, Rivers, and Stankiewicz (1956); Goldberg, Kelly, and Frankenthaler (1957); Müller and Schueler (1958); Jean Follett, Gabriel Kohn, Jack Youngerman, and Kaprow (1959); Myron Stout and Alfred Jensen (1960).[33]

In 1958, Pavia began to publish *It Is*, a magazine written mainly by the gestural abstract artists of the New York School. *It Is* consisted of color and half-tone reproductions, statements, and articles. Although the magazine aimed to promote Abstract Expressionism, the five issues that appeared between 1958 and 1960 turned out to be more than anything else a valuable historical documentation of the three years.[34]

In the fall of 1956, Fitzsimmons started a magazine, *European Art This Month*. In

1958, he changed the name to *Art International* and expanded the coverage to include American art, publishing articles, reviews, and a monthly "New York Letter," at first by Rubin, Goossen, and Alloway, and by the end of 1960 by Greenberg, Rosenblum, and me, among others. We critics repeatedly called attention to "the extraordinary high caliber of the *second generation* of New York School painters."[35] In 1960, *Art International* also began to publish articles on younger American painters, the first of which was on Dan Rice (by Jonathan Williams); followed by Louis and Noland (by Greenberg) and Johns (by Rosenblum),[36] and to reproduce their works on its covers: Stella (Number 1, 1960); Parker (25 May 1960); and Johns (24 September 1960).

Art writers of the fifties also began to include second-generation artists in their books on contemporary art. In 1956, Rudi Blesh published *Modern Art USA: Men, Rebellion, Conquest, 1900–1956,* which he ended by calling attention to emerging young artists.[37] So did Sam Hunter two years later in the American section of a lavishly illustrated book entitled *Art Since 1945,* composed of chapters on various countries and regions.[38] The most important book published on the second generation during the fifties was *School of New York: Some Younger Artists* (1959), a compilation of illustrated essays on eleven artists, introduced by Friedman. The artists included were Frankenthaler, Goodnough, Hartigan, Johns, Leslie, Mitchell, Parker, Rauschenberg, Rivers, Schueler, and Stankiewicz.[39] It was not Friedman's intention to make a critical choice, but in 1959, he could not help but try to feature the best artists of the second generation. His selection typified in general the taste of the New York School and its audience at that time.

The most influential taste-maker in matters of modern art in America (and highly respected abroad) was the Museum of Modern Art under the leadership of Alfred H. Barr, Jr. The museum had recognized the first generation in its *Fifteen Americans* show of 1952, one of a prestigious series organized by Dorothy C. Miller.[40] Indeed, as the fifties progressed, the Museum of Modern Art was widely seen as a champion of the New York School, so much so that in 1959, England's *Times Literary Supplement* noted "that the current style of painting known as Abstract Expressionism radiates the world over from Manhattan Island, more specifically from West Fifty-third Street, where the Museum of Modern Art stands as the Parthenon on this particular acropolis."[41] As early as 1950, the museum began to exhibit second-generation artists in a series of three-man *New Talent* shows.[42] But it was not until 1956 that the museum "officially" accepted four second-generation painters—Briggs, Francis, Hartigan, and Rivers—by including them in a *12 Americans* show. This event probably more than any other signaled—as it contributed to—the arrival of the younger New York School artists.[43]

208, 209

But the museum did much more on behalf of the New York School, building its reputation internationally as only that museum could do.[44] In 1957, it chose the Americans represented at the Fourth Bienal at São Paulo, Brazil. One section was a large exhibition of Pollock's pictures; the other, consisting of five works each by three sculptors and five painters, included Hartigan and Rivers. In 1958, the museum organized a major show of Abstract Expressionist painting, composed of fifteen older artists and two

208   Larry Rivers, *Berdie in a Red Shawl,* 1953.
53″ x 65″. Whitney Museum of American Art, New York.

younger ones, Hartigan and Francis. Entitled *The New American Painting,* the show
circulated throughout Europe, visiting Basel, Milan, Berlin, Brussels, Paris, London,
and other cities, and generating enormous interest in them all.[45] Contributing further to
Europe's recognition of the New York School was the enormous impact made by the
American section at *II Documenta '59,* in Kassel, Germany, the whole show consisting
of works by some 340 artists.[46] The American section, composed of twenty-seven
painters and seven sculptors, was chosen by Porter McCray of the Museum of Modern
Art. It included the second-generation painters Bluhm, Francis, Frankenthaler, Goldberg, Hartigan, Mitchell, and Rauschenberg.

 Shows such as *The New American Painting* and *II Documenta '59* established the international reputation of the New York School. This helped prompt the prestigious *Times Literary Supplement* to devote a special number to "The American Imagination: Its Strength and Scope" (which in itself contributed to the success of American art). The *TLS* proclaimed that "it is true to say that the flowering of the American imagination has been the chief event in the sphere of living art since the end of the First World War." [47]

In 1959, under the auspices of the museum's international program, Peter Selz chose twelve Americans for the first *Paris Biennale*, a show of artists under thirty-five years of age. Most were Californians, but also included were Frankenthaler, who won the first prize, and Rauschenberg. In the same year, the International Council recommended to the authorities of the *Fifth São Paulo Bienal* that the Minneapolis Institute of Art select the United States section. It consisted of three parts: one-man shows of the works of David Smith and Guston, and *Ten Painters and Sculptors*, which included Francis, Frankenthaler, Goldberg, Gabriel Kohn, Leslie, Mitchell, and Rauschenberg.

As important as the Museum of Modern Art's impact internationally was its influ-

209   Grace Hartigan, *Shop Window,* 1955.
63″ x 81″. Neuberger Museum, State University of New York at Purchase.

ence domestically. Not all of its shows were significant. The *New Images of Man* exhibition[48] in the fall of 1959 made little lasting impression, but the *Sixteen Americans*[49] which followed it in the winter created enormous interest. With this show the museum conferred its recognition on the non- and anti-gestural styles of Kelly and Stella (whose black pictures provoked immediate controversy), and on the so-called Neo-Dadas Johns, Rauschenberg, and Stankiewicz, and related assemblagist Louise Nevelson. It is noteworthy that only one gesture painter of the New York School, Leslie, was selected,

210

210  Alfred Leslie, *#3339 Fountain,* 1958.
60″ x 66″. Harry N. Abrams Family Collection, New York.

indicating that the decision-makers at the museum had lost interest in that tendency.

The Whitney Museum began to include numbers of second-generation artists in its large annual exhibitions after 1955. But it was not until two years later that its support began to count. In its *Young America 1957* show of thirty artists under thirty-five years of age, a third were New Yorkers, among them Rosemarie Beck, Frankenthaler, Goldberg, Angelo Ippolito, Paul Jenkins, Kelly, Müller, and Stankiewicz.[50] The percentage looms even larger when it is considered that the Whitney's policy was to give coverage to all styles and regions. In 1958, of the painters represented in the *Nature in Abstraction* show, roughly one-sixth were second generation, including Beck, Frankenthaler, Goodnough, Ippolito, Jenkins, Mitchell, and Schueler.[51] *Young America 1960*, consisting of thirty painters, included eleven identified with the New York School, among them Alex Katz.[52] The Solomon R. Guggenheim Museum was relatively inactive during the fifties, awaiting the opening of its new building by Frank Lloyd Wright at the end of 1959. The museum did not deal adequately with advanced American art until 1961, when it presented its massive *American Abstract Expressionists and Imagists* show, consisting of sixty-four painters of whom twenty were born after 1920.[53]

Assemblage was first recognized by the Museum of Modern Art in its *Sixteen Americans* show in 1959. Individual young artists had already made some reputation for themselves, notably Stankiewicz and Rauschenberg. They were joined by Johns in 1957, when his pictures were first shown at the Jewish Museum. The Castelli Gallery soon gave him a show; *Art News* reproduced *Target* on its cover in January 1958; Barr acquired work for the Museum of Modern Art. Johns was also included in a special section of the Venice Biennale, and at the Carnegie International, he was the only American to win a prize.[54] In 1960, a two-part show entitled *New Media—New Forms* was presented at the Jackson Gallery.[55] The following year, the Museum of Modern Art conferred its "official" stamp of approval in its comprehensive *The Art of Assemblage* show, organized by Seitz, who also wrote the book-size catalogue. In 1958, Kaprow began to make his bid to achieve recognition for Environments and Happenings by publishing articles and letters in *Art News*, *It Is*, and *Arts*.

There was a slow build-up of understanding and appreciation of alternatives to gesture painting, beginning in 1955 with the publication of Greenberg's " 'American-Type' Painting."[56] Hard-edge abstraction began to be noticed with Kelly's inclusion in the *Young America 1957* show at the Whitney Museum, but it was not until the end of the following year, when Gordon Washburn selected Kelly, Stout, and Nassos Daphnis for the Carnegie International Exhibition, that widespread interest was generated. In an article on the show, Kramer commented on Washburn's "keen eye in selecting the work of younger or lesser known artists. . . . Indeed, it is precisely this *currency* which characterizes the International as an exhibition."[57] The implication was that hard-edge abstraction's time had come.[58] Kelly's "official" recognition came with his inclusion in the *Sixteen Americans* show at the Museum of Modern Art.

Greenberg was largely responsible for the acceptance of the stain painting of Louis and Noland, by getting them shows at the French and Company Gallery in 1959 and

211

211   Robert Rauschenberg, *Winter Pool,* 1959.
88¹/₂″ x 58¹/₂″ x 3″. Collection, Mr. and Mrs. Victor W. Ganz, New York.

1960 and by featuring them in major articles in 1960 and 1962.[59] But Greenberg's reputation had declined somewhat in the late fifties. It was bolstered when younger critics such as William S. Rubin began to deal seriously with his ideas and with color-field painting. By 1960, Rubin had accepted Greenberg's contention that the de Kooning-Kline influence was a losing proposition. He was taken, moreover, with Greenberg's "preference for the directions pointed by Still and Newman [which] showed extraordinary prophetic insight in terms of where the younger painters of quality find themselves today."[60] Rubin went on to say that Louis's last show "seemed to me one of the most significant in years. . . . he may be emerging with a painterly profile comparable in stature to those of the 'first wave' pioneers."[61] Greenberg's influence grew with the publication of *Art and Culture*, 1961,[62] so much so that he became the mentor of a new generation of critics; "the dean of post-war American critics," as Rubin called him.[63]

Although the *American Abstract Expressionists and Imagists* show at the Guggenheim Museum in 1961 was meant to deal with the movement as a whole, it ended up promoting the Imagist wing, and that was part of the intention of its organizer, H. Harvard Arnason. He not only established a new category, "imagism," by which he meant abstract painting composed of simple forms and flat colors, e.g., Newman's, Rothko's, or Parker's, but in his introduction to the catalogue he called attention to the "continually increasing influence of the 'Imagist' wing of 'Abstract Expressionism.' "[64]

During the fifties, outside of New York City, there emerged two movements that achieved national recognition: one, the San Francisco figurative school; the other, the Chicago Monster Roster. The Chicagoans became known in New York beginning in 1954, the year Leon Golub and George Cohen were first shown there. Articles in art magazines kept the New York School informed of them,[65] but it was not until 1959 that they took the limelight momentarily in the *New Images of Man* show organized by Peter Selz at the Museum of Modern Art, which included Cosmo Campoli, Golub, and H. C. Westermann. Selz promoted the notion that man in a post-Buchenwald-Hiroshima age was plagued by existential feelings of despair, anxiety, and solitude.[66] The critical response to the idea of the show was generally negative, although individual artists in it were acclaimed.[67] Diebenkorn was also in the *New Images of Man* show. He and, to a lesser degree, Park and Bischoff became known in New York in 1957 as the leaders of a school of figurative artists in San Francisco who had created their own variant of gestural realism.[68]

In conclusion, with regard to the exposure of the paintings and sculptures of the second generation of the New York School to the public—in galleries, museums, and art periodicals—1956 can be considered the "breakthrough" year. For example, the Stable Gallery presented Hess's *U.S. Paintings: Some Recent Directions* and Morris's *Vanguard 1955*; and the Museum of Modern Art, its *12 Americans* show. Subsequently, promotional activities only intensified and broadened, particularly with the proliferation of the Tenth Street galleries.

At this time, too, critics, curators, and other taste-makers began to shift from general support of the second generation to critical selection, and a consensus as to who was

212   Robert Goodnough, *Summer III,* 1959.
50″ x 66″. Whitney Museum of American Art, New York.

best developed. It is difficult to determine why one artist received greater recognition than another. Undoubtedly the quality of the work was largely responsible—even though there are no demonstrable criteria. But there were other factors. Certain significant occurrences, more or less independent of each other, notably exhibitions and publications, contributed to the formation of the consensus. Among them, as I see it, were participation in the *New Talent* show, selected by Greenberg and Shapiro; the Ninth Street Show; Hess's *U.S. Painting: Some Recent Directions*; the shows organized by the Museum of Modern Art—*12 Americans, The New American Painting, II Documenta '59,* and *Sixteen Americans*; and inclusion in B. H. Friedman's *School of New York: Some Younger Artists.* Of the many artists dealt with in this study, seven can be singled out because they more than their colleagues were included in the above events. They were Frankenthaler, Goodnough, Hartigan, Leslie, Mitchell, Rauschenberg, and Rivers. They can be taken to represent what the New York School in the fifties considered the best and liveliest artists of the second generation.[69]

# Notes

1. "The Metropolitan and Modern Art," *Life*, 15 January 1951, p. 34. The caption to the photograph read: "Irascible Group of Advanced Artists Led Fight Against Show." See Sandler, *The Triumph of American Painting*, frontispiece and p. 213.

2. Critics generally were a conservative lot; the tastes of those writing for seven leading periodicals could be gauged in 1952 when each was asked to select his ten favorite American paintings since 1900 for a show at the Wildenstein Gallery. The leaders were John Marin and Edward Hopper (with five votes); then Ben Shahn and George Bellows (with four votes); then Stuart Davis, Charles Demuth, Marsden Hartley, Lyonel Feininger, and Willem de Kooning (with three votes); followed by Arshile Gorky, Karl Knaths, Loren MacIver, Mark Tobey, Max Weber, and Andrew Wyeth (with two votes each). Aside from Gorky and de Kooning, the other leading Abstract Expressionists chosen were Baziotes, Hofmann, Kline, and Pollock (with only one vote). See "Critics: They Know What They Like," *Art Digest*, 1 March 1952, pp. 8–9, and Ad Reinhardt, "Our Favorites," *Art News*, March 1952, pp. 28–29, 67.

3. Clement Greenberg, "Art," *Nation*, 8 March 1947, p. 284. Many of Blaine's fellow artists shared Greenberg's high opinion of her. Rivers and Freilicher even studied with her.

4. Clement Greenberg, "Art," *Nation*, 16 April 1949, pp. 453–54.

5. Hess, "Seeing the Young New Yorkers," p. 23.

6. Motherwell and Reinhardt, eds., *Modern Artists in America*, p. 6.

7. Clement Greenberg, Statement, *New York Artists Annual*, exhibition announcement (New York: Stable Gallery, 1953), unpaginated.

8. Ibid.

9. Kramer, "As Artists See Themselves: The Stable Show," *Arts*, June 1956, p. 14.

10. Hess, "U.S. Painting: Some Recent Directions," p. 81.

11. Kyle Morris, Introduction, *Vanguard 1955*, exhibition catalogue (New York: Stable Gallery, 1955), unpaginated.

12. For example, when in 1956, the prestigious Sidney Janis Gallery which by then represented most of the pioneers of Abstract Expressionism presented a *Four Americans* exhibition of second-generation painters, it consisted of Goodnough, Mitchell, Goldberg, and Brach.

13. See note 2.

14. Thomas B. Hess, "Miracle at Schenley Park," *Art News*, November 1952, p. 30. Other early articles by Hess on second-generation artists were "Seeing the Young New Yorkers," pp. 23, 60, and "Invited Guests at the Whitney," *Art News*, December 1950, pp. 32–33, 63.

15. Fairfield Porter, "Rivers Paints a Picture," *Art News*, January 1954, pp. 56–59, 81–83; O'Hara, "Porter Paints a Picture," pp. 38–41, 66–67; Porter, "Stankiewicz Makes a Sculpture," pp. 36–39, 62–63; Porter, "Jane Freilicher Paints a Picture," pp. 46–49, 65–66; Parker Tyler, "The Purple-patch of Fetichism," *Art News*, March 1957, pp. 40–43, 52–53 (on Larry Rivers); Sandler, "Mitchell Paints a Picture," pp. 44–47, 69–70; Lawrence Campbell, "Resnick Paints a Picture," *Art News*, December 1957, pp. 38–66; Eleanor C. Munro, "De Niro Works on a Series of Pictures," *Art News*, May 1958, pp. 38–41, 48–50; James Schuyler, "Bell Paints a Picture," *Art News*, September 1958, pp. 42–45, 61–62; Campbell, "Blaine Paints a Picture," pp. 38–41, 61–62; Lawrence Campbell, "Elaine de Kooning Paints a Picture," *Art News*, December 1960, pp. 40–44, 61–63.

16. De Kooning, "Subject: What, How or Who?" and Finkelstein, "New Look: Abstract-Impressionism."

17. "The Year's Best: 1952," *Art News*, January 1953, p. 43; A[lfred] F[rankfurter], "The Year's Best: 1955," *Art News*, January 1956, p. 40; T[homas] B. H[ess], "Editorial: The Year's Best: 1956," *Art News*, January 1957, p. 27; T[homas] B. H[ess], "The Year's Best: 1957," *Art*

*News*, January 1958, pp. 45, 62; T[homas] B. H[ess], "The Year's Best: 1958," *Art News*, January 1959, pp. 44–45; A[lfred] F[rankfurter], "Editorial: The Year's Best: 1959," *Art News*, January 1960, p. 23; T[homas] B. H[ess], "Editorial: The Year's Best: 1960," *Art News*, January 1961, p. 25.

18. Jasper Johns's *Target*, *Art News* cover, January 1958. The caption on p. 5 characterized it as "Neo-Dada" and related it to the work of "such better known colleagues as Rauschenberg, Twombly, Kaprow, and Ray Johnson."

19. Nicolas Calas, "ContiNuance," *Art News*, February 1959, pp. 36–39.

20. See Kaprow, "The Legacy of Jackson Pollock."

21. Belle Krasne was appointed editor in 1951 and remained in that capacity until 15 February 1954, when Jonathan Marshall assumed the position of publisher, retaining Crehan as managing editor until 1 March 1955. In that month, Marshall became editor and publisher, and Hilton Kramer was made second in command as feature editor, promoted on 15 September 1955 to managing editor, and in October 1958 to editor. Among the critics whose writings appeared in *Art Digest*, *Arts Digest*, and *Arts*, were Dore Ashton, Paul Brach, James Fitzsimmons, Sidney Geist, Sam Feinstein, Sam Hunter, Martica Sawin, Robert Rosenblum, Al Newbill, Leo Steinberg, Barbara Butler, Vincent Longo, Anita Ventura, Bernard Chaet, James Mellow, Helen De Mott, and Sidney Tillim.

22. Sidney Geist, "Stankiewicz: Miracle in the Scrapheap," *Art Digest*, 1 December 1953, p. 10.

23. Mary Fuller, "Edward Corbett: A Profile," *Art Digest*, 1 January 1954, pp. 21–23; Sam Feinstein, "Jon Schueler: A Vision of Nature," *Art Digest*, 1 March 1954, pp. 14, 25; and C[rehan], "Edward Dugmore," *Arts Digest*, 15 October 1954, p. 9.

24. Martica Sawin, "Hyde Solomon," *Arts*, November 1958, pp. 38–43; Sawin, "Jan Müller; 1922–1958," *Arts*, February 1959, pp. 38–45; Geist, "A New Sculptor: Mark di Suvero," *Arts*, December 1960, pp. 40–43.

25. Leo Steinberg, January 1956, pp. 46–47 (on Goldberg, Mitchell, Pasilis, Blaine, and Goodnough); Hilton Kramer, December 1956, pp. 47–48 (on Stankiewicz); Hilton Kramer, March 1957, pp. 48–49 (on Pearlstein); Hilton Kramer, January 1959, pp. 50–51 (on Stankiewicz); Martica Sawin, March 1959, pp. 47–49 (on Resnick and Johnson); Sidney Tillim, October 1959, pp. 48–50 (on Kelly); Sidney Tillim, December 1960, pp. 45–47 (on Porter and Solomon).

In 1957, *Arts* began to publish *Arts Yearbook*. The third annual, titled *Paris/New York* (1959), included color reproductions of works by "24 Painters of the 1950s," among them Müller, Johnson, Follett, and Pearlstein. The other articles were mostly devoted to contemporary masters but included Sidney Tillim, "Profile: Ellsworth Kelly," and Martica Sawin, "Profile: Richard Stankiewicz." *Arts Yearbook 4* (1960) contained an article, "Artists on the Current Scene: A portfolio of notable paintings and sculpture by American artists," which featured Kohn, Chamberlain, and Noland.

26. Hilton Kramer, "Pittsburgh's International," *Arts*, November 1955, pp. 18–20.

27. See Hilton Kramer, "Month in Review," *Arts*, September 1959, p. 56; "Critics of American Painting," *Arts*, October 1959, pp. 26–29; and "Editorial: The Coming Political Breakthrough," *Arts*, January 1960, p. 13.

28. Hilton Kramer, "Notes on Painting in New York," *Arts Yearbook: New York: The Art World* 7 (1964): 11–12.

29. Ibid., p. 10.

30. Dore Ashton, "Art," *Arts and Architecture*, February 1956, p. 10.

31. Dore Ashton, "Art," *Arts and Architecture*, March 1956, pp. 15, 43.

32. See Dore Ashton, "Some Lyricists of the New York School," *Art News and Review* 22 (November 1958): 3, 8. In 1959, Ashton with Bernard Dorival chose the American section of an exhibition titled *New York and Paris: Paintings of the 1950s* at the Museum of Fine Arts, Hous-

ton, Texas. Of the fifteen artists they selected, two were of the second generation: Mitchell and Hartigan.

33. John I. H. Baur, "George Hartigan," *Art in America*, Winter 1954, pp. 18–19 (for a period of time Hartigan replaced Grace with George as her first name); "Painters," *Art in America*, February 1956, pp. 22–23 (Hultberg), p. 24 (Rivers), and "Sculptors," *Art in America*, February 1956, pp. 46–47 (Stankiewicz); "New Talent in the U.S.A.: Painters," *Art in America*, February 1957, p. 17 (Goldberg), p. 21 (Kelly), pp. 28–29 (Frankenthaler); "New Talent in the U.S.A.," *Art in America*, Spring 1958, p. 16 (Müller), p. 22 (Schueler); "New Talent in the U.S.A. 1959," *Art in America* 1 (1959): 39 (Follett), p. 43 (Kohn), p. 47 (Youngerman), p. 58 (Kaprow); "New Talent U.S.A.," *Art in America* 1 (1960): 22 (Stout), p. 26 (Jensen).

34. *It Is* 1 (Spring 1958); *It Is* 2 (Autumn 1958); *It Is* 3 (Spring 1959); *It Is* 4 (Autumn 1959); *It Is* 5 (Spring 1960). A sixth issue of *It Is* was published in the autumn of 1965.

35. William S. Rubin, "Pittsburgh's Carnegie International," *Art International* 3, no. 1–2 (1959): 19.

36. Jonathan Williams, "The Paintings of Dan Rice," *Art International* 4, no. 1 (1960): 54–56; Greenberg, "Louis and Noland"; and Robert Rosenblum, "Jasper Johns," *Art International*, 25 September 1960, pp. 75–77.

37. Rudi Blesh, *Modern Art USA: Men, Rebellion, Conquest, 1900–1956* (New York: Alfred A. Knopf, 1956), pp. 291–94. Blesh singled out Mitchell, Kahn, Goodnough, Brach, and Stankiewicz, and ex-students of the California School of Fine Arts, such as Briggs, Grillo, Diebenkorn, Francis, and Hultberg, with special emphasis on Hultberg and Francis.

38. Sam Hunter, "USA," in *Art Since 1945* (New York: Harry N. Abrams, 1958), pp. 328–30. Hunter dealt with Hartigan, Mitchell, Leslie, Resnick, Francis, and Frankenthaler, and reproduced works by Francis and Hartigan. Hunter, in *Modern American Painting and Sculpture* (New York: Laurel Edition, Dell Publishing Company, 1959), did not discuss any artist of the second generation but included colorplates of works by Helen Frankenthaler and Grace Hartigan.

39. B. H. Friedman, ed., *School of New York: Some Younger Artists* (New York: Grove Press, 1959). The writers were as follows: Sonya Rudikoff on Helen Frankenthaler; Barbara Guest on Robert Goodnough; Emily Dennis on Grace Hartigan; Ben Heller on Jasper Johns; James Schuyler on Alfred Leslie; Irving Sandler on Joan Mitchell; Bill Godden on Raymond Parker; David Myers on Robert Rauschenberg; Frank O'Hara on Larry Rivers; Alastair Reid on Jon Schueler; and Fairfield Porter on Richard Stankiewicz.

40. Dorothy C. Miller, ed., *Fifteen Americans*, exhibition catalogue (New York: Museum of Modern Art, 1952).

41. "The Realist Predicament: Past and Present Traditions of the National Scene," *Times Literary Supplement*, 6 November 1959, p. xxix.

42. The first of these exhibitions consisted of Raymond Parker, William King, and Seymour Drumlevitch. Later shows included John Hultberg (1952); Nora Speyer (1956); and Gabriel Kohn and Miriam Schapiro (1957).

43. Dorothy C. Miller, ed., *12 Americans*, exhibition catalogue (New York: Museum of Modern Art, 1956). Also represented in the show were James Brooks, Philip Guston, and Franz Kline, three older gesture painters who emerged somewhat later than the originators of the movement.

Sam Francis is a special case. After his first show in Paris in 1952, Francis achieved a greater reputation in Europe than any member of the first generation with the possible exception of Pollock. (The only American whose fame surpassed Francis's was Tobey, another West Coast painter.) This recognition was augmented by the active sponsorship of the Museum of Modern Art, which in 1955 was the first public institution to acquire his work, introducing it to New York, and which included him not only in the *12 Americans* but in *The New American Painting*, 1958–59, which with the exception of him and Hartigan was a first-generation show. The powerful support that Francis had abroad and at home generated considerable resentment within the New York School, and naturally so, since it was widely believed that Francis's reputation as the "American" painter of the postwar era was based more on the fact that he lived in Paris than on the quality of his work, which, no matter how high, was not considered on a par with a Gorky, a Rothko, or a Still, all of whom influenced him. More than that, it was accepted by many that Francis's lack of identification with the New York School was partly accountable for his success, since the cultural institutions that supported the School of Paris were engaged in an art political struggle to regain world leadership in the visual arts. By establishing Francis and Tobey as the "American" painters, and the French went so far as to invent an École du Pacifique, the stature of the New York School would be diminished.

44. The Museum of Modern Art was not alone in introducing American vanguard art abroad. In 1951, Leo Castelli and Sidney Janis selected a show entitled *American Vanguard* which was exhibited at the Sidney Janis Gallery, New York, and the Galerie de France, Paris. Twenty artists were represented, including Robert Goodnough and Alfred Russell.

An important source of information was Meyer Schapiro, "The Younger American Painters of Today," *Listener* 60 (January 1956): 146–47. Although Schapiro concentrated on the first generation, he called attention to Robert de Niro, Wolf Kahn, and Gandy Brodie.

45. *The New American Painting* (New York: Museum of Modern Art, 1959).

46. See John Anthony Thwaites, "Report on Documenta II," *Arts*, November 1959, pp. 44–49.

47. "Wholly American" (an editorial), *Times Literary Supplement*, 6 November 1959, p. 643. Hilton Kramer was so appalled by the *TLS*'s sympathetic treatment of Abstract Expressionism that he protested in an "Editorial," *Arts*, December 1959, p. 15:

> The *Times Literary Supplement* speaks for the cultivated Briton at his snobbish best. It represents itself as standing for responsible literary taste, for scrupulous scholarship in history and the arts and for literary and artistic values of a seriousness which precludes the least vulnerability to passing fads. Many Americans read the *TLS* as an aesthetic fairy tale in which "good" (classical learning, French literature and truly interesting historical personalities) always triumphs over "evil" (boorish American scholarship, contemporary novels and bothersome social issues).

48. Peter Selz, *New Images of Man*, exhibition catalogue (New York: Museum of Modern Art, 1959.

49. Dorothy C. Miller, ed., *Sixteen Americans*, exhibition catalogue (New York: Museum of Modern Art, 1959).

50. *Young America 1957*, exhibition catalogue (New York: Whitney Museum of American Art, 1957).

51. John I. H. Baur, *Nature in Abstraction*, exhibition catalogue (New York: Whitney Museum of American Art, 1958).

52. *Young America 1960*, exhibition catalogue (New York: Whitney Museum of American Art, 1960).

53. H. H. Arnason, *American Abstract Expressionists and Imagists*, exhibition catalogue (New York: Solomon R. Guggenheim Museum, 1961). The twenty were Norman Bluhm, Jimmy Ernst, Sam Francis, Helen Frankenthaler, Michael Goldberg, Grace Hartigan, Al Held, Ralph Humphrey, Paul Jenkins, Jasper Johns, Ellsworth Kelly, Alfred Leslie, Joan Mitchell, Kenneth Noland, Raymond Parker, Robert Rauschenberg, William Ronald, Theodoros Stamos, Frank Stella, and Jack Youngerman. Milton Resnick, born 1917, was also included.

54. Critics quickly responded to Johns's work. See R[obert] R[osenblum], "In the Galleries," *Arts*, January 1958, pp. 54–55, and "Jasper Johns," pp. 75–77. (A drawing by Johns was reproduced on the cover of *Art International*, 25 September 1960.) Ben Heller, "Jasper Johns," in

Friedman, ed., *School of New York: Some Younger Artists*, pp. 30–35. Steinberg, "Jasper Johns," pp. 87–109, and *Jasper Johns*.

55. See Sandler, "Ash Can Revisited," a review of this show and the first major article on Assemblage.

56. See also Raymond Parker, "Intent Painting," *It Is* 2 (Autumn 1958): 8–9; and Paul Brach, "Statement," *It Is* 3 (Winter–Spring 1959): 26.

57. Hilton Kramer, "Report on the Carnegie International," *Arts*, January 1959, p. 32.

58. See Sidney Tillim, "What Happened to Geometry?" *Arts*, June 1959, pp. 33–44, which features Kelly, Leon Polk Smith, Stout, and Daphnis; Tillim, "Profile: Ellsworth Kelly,"; "Month in Review," *Arts*, October 1959, pp. 48–50, which acclaims Kelly; and Hilton Kramer, "Constructing the Absolute," *Arts*, May 1960, pp. 39, 41, which singles out Smith.

59. Greenberg, "Louis and Noland," pp. 26–29; and "After Abstract Expressionism," pp. 24–32.

60. William Rubin, "Younger American Painters," *Art International* 4, no. 1 (1960): 26. Rubin's attitude toward Barnett Newman changed after 1958. In his two-part article, "The New York School—Then and Now," *Art International*, March–April 1958 and May–June 1958, he does not even mention Newman.

61. Rubin, "Younger American Painters," p. 28.

62. Clement Greenberg, *Art and Culture: Critical Essays* (Boston: Beacon Press, 1961).

63. Rubin, "Younger American Painters," p. 26.

64. Arnason, Introduction, *American Abstract Expressionists and Imagists*, p. 24. The "imagist" tendency emerged even more clearly in two more shows. One was *Toward a New Abstraction*, organized by Ben Heller (New York: Jewish Museum, 1963), consisting of works by Brach, Held, Kelly, Louis, Noland, Ortman, Parker, Schapiro, and Stella. The other, organized by Clement Greenberg, was titled *Post Painterly Abstraction* (Los Angeles, Calif.: Los Angeles County Museum of Art, 1964); it contained thirty-one painters, including Dzubas, Francis, Frankenthaler, Held, Jensen, Kelly, Krushenick, Louis, Noland, Olitski, Parker, and Stella.

65. See Leon Golub, "A Critique of Abstract Expressionism," *College Art Journal* 14 (Winter 1955): 142–47; Malone and Selz, "Is There a New Chicago School?" pp. 36–39, 58–60; Peter Selz, "A New Imagery in American Painting," *College Art Journal* 15 (Summer 1956): 290–301; Thomas B. Folds, "The New Images of the Chicago Group," *Art News*, October 1959, pp. 40–41, 52–53.

66. Selz, *New Images of Man*, pp. 11–12.

67. See Manny Farber, "New Images of (ugh) Man," *Art News*, October 1959, pp. 38–39, 58; Jerrold Lanes, "Brief Treatise on Surplus Value; or, The Man Who Wasn't There," *Arts*, November 1959, pp. 28–35; and William S. Rubin, "New Images of Man," *Art International* 3, no. 9 (1959): 1–5.

68. See Herschel B. Chipp, "Diebenkorn Paints a Picture," *Art News*, May 1957, pp. 44–47, 54–55; "Figurative Painters in California," *Arts*, December 1957, pp. 26–27; "San Francisco," *Art News*, December 1957, p. 50; and Hilton Kramer, "Month in Review: Elmer Bischoff and the San Francisco School of 'Figuratives,' " *Arts*, January 1960, pp. 42–45.

69. I must stress that the estimation of the importance of certain events is mine alone. I have tried to be objective, but I can imagine other criteria of judgment which would yield different names.

# 13

# The New Academy

As THE FIFTIES progressed, the premises of Abstract Expressionism, particularly those of gesture painting both abstract and figurative, became increasingly known. Several of the innovating artists were metamorphosed from avant-garde pariahs into culture heroes, the latest masters, and a large number of artists at home and abroad submitted to their influence. This led to the growing belief that gesture painting had or was rapidly becoming an established style, and there ensued a controversy over whether it continued to be a viable tendency or had become an academic dead end.

Troublesome questions were raised. Could a valid Expressionist art be created in an established style? Or had Abstract Expressionism lapsed into empty bombast and decoration? Were the newcomers and perhaps even some of the pioneers becoming school artists, interested more in the joys of belonging than in the non-conformist struggle for personal expression, comfortably settled into style and thus deficient in ambition, daring, and originality? If they were, was this not a betrayal of the urgent purpose of the innovators, namely, to venture into the unknown? To put it another way: Was not the "professional" or craftsmanlike imitator, who was presumed to be interested more in an innovator's means of painting than in his (or any) vision, the enemy of originality and the exemplar of academicism? Was the painting of the followers really the issue of moments of inspiration or had it succumbed to habit, mannerism, or parody? Was not the similarity in the "look" of the pictures of so many artists proof of the latter? Could there be, as Reinhardt quipped, " 'Divine madness' in the third Abstract-Expressionist generation"?[1]

For most in the early wave, the answer to Reinhardt's question was: yes—at least until 1957 or 1958. A few believed that gesture painting by its very nature, if genuine of course, could not be academic. Tworkov defined it only as "painting that does not lean on references to recognizable objects on the one hand, nor on geometric patterning on the other." He insisted that it "has no rules, no specific character, attitude or face. It does not even exclude the use of representation or geometry. It merely claims to be able to do without them. As such it is now everybody's idea, which is academic when the idea is merely being demonstrated, but is non-academic if you realize that, given the idea, everything else in a picture still remains to be done—you cannot predict in advance what its look ought to be."[2]

But dissenting voices began to be raised. By the middle of the decade, Greenberg came to believe, as he announced at the Club, that gesture painting had become "timid, handsome, second generation . . . in a bad way."[3] Color-field abstraction had replaced it as the avant-garde direction. Others in the art world who were having doubts were not as clear as to the course advanced art was or ought to be taking; yet they felt increasingly uneasy about the mushrooming quantity of gesture painting and the concomitant decrease in its quality. They also questioned the intentions of the imitators. But such reservations were not publicized beyond the pale of the New York School until late in the fifties. Sympathetic to gesture painting and not sure that it had ceased to be radical, most of those who were becoming critical did not desire to make premature judgments that might subvert it.

Thus, it was those who believed that gesture painting still had potential for growth who had the first say in public. Most granted that a change in the art had occurred: a movement toward "consolidation" or "good painting." As they saw it, this did not constitute an academic betrayal but a necessary and healthy development. And yet, there was generally an element of defensiveness or ambiguity in their assertions. For example, Ferren, in reviewing the Stable Annual of 1955, remarked that it was "a parochial show," yet "singularly impervious to the traps of academic procedure." But he implied that if the participants were not academic, neither were they avant-garde. "From my chair, I see a general consolidation. What new frontiers there are are implicit developments rather than surprises." Ferren hastened to add: "Consolidation is a conquest too, and a meaningful one. . . . Abstract Expressionism has become more refined and relaxed, fewer nerves and more gray matter back of the eyes. In a word, better painted." Ferren concluded: "It could become an academy but it hasn't. It is a movement and it knows it. It does not think it is a school because it has no one technique."[4]

Ashton was more positive in her justification of consolidation. Maintaining that an international style of slapdash Abstract Expressionism was being proclaimed falsely as advanced art, she proposed that "the real *avant garde* today consist of those who have acknowledged the victories and lessons of the 20th-century revolution and who calmly develop in a progressive, but defined, line."[5] Ashton was critical of the eclecticism and derivativeness of many young artists, their cultivation of "elegant manners at the expense of magnificent dreams,"[6] but she acclaimed those who are "talented pros," concerned with craft, "with such old fashioned considerations as quality of paint, durability of technique, and possibilities of subtlety within painting."[7]

Hess was the most vocal champion of the second generation. As early as 1954, he noted a difference in attitude between the first and second generations. In his review of the third Stable Annual, he remarked that the work of his younger contributors on the whole was personal, professional, and provincial.[8] Two years later, Hess discussed the second-generation's proclivity for aesthetic incest which shaped the art produced—for the better, in his opinion, because "by stealing frequently from each other, painters . . . [quickly force an idea] to all possible mutations, . . . [which] can be used or discarded by anyone, . . . . This orients the individual to his basic talent, because he knows that alone remains his."[9]

Thus, Hess made a virtue of eclecticism, an attitude shared by many in the second generation, the idea being that choosing from diverse existing options could lead to individuality, if not originality.[10] At the time it seemed to, if only because artists and critics were willing to consider an artist's style on its own exclusive terms. A later generation would insist on seeing only a general tendency and not the individuals in it, and branding it all academic.

But Hess was also ambivalent. In 1956, he worried about the Stable Annual's "decline in vitality and variety," its forced look—for the first time. "The quantity of quality remains surprisingly high, but an air of good taste and conformity has been added." He concluded: "Perhaps the moment of inspired collective activity that such an exhibition marks has passed, and . . . [it] is undergoing the historical change of fossilization."[11] The artist-organizers of the Stable Annuals appear to have agreed with Hess, for they terminated the series in 1957.

But on the whole, Hess refused to accept the fact that Abstract Expressionism was a dying or dead orthodoxy. Instead, in 1957, he launched a vigorous attack on the detractors of gesture painting, particularly its former friends who were growing in number, as Hess acknowledged. His primary target was the idea that "the situation of 1950–55 *should* have changed as drastically as it did in 1945–50. And by not changing, has stopped living."[12] As Hess saw it, the model for this kind of thinking was the series of artistic revolutions that occurred in Paris from 1907 to 1937. The establishment of a school implied the need to overthrow it. But the situation of the New York School was different, closer to that of the Impressionists who created "a look that was not erased in the work of the following generation: Cézanne wanted to make something solid of Impressionism, not cut its throat; . . . The school was not overthrown like a tyrant, but spread like a tree, influencing artists throughout Europe and America and attracting them to its center (as New York art is doing today)."[13]

It followed that artists had to consciously relate their style to Abstract Expressionism in its varied manifestations—to know what was going on and to use such information to find their individual ways. However, the growth in size of the second generation made Hess nervous. He insisted with justification that bad art in no way invalidated good art. Still, he began to make distinctions, and he did so on the basis of how much young artists seemed to be aware of advanced art in New York. This led him to elevate artists who lived and worked there on the assumption that their close proximity to the center of creativity would enable them to better partake of its creative spirit and gain the information required to make independent moves.

Hess was justified in thinking that to be in the know, an artist had to be physically *in* the New York art scene. Artists in the "provinces" did get the word later, generally garbled, from *Art News*. The practice out-of-town was to execute variations of illustrations in magazines, as best they could, given the distortions in scale, color, and texture. The resulting pictures were more often than not well-crafted but made without understanding the premises of what was emulated and away from the pressures exerted by critical peers. However, the ranks of resident New York artists had grown so that it was obvious large numbers could only be academic followers who fabricated pictures in someone else's manner, with minor deviations to be sure, or who mixed the styles of others, contriving a measure of "originality."

Moreover, the "in group" of the New York School was rarely as critical as Hess would have liked to think. It was common to accept an artist's intention and not worry too much about the work it yielded. All too frequently value judgments were made on the basis of friendship, or social pressures and manipulation, or a sense of mission. Many devoted to the cause of American vanguard art, the alive art of one's generation, avoided making accusations of plagiarism or eclecticism or negative value judgments since internal arguments might break the ranks of artists, when holding together seemed necessary in the face of hostile public opinion, and would hurt the efforts to achieve public acceptance. However others, equally sympathetic to the New York School, questioned the continuing and even growing clannishness and the uncritical attitude that it bred. Goldwater asserted in 1959: "Given recent 'successes,' massive defense is not only no longer necessary, but positively harmful."[14] If artists refuse to make distinctions, they will abdicate this essential activity to others.

In 1958, Hess intensified his attack on the detractors of the New York School. He categorically denied the existence of an establishment, a style, or an aesthetic against which a young artist should or even could react. Instead, he found "an atmosphere of individual freedom." *"There is no Revolution any more,"* he proclaimed. "It is . . . quixotic to expect [artists] . . . to abandon a movement they never joined. . . . The avant-garde artist, without capital letters, is the one with his own vision of what is going to be going on."[15] Rebutting proclamations of Abstract Expressionism's death, Hess called attention to its "heterogeneity and depth," to "its signs of life."[16]

Hess also began to castigate, with growing vehemence, the conservative enemies of the New York School, pointing to their obituaries of Abstract Expressionism as proof of its continuing life. The premise was that if the philistines do not like us, we must still be avant-garde. The primary target was John Canaday, who had been appointed art editor of the *New York Times* in September 1959. Canaday immediately set out to destroy the Abstract Expressionists by accusing them of being frauds, freaks, charlatans, and worse, and being a skillful journalist, he stirred up controversy.[17] In the winter of 1961, a group of artists, critics, curators, and collectors, invited by Ferren and me, met and framed a letter to the *Times* protesting against Canaday's "consistent practice of going beyond the discussion of exhibitions in order to impute to living artists en masse, as well as to critics, collectors and scholars of present-day American art, dishonorable motives, those of cheats, greedy lackeys or senseless dupes."[18] The letter, quoting scurrilous excerpts from Canaday's articles and concluding that they comprised the writing "not of a

critic but of an agitator," was signed by forty-nine leading figures in the arts and published in the *Times* on 26 February 1961.[19] The protest letter provoked considerable
controversy; hundreds of letters were received by the *Times*, running twelve to one in
Canaday's favor.[20] None of the contestants seemed aware of the irony of the situation.
All felt "embattled" and accused the other of being the "Establishment"—Canaday in
America's most prestigious newspaper and the Abstract Expressionists who had achieved
national and international acclaim.

The Abstract Expressionists and their spokesmen also disparaged any approach, no
matter how sympathetic, which even hinted that Abstract Expressionism might have entered middle or old age. This included all historical treatment, because it focused on the
"dead" past, and stylistic analysis, because it suggested that pictorial attributes had
become familiar and fixed enough to be categorized. Arguments and actions against detractors, much as they appeared to be assaults, were defenses, the last remaining ones.
Earlier the Abstract Expressionists would have ignored Canaday as they had other of
their detractors. After 1959, they felt the need to respond, and their counterattacks could
not help but reveal their underlying insecurity.

Beginning in 1958, the issue of whether gesture painting had become academic
was openly debated within the New York School. In that year, there took place at the
Club a panel entitled "Has the Situation Changed?"; and a compilation of statements by
artists under the heading "Is Today's Artist With or Against the Past?" was published in
*Art News*. In 1959, there was another series of panels at the Club entitled "What is the
New Academy?" The issues were defined by Raymond Parker, who moderated one of
the panels. He asked the following questions, among others. Was what was being called
a new academy perhaps a new tradition? Was academic to be defined as imitation, that
is, following rules or rehashing settled questions? Was there anything wrong with painting what was already known? Was originality important as a goal or was it a result?
Could new means be evolved through variations of old themes?[21]

Perhaps the earliest attack on gesture painting of consequence was that of Barr, the
head of the Museum of Modern Art, in 1958, while he was participating with Hess and
Rosenberg on a panel at the Club. Barr challenged the audience with a series of questions: Is the younger generation rebellious or is it basking in the light of half a dozen
leaders? Are Tenth Street artists living on the energies of the painters of the forties and
early fifties? Should there have been a rebellion by now? (Barr said that he looked
forward to it but had not seen it yet.) Are painters continuing a style when they should
be bucking it?

Hess protested that Barr was imposing a pattern of rebellion that did not apply.
Rosenberg added that young artists were justified in following a style until something
new came along, and that had not happened. Artists in the audience also rebutted Barr.
Michael Goldberg called him a grave digger. The revolution was going on and he did
not even recognize it. Sidney Gordin insisted that revolution had become fashionable,
that there was now an academy of revolution. Ludwig Sander maintained that the
young had nothing to revolt against since the leaders were themselves in revolt; an official art did not exist.

Barr acknowledged that the vein of gesture painting might be rich enough for a whole generation to mine, and more time might be required for boredom to set in. But even so, working veins that were already opened could only yield minor discoveries, and Barr again called upon younger artists to reject their elders more strongly. [22]

Among the most vocal critics of gesture painting initially were the makers (and supporters) of assemblages, Environments, and Happenings within the early wave of the second generation. Although aesthetically on the fringe, they were accepted, at least as *enfants terribles* who enlivened things without constituting a threat, or more seriously, because their work possessed a kinship in look to gesture painting, and even if frivolous, was felt to be of a certain quality. But the so-called Neo-Dadas resented being patronized by artists they had ceased to respect. The strongest attack on second-generation gesture painting came from Kaprow. Using Pollock's death in 1956 as his symbol he wrote: "The 'Act of Painting,' the new space, the personal mark that builds its own form and meaning, the endless tangle, the great scale, the new materials, etc. are by now clichés of college art departments. The innovations are accepted. They are becoming part of text books." [23] Elsewhere, Kaprow remarked "that from 1951 to the present there had been . . . a tremendous amount of dullness in abstract expressionism and impressionism: 10th Street, for example." [24]

Kelly, Louis, Noland, and Stella did not participate in the polemics of the New York School during the fifties. But Greenberg did, and toward the end of the decade he intensified his attack on gesture painting, summing it up in 1964 as follows: "Abstract Expressionism was, and is, a certain style of art, and like other styles of art, having had its ups, it had its downs. Having produced art of major importance, it turned into a school, then into a manner, and finally into a set of mannerisms. Its leaders attracted imitators, many of them, and then some of these leaders took to imitating themselves." [25] Other writers began to support Greenberg's position. In 1960, Rubin wrote that he was struck "by the poor quality of contemporary Abstract-Expressionist or de Kooning style painting." It was "rendered decorative by painters who have converted it into a formula and given it 'professional' finish and polish. This happens only after a style has passed its period of vitality, when the metaphor becomes the cliché." [26]

Post-gestural artists within the New York School also went on the attack. For example, during a panel at the Club in 1961 on the Guggenheim Museum's *American Abstract Expressionists and Imagists* show, one participant condemned the coldness, arrogance, elegance, and calculation of much of recent abstraction. Brach responded: "That's marvelous. I liked the picture by Newman. The Imagist tendency offers possibilities to my generation that the *école* de Kooning doesn't. I changed. I didn't know how good Newman was." [27] In retrospect, Parker recalled that what began to interest him about "intent painting" was a decline in the credibility of "direct painting." One of the faults of the latter

> . . . was the proliferation of some easily available and relatively simple ideas, so that there were perhaps a thousand too many artists working in a pretty easily formulated style of improvisation. The result was that the paintings of all looked alike, and one might conclude from that that the painters who made them

really did know what they were doing—and in that case there wasn't any value to the idea of improvisation, since the paintings always turned out pretty much the same anyway.[28]

Kramer, soon to be followed by Tillim, joined in the attack on gesture painting, but their interest was more in the figurative variant than in the abstract. They objected to the introduction of figuration into gesture painting without adequate consideration of the meaning of the subject matter. Using Park, Bischoff, and Diebenkorn as examples, Kramer wrote: "These painters leave painting in exactly the same state of exhaustion in which they found it. They refuse to bring any ideas to their work which might violate the painting method they favor, a method they have inherited but not enlarged."[29]

It was above all the glut of followers in New York, throughout the nation, and the Western world that called into question the viability of gesture painting as avant-garde. An avant-garde which turns into a mass movement becomes a parody of itself. The increase in numbers was also a reason for the deterioration of the community of the New York School. Too many of the newcomers had nothing at all fresh to say or were intent primarily on practicing "the art of the life of art," as Reinhardt observed.[30] But there were other reasons for the decline. One was the substantial success of a few artists. This subverted the condition of equality which facilitated easy relationships. It was hard for "winners" and "losers" to communicate. A second was the growth in number and intensity of attacks on gesture painting within the New York School. A third reason was the emergence of a vocal new generation with values different from, and in many cases antithetical to, gesture painting.

These values were articulated in 1960 by Stella, perhaps the most influential of the newcomers. While participating in a panel at New York University, he remarked that he could find few creative ideas in current art; there were not even enough good gimmicks. He claimed that his own painting aimed for unoriginality—originality gone dead. What interested him most was a good idea rather than the process of painting; he could not see why it was bad for an artist who had a good idea just to paint it. So intent was Stella on presenting his pictorial concepts that he said he would welcome mechanical means to paint his pictures, that is, to translate ideas into painting. He referred to a certain artist who had sent his pictures out to be painted as an executive artist, commenting that he was a good painter when he did not paint. He also said that his idea of a picture was one that was the same all over and the same in the next painting, one in which only paint was used and none of himself. Stella concluded by saying that he did not know why he was an artist, or even if he was one.[31] Stankiewicz, another panelist, who was still being ridiculed as a Neo-Dada, was so incensed by Stella's remarks that he blurted out, "Nonsense."[32]

Such statements as Stella's could not but shock and dismay those nurtured on Abstract Expressionist values. The more sensitive were appalled by what they took to be the anti-humanistic aesthetics advanced by younger artists and the seemingly impoverished art that they created, experiencing a profound sense of loss in the denial of their heroic and sublime aspirations. This anguished sense of deprivation aggravated by an awareness of decline gave rise to a growing aggressiveness in the stance of the older artists. Their values were worth a strong defense—in the cause of art and man. Others, not so idealistic, were angry because of the threats to their careers. O'Doherty called them "a young breed of tough guys who thought their certificates of inheritance had been stamped by Pollock and Kline and de Kooning and that the future was theirs by divine right."[33]

But waging war against young artists claiming to be creating *the* advanced art was not easy. An old vanguard cannot attack a new one with strong assurance since to believe that its revolution had been the last one or the last worthwhile one goes against the very conception of avant-garde. But initially, the Abstract Expressionist offensive was successful. Young artists who were diverging from or challenging gesture painting faced the formidable problem of establishing their art as *serious*. More than any other artist of his generation, Stella was the butt of ridicule, treated by his elders as the juvenile delinquent of contemporary art.

Adding irritation to the dismay of the Abstract Expressionists was the way in which the newcomers managed again and again to hold the center of interest, as Stella did at the panel at New York University. First- and second-generation artists resented "young kids," seemingly frivolous and certainly disrespectful of them and of their art, indeed, it seemed of art itself, muscling into the limelight, crowding out those who in their opinion had earned attention, making them appear old hat and boring. And what was worse, these upstarts attracted many art critics and curators, including some who had been old allies of the Abstract Expressionists, such as Dorothy C. Miller, who had selected Stella for her prestigious *Sixteen Americans* show at the Museum of Modern Art; Leo Castelli, who became his dealer; and William C. Seitz, who had been his teacher.

In this situation, the joining together of the Abstract Expressionists to publicly censure Canaday can be seen as a sign of crisis and paradoxically of a weakening of their community. Irving Howe observed that when groups fall apart, "there comes that tremor of self-awareness which no one would have troubled to feel during the years of energy and confidence. A tradition in process of being lost, a generation facing assault and ridicule from ambitious younger men—the rekindled sense of group solidarity is brought to a half-hour's flame by the hardness of dying."[34]

The Abstract Expressionists' loss of confidence was hidden (but only barely) by their aggressiveness. Ironically, the bluster generated a hostile atmosphere which caused the decline of the Club, the core of Abstract Expressionist activities, around 1960 (although it lingered on some three years more). Artists venturing in new directions simply stopped coming. Most of the Abstract Expressionists themselves were repelled by the Club's atmosphere, which made an open exchange of ideas impossible. What remained were a dwindling number of diehards muttering bitterly to themselves.

Like the Club, the Tenth Street galleries declined in the late fifties and early sixties, closing one by one. For example, the Tanager closed in June 1962. Earlier in the decade, the status of the cooperatives was sustained by the strong assertion (if not always by an equally strong conviction) by their artist-members that exhibition downtown was important, perhaps more important than showing uptown, since the primary audience was composed of artists and only their opinion mattered; what non-artists, particularly in the art establishment, thought was of no account. This aura of confidence attracted critics, curators, commercial gallery dealers, and a few collectors, all of whom were welcomed by the artists, if somewhat haughtily, considering the rhetorical stance against non-artist opinion. By 1959, the attitude of these "guests" had changed. Noting their growing indifference to the Club—and by inference to the Tenth Street galleries—Goldwater wrote: "At the beginning only those who were known to have nothing to do with the authorities were allowed to play; now it is the other way around, most of the uptown men won't come in the door."[35] But perhaps more important, the best of the Tenth Street artists were taken by uptown commercial galleries, and with very few exceptions those that continued to show on Tenth Street were the mediocrities.

Last to go was the sense of camaraderie, and the success of a small number of New York School artists was largely responsible. Ashton recalled:

> In the spring of 1961 a great party was given by three of the most celebrated New York School painters. It represented the end of an era. . . . [It] was more like an embassy reception than the spontaneous revels of old bohemia— . . .
>
> This party took place in a loft, but a loft with parquet floors, spotless walls, and a majestic colonnade running its length. Many of the old restless spirits were present, but then, so were some 800 others, including collectors, dealers, museum officials, and assorted functional members of a greatly enlarged art world. They were there by written invitation and checked carefully at the door by armed Pinkerton men. Once upon a time, a famous poet remarked, Pinkerton men had been used to chase disreputable elements such as artists. Now the artists do the chasing.[36]

A few critics maintained that the success in terms of rapidly growing sales and recognition from art institutions of Abstract Expressionist work was the primary cause of its decline. The dramatic "signal that there has been a radical change in the situation" was the Metropolitan Museum's purchase of Pollock's *Autumn Rhythm* for $30,000. As Crehan saw it in 1958: "Success is likely to be the most problematical thing about the American abstract art movement. How the artists deal with it!"[37] Kramer was not sure that artists had much choice in the matter. It was too much to resist. The changed situation would be the determining factor. In 1959, he wrote:

> We have lately been so overcome with self-congratulation at the way the public at large has interested itself in "advanced" art that we have quite forgotten the implications of this interest. We are amused when conservative universities invite the most "experimental" artists to exhibit in their halls and address their solemn symposia; and we are only a little astonished when the big commercial galleries decide to crash the market in contemporary abstract painting now that it commands generous five-figure prices. We are not even bothered much any more at the way artists themselves have begun to complain at cocktail parties about their income-tax problems. The boom is in full swing, and it was perhaps too much to

expect that artists might resist the habits of mind and speech which have long characterized both Wall Street and Madison Avenue.[38]

And that was not all, for as far as Kramer was concerned, *The New American Painting* exhibition at the Museum of Modern Art was "its official installation as a department of American culture."[39]

However, artists countered that just as they had been inured to poverty, so would they be inured to success. As Hartigan remarked at the Club: "If an artist can be corrupted, he's corruptible. It's not an important issue."[40] In the end, it was not corruptibility but massive mediocrity that made the difference. The movement could not remain fresh in the face of it, and even the reputations of the best artists suffered.

# Notes

1. Ad Reinhardt, "44 Titles for Articles for Artists Under 45," *It Is* 1 (Spring 1958): 22.

2. Jack Tworkov, statement in "Is There A New Academy?" *Art News*, September 1959, p. 38.

3. Club panel, "The Role of the Critic in Contemporary Art," 25 May 1956, John Ferren (moderator), Robert Goldwater, Clement Greenberg, Thomas B. Hess, and Stuart Preston (notes taken by me).

4. Ferren, "Stable State of Mind," pp. 22–23, 64. Ferren noted that the Stable Annual had its *enfants terribles*, e.g., Rauschenberg and Stankiewicz. On p. 62, he remarked: "But this year there is not the intensity of experiment and the sometimes outrageous personal gesture of other times. There is instead the intensity of the finished picture."

5. Dore Ashton, "What is 'avant-garde'?" *Arts Digest*, 15 September 1955, p. 8. Hilton Kramer was thinking along lines similar to Ashton. In "Pittsburgh's International," p. 20, he singled out pictures which "are painted with a modesty and seriousness which focuses all energies on the prosaic tasks of making a good picture. . . . They offer a quiet kind of evidence that the noisy American 'presence' which everywhere announces itself in the International is not the whole story of American art today."

6. Dore Ashton, "Art," *Arts and Architecture*, September 1956, p. 4.

7. Dore Ashton, "Art," *Arts and Architecture*, February 1956, p. 10.

8. Hess, "The New York Salon," p. 57.

9. Hess, "U.S. Painting: Some Recent Directions," p. 90.

10. Other critics had strong reservations about the value of eclecticism. Leo Steinberg, "Month in Review," *Arts*, January 1956, p. 47, wrote in a review of Hess's show *U.S. Painting: Some Recent Directions*, that many of the works "demonstrate the impasse of expressionism settling into style and turning to habit. The raw, rash, rapid handling of paint is the Hofmannerism of our day."

11. Thomas B. Hess, "Great Expectations, Part II," *Art News*, Summer 1956, p. 38.

12. Thomas B. Hess, "Younger Artists and the Unforgivable Crime," *Art News*, April 1957, p. 47.

13. Ibid., p. 48.

14. Robert Goldwater, " 'Everyone Knew What Everyone Else Meant,' " *It Is* 4 (Autumn 1959): 35.

15. Thomas B. Hess, "Inside Nature," *Art News*, February 1958, pp. 64–65.

16. Thomas B. Hess, "Editorial: The Many Deaths of American Art," *Art News*, October 1960, p. 25.

17. See John Canaday, *Embattled Critic* (New York: Noonday Press, 1962), for a collection of essays.

18. "Letter to the *New York Times*," 26 February 1961, sec. 2, p. 19. The "Letter" was reprinted in Canaday, *Embattled Critic*, pp. 219–23.

Among the forty-nine signers of the "Letter" were James Ackerman, William Barrett, James Brooks, John Cage, Howard Conant, Stuart Davis, Edwin Denby, Adolph Gottlieb, David Hare, Thomas B. Hess, Hans Hofmann, Sam Hunter, Kenneth Koch, Willem de Kooning, Stanley Kunitz, Robert Motherwell, Barnett Newman, Raymond Parker, Phillip Pavia, Fairfield Porter, Harold Rosenberg, Robert Rosenblum, David Smith, Meyer Schapiro, and Paul Weiss.

19. Ibid.

20. For a selection of letters, see Canaday, *Embattled Critic*, pp. 223–38.

21. Club panel, "What is the New Academy? Part 3," 10 April 1959, Ben Heller, Alex Katz, Raymond Parker (moderator), Larry Rivers, and David Slivka (notes taken by me).

22. Club panel, "Has the Situation Changed?" Around this time, Barr began to promote Jasper Johns as the alternative to Abstract Expressionist academicism. It is also noteworthy that the *Sixteen Americans* show at the Museum of Modern Art in 1959 included only one gesture painter of the New York School, Alfred Leslie. In 1961, only three of the twenty-three artists under thirty-five years of age whose works the museum acquired painted in an Abstract Expressionist manner. See John Canaday, "Art: The Modern's New Acquisitions," *New York Times*, 20 December 1961, p. 38.

23. Kaprow, "The Legacy of Jackson Pollock," p. 26.

24. Allan Kaprow, "Editor's Letters," *Art News*, February 1959, p. 6.

25. Greenberg, Introduction, *Post Painterly Abstraction*, unpaginated.

26. Rubin, "Younger American Painters," p. 25.

27. Club panel, "The Guggenheim Image," 27 October 1961, Paul Brach, Paul Burlin, Louis Finkelstein (moderator), Elaine de Kooning, Nicholas Marsicano, Raymond Parker, and Jon Schueler (notes taken by me).

28. "The New Abstraction: A Discussion Conducted by Bruce Glaser" (with Paul Brach, Al Held, and Raymond Parker), *Art International*, 20 February 1966, p. 42. Held agreed with Parker but blamed the rhetoric of gesture painting, e.g., that of Rosenberg. Once one disregarded the verbiage, it was clear that a de Kooning or a Pollock *knew* what they were doing since the pictures of each looked alike.

29. Hilton Kramer, "Month in Review," *Arts*, January 1960, p. 45.

30. Reinhardt, "44 Titles for Articles for Artists Under 45," p. 22.

31. Panel, "Art 1960," New York University, New York, 21 April 1960, Robert Goldwater (moderator), Jasper Johns, Alfred Leslie, Robert Mallary, Louise Nevelson, Richard Stankiewicz, and Frank Stella, organized by Howard Conant (notes taken by me).

32. Ibid.

33. Brian O'Doherty, "Master of a Movement Manqué," *Arts Magazine*, April 1966, p. 28.

34. Irving Howe, *Decline of the New* (New York: Harcourt, Brace and World, 1970), p. 214.

35. Goldwater, " 'Everyone Knew What Everyone Else Meant,' " p. 35.

36. Ashton, *The New York School: A Cultural Reckoning,* p. 229.

37. Hubert Crehan, "Recent Attacks on Abstract Art," *It Is* 1 (Spring 1958): 62–63.

38. H[ilton] K[ramer], "Editorial," *Arts,* February 1959, p. 13.

39. Hilton Kramer, "Month in Review," *Arts,* September 1959, p. 58.

40. Club panel, "Tastemakers in American Art," 8 February 1957, Hermann Cherry (moderator), Ibram Lassaw, Al Newbill, Milton Resnick, and George Spaventa (notes taken by me).

# 14
# Circa 1960:
# A Change in Sensibility

IN THE PRECEDING chapters, I attempted a more or less chronological development of the New York School in the fifties, beginning at the beginning and reconstructing what occurred. My aim was to think from within the period, governed by its attitudes and values, by its sense of quality. This chapter begins from the vantage point of the end of the fifties, looking back but with an eye for what occurred in the following period, influenced by its outlook. My problem was to treat fairly the self-judgment of the fifties while considering the retrospective judgment (based on its own self-judgment) of the sixties, determined by what the latter took to be of continuing viability and quality.

I assumed that the aesthetic judgment of one generation is neither better nor worse than that of another. In aesthetic matters, the objectivity supposedly engendered by historical distance is largely a myth. What hindsight creates is different criteria for judgment. To put it bluntly, each generation, responding to its own changed needs, rewrites art history, and furthermore, what any generation finds of significance is significant, and what is not, is not—for its time, of course. Although there are no demonstrable criteria to determine quality, the awareness of quality exists, and this awareness causes certain works and bodies of work to grow in stature in time. But it is not only quality that guarantees longevity. The possibilities that a work possesses for future development can cause it to remain interesting, whether it has aesthetic quality or not, as the continuing fame of Duchamp indicates. In most cases quality and the potential of further development come together in an artist's work, but not necessarily.

I also assumed that each generation is intent on weighing aesthetic possibilities in order to discover the main sources of energy at the moment, what appears alive and dead or boring in current art. At every moment ambitious young artists—ambitious in that they do not want to merely imitate past styles—each face a "crisis." The pressure on them is simultaneously to ascertain what in existing art has become too familiar and overused to continue to challenge perception; what seems open for fresh extension; what constitutes the particular sensibility of their generation, its particular manner of experiencing as distinct from any other; and what each artist desires or feels compelled to say. Thus, the task of an artist is to achieve a style which embodies his or her private insights while forming the sensibility of the time. If the artist succeeds, his or her individual statement relates to that of his or her most relevant contemporaries.

These individual styles in aggregate constitute a manner which possesses the energy to command an audience for advanced art, an audience that, to the surprise of the artists, seemed to have been waiting for a new art to clarify its latent self- and generational-awareness, initially in the face of ridicule and hostility. The most influential members of such an audience are the artists themselves, who naturally evaluate present and past art from the vantage point of their own appetites and aesthetics. It is not quite so simple, of course. Other taste-makers exert influence on the public, but generally they are close to the artists who provide them with cues.[1] Of particular importance are older taste-makers (including curators, critics, dealers, and collectors) who, like the venturesome artists, have become tired of the old styles they had been influential in "establishing." Indeed, fatigue is a primary cause of the decline of a prevailing vanguard which has exhausted the potential of its aesthetic premises and whose premises have become well-known and successful enough to attract large numbers of followers. Most of these latecomers at best try to extend the style whose potential for fresh development has diminished, and at worst, craft the "look" of the style, producing a glut of stale, unchallenging, or academic work, generating ever more fatigue.

The audience for new art recognizes a style by focusing attention on it and in so choosing disregards competing styles, generally exempting a few leading artists in each. The few exceptions, in most cases the initiators of the established styles, come to be viewed as individual artists rather than as members of a "school." In time, the achievement of such individuals counts for more and more and continues to engage the public for advanced art long after the style of which it is a part ceases to be of interest.

One would suppose that it would be difficult to determine with any certainty which tendency at any time best exemplifies that time. However, it appears that the audience for advanced art is somehow agreed on what is of value, notwithstanding inevitable differences of individual opinion. Such consensuses are not founded on "objective" (not to mention "universal") criteria for judging the importance and quality of art works, since these accords are constantly changing. Even if such criteria do exist (and it is doubtful), none that have been offered to date have seemed credible enough to be widely accepted, even among those who yearn for them. Thus the only basis for evaluation remains the "subjective" taste or appetite of individuals or groups of individuals. But these individuals do possess a similar culture. Thus if a significant number of artists, curators, and critics in the milieu of the New York School in 1960 were each asked to name the outstanding young artists, it is likely that Frankenthaler, Goodnough, Hartigan, Leslie, Mitchell, Rauschenberg, and Rivers would have appeared on most lists.

In the fifties, it was generally accepted within the New York School that the major avant-garde style was gesture painting. Most young painters had been so stunned by the painting of de Kooning, Kline, or Guston, had felt so liberated by its freedom and sweep, that they thought it trivial to work in any other direction. It also occurred to them that by starting with de Kooning rather than with Picasso or Miró, they faced a better chance of finding independent styles. At least, their painting felt more challenging, livelier, and up-to-date. By 1957 or 1958, some younger artists were becoming critical of gesture painting—not that of the pioneers but of the growing number of followers—and of the romantic rhetoric justifying it. Increasingly, questions were raised as to whether gesture painting, particularly in the vein of de Kooning, had anything fresh to say. And if not, was it not necessary to attempt alternatives—non-gestural styles, perhaps? Growing numbers of artists thought so and began to experiment with cleanly defined forms and colors. In retrospect, the contrast between generational manners is pronounced, indeed, dramatic. The stylistic common denominator of fifties art was the "hot," "dirty," painterly look, and of sixties art, the "cool," "antiseptic," mechanistic look. In fact, the more art was based on clearly defined forms of unmodulated colors, the more of the sixties it looked, so much so that until late in the decade, painterly painting received very little critical attention.

A few strong young artists were able to continue their gesture painting with confidence, notably Mitchell and Hartigan (both of whom left New York) and Frankenthaler. However, only Frankenthaler continued to command a considerable audience (and a growing one), most likely because her technique was innovative and was a major influence on stained color-field abstraction, and because her work was exceptional in that it was not closely identified with the "school" of de Kooning. The rest of the second generation of gesture painters was caught in a creative crisis. Many tried to change styles, for example, moving from abstraction to gestural figuration, but that did not help, since the latter was commonplace. Others simplified their gesture painting, articulating structure and color. But in this they were anticipated—and eclipsed—by Kline's black-and-white abstractions and de Kooning's abstract "landscapes" of the late fifties.

However, there were related artists who were unaffected by the debilitation, those venturing into assemblage, unaffected, that is, until after 1961 or 1962. Indeed, of the directions taken by fifties artists, the one that appeared most problematic and controversial, thus most vanguard, toward the end of the decade was Neo-Dada, as junk assemblage was then commonly called, and related tendencies, such as Environments and Happenings, that shortly emerged. But junk relief and sculpture were made respectable by the Museum of Modern Art's *The Art of Assemblage* in 1961. This show confirmed what I had noted a year earlier, that assemblage had become "a mass manner. Artists still under forty such as Rauschenberg, Johns, Stankiewicz [all of whom were included in the museum's *Sixteen Americans*, 1959], and Kaprow find themselves in the ironic position of old masters."[2]

One event that helped undermine the avant-garde status of assemblage, although it was meant to do just the opposite, was Jean Tinguely's *Homage to New York*, presented in the sculpture garden of the Museum of Modern Art in 1960. A kinetic, environmental, junk construction, it was meant to self-destruct. As described by Seitz, Tinguely's "melange of materials ranging from bicycle wheels and dishpans to an upright piano, vibrated and gyrated, painted pictures, played music, and . . . sawed, shook, and burned itself to rubble and extinction." [3] This sculpture-event, witnessed by several hundred members of the museum's art world, became the occasion of fashion, " 'Black-Tie Dada.' " [4] Tinguely's work most likely appealed to art officialdom and the world of fashion because it seemed to be a sophisticated spoof of assemblage and a familiar, eclectic fabrication in the vein of Rauschenberg and Stankiewicz.

Unaffected by the falling off of assemblage as a tendency were Rauschenberg, a member of the early wave, and Chamberlain and di Suvero, who matured late in the fifties. [5] During the same period, the reputation of Stankiewicz, who had been the first of his generation to weld sculpture from junk metal exclusively and who had achieved more acclaim than Rauschenberg during the fifties, went into a decline. The probable reason was that the bizarre images improvised by Stankiewicz, personal and masterful though they are, call to mind too insistently the tradition of Surrealist biomorphic fantasy, a figurative tradition that seemed outworn.

In contrast to Stankiewicz's welded sculptures, Rauschenberg's combines were not seen as possessing Surrealist content. There was that possibility, for in the combines incongruous images and materials are juxtaposed, but they refer not to the unconscious but to the urban environment, more like Schwitters's Dadaist collages. The greater difficulty in the acceptance of the combines should have resulted from their references to de Kooning's painting, but that was not the case. Rauschenberg appeared to have radically transformed the gestural manner of Abstract Expressionism by introducing real objects, taken from "life." Indeed, he substituted Cagean life-art strategies for de Kooningesque *angst*. Thus the decline of gesture painting did not affect Rauschenberg's reputation. In fact, during the sixties considerable numbers of younger artists began to work in the gap between "life" and "art," and Rauschenberg was hailed as a progenitor, assuming an ever-larger historical stature.

Like Rauschenberg's combines, the junk constructions of Chamberlain and di Suvero refer to the American scene. But such associations were frequently disregarded by a new, sympathetic audience, formalist in sensibility. [6] Like Rauschenberg's combines, the constructions of the two younger artists overcame allusions to the gesture painting of de Kooning (in Chamberlain's case) and Kline (in di Suvero's) by being projected in three dimensions. The audience for sixties art found the improvisational painterly look retarded in painting but advanced in assemblage.

Di Suvero and Chamberlain also diverged from the welded sculpture of the fifties by clarifying and articulating structure, and to further make it visible, by enlarging their works. Instead of drawing in space with intricate, often ambiguously busy, richly textured, linear elements, di Suvero used wooden beams, chains, and other massive elements, and Chamberlain, more or less simple planar elements cut and shaped from scrunched automobile parts, all of which were readily identifiable as discrete parts, to compose legible structures.

Johns, like Rauschenberg, was able to cultivate the look of gesture painting without    213

213  Jasper Johns, *Flag Above White,* 1954.
22″ x 19″. Private Collection, New York.

appearing retrogressive. Rauschenberg succeeded by mixing real objects with painted areas; Johns, by overlaying images that looked like real things, such as American flags or targets, with facture that resembled that of Guston and, to a lesser degree, de Kooning.

And yet Johns pointed the way in form and context to a number of new styles that emerged in the sixties. Within the style of painterly painting, he introduced hard edges which delineated representational subjects—flags, targets, letters, numbers—in a literal manner. Johns's clear and factual presentation of commonplace subjects prompted Oldenburg and Dine, on the one hand, and Roy Lichtenstein, Andy Warhol, and James Rosenquist, on the other hand, to choose similar subjects, often from the mass media, inaugurating the movement commonly called Pop Art. Johns occasionally set off stenciled images against brushy areas, showing the way to Warhol and Lichtenstein, who relied even more on mechanical devices because they eliminated painterly facture.[7] Pop Art was the parent of Photo-realism; thus Johns can be considered a grandparent.

Johns was also an influence on Stella. The clarity of his flags and targets, composed of simple stripes and concentric circles, impressed the younger artist. Furthermore, as Stella said: "The thing that struck me most was the way he stuck to the motif . . . the

214, 215
216

214   Roy Lichtenstein, *Girl with Ball*, 1961.
60¼″ x 36¼″. Private Collection.

215   Andy Warhol, *Water Heater,* 1960.
44¾″ x 40″. The Museum of Modern Art, New York.

216 James Rosenquist, *Look Alive,* 1961.
67″ x 58⅛″. Harry N. Abrams Family
Collection, New York.

idea of stripes—the rhythm and interval—the idea of repetition. I began to think a lot about repetition."[8] The unitary nature of Johns's work, that is, the identification of a single subject such as a flag with the painted image of the flag, with the whole picture plane, which was the exact shape and size of the flag, strongly impressed Stella and innovators of "minimal" or "unitary" sculpture, such as Robert Morris and Donald Judd.[9]

Stella was also taken with the fact that Johns's repetitive images were preconceived and that his painterly surfaces were coolly formed, "made" and not "found" in the process of painting, subverting the rhetoric of gesture painting. He crafted the impulsive look of gesture painting while denying its extra-aesthetic, romantic content, elevating the self-detached exercise of picture-making to a primary end in art. The importance of ideas to Johns, that is, of the conceptual component in art, e.g., the idea of painting a flag or a target to look like the real thing, gave a Stella, a Warhol, and a Morris[10] permission to base their works on predetermined concepts and led ultimately to a purely conceptual art. To sum up, Johns can be considered a main artery from Abstract Expressionism to Pop, Minimalism, and Conceptual movements. Equally important, Johns's body of painting and sculpture impressed young artists with its masterly quality, this augmenting the influence of his ideas.

Although Johns did not directly influence Pearlstein or Katz, he anticipated the course their painting would take. However, their development was shaped essentially by contradictions that appeared within gestural realism and the fact that it had become university-type art.[11] In 1959, Kramer became troubled by a "crisis" in gestural realism: the equivocation between the role of the subject and the manner of painting, between realism and abstraction. Using David Park as the exemplar of such San Francisco figurative artists as Richard Diebenkorn and Elmer Bischoff, Kramer wrote of his painting, "that the only real interest . . . consisted in the fact that it was *not* abstract." Park merely introduced into gesture painting "some crude cartoons of the human figure," which Kramer found "completely devoid of pictorial expression." Thus Park and his fellow San Franciscans were painting the figure "in a serious way without any real decision about its meaning. . . . psychological or . . . plastic . . . It lacks necessity. Now it strikes me as somehow decadent to use the figure merely as a spatial counter." Summing up, Kramer wrote: "Far from constituting a 'way out' of the current impasse in abstract painting, the figurative work of these three painters is actually a chapter in the crisis of abstract painting at the present moment."[12]

Tillim too became dissatisfied with the prevailing compromise of the abstract and the representational, exemplified by Park, Bischoff, and Diebenkorn. Their use of the figure was "not only less important than the style in which it was painted," but "the figure did not experience any revitalization in the effort."[13] Tillim was more respectful of certain painterly realists identified with the New York School, particularly Porter. But he became increasingly interested in a group of "revisionists," including Katz (who had

217

217   David Park, *Four Men*, 1958.
57″ x 92″. Whitney Museum of American Art, New York.

long been at the realist edge of gestural realism) and Pearlstein, who "have reopened the case for subject matter as more than merely a pretext for a painting."[14] Tillim believed that conditions were ripe for a new realism, but much as he initially found it too flawed to be a serious contender of abstract art,[15] he soon became one of its champions.

218     Pearlstein took on the task of discovering a new content for figurative painting and developing the technical skills necessary to achieve it, and the latter was the primary challenge.[16] He resolved to make representational art truly representational by attempting to record his subjects as matter-of-factly as he could, coolly and painstakingly depicting only that which he could observe, avoiding any and all interpretation.[17] Pearlstein also formulated the aesthetic rationale for the new realism, an intellectual framework that caused it to be taken seriously. In an article of 1962, he enumerated the variety of "acceptable" contemporary figurative styles. Unsympathetic to them all, he wrote: "It

218     Philip Pearlstein, *Male and Female Models Sitting on the Floor*, 1962. 44″ by 50″. Courtesy Allan Frumkin Gallery, New York.

seems madness on the part of any painter educated in the twentieth-century modes of picture-making to take as his subject the naked human figure, conceived as a self-contained entity possessed of its own dignity, existing in an inhabitable space, viewed from a single vantage point. For as artists we are too ambitious and conscious of too many levels of meaning. The description of the surface of things seems unworthy."[18]

Nevertheless, Pearlstein set out to imitate reality. His intention led him to rid his art of two "tyrannies." One was the concept of pictorial flatness—the primary demand of modernist dogma. Pearlstein considered the ban on spatial illusionism arbitrary, a matter of personal choice. He would choose to disregard it. He also ignored the second tyranny, the "roving point-of-view," which was the way most modern artists tried to see, in response to the idea that reality constantly changes.[19] Given his attitude, Pearlstein reinterpreted the history of modern art, and came to think that the evolution of realism in the nineteenth century was aborted by the Impressionists. Much as they aimed to be perceptual, they dematerialized matter and flattened pictorial space into a screen of light, and thus ushered in modernist painting. Therefore, Pearlstein turned back in time from Impressionism and used the early Manet and Courbet as his points of departure, proposing to develop an even more factual realism than they had.

Intending to represent literally a solid figure in a believable space, to tell the truth uncompromisingly about what he saw, Pearlstein suppressed signs of facture, tightening his earlier loose brushhandling in order to render details closely. So single-minded was he in restituting the figure that Tillim remarked: "For the moment, then, a new realism would be anti-expressionist, anti-rhetorical."[20] But it turned out to be more than just for the moment. Pearlstein's anti-romantic aesthetic remained at the heart of realist thinking throughout the sixties, indeed at the heart of basic aesthetics of the decade, related in outlook to Warhol, Lichtenstein, and other Pop artists, and Stella and other Minimalist artists. Pearlstein recognized this affinity: "The sensibility of the *first half* of the sixties has hardened. Pop art, constructions of all kinds, hard-edge abstraction, and my own kind of hard realism—it's all 'hard'—sharp, clear, unambiguous. In the fifties everything was ambiguous."[21]

Like Pearlstein, Katz aimed to represent what he saw—the likeness and gestures of his sitters, the specific light of a moment in time, and the particular surface texture and density of bodies and things. During the fifties, his style had been less brushy than that of any of the gestural realists, and in the early sixties, he hardened it even more and enlarged his formats, so that his work would compete in scale with ambitious abstract art of the time, a contribution of great consequence for the new realism. However, Katz, unlike Pearlstein, tried to reconcile realism with modernism, and he flattened his subjects but without sacrificing literalness.

Just as assemblage became familiar in the early sixties, so did Environments and Happenings, and they suffered a similar loss of a serious audience. The number of Happenings fell off, particularly after the Reuben Gallery closed in 1961. Several of the initiators turned to the creation of art objects rather than theatrical events, in the cases of Dine and Grooms, as early as 1960. They reacted against the expendability of their theater pieces, as Dine said, "because I felt anyone could do anything and be liked. It was

219

220

219   Alex Katz, *Red Smile,* 1963.
78″ x 120″. Collection, the artist.

becoming so chic. The audiences were laughing at everything." [22] Oldenburg continued to produce Happenings while making art objects until 1963, after which he curbed but did not stop his theatrical activities.

The paintings, collages, assemblages, and sculptures made by the three artists (and Segal, who was closely associated with them) were often environmental in size and were infused with the spirit of Happenings, so much so that many could have been "props" in the earlier events. For example, Oldenburg conceived of each object in a Happening as having a life of its own, of being a "charged object ('living')." [23] The animistic attitude with its carry-overs of expressionism in the works of Oldenburg, Dine, Grooms, and Segal separated them from Warhol, Lichtenstein, and most other Pop artists with whom they were commonly identified. [24]

The spirit of Happenings also entered into other art forms that emerged in the sixties or helped to change existing ones. It is not always possible to establish a direct influence. Perhaps there was "something in the air," a convergence of sensibility that caused, for example, the visual arts to tend toward theater, or theater to emphasize its physical and visual components, the *mise en scène*.

Most directly related to Happenings was a series of events by artists who called themselves Fluxus. Initiated by George Maciunas in collaboration with Wolf Vostell

221

222

220   Jim Dine, *Flesh Striped Tie,* 1961. 60¹/₄″ x 50″. Hirshhorn Museum and Sculpture Garden, Smithsonian Institution, Washington, D.C.

221   George Segal, *Man at Table,* 1961.
338″ x 305″ x 305″. Städtisches Museum Mönchengladbach, Germany.

and Nam June Paik in Wiesbaden, Germany, in 1962, Fluxus remained active in Europe and America during the next few years.[25] Although its events were not produced until some three years after the first Happening, the influence of the one on the other was probably not too strong, since the relations between the artists in the two groups were not particularly close. However, several of Kaprow's fellow students in Cage's class at the New School for Social Research—Dick Higgins, George Brecht, Al Hansen, Jackson MacLow, and Richard Maxfield—were early participants in Fluxus and shaped its thinking. Higgins was of particular importance to Fluxus—as its major historian and, after he founded the Something Else Press in 1964, as the primary publisher and distributor of its literature.[26]

Fluxus events differed from Happenings in that they tended to be simple, short, sound-producing actions rather than complex, lengthy, visually oriented productions. Typically, a "monostructural" Fluxus event would involve one performer, in most cases the composer, in a concert setting with few or no environmental elements and would be part of a program of other similar events.[27] (Many Fluxus actions were non-physical, purely verbal or conceptual, for example, giving participants a simple instruction or making a statement.[28]) Moreover, Fluxus artists were unsympathetic to the Expressionist

222   Claes Oldenburg, *Red Tights with Fragment 9*, 1961.
69⅝" x 34¼" x 8¾".
The Museum of Modern Art, New York.

and symbolic aspect—they called it "operatic" and "baroque"—of most Happenings. Indeed, Fluxus artists tried to demythologize the artist and his art. As Maciunas wrote in a manifesto more Duchampian than any Happening-makers, Fluxus art is an amusement which "forgoes distinction between art and non-art, forgoes artists' indispensability, exclusiveness, individuality, ambition, forgoes all pretension towards a significance, variety, inspiration, skill, complexity, profundity, greatness, institutional and commodity value. It strives for nonstructural, non-theatrical, nonbaroque, impersonal qualities of a simple, natural event, an object, a game, a puzzle or a gag. It is a fusion of Spike Jones, gags, games, Vaudeville, Cage and Duchamp." [29]

But Happenings and Fluxus artists shared a similar attitude to the objects they used in their events. Higgins remarked that Fluxus performers were irrationally fetishistic in the way they "idealized the most direct relationship with 'reality,' " specifically objective reality. "The lives of objects, their histories and events were considered somehow more realistic than any conceivable personal intrusion on them." [30]

Most Fluxus events occurred from 1962 to 1964. In the latter year, internal dissension caused a decline in performances. The emphasis then shifted to publications, substantial numbers of which were produced by Higgins and Maciunas until about 1966. [31]

Avant-garde dance in the sixties was strongly influenced by Happenings, Cage, and Cunningham. In 1962, a group of dancers, among them Yvonne Rainer, Steven Paxton, Judith Dunn, Deborah and Alex Hay, formed a dancers' workshop in the Judson Church (where earlier Oldenburg and Dine had produced their first Happenings) and called it the Judson Dance Theater. [32] During the previous two years, its founders had studied at Cunningham's studio with composer Robert Dunn, assisted by his wife Judith, from whom they learned of Cage's ideas and methods. [33] They also were inspired by Happenings, such as the one by Simone Morris (Forti) in 1960 at the Reuben Gallery. [34]

The Judson dancers took as their point of departure Cunningham's idea that any movement could be part of a dance and that dance should take into account the kind of movement natural to an individual performer. Under the inspiration of Happenings they limited their choreography to more or less ordinary activities that did not require dance training, a practice spurned by Cunningham, although he had himself anticipated it. [35] The members of the Judson Dance Theater often used commonplace objects, e.g., rope, poles, planks, doing simple things with them, like tasks, much in the manner of Happenings or Fluxus events. For example, in *Terrain*, Rainer played with a red ball, employing movements—bouncing, throwing, catching—which are appropriate to the object and nothing more than that. (Robert Morris manipulated oblong columns in a dance in 1960; these were the precursors of his Minimalist sculpture, indeed of Minimalist Art, for he was one of its innovators.)

The ideas of Cage also prompted Billy Klüver, an engineer, Rauschenberg, and a group of their friends, to organize 9 *Evenings: Theatre and Engineering* which were held at the Twenty-fifth Street Armory (the site of the Armory Show of 1913) in October 1966. The participating artists, most of them associated with the Judson Dance Theater, were Cage, Lucinda Childs, Oyvind Fahlström, Alex and Deborah Hay, Paxton, Rainer, Rauschenberg, David Tudor, and Whitman. They collaborated with more than thirty engineers from Bell Telephone Laboratories, Inc., who subscribed to the motto: "Technology for Art's Sake."[36] The 9 *Evenings* were less than an aesthetic success, flawed by engineering breakdowns and aesthetic confusion, but they made artists aware of the potential of the new technology and led the following month to the active organization of Experiments in Art and Technology, or EAT, as it was commonly called.[37]

The prime movers of EAT were Klüver, Rauschenberg, and Whitman. Their rationale was a simple one. If, as Cage said, the fusion of art and life was desirable, and if technology was central to contemporary life, then art and technology ought to merge. The purpose of the organization was to make the most advanced technology available to artists, at first by matching artists who needed technical assistance with engineers, and later by establishing more organic collaborations.

In 1968, EAT, in conjunction with the Brooklyn Museum and the Museum of Modern Art, organized *Some More Beginnings*, an exhibition of some 120 works involving technical materials and processes.[38] In 1970, EAT designed a pavilion for the Pepsi-Cola Company which was built at *Expo '70* in Osaka, Japan.[39] Extending the thinking of EAT in a somewhat different direction, Jack Burnham organized a show exploring the potential of computer technology for art at the Jewish Museum in 1971; and Maurice Tuchman, chief curator of the Los Angeles County Museum of Art, arranged for more than twenty artists to work in West Coast industrial and other companies from 1967 to 1971.[40] However, as the seventies progressed there was a sharp decline of interest in art using new technology.

An important influence of Happenings on cultural life in America was outside of the visual arts, first on avant-garde theater and then on the "legitimate" stage. This is somewhat ironic, since those connected with the established theater rarely attended Happenings, and drama critics did not write about them seriously until 1965.[41] There were affinities between Happenings, and the Living Theater on the one hand, and on the other hand, such popular plays as Peter Brook's production of Peter Weiss's *The Persecution and Assassination of Marat as Performed by the Inmates of the Asylum of Charenton under the Direction of the Marquis de Sade* or, as it came to be called, *Marat/Sade* (1965) and the Public Theater's production of *Hair* (1967).

The Living Theater was the first theatrical company to grow impatient with the limitations of scripts. Judith Malina (Beck) and Julian Beck, who founded the company, began with *The Brig* in 1963 to de-emphasize the texts of plays and emphasize acting and staging techniques, theater as spectacle. Before then, the Becks had been close to Cage-inspired artists, as early as 1960 presenting three concerts of their music and Jackson MacLow's *The Marrying Maiden*.[42] The Becks were also friendly with the artists of the New York School, for example, organizing a panel at the Club.[43]

As Kirby saw it, the influence of Happenings on the avant-garde theater which followed it in time was significant. He implied that the Living Theater's *Mysteries—and Smaller Pieces* and *Paradise Now* produced in America in 1968–69 were Happenings in everything but name.[44] Kirby somewhat overstated his case, for the Happenings artists were substantially different in outlook from the Living Theater and most other avant-garde theater groups in the sixties, the time of the Vietnam War. Happenings were created by individual artists and were generally apolitical, unlike the Living Theater, which insisted on the fusion of radical theater, pacificist-anarchist politics, and communal life.

However, Happenings showed the way to the later theater companies to use compartmented structure; to involve the spectator in the performance; to avoid formal theaters, as in the case of Richard Schechner's Performance Group which presented *Dionysus in 69* in a redesigned garage; to stress physicality, energy, and freedom, the visual rather than the literary; to possess a "homemade," primitive quality, as in Peter Schumann's Bread and Puppet Theater; and to organize the theater company as a cooperative group rather than an authoritarian hierarchy.[45] Another theater group which employed techniques first used in Happenings was the Open Theater, headed by Joseph Chaikin, an alumnus of the Living Theater.[46] The Open Theater was started in 1963, the year that saw the inauguration of Ellen Stewart's Café La Mama, Café Cino, and the general upsurge of experimental theater in America. During the early seventies, the avant-garde theater that had emerged in the previous decade declined. The Living Theater and Open Theater were disbanded, and the Performance Group was reorganized, but its new productions were unsuccessful.

Happenings also influenced "guerrilla theater," and even discotheques, rock festivals, and light shows, most of which were commercialized corruptions of Happenings and experimental theater.[47] The guerrilla theater, also called "radical," "alternative," "street," or "people's" theater, carried the action component of Happenings into the political arena, proposing to confront and change social attitudes by reaching people in the street or through television and radio. The assaulting of the Pentagon during the Vietnam War and the trial of the "Chicago Seven" were seen by many of their participants as spectacles for the mass media.[48]

Summing up the activities of the original Happening-makers, Grooms, Oldenburg, and Dine abandoned theatrical events for the making of art objects, imbued with the spirit of Happenings, to be sure, but also related to the Pop Art of Warhol, Lichtenstein, and others. Kaprow ventured in an opposite direction away from "art," particularly in the form of an object, toward "non-art" or "life." In 1966, he summed up his thinking in an article entitled, "The Happenings Are Dead—Long Live the Happenings." Kaprow enumerated seven "principles of action":

1. THE LINE BETWEEN THE HAPPENING AND DAILY LIFE SHOULD BE KEPT AS FLUID AND PERHAPS INDISTINCT AS POSSIBLE. . . .

2. THEMES, MATERIALS, ACTIONS AND THE ASSOCIATIONS THEY EVOKE, ARE TO BE GOTTEN FROM ANYWHERE EXCEPT FROM THE ARTS, THEIR DERIVATIVES AND THEIR MILIEU. . . .

3. THE HAPPENING SHOULD BE DISPERSED OVER SEVERAL, WIDELY-SPACED, SOMETIMES MOVING AND CHANGING, LOCALES. . . .

4. TIME, CLOSELY BOUND UP WITH THINGS AND SPACES, SHOULD BE VARIABLE AND INDEPENDENT OF THE CONVENTION OF CONTINUITY. . . .

5. THE COMPOSITION OF ALL MATERIALS, ACTIONS, IMAGES, AND THEIR TIMES AND SPACES, SHOULD BE UNDERTAKEN IN AS ARTLESS, AND, AGAIN, PRACTICAL, A WAY AS POSSIBLE. . . .

6. HAPPENINGS SHOULD BE UNREHEARSED, AND PERFORMED BY NON-PROFESSIONALS, ONCE ONLY. . . .

7. IT FOLLOWS THAT THERE SHOULD NOT BE (AND USUALLY CANNOT BE) AN AUDIENCE OR AUDIENCES TO WATCH A HAPPENING.[49]

With a few exceptions, the artists who matured in the fifties who commanded the most interest in the following decade were those who responded to the crisis in gesture painting by suppressing painterly facture and relational design and creating what might be called a post-gestural manner, notably Kelly, Louis, Noland, and Held in abstract art, and Pearlstein and Katz in figurative art.[50] Indeed, the styles of these artists are closely related to new ones emerging in the sixties, such as minimalist abstraction, Pop Art and other variants of new realism, and optical art.

Fifties gestural and sixties post-gestural styles, each taken as a whole, can be thought of as two competing paradigms. The exemplar of the one was de Kooning; of the other, Stella. As Rosenblum wrote, the latter's "art directly intersects almost every important pictorial preoccupation of his time."[51] In the black stripe canvases that Stella first exhibited in 1959, he seemed to willfully challenge, indeed invert, every pictorial conception and romanticist justification of gesture painting "with a cold, smartaleck, humorless methodicalness that showed up, in the paintings . . . like a slap in the face."[52] In retrospect, it seems as if Stella took on the ambitious task of destroying the paradigm of gesture painting and establishing a new one instead. He aimed to be central to sixties art, as he said: "The idea in being a painter is to declare an identity. Not just my identity, an identity for me, but an identity big enough for everyone to share in. Isn't that what it's all about?"[53]

Stella began by questioning gesture painting:

> I think I had been badly affected by . . . the romance of Abstract Expressionism, . . . particularly as it filtered out to places like Princeton and around the country, which was the idea of the artist as a terrifically sensitive ever-changing, ever ambitious person—particularly (as described) in magazines like *Art News* and *Arts*, which I read religiously. It began to be kind of obvious and . . . terrible, and you began to see through it. . . . I began to feel very strongly about finding a way that wasn't so wrapped up in the hullabaloo, . . . something that was stable in a sense, something that wasn't constantly a record of your sensitivity, a record of flux.[54]

This Stella achieved in his black paintings, whose stark patterns of unmodulated black stripes, in contrast to gesture painting, "looked insolently static, intractably simple-minded,"[55] impersonal and cold. Moreover, like the gesture painters who tried to

223, 224
225

224

223  Frank Stella, *The Marriage of Reason and Squalor*, 1959.
90³/₄″ x 132³/₄″. The Museum of Modern Art, New York.

224  Frank Stella, *Coney Island*, 1958.
85¹/₄″ x 78³/₄″. Yale University Art Gallery, New
Haven, Connecticut.

formulate their emotive images in the improvisational act of painting, Stella preconceived his configurations, basing them on ideas so inflexible that the painting process seemed negligible—a shocking approach at the time.[56] And his primary concept was to *deduce* design from the literal shape of the canvas and the width of the stretcher. The result was a design of concentric rectangular stripes the same width as the stretcher. The internally consistent scheme seemed utterly self-referential, of and for itself, devoid of the extra-aesthetic polyreferentiality associated with gesture painting.

Carl Andre emphasized the self-referentiality of Stella's abstractions in the first statement written about them in 1959. "Stella is not interested in expression or sensitivity. He is interested in the necessities of painting. . . . His stripes are the paths of brush on canvas. These paths lead only into painting."[57] Stella himself said: "My painting is based on the fact that only what can be seen there *is* there. It really is an object. . . . If the painting were lean enough, accurate enough or right enough, you would just be able to look at it. All I want anyone to get out of my paintings, and all I ever get out them, is the fact that you can see the whole idea without any confusion. . . . What you see is what you see."[58]

There is a purist tenor in this remark, partaking of Reinhardt's aesthetics, and thus at odds with all of Abstract Expressionist thinking. Indeed, it was as if Stella took per-

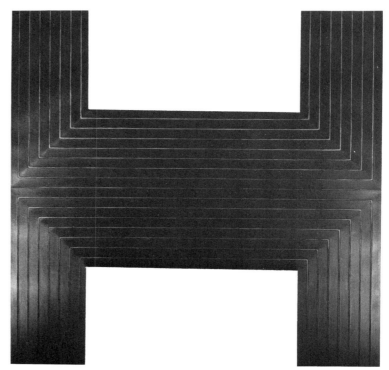

225  Frank Stella, *Pagosa Springs*, 1961. 99¼" x 99¼". Hirshhorn Museum and Sculpture Garden, Smithsonian Institution, Washington, D.C.

sonally Reinhardt's witty dictum: "A cleaner New York School is up to you."[59] And yet, Stella's painting can be viewed as a continuation of Abstract Expressionism, notably the color-field tendency. For example, their abstractness, large scale, openness, and non-painterly quality is reminiscent of Newman's work. Some critics, even while acknowledging their deadpan, cool aspect and polemical negation of Abstract Expressionism, saw them as romantic, mysterious.[60] But Stella's own generation was moved by the anti-romantic attributes of his pictures. As Lucy Lippard wrote, his "unequivocal rejections of illogic, illusion, and allusion, his advocacy of symmetry, impersonalism and repetition, was unique in its impact on younger artists, most of whom were older than Stella himself. He did not write, but his ideas spread through conversations and through criticism. . . . It seemed as though he had looked at painting as it *was* in 1959, brilliantly diagnosed its symptoms and prescribed the 'right' cure."[61]

Stella influenced the form of Pop Art, for example that of Lichtenstein and Warhol, which began to emerge two years or so after his black paintings were first shown.[62] But the more significant impact of Stella's work and thinking was on the development of the two main tendencies in sixties abstract art. The first conceived of a picture or a sculpture as a literal thing which derives "its strength from the affirmation of the *objectness* of the painting and from the directness of the artist's relations to his materials."[63] The second conceived of a picture as an allover field; "objectness was the thing to beat . . . [in order to] breakthrough to an inspired two-dimensionalism, and . . . the way to do it was through *color*, and, as much as possible, through color alone."[64]

Leider called these competing tendencies "literalism" and "abstraction." They were often thought of as contradictory, and artists and critics took sides. It is to the credit of Stella's painting that it was generally embraced (for different reasons, of course) by proponents of both directions. Because Stella's pictures had deep stretchers, literalists took them as an indication and then proof that "the best painting was moving inevitably toward three dimensions." For artists venturing into sculpture, "there is no sense in making art in three dimensions that tries to approximate the sensations or appearances of two-dimensions."[65] This attitude shaped the work of artists as diverse as Carl Andre, Dan Flavin, Michael Heizer, Don Judd, Robert Morris, Bruce Nauman, Alan Saret, Richard Serra, Robert Smithson, and Keith Sonnier.

Abstract painters saw in Stella's pictures an alternative to fifties painterly painting, that is, they were non-gestural; non-referential in image, color, and space; non-relational in design; and above all, non-illusionistic or flat. Stella so ruthlessly banished every traditional painterly variation, accent, and nuance that his pictorial space seemed ironed out to an unprecedented flatness.[66] This was of utmost importance to two kinds of Stella's admirers: the purists who believed that painting was fundamentally an art of surface, and the avant-gardists who proclaimed that his extreme renunciation of illusionism was a prophetic move.[67]

Stella's antipathy to gesture painting and Cubist-inspired relational design was shared by Louis and Noland. This was one reason that their names were often linked, even though Stella's anti-romantic black abstractions were far different in spirit from

Louis's and Noland's expressive color-fields. However, there was another, more important reason for considering Stella, Louis, and Noland as a group. The critical frame of reference in which stain painting came to be discussed (indeed, which shaped the way in which it was seen) was a formalist one first formulated by Greenberg. Actually this approach was applicable more to Stella's pictures than to stain painting, ironically so because Greenberg was unsympathetic to Stella's work.[68] Although Stella's painting was more germinal in the art of the sixties than Louis's or Noland's, Greenberg's formalist conception came to dominate the aesthetic discourse of the decade.

At the core of Greenberg's thinking was the notion that in the modern era, each of the arts was impelled toward "purity," that is, toward what was unique and irreducible in the nature of its medium, toward "self-definition." The urge of each art was to dissociate itself from the other arts. With reference to painting, this meant the elimination of such impurities as representation and illusion. Changes in style issued from the progressive reduction of the impurities which deny the medium and from the concomitant exploitation of its expressive resources. This process was achieved through aesthetic self-criticism, by purging "any and every effect that might conceivably be borrowed from or by the medium of any other art. Thus would each art be rendered 'pure,' and in its 'purity' find the guarantee of its standards of quality as well as of its independence."[69]

As Greenberg saw it, painting's unique qualities were "the flat surface, the shape of the support, the properties of pigment," and, most important, flatness, for it alone was "exclusive to pictorial art." He went on to say: "To achieve autonomy, painting has had above all to divest itself of everything it might share with sculpture."[70] As a purely optical art, painting had to get rid of tactile associations.[71]

Self-criticism was a historical process, seemingly determined by historical necessity, a notion that Greenberg probably borrowed from Marxism. He conceived of the history of modern art as a succession of styles, evolving and dying as if predestined, each of which (inevitably) moved art closer to self-definition. Moreover, "the more closely the norms of a discipline become defined, the less freedom they are apt to permit in many directions."[72] Once a style was established as modernist, all others were superseded. There was only one correct style at any one time and only one way of correctly perceiving it. The single-minded narrowness yet comprehensiveness of this reductive view of modern art, so internally consistent that there seemed to be no loose ends, was the source of its enormous power as polemic.

Also responsible for the influence of formalist criticism was Greenberg's brilliance, his persuasiveness, and his historical role. He had been among the earliest champions of Abstract Expressionism, testifying to the quality of his taste. Although he had largely withdrawn from the New York art world in the middle fifties, he reentered the scene in 1959 as the consultant of the French and Company Gallery. Moreover, his writing was made fully available in 1961 with the publication of *Art and Culture: Critical Essays*. Greenberg's point of view seemed to many to best illuminate "post-painterly" abstraction in all of its manifestations.

Many artists and a growing number of young critics and historians, e.g., Michael

Fried and Rosalind Krauss, found in Greenberg's writing an attractive alternative to the frequently excessive romantic or existentialist "poetic" criticism prevalent in the fifties, criticism based on such unverifiable notions as creative agony, self-discovery, and visions of the sublime. Young writers in the sixties refused to concern themselves with the subjective, symbolic, or visionary content of art and instead focused exclusively on the formal components of work, what they could point to and thus claim to be "objective" about.

Formalist rhetoric can be considered a verbal weapon used by sixties artists and critics to compete with Abstract Expressionist rhetoric which earlier had been used to attack the rationales of thirties geometric abstraction. In retrospect, it appeared that each generation devised a language that most suited the art of its time and that challenged the manner of the preceding generation. In the art-critical war, the main formalist target was Harold Rosenberg's writing, particularly the article on "action painting," which was taken (or more accurately, mistaken) for the quintessence of Abstract Expressionist thinking. Greenberg pinpointed the target in an article entitled, "How Art Writing Earns Its Bad Name," published in 1962. He called Rosenberg and all who took him seriously "inveterate futurists, votaries of false dawns, sufferers from the millennial complex . . . comedians." As Greenberg viewed it, Rosenberg's treatment of "action painting" put it outside the limits of art, and this angered him because the art was liable to be dismissed as non-art. Greenberg ridiculed "perversions and abortions of discourse: pseudo-description, pseudo-narrative, pseudo-exposition, pseudo-history, pseudo-philosophy, pseudo-psychology, and—worst of all—pseudo-poetry (which represents the abortion, not of discourse, but of intuition and imagination)." He concluded: "The pity, however, is not in the words; it is in the fact that art itself has been made to look silly."[73]

Greenberg's thinking exerted a powerful pressure on sixties criticism. Leider recalled that the publication of Rosenberg's essay on "action painting" in 1952 was felt to be "the precise moment at which the American artist was distorted into a gesturing existentialist, committing his romantic despair to canvas in a spurt of unpremeditated activity," and with no thought to art.[74] However, Leider was moved to defend Rosenberg against simplistic interpretations of his ideas. In this, he differed from most of his contemporaries generally who accepted Greenberg's opinions with few if any reservations.

Much as Greenberg claimed to want to protect what he called "painterly painting" from Rosenbergian rhetoric, to save the art from its friends, he himself was intent on denigrating it—because the looseness of its facture denied pictorial flatness and suggested illusionistic space, which even at its most abstract could not help but invite associations with nature. Besides, he believed that painterly painting had become too virtuoso, too much a matter of performance. To be sure, it had shown the way to making Cubist drawing painterly and that was an advance, but by 1955: "The look of the accidental had become an academic, conventional look."[75]

The butt of Greenberg's attack was the school of de Kooning, what he called "Tenth Street Painting," and in time, de Kooning himself, whose towering presence seemed to stand in the way of younger artists venturing in other directions much as Picasso had once blocked the way of de Kooning. The tactic used to topple de Kooning from his pedestal was to overstress his ties to tradition, and particularly to Cubism, and then to relegate any contemporary Cubist-inspired manner to the dust bin of history. Greenberg announced that the *new* abstract art "grows out of Painterly Abstraction" but "puts the main stress on color as hue. For the sake of this stress painterliness is being abandoned."[76] The future for at least one more generation of major artists was with stain painting, which staked all on open, optical color.

Greenberg claimed that his estimate of what the future would hold for modernist art was based on an evaluation of aesthetic quality. Indeed, he insisted that the sole issue of consequence for art criticism was whether a work of art was good or bad—and only taste could determine that. However, Greenberg did formulate an historico-aestheticist theory of the development of modernist art. Undeterred by the potential conflict between taste and dogma, he insisted that both led him to a single style and the same artists. He seems to have been uncomfortable with the "subjective" authority of taste alone (no matter how commanding) and needed an appeal to the "objective" authority of purist aesthetics and art history.

Greenberg's appeal to history was enormously attractive, doubly so because it was accompanied by an appeal to visually verifiable criteria. Krauss described the method and the psychological comfort of "the clear provability of an 'if x then y.' " "The syllogism we took up was historical in character, which meant that it read only in one direction; it was progressive. . . . [History] was like a series of rooms *en filade*. Within each room the individual artist explored, to the limits of his experience and his formal intelligence, the separate constituents of his medium. The effect of his pictorial act was to open simultaneously the door to the next space and close out access to the one behind him."[77]

Krauss went on to say: "I never doubted the absoluteness of that history. It was out there, manifest in a whole progression of works of art, an objective fact to be analyzed. It had nothing to do with belief, or privately held fantasies about the past. Insofar as modernism was tied to the objective datum of that history, it had, I thought, nothing to do with 'sensibility.' "[78] Krauss's comments reveal how art history based on notions of art's inexorable progression toward purity can become a mystique which allows a critic to transcend self by idolizing history.

Poggioli considered the purist mystique ultraist or hyperbolic in its extremeness and masochistic and decadent in its self-abnegation,[79] but Greenberg's disciples chose to disregard these effects throughout the sixties; after all, they were on the side of history, or so they doggedly believed. As Poggioli saw it, purists such as Greenberg developed a system which was first conceived of as an *effect* of modernism, which was then turned into a *cause* and finally into a *dogma* and a *mystique*. This in turn invaded and conquered the historical and critical disciplines, and ultimately operated as a criterion of judgment. Tillim remarked on how Greenberg was able to use history to validate his taste. His "linear view of art history necessarily interprets art in terms of a mainstream that issues from constantly evolving solutions to a formal problem. As the mainstream is by definition also the best art, i.e., major, all other art *must* pursue other enterprises for which reason it is minor—*if that*. Formalism, then, does not so much interpret history as it interprets *quality*, or rather it sees the history of art as the history of quality."[80]

But in the end, Greenberg was using ideology to validate *his* personal taste, for it was he who did the interpreting of what the next move in art was to be. Because of this, it is instructive to examine Greenberg's underlying tastes or appetites in art. These do not appear to have changed much since 1947, although his assessments of specific movements and artists have. In that year, Greenberg called for an "Apollonian" art, open, ample, hedonistic, and impassive; for "the development of a bland, large, balanced Apollonian art . . . [which] takes off from where the most advanced theory stops, and in which an intense detachment informs all."[81] Above all, Greenberg was disposed to openness, and thus to Impressionist-inspired field painting, an appetite shared generally by the sixties audience for advanced art.[82] Although Greenberg championed the first generation of the New York School, that generation did not create the hedonistic art that fit his theories and his sensibility. However, Louis, Noland, and somewhat later, Olitski, and their progeny in the sixties fulfilled Greenberg's requirements.

To sum up, there were two major thrusts in sixties aesthetics. One, inspired by the Duchamp-Cage impurist aesthetics, led artists beyond the realm of the traditional visual arts toward theater and the other arts, and toward "non-art" or "life," even though it continued to fertilize painting, sculpture, and collage. The other tended to emphasize the art object as an impersonal thing in itself rather than as an object expressive of its creator, although many were that, if inadvertently. The aim of the second thrust was on the one hand purist or art-for-art's-sake—to reveal the physical or aesthetic properties of painting or sculpture (e.g., Stella)—and on the other hand, realist—to describe things in the world (e.g., Warhol and Lichtenstein). In both cases, the treatment was factual or specific or literal rather than interpretive. It is difficult to account for this shift in sensibility. It may have been, as Alain Robbe-Grillet, a spokesman for a new "objectivity" in literature, insisted, that every psychological, emotional, and intellectual comment that an artist might make about human experience had been exhausted. What remained was to coolly describe the surface of the world, impervious to any system of meaning.[83]

Artists themselves were generally agreed that art had undergone a drastic change, whether they favored the new developments or not. In 1967, Barbara Rose and I published a series of thirty-five statements by artists under the heading, "Sensibility of the Sixties." We wrote in summary that the respondents as a whole "characterized the sensibility of the sixties as slick, hard-edge and impersonal."[84] They concurred on the other matters as well, notably about the changed condition of their lives, their "success," as it were.

> The artist is now, in Allan Kaprow's words, "a man of the world." . . . The traditional alienation of an avant-garde from society, however, does not seem diminished . . . Beneath the relative optimism runs an undertone of discontent.

Although the artist is now being feted, there is the suspicion that his works are being consumed rather than understood. . . .

There emerges a collective portrait of the artist in the sixties as an individual enjoying relative physical comfort but subject to continued emotional uneasiness. . . . Despite the fantastic amount of activity generated in and around the art world, despite the fact that artists are (often literally) pursued by an over-eager public and sought after as never before, as Paul Brach summed it up succinctly, "It's still lonely in the studio."[85]

# Notes

1. However, during the sixties, the pressure of commerce and fashion was exerted on avant-garde taste as never before. A new audience emerged that seemed excited by novelty, not quality, by the artist as celebrity, not by his or her art. (See Brian O'Doherty, "Vanity Fair: The New York Art Scene," *Newsweek*, 4 January 1965, pp. 54–59.) As art became increasingly fashionable, the fashion world entered the art world bringing its own aims, a few of which seemed similar to those of the avant-garde artists, such as the pursuit of the new and refusal to redo what had been done. But the values of the New York School were substantially different than those of the fashionable (with the exception, of course, of the few seriously interested in art); the one, intent on the expansion of perception, on achieving new visions; the other, on novelties that titillate, replaced by others with such regularity that they appear to have planned obsolescence built into them. Still, the fashion world exerted on the art world a growing demand for novelty and for a more rapid rate of style change—exacerbating the development of avant-garde art.

The pressures of fashion on art and the problems raised by them were intensified, but they were not new. Poggioli, in *The Theory of the Avant-Garde*, p. 79, saw them as inherent in the condition of the avant-garde: "The chief characteristic of fashion is to impose and suddenly to accept as a new rule or norm what was, until a minute before, an exception or whim, then to abandon it again after it has become a commonplace, everybody's 'thing.' " On p. 82, Poggioli went on to say that "the avant-garde is condemned to conquer, through the influence of fashion, that very popularity it once disdained—and this is the beginning of its end."

2. Sandler, "Ash Can Revisited," p. 30.

3. Seitz, *The Art of Assemblage*, p. 89. See also Tomkins, *The Bride and the Bachelors*, pp. 116–82.

4. T[homas] B. H[ess], "Reviews and Previews: Jean Tinguely," *Art News*, April 1960, pp. 16, 54.

5. Oldenburg's early assemblages, 1959–61, are among the most expressive of the time, but he did not continue to work with found substances.

6. Barbara Rose, in "How to Look at John Chamberlain's Sculpture," *Art International*, 16 January 1964, pp. 36–38, aimed, as she said, "to correct . . . a gross misconception of his [Chamberlain's] intentions and a faulty experiencing of his works." She denied the validity of making social allusions and insisted that the constructions be seen only as abstract art, "fully realized, articulate, sophisticated . . . sculpture." Donald Judd, in "Chamberlain: Another View," pp. 38–39, also emphasized the formal qualities of Chamberlain's sculpture.

7. Rivers's combination of gesture painting and commonplace motifs, e.g., Buick automobiles, also prepared the ground for Pop Art, but his influence was not as strong as Johns's.

8. William S. Rubin, *Frank Stella*, exhibition catalogue (New York: Museum of Modern Art, 1970), p. 12.

9. See Robert Morris, "Notes on Sculpture: Part 4," *Artforum*, April 1969, pp. 50–54. On p. 50, Morris wrote about the *Flags:* "Johns took the background of the painting and isolated the thing. The background became the wall. What was previously neutral became actual, while what was previously an image became a thing."

10. Johns also influenced Morris's pre-Minimalist work. John Tancock in "The Influence of Marcel Duchamp," *Marcel Duchamp*, exhibition catalogue (New York: Museum of Modern Art and Philadelphia: Philadelphia Museum of Art, 1973), p. 173, remarked that Morris's early work is "virtually a commentary on certain issues raised by Duchamp (frequently by way of Jasper Johns), . . . [Dissatisfied] with the painterly style of the 1950s, . . . [Morris] began producing objects that . . . enmeshed visual and verbal information in the most curious manner."

11. See Sidney Tillim, "The Figure and the Figuration in Abstract Expressionism," *Artforum*, September 1965, p. 45.

12. Hilton Kramer, "Month in Review," *Arts*, January 1960, p. 45.

13. Sidney Tillim, "The Present Outlook on Figurative Painting," *Arts Yearbook: Perspectives on the Arts* 5 (1961): 40.

14. Ibid., p. 56.

15. Ibid., p. 59.

16. See Philip Pearlstein, "Whose Painting Is It Anyway?" *Arts Yearbook: New York: The Art World* 7 (1964): 129–32.

17. Pearlstein's new realism was anticipated by Rivers in the middle fifties. However, Pearlstein carried literal rendering to an extreme with a rigor lacking in Rivers's most factual works, sections of which were more or less painterly. Moreover, Rivers painted in an extreme realist manner for only a short time, from 1954 to 1955.

18. Philip Pearlstein, "Figure Paintings Today Are Not Made in Heaven," *Art News*, Summer 1962, p. 39.

19. Ibid., p. 52.

20. Sidney Tillim, "Month in Review," *Arts Magazine*, April 1963, p. 46.

21. Barbara Rose and Irving Sandler, "Sensibility of the Sixties," *Art in America*, January–February 1967, p. 53.

22. Kirby, *Happenings*, p. 188. Dine did one more Happening, *Natural History* (*The Dreams*), New York, 1965.

23. Oldenburg, *Store Days*, p. 8. Oldenburg was also thinking of Pollock's conception of a picture with a life of its own.

24. It is noteworthy that Lichtenstein acknowledged a debt to Happenings. See Alloway, *American Pop Art*, p. 20.

25. See Higgins, *Postface*, p. 66. Prior to the organization of Fluxus, Maciunas ran the AG Gallery in New York, where he presented performances by Higgins, Maxfield, MacLow, Flynt, and Ray Johnson, among others.

In May 1963, nine months after the Festival at Wiesbaden, Fluxus artists came to the United States. George Brecht and Robert Watts arranged a Yam (May spelled backwards) Festival, a series of events and performances held at George Segal's farm in New Jersey, the Smolin Gallery, then managed by Al Hansen, and the Hardware Poets' Playhouse.

26. See Higgins's *Postface* for the fullest account of the movement, pp. 66–86.

27. Adrian Henri, *Total Art: Environments, Happenings, and Performance* (New York: Praeger Publishers, 1974), p. 157.

28. See Jan van der Marck, "George Brecht: An Art of Multiple Implications," *Art in America*, July–August 1974, pp. 48–52. Such Fluxus actions are precursors of Conceptual Art.

29. Henri, *Total Art*, p. 159.

30. Dick Higgins, "Something Else about Fluxus," *Art and Artists*, October 1972, pp. 17–18.

31. See ibid., p. 20. For a listing of Fluxus performances, see Sohm, ed., *Happenings & Fluxus*; Becker and Vostell, eds., *Happenings: Fluxus: Pop Art: Nouveau Realisme*; and David Mayor, ed., *Fluxshoe* (Cullompton, Devon, England: Beau Geste Press, 1972).

For an account of the continuing influence of Fluxus, see *Art and Artists*, October 1972, most of which is devoted to Fluxus, and Henri, *Total Art*, pp. 156–61.

In New York, the Fluxus spirit is perpetuated in the Annual Avant-Garde Festivals, whose prime movers are Charlotte Moorman and Nam June Paik. The thirteenth festival took place in 1977, and approximately five hundred artists participated.

32. For a listing of the performances and the participants of the Judson Dance Theater from 1962 to 1967, see "Judson: A Dance Chronology," *Ballet Review* 1:6 (1967): 54–72. Other participants were: George Brecht, Trisha Brown, Remy Charlip, Lucinda Childs, Philip Corner, Al Hansen, Fred Herko, Robert Huot, Simone Forti, Ray Johnson, Jill Johnston, John Herbert McDowell, Meredith Monk, Robert Morris, Aileen Passloff, Robert Rauschenberg, Charles Ross, Carolee Schneeman, Elaine Summers, Twyla Tharp, and James Waring.

33. Jill Johnston, "The New American Modern Dance," in Richard Kostelanetz, ed., *The New American Arts* (New York: Collier Books, 1967), p. 182. On p. 183, Johnston remarked: "In Dunn's class the limits of dance expanded to include any kind of activity at all. Non-dancers participated from the beginning."

34. Ibid., p. 183. Johnston stressed the influence of Ann Halprin, with whom several of the dancers in Dunn's class, including Forti, had studied on the West Coast. See also "Yvonne Rainer Interviews Ann Halprin," *Tulane Drama Review* 10 (Winter 1965): 142–66.

Yvonne Rainer, in *Works 1961–73* (New York: New York University Press, 1974), p. 5, describes the effect on her of an improvisation Forti did in 1960. "She scattered bits and pieces of rags and wood around the floor, landscape-like. Then she simply sat in one place for awhile, occasionally changed her position or moved to another place. I don't know what her intent was, but for me what she did brought the god-like image of the 'dancer' down to human scale more effectively than anything I had seen."

35. Johnston, "The New American Modern Dance," p. 184. Cunningham's *Collage*, 1953, composed for the first Creative Arts Festival at Brandeis University, used fifteen people from the university who were not trained dancers. They performed a number of natural gestures, e.g., combing hair, skipping, walking, and turning somersaults.

36. See Billy Klüver, Introduction, 9 *Evenings: Theatre and Engineering*, exhibition catalogue (New York: Foundation for Contemporary Performance Arts in cooperation with Experiments in Art and Technology, 1966).

37. For a discussion of the inception and evolution of EAT, see Barbara Rose, "Art as Experience, Environment, Process," in Billy Klüver, Julie Martin, and Barbara Rose, eds., *Pavilion by Experiments in Art and Technology* (New York: E. P. Dutton & Co., 1972), pp. 91–96.

38. See *Some More Beginnings: An Exhibition of Submitted Works Involving Technical Materials and Processes*, exhibition catalogue (New York: Experiments in Art and Technology, 1968). The show was an extension of *The Machine as Seen at the End of the Mechanical Age*, an exhibition organized at the Museum of Modern Art by Pontus Hultén, 1968.

39. See Klüver, Martin, and Rose, eds., *Pavilion by Experiments in Art and Technology*.

40. See Jack Burnham, *Software: Information Technology: Its New Meaning for Art*, exhibition catalogue (New York: Jewish Museum, 1970) and Maurice Tuchman, ed., *Art and Technology: A Report on the Art and Technology Program at the Los Angeles County Museum of Art 1967–71* (New York: Viking Press, 1971).

41. The *Tulane Drama Review* 10 (Winter 1965), edited by Richard Schechner, was devoted to Happenings and related events. Michael Benedikt, an art as well as drama critic, in-

cluded Happenings in his anthology of plays, *Theatre Experiments*, published in 1967.

42. The first concert in January 1960 was by the New York City Audio-Visual Group, including Higgins, Hansen, Poons, MacLow, Daniels, LaMonte Young, and Ray Johnson. The second concert in March contained works by Kaprow, Brecht, Rauschenberg, Johnson, Richard Maxfield, Cage, Hansen, and McDowell. The third concert in August was by the New York City Audio-Visual Group. The Living Theater later made its space available to Philip Corner and Carolee Schneeman.

MacLow's *The Marrying Maiden* was a work of "Chance Theater," in which unrelated lines were delivered according to throws of the dice.

43. Club panel, "Avant-Garde Theater," 12 February 1960. The participants were Julian Beck, Judith Malina, and others of the Living Theater.

44. Michael Kirby, "The Influence of Happenings and Events," unpaginated (a pamphlet inserted in Sohm, ed., *Happenings and Fluxus*). Kirby lists a number of theatrical companies active in 1970 who employed techniques borrowed from Happenings.

Margaret Croyden, in *Lunatics, Lovers and Poets: The Contemporary Experimental Theatre* (New York: McGraw-Hill Book Company, 1974), Introduction to chapter 5, corroborated Kirby's opinion. On pp. 87–88, Croyden wrote: "For all its shortcomings, the happening had a decisive influence on the arts, and on the theatre of the sixties in particular. . . . [It] helped usher in the Living Theatre." Croyden titled her next chapter, six, "The Living Theatre—The Mother of Them All," meaning later experimental theaters in America.

45. Kirby, "The Influence of Happenings and Events," unpaginated. It is noteworthy that Schechner had presented a Happening in New Orleans prior to founding the Performance Group.

46. Chaikin worked with Jean Claude Van Itallie and Megan Terry, authors respectively of *America Hurrah* (1966) and *Viet Rock* (1966).

47. See Kirby, "The Influence of Happenings and Events," unpaginated.

48. For an international listing of groups committed to political action that engage in theatrical activities, see Henri, *Total Art*, pp. 176–85; Eleanor Lester, "Is Abbie Hoffman the Will Shakespeare of the 1970's?" *New York Times*, 11 October 1970, sec. 11, pp. 3, 5; John Weisman, *Guerrilla Theatre* (Garden City, N. Y.: Anchor Books, 1973); and Henry Lesnick, ed., *Guerrilla Street Theater* (New York: Bard Books, 1973).

49. Allan Kaprow, "The Happenings Are Dead—Long Live the Happenings," *Artforum*, March 1966, pp. 37, 39.

50. It is noteworthy that Kelly's hard-edge abstraction, first exhibited in 1956, was peripheral until the sixties when it entered the main manner, that is, post-gestural painting.

51. Robert Rosenblum, *Frank Stella* (Harmondsworth, Middlesex, England: Penguin Books, 1971), p. 52.

52. Philip Leider, "Literalism and Abstraction: Frank Stella's Retrospective at the Modern," *Artforum*, April 1970, p. 45.

53. Ibid., p. 44.

54. Rubin, *Frank Stella*, p. 13.

55. Rosenblum, *Frank Stella*, p. 16.

56. Taking his cues from Johns, Stella grasped the major weakness in the aesthetics of gesture painting: the impossibility of determining whether a picture was "found" in the improvisational process of painting, as all gesture painters claimed, or whether it was deliberately "made." Stella articulated the growing suspicion that pictures that looked "found" were actually "made," and that this did not make them better or worse in quality. He then proposed that a valid painting could be predetermined and methodically executed.

57. Carl Andre, "Preface to Stripe Painting," in Miller, ed., *Sixteen Americans*, p. 76.

58. Bruce Glaser, interviewer, and Lucy R. Lippard, ed., "Questions to Stella and Judd," *Art News*, September 1966, pp. 58–59.

59. Lucy Lippard, "Ad Reinhardt: One Art," *Art in America*, September–October 1974, p. 72.

60. See Rubin, "Younger American Painters," p. 24; Rosenblum, *Frank Stella*, p. 18; and Betsy Baker, "Frank Stella: Perspectives," *Art News*, May 1970, p. 62.

61. Lucy R. Lippard, "Constellation in Harsh Daylight: The Whitney Annual," *Hudson Review* 21 (Spring 1968): 177–78.

62. See Alloway, *American Pop Art*, p. 19. Lucy R. Lippard, in *Pop Art* (New York: Praeger Publishers, 1966), p. 9, wrote that Pop Art "is the heir to an abstract rather than a figurative tradition."

In *Artforum*, February 1966, pp. 20–24, Lichtenstein said that he desired an impersonal look, and that unlike the artists who preceded him, he did not invent his images.

63. Leider, "Literalism and Abstraction," p. 45.

64. Ibid.

65. Ibid., p. 46.

66. Rosenblum, *Frank Stella*, pp. 16–17.

67. See Sheldon Nodelman, "Sixties Art: Some Philosophical Perspectives," *Perspecta: The Yale Architectural Journal* 11 (1967).

68. Stella himself recognized the ambiguous position of stain painting when he said: "Louis is the really interesting case. In every sense his instincts were Abstract Expressionist, and he was terribly involved with all of that, but he felt he had to move, too." Glaser and Lippard, "Questions to Stella and Judd," p. 58.

69. Clement Greenberg, "Modernist Painting," *Arts Yearbook* 4 (1960): 103–4.

70. Ibid.

71. Ibid., p. 105. Although Greenberg called for painting to rid itself of the sculptural, sculpture was not to rid itself of the pictorial. Paradoxically, he conceived of modernist sculpture as being "almost as exclusively visual in its essence as painting itself. It has been 'liberated' from the monolithic." See Greenberg, "Sculpture in Our Time," p. 23.

72. Greenberg, "Modernist Painting," p. 106.

73. Clement Greenberg, "Art: How Art Writing Earns Its Bad Name," *Encounter* 19 (December 1962): 70–71.

74. Philip Leider, "The New York School in Los Angeles," *Artforum*, September 1965, p. 5.

75. Greenberg, "The 'Crisis' of Abstract Art," p. 91.

76. Ibid., p. 92.

77. Rosalind Krauss, "A View of Modernism," *Artforum*, September 1972, p. 49. Greenberg believed that when a style became too familiar, and thus safe and lacking in difficulty, it had to be discarded. Responsible in part for this view was his dislike of "Kitch" art, easy and, hence, debased art.

78. Ibid., pp. 49–50.

79. Poggioli, *The Theory of the Avant-Garde*, p. 201.

80. Sidney Tillim, "Evaluations and Re-Evaluations," *Artforum*, Summer 1968, p. 22.

81. Clement Greenberg, "The Present Prospects of American Painting," *Horizon*, October 1947, pp. 27–28.

82. The painters whose work developed counter to this "Impressionist" tendency, such as Kelly, who emphasized shape as much as color, and, particularly, Held, who aimed to make his forms weighty and seemingly separable, did not receive as much recognition during the sixties as did Stella, Louis, and Noland. In the case of Held's work, an implicit Expressionist component also ran counter to the sensibility of the decade. Romantic content was not necessarily taboo if it was hedonistic, as was the stained painting of Louis and Noland.

83. See Alain Robbe-Grillet, *For A New Novel: Essays on Fiction* (New York: Grove Press, 1965).

84. Rose and Sandler, eds. "Sensibility of the Sixties," p. 44.

85. Ibid.

# Appendix A

*First-Generation Painters, Dates and Places of Birth*

BAZIOTES, William, born 1912, Pittsburgh, Pa.

BROOKS, James, born 1906, St. Louis, Mo.

FERREN, John, born 1905, Pendleton, Ore.

GORKY, Arshile, born 1905, Hayotz Dzore, Turkish Armenia

GOTTLIEB, Adolph, born 1903, New York City

GUSTON, Philip, born 1913, Montreal, Canada

HOFMANN, Hans, born 1880, Weissenburg, Germany

KLINE, Franz, born 1910, Wilkes-Barre, Pa.

DE KOONING, Willem, born 1904, Rotterdam, Holland

MCNEIL, George, born 1908, New York City

MOTHERWELL, Robert, born 1915, Aberdeen, Wash.

NEWMAN, Barnett, born 1905, New York City

POLLOCK, Jackson, born 1912, Cody, Wyo.

POUSETTE-DART, Richard, born 1916, St. Paul, Minn.

REINHARDT, Ad, born 1913, Buffalo, N.Y.

ROTHKO, Mark, born 1903, Dvinsk, Russia

STAMOS, Theodoros, born 1922, New York City

STILL, Clyfford, born 1904, Grandin, N. D.

TOMLIN, Bradley Walker, born 1899, Syracuse, N.Y.

TWORKOV, Jack, born 1900, Biala, Poland

VICENTE, Esteban, born 1906, Segovia, Spain

# Appendix B

*Second-Generation Artists, Dates and Places of Birth,*
*Art Education, and One-Person Shows in New York,*
*1950–1960*

BELL, LELAND: painter; born 1922; Cambridge, Md.; self-taught; exhibited at Hansa Gallery, 1955; Poindexter Gallery, 1957; Zabriskie Gallery, 1959.

BLADEN, RONALD: sculptor; born 1918; Vancouver, British Columbia; studied at Vancouver School of Art; California School of Fine Arts, San Francisco; exhibited at Brata Gallery, 1958.

BLAINE, NELL: painter; born 1922; Richmond, Va.; studied at Hans Hofmann School and with Stanley William Hayter; exhibited at Tibor de Nagy Gallery, 1953, 1954; Poindexter Gallery, 1956, 1958, 1960.

BLUHM, NORMAN: painter; born 1920; Chicago, Ill.; self-taught; exhibited at Castelli Gallery, 1957, 1959, 1960.

BRACH, PAUL: painter; born 1924; New York City; studied at University of Iowa; exhibited at Castelli Gallery, 1957, 1959.

BRIGGS, ERNEST: painter; born 1923; San Diego, Calif.; studied at California School of Fine Arts, San Francisco; exhibited at Stable Gallery, 1954, 1955; Wise Gallery, 1960.

BRODIE, GANDY: painter; born 1925; New York City; self-taught; exhibited at Urban Gallery, 1954; Durlacher Gallery, 1955, 1957, 1959.

CHAMBERLAIN, JOHN: sculptor; born 1927; Rochester, Ind.; studied at Art Students League, New York; exhibited at Jackson Gallery, 1960.

DE KOONING, ELAINE: painter; born 1920; New York City; studied at Leonardo da Vinci Art School, New York; American Artists School, New York; and with Willem de Kooning; exhibited at Stable Gallery, 1954, 1956; de Nagy Gallery, 1957; Graham Gallery and Tanager Gallery, 1960.

DE NIRO, ROBERT: painter; born 1922; Syracuse, N.Y.; studied at Syracuse Museum; Hans Hofmann School; Black Mountain College, N.C.; exhibited at Art of this Century Gallery, 1946; Egan Gallery, 1951, 1953, 1955; Poindexter Gallery, 1956; Zabriskie Gallery, 1958, 1960.

DIEBENKORN, RICHARD: painter; born 1922; Portland, Ore.; studied at Stanford University; California School of Fine Arts, San Francisco; University of New Mexico; exhibited at Poindexter Gallery, 1956, 1958.

DINE, JIM: painter, Happening-maker; born 1935; Cincinnati, Ohio; studied at Cincinnati Art

Academy; exhibited at Reuben Gallery, 1960; Happenings at Judson Gallery and Reuben Gallery, 1960.

DI SUVERO, MARK: sculptor; born 1933; Shanghai, China; studied at University of California, Berkeley; exhibited at Green Gallery, 1960.

DUGMORE, EDWARD: painter; born 1915; Hartford, Conn.; studied at Hartford Art School; California School of Fine Arts, San Francisco; University of Guadalajara, Mexico; exhibited at Stable Gallery, 1953, 1954, 1956; Wise Gallery, 1960.

DZUBAS, FRIEDEL: painter; born 1915; Berlin, Germany; studied at State Academy of Fine Arts, Berlin, and with Paul Klee; exhibited at de Nagy Gallery, 1952; Castelli Gallery, 1958; French and Company Gallery, 1959.

FORST, MILES: painter; born 1923; New York City; studied at Art Students League, New York; Hans Hofmann School; exhibited at Hansa Gallery, 1953, 1954, 1955, 1958.

FRANCIS, SAM: painter; born 1923; San Mateo, Calif.; studied at University of California, Berkeley; exhibited at Jackson Gallery, 1956, 1959.

FRANKENTHALER, HELEN: painter; born 1928; New York City; studied at Bennington College, Vt.; Art Students League, New York; Hans Hofmann School; exhibited at de Nagy Gallery, 1951, 1954, 1956, 1957, 1958; Emmerich Gallery, 1959, 1960.

FREILICHER, JANE: painter; born 1924; New York City; studied at Hans Hofmann School; exhibited at de Nagy Gallery, 1952, 1953, 1954, 1955, 1956, 1958, 1960; Tanager Gallery, 1960.

GOLDBERG, MICHAEL: painter; born 1924; New York City; studied at Art Students League, New York; Hans Hofmann School; exhibited at de Nagy Gallery, 1953; Poindexter Gallery, 1956, 1958; Jackson Gallery, 1960.

GOODNOUGH, ROBERT: painter; born 1917; Cortland, N.Y.; studied at Syracuse University, N.Y.; Ozenfant School of Fine Arts, New York; Hans Hofmann School; New York University; exhibited at de Nagy Gallery, 1952, 1953, 1954, 1955, 1956, 1957, 1958, 1959, 1960.

GRILLO, JOHN: painter; born 1917; Lawrence, Mass.; studied at Hartford Art School, Conn.; California School of Fine Arts, San Francisco; Hans Hofmann School; exhibited at de Nagy Gallery and Tanager Gallery, 1953; Schaefer Gallery, 1957, 1959.

GROOMS, RED: sculptor, Environment-maker, and Happening-maker; born 1937; Nashville, Tenn.; studied at Art Institute of Chicago; Peabody College, Nashville; New School for Social Research, New York; Hans Hofmann School; exhibited at City Gallery, 1958, 1959; Reuben Gallery, 1960; Happenings at Delancey Street Museum, 1959; Reuben Gallery, 1960.

HARTIGAN, GRACE: painter; born 1922; Newark, N.J.; studied with Isaac Lane Muse; exhibited at de Nagy Gallery, 1951, 1952, 1953, 1954, 1955, 1957, 1959.

HELD, AL: painter; born 1928; New York City; studied at Art Students League, New York; Académie de la Grand Chaumière, Paris; exhibited at Poindexter Gallery, 1958, 1960.

JOHNS, JASPER: painter; born 1930; Allendale, S.C.; studied at University of South Carolina; exhibited at Castelli Gallery, 1958, 1960.

JOHNSON, LESTER: painter; born 1919; Minneapolis, Minn.; studied at St. Paul Art School, Minn.; Minneapolis Art Institute; exhibited at Artists Gallery, 1951; Korman Gallery, 1954; Korman-Zabriskie Gallery, 1955; Zabriskie Gallery, 1957, 1959; City Gallery, 1959.

KAHN, WOLF: painter; born 1927; Stuttgart, Germany; studied at Hans Hofmann School; exhibited at Hansa Gallery, 1953, 1955; Borgenicht Gallery, 1956, 1959.

KAPROW, ALLAN: painter, Happening-maker; born 1927; Atlantic City, N.J.; studied at Hans Hofmann School; exhibited at Hansa Gallery, 1953, 1954; Urban Gallery, 1955; Bernard-Ganymede Gallery, 1956; Hansa Gallery, 1957, 1958; Happenings at Reuben Gallery, 1959; Judson Gallery and Reuben Gallery, 1960.

KATZ, ALEX: painter; born 1927; New York City; studied at Cooper Union, New York; Skowhegan School of Painting and Sculpture, Me.; exhibited at Roko Gallery, 1954, 1957; Tanager

Gallery, 1959; Stable Gallery, 1960.

KELLY, ELLSWORTH: painter; born 1923; Newburgh, N.Y.; studied at Boston Museum School; École des Beaux-Arts, Paris; exhibited at Parsons Gallery, 1956, 1959.

LESLIE, ALFRED: painter; born 1927; New York City; studied at New York University; exhibited at de Nagy Gallery, 1951, 1952, 1953, 1954, 1957; Hansa Gallery, 1956; Jackson Gallery, 1960.

LOUIS, MORRIS: painter; born 1912; Baltimore, Md.; studied at Maryland Institute of Art; exhibited at Jackson Gallery, 1957; French and Company Gallery, 1959, 1960.

MITCHELL, JOAN: painter; born 1926; Chicago, Ill.; studied at Smith College, Northampton, Mass.; Art Institute of Chicago; exhibited at New Gallery, 1952; Stable Gallery, 1953, 1957, 1958.

MÜLLER, JAN: painter; born 1922; Hamburg, Germany; died 1958; studied at Hans Hofmann School; exhibited at Hansa Gallery, 1953, 1954, 1955, 1956, 1957, 1958, 1958–59.

NOLAND, KENNETH: painter; born 1924; Asheville, N.C.; studied at Black Mountain College, N.C. and with Ossip Zadkine; exhibited at de Nagy Gallery, 1957; French and Company Gallery, 1959.

OLDENBURG, CLAES: sculptor, Happening-maker; born 1929; Stockholm, Sweden; studied at Yale University; Chicago Art Institute; exhibited at City Gallery, 1957–58; Cooper Union Museum Library and Judson Gallery, 1959; Reuben Gallery, 1960; Happening at Judson Gallery, 1960.

ORTMAN, GEORGE: painter, wood-relief maker; born 1926; Oakland, Calif.; studied at California College of Arts and Crafts, Oakland; with Stanley William Hayter; at Atelier André Lhote, Paris; Hans Hofmann School; exhibited at Tanager Gallery, 1953; Wittenborn Gallery, 1955; Stable Gallery, 1957, 1960.

PARKER, RAYMOND: painter; born 1922; Beresford, S.D.; studied at University of Iowa; exhibited at Widdifield Gallery, 1957, 1959; Kootz Gallery, 1960.

PASILIS, FELIX: painter; born 1922; Batavia, Ill.; studied with William Calfee and at Hans Hofmann School; exhibited at Hansa Gallery, 1953; Urban Gallery, 1954; Wittenborn Gallery, 1954; Bernard-Ganymede Gallery, 1956; de Nagy Gallery, 1957; Zabriskie Gallery, 1957; Nonagon Gallery, 1959; Marino Gallery, 1959; Great Jones Gallery, 1960.

PEARLSTEIN, PHILIP: painter; born 1924; Pittsburgh, Pa.; studied at Carnegie Institute of Technology; exhibited at Tanager Gallery, 1955; Peridot Gallery, 1956, 1957, 1959; Tanager Gallery, 1959.

PORTER, FAIRFIELD: painter; born 1907; Winnetka, Ill.; studied at Art Students League, New York; exhibited at de Nagy Gallery, 1952, 1954, 1955, 1956, 1958, 1959, 1960.

RAUSCHENBERG, ROBERT: assemblage-maker; born 1925; Port Arthur, Tex.; studied at Kansas City Art Institute; Académie Julian, Paris; Black Mountain College, N.C.; Art Students League, New York; exhibited at Parsons Gallery, 1951; Stable Gallery, 1953; Egan Gallery, 1955; Castelli Gallery, 1958.

RESNICK, MILTON: painter; born 1917; Bratislav, Russia; studied at Pratt Institute; American Artists School; Hans Hofmann School; exhibited at Poindexter Gallery, 1955, 1957, 1959; Howard Wise Gallery, 1960.

RIVERS, LARRY: painter; born 1923; New York City; studied at Hans Hofmann School; New York University; exhibited at de Nagy Gallery, 1951, 1952, 1953, 1954; Stable Gallery, 1954; de Nagy Gallery, 1955, 1956, 1957, 1958, 1959.

SCHUELER, JON: painter; born 1916; Milwaukee, Wis.; studied at California School of Fine Arts, San Francisco; exhibited at Stable Gallery, 1954; Castelli Gallery, 1957, 1959.

SEGAL, GEORGE: painter, sculptor; born 1924; New York City; studied at New York University; exhibited at Hansa Gallery, 1956, 1957, 1958, 1959; Green Gallery, 1960.

SMITH, LEON POLK: painter; born 1906; Chickasha, Okla.; studied at Oklahoma State College;

Columbia University; exhibited at Mills College, New York, 1955, 1956; Camino Gallery, 1956, 1958; Section II Gallery, 1958, 1960.

SOLOMON, HYDE: painter; born 1911; New York City; studied at Pratt Institute, New York, and with Chaim Gross and Ossip Zadkine; exhibited at Peridot Gallery, 1954, 1955, 1956; Poindexter Gallery, 1958, 1960.

STANKIEWICZ, RICHARD: sculptor; born 1922; Philadelphia, Pa.; studied at Hans Hofmann School, and with Fernand Léger and Ossip Zadkine, Paris; exhibited at Hansa Gallery, 1953, 1954, 1955, 1956, 1957, 1958; Stable Gallery, 1960.

STELLA, FRANK: painter; born 1936; Malden, Mass.; studied at Princeton University, N.J.; exhibited at Castelli Gallery, 1960.

SUGARMAN, GEORGE: sculptor; born 1912; New York City; studied with Zadkine in Paris; exhibited at Widdifield Gallery, 1960.

WHITMAN, ROBERT: Happening-maker; born 1935; New York City; studied at Rutgers University, N.J.; Columbia University; exhibited at Hansa Gallery, 1959; Reuben Gallery, 1959; Happenings at Reuben Gallery, 1959, 1960.

# Bibliography

## BOOKS

Allen, Donald, and Warren Tallman, eds. *The Poetics of the New American Poetry* (New York: Grove Press, 1973).

Allen, Donald, ed. *The New American Poetry 1945–1960* (New York: Grove Press, 1960).

Alloway, Lawrence. *American Pop Art* (New York: Macmillan Co., Collier Books, 1974).

———. "Jasper Johns and Robert Rauschenberg," in *Art Since Mid-Century: The New Internationalism*, Vol. II, "Figurative Art" (Greenwich, Conn.: New York Graphic Society, 1971).

Amaya, Mario. *Pop Art . . . and After* (New York: Viking Press, 1966).

American Abstract Artists, ed. *The World of Abstract Art* (New York: George Wittenborn, 1958).

Anderson, Wayne. *American Sculpture in Process: 1930/1970* (Boston: New York Graphic Society, 1975).

Artaud, Antonin. *The Theatre and Its Double* (New York: Grove Press, 1958).

Ashton, Dore. *The New York School: A Cultural Reckoning* (New York: Viking Press, 1973).

———. *Modern American Sculpture* (New York: Harry N. Abrams, 1968).

———. *Rauschenberg: XXXIV Drawings for Dante's Inferno* (New York: Harry N. Abrams, 1964).

———. *The Unknown Shore: A View of Contemporary Art* (Boston, Mass., and Toronto, Ont.: Little, Brown, 1962).

Baro, Gene. *Claes Oldenburg: Drawings and Prints* (New York: Chelsea House, 1969).

Battcock, Gregory, ed. *The New Art: A Critical Anthology* (New York: E. P. Dutton, 1969).

———. *Minimal Art: A Critical Anthology* (New York: E. P. Dutton, 1968).

Becker, Jürgen von, and Wolf Vostell, eds. *Happenings: Fluxus: Pop Art: Nouveau Realisme* (Reinbek near Hamburg: Rowohet, 1965).

Benedikt, Michael. *Theatre Experiments* (New York: Doubleday, 1967).

Berkson, Bill, and Irving Sandler, eds. *Alex Katz* (New York: Praeger Publishers, 1971).

Blesh, Rudi. *Modern Art U.S.A.: Men, Rebellion, Conquest 1900–1956* (New York: Alfred A. Knopf, 1956).

Cage, John. *A Year from Monday* (Middletown, Conn.: Wesleyan University Press, 1969).

———. *Silence: Lectures and Writings* (Cambridge, Mass.: M.I.T. Press, 1967).

Calas, Elena and Nicolas. *Icons and Images of the Sixties* (New York: E. P. Dutton, 1971).

Calas, Nicolas. *Art in the Age of Risk and Other Essays* (New York: E. P. Dutton, 1968).

Canaday, John. *Embattled Critic* (New York: Noonday Press, 1962).

Celentano, Francis. "The Origins and Development of Abstract Expressionism in the United States." Unpublished Master's thesis, New York University, 1957.

Chassman, Neil A., ed. *Poets of the Cities New York and San Francisco 1950–1965* (New York: E. P. Dutton, 1974).

Chernow, Burt. *Lester Johnson* (New York: David Anderson Publications, 1975).

Coplans, John. *Ellsworth Kelly* (New York: Harry N. Abrams, 1973).

———, ed. *Roy Lichtenstein* (New York: Praeger Publishers, 1972).

————. *Andy Warhol* (Greenwich, Conn.: New York Graphic Society, 1971).

Crichton, Michael. *Jasper Johns* (New York: Harry N. Abrams, 1977).

Crone, Rainer. *Andy Warhol* (New York: Praeger Publishers, 1970).

Croyden, Margaret. *Lunatics, Lovers and Poets: The Contemporary Experimental Theatre* (New York: McGraw-Hill, 1974).

Davis, Douglas. *Art and the Future: A History/Prophecy of the Collaboration Between Science, Technology and Art* (New York: Praeger Publishers, 1973).

Denby, Edwin. *Dancers, Buildings, and People in the Streets* (New York: Horizon Press, 1965).

Duberman, Martin. *Black Mountain: An Exploration in Community* (New York: E. P. Dutton, 1972).

Field, Richard S. *Jasper Johns: Prints 1960–1970* (New York: Praeger Publishers, 1970).

Finch, Christopher. *Pop Art: Object and Image* (London: Studio Vista, and New York: E. P. Dutton, 1968).

Forge, Andrew. *Robert Rauschenberg* (New York: Harry N. Abrams, 1969).

Fried, Michael. *Morris Louis* (New York: Harry N. Abrams, 1970).

Friedman, B. H., ed., *School of New York: Some Younger Artists* (New York: Grove Press, 1959).

Friedman, B. H., and Barbara Guest. *Goodnough* (Paris: The Pocket Museum, Editions Georges Fall, 1962).

Geldzahler, Henry. *New York Painting and Sculpture: 1940–1970* (New York: E. P. Dutton, 1969).

————. *American Painting in the Twentieth Century* (New York: Metropolitan Museum of Art, 1965).

Greenberg, Clement. "Avant-Garde Attitudes: New Art in the Sixties," in Bernard Smith, ed., *Concerning Contemporary Art: The Power Lectures* (Oxford: Clarendon Press, 1975).

————. *Art and Culture: Critical Essays* (Boston: Beacon Press, 1961).

————. *Hofmann* (Paris: The Pocket Museum, Editions Georges Fall, 1961).

Gruen, John. *The New Bohemia: The Combine Generation* (New York: Grosset & Dunlap, 1967).

————. *The Party's Over Now* (New York: Viking Press, 1972).

Hansen, Al. *A Primer of Happenings Time/Space Art* (New York: Something Else Press, 1965).

Henri, Adrian. *Total Art: Environments, Happenings, and Performance* (New York: Praeger Publishers, 1974).

Heron, Patrick. *The Changing Forms of Art* (London: Routledge and Kegan Paul, 1955).

Hess, Thomas B. *Barnett Newman* (New York: Walker and Co., 1969).

————. *Abstract Painting: Background and American Phase* (New York: Viking Press, 1951).

Higgins, Dick. *Postface* (New York: Something Else Press, 1964).

Hofmann, Hans. *Search for the Real* (Cambridge, Mass.: M.I.T. Press, 1967).

Holmes, John Clellon. *Nothing More to Declare* (New York: E. P. Dutton, 1967).

Hunter, Sam. *American Art of the Twentieth Century: Painting, Sculpture, Architecture* (New York: Harry N. Abrams, 1974).

————. *Larry Rivers* (New York: Harry N. Abrams, 1969).

————. "USA," in *Art Since 1945* (New York: Harry N. Abrams, 1958).

Janis, Harriet, and Rudi Blesh. *Collage: Personalities, Concepts, Techniques* (Philadelphia: Chilton Books, 1962).

Johnson, Ellen H. *Claes Oldenburg* (Baltimore: Penguin Books, 1971).

Kaprow, Allen. *Assemblage, Environments & Happenings* (New York: Harry N. Abrams, 1966).

————. *Some Recent Happenings* (New York: Something Else Press, 1966).

Kirby, Michael. *The Art of Time: Essays on the Avant-Garde* (New York: E. P. Dutton, 1969).

————. *Happenings, An Illustrated Anthology* (New York: E. P. Dutton, 1965).

Kluver, Billy, Martin, Julie, and Barbara Rose, eds. *Pavillion by Experiments in Art and Technology* (New York: E. P. Dutton, 1972).

Kostelanetz, Richard, ed. *The New American Arts* (New York: Collier Books, 1967).

Kozloff, Max. *Renderings: Critical Essays on a Century of Modern Art* (New York: Simon & Schuster, 1968).

————. *Jasper Johns* (New York: Harry N. Abrams, 1967).

Kramer, Hilton. *The Age of the Avant-Garde: An Art Chronicle of 1956–1972* (New York: Farrar, Straus & Giroux, 1973).

Kultermann, Udo. *New Realism* (Greenwich, Conn.: New York Graphic Society, 1972).

————. *Art and Life* (New York: Praeger Publishers, 1971).

————. *The New Painting* (New York: Praeger Publishers, 1969).

————. *The New Sculpture, Environments and Assemblages* (New York: Praeger, Publishers, 1969).

Lebel, Robert. *Marcel Duchamp* (New York: Grove Press, 1959).

Lippard, Lucy R. *Changing: Essays in Art Criticism* (New York: E. P. Dutton, 1971).

————. *Pop Art*. With contributions by Lawrence Alloway, Nancy Marmer and Nicolas Calas (New York: Praeger Publishers, 1966).

Lucie-Smith, Edward. *Late Modern: The Visual Arts Since 1945* (New York: Praeger Publishers, 1969).

McDarrah, Fred W. *The Artist's World in Pictures* (New York: E. P. Dutton, 1961).

McDonagh, Don. *The Rise and Fall of Modern Dance* (New York: Outerbridge and Dienstfrey, 1970).

Moore, Ethel, ed. *Contemporary Art 1942–72: Collection of the Albright–Knox Art Gallery.* With contributions by Irving Sandler, Edward F. Fry, John Russell, R. W. D. Oxenaar, Lawrence Alloway, Jan van der Marck, George Rickey, and Henry Geldzahler (New York: Praeger Publishers, 1973).

Motherwell, Robert, and Ad Reinhardt, eds. *Modern Artists in America* (New York: Wittenborn, Schultz, 1952).

Motherwell, Robert, ed. *The Dada Painters and Poets* (New York: Wittenborn, Schultz, 1951).

O'Doherty, Brian. *American Masters: The Voice and the Myth* (New York: Ridge Press/Random House, 1973).

O'Hara, Frank. *Art Chronicles: 1954–1966* (New York: Braziller, 1975).

———. *Standing Still and Walking in New York* (Bolinas, Calif.: Grey Fox Press, 1975).

———. "A Memoir," in Sam Hunter, ed., *Larry Rivers* (New York: Harry N. Abrams, 1969).

———. *In Memory of My Feelings* (New York: Museum of Modern Art, 1967).

Oldenburg, Claes. *Claes Oldenburg: Proposals for Monuments and Buildings, 1965–1969* (Chicago: Big Table Publishing Co., 1969).

———. *Store Days* (New York: Something Else Press, 1967).

Plagens, Peter. *Sunshine Muse: Contemporary Art on the West Coast* (New York: Praeger Publishers, 1974).

Poggioli, Renato. *The Theory of the Avant-Garde* (Cambridge, Mass.: Belknap Press/Harvard University Press, 1968).

Rainer, Yvonne. *Works, 1961–73* (New York: New York University Press, 1974).

Rodman, Selden. *Conversations with Artists* (New York: Devin-Adaro, 1957).

Rose, Barbara. *American Art Since 1900: A Critical History* (New York: Praeger Publishers, 1975).

———. *Helen Frankenthaler* (New York: Harry N. Abrams, 1971).

———. *American Painting: The Twentieth Century,* 2 vols. (New York: Skira, 1970).

Rosenberg, Bernard, and Norris Fliegel. *The Vanguard Artist: Portrait and Self-Portrait* (Chicago: Quadrangle Books, 1965).

Rosenberg, Harold. *Discovering the Present: Three Decades in Art, Culture, and Politics* (Chicago: University of Chicago Press, 1973).

———. *The De-Definition of Art: Action Art to Pop to Earthworks* (New York: Horizon Press, 1972).

———. *Artworks and Packages* (New York: Horizon Press, 1969).

———. *The Anxious Object: Art Today and Its Audience* (New York: Horizon Press, 1966).

———. *Tradition of the New* (New York: Horizon Press, 1959).

Rosenblum, Robert. *Frank Stella* (Harmondsworth, Middlesex, England: Penguin Books, 1971).

Rubin, William S. *Frank Stella* (New York: Museum of Modern Art, 1970).

Rublowsky, John. *Pop Art* (New York: Basic Books, 1965).

Russell, John, and Suzi Gablik. *Pop Art Redefined.* (London: Thames and Hudson, 1969).

Sandler, Irving. *The Triumph of American Painting: A History of Abstract Expressionism* (New York: Icon Editions/Harper & Row, 1970).

Schapiro, Meyer. "Rebellion in Art," in Daniel Aaron, ed., *America in Crisis* (New York: Alfred A. Knopf, 1952).

Schultze, Franz. *Fantastic Images: Chicago Art Since 1945* (Chicago: Follett Publishing Co., 1972).

Seitz, William. *George Segal* (New York: Harry N. Abrams, 1972).

———. *The Art of Assemblage* (New York: Museum of Modern Art, 1961).

———. Abstract Expressionist Painting in America. Unpublished Ph.D. dissertation, Princeton University, 1955.

Smith, Terence. "Abstract Expressionism: Ethical Attitudes and Moral Function." Unpublished Master's thesis, University of Sydney (Australia), 1974.

Solomon, Alan R. *New York: The New Art Scene* (New York: Holt, Rinehart and Winston, 1967).

Steinberg, Leo. *Other Criteria: Confrontations with Twentieth-century Art* (New York: Oxford University Press, 1972).

———. *Jasper Johns* (New York: George Wittenborn, 1963).

Tomkins, Calvin. *The Bride and the Bachelors* (New York: Viking Press, 1968).

———. *The World of Marcel Duchamp* (New York: Time-Life Library of Art, 1966).

Tuchman, Maurice. *Art and Technology: A Report on the Art and Technology Program at the Los Angeles County Museum of Art 1967–71* (New York: Viking Press, 1976).

Waldman, Diane. *Ellsworth Kelly: Drawings, Collages and Prints* (Greenwich, Conn.: New York Graphic Society, 1971).

———. *Roy Lichtenstein: Drawings and Prints* (New York: Chelsea House, 1969).

Wescher, Herta. *Collage,* trans. by Robert E. Wolf (New York: Harry N. Abrams, 1968).

## EXHIBITION CATALOGUES

Alloway, Lawrence. *Leon Polk Smith's Geometric Paintings 1945–1953* Galerie Chalette, New York, 1970.

———. *Eleven from the Reuben Gallery,* Solomon R. Guggenheim Museum, New York, 1965.

———. "Junk Culture as a Tradition," *New Forms—New Media I,* Martha Jackson Gallery, New York, 1960.

———. *Leon Polk Smith,* San Francisco Museum of Art, San Francisco, Calif., 1968.

———. *Morris Louis 1929–1962*, Solomon R. Guggenheim Museum, New York, 1963.

———. *Six Painters and the Object*, Solomon R. Guggenheim Museum, New York, 1963.

———. *Systemic Painting*, Solomon R. Guggenheim Museum, New York, 1966.

Arnason, H. Harvard. *American Abstract Expressionists and Imagists*, Solomon R. Guggenheim Museum, New York, 1961.

———. *60 American Painters, 1960: Abstract Expressionist Painting of the Fifties*, Walker Art Center, Minneapolis, Minn., 1960.

Ashton, Dore, and Bernard Dorival. *New York and Paris: Paintings of the 1950s*, Museum of Fine Arts, Houston, Tex., 1959.

Baro, Gene. *Paul Feeley 1910–1966*, Solomon R. Guggenheim Museum, New York, 1968.

Baur, John I. H. *Nature in Abstraction*, Whitney Museum of American Art, New York, 1958.

———. *The New Decade: 35 American Painters and Sculptors*, Whitney Museum of American Art, New York, 1955.

Bryant, Edward. *Nell Blaine, Works, 1955–1973*, Picker Gallery, Hamilton, N.Y., 1974–75.

Buck, Robert T., with Linda L. Cathcart, Gerald Nordland, and Maurice Tuchman. *Richard Diebenkorn*, Albright–Knox Art Gallery, Buffalo, N.Y., 1976.

Buck, Robert T. *Sam Francis Paintings 1947–1972*, Albright–Knox Art Gallery, Buffalo, N.Y., 1972.

Burnham, James. *Software: Information Technology: Its New Meaning for Art*, Jewish Museum, New York, 1970.

Bush, Martin H., and Kenward, Moffett, *Goodnough*, Wichita, Kansas: Wichita State University, 1973.

Cathcart, Linda L., and Marcia Tucker. *Alfred Jensen: Paintings and Diagrams from the Years 1957–1977*, Albright–Knox Art Gallery, Buffalo, N.Y., 1978.

Coe, Ralph T. *Popular Art*, Nelson Gallery–Atkins Museum, Kansas City, Mo., 1963.

Colt, Priscilla. *Color and Field 1890–1970*, Albright–Knox Art Gallery, Buffalo, N.Y., 1970.

*Contemporary American Painting and Sculpture*, University of Illinois, Urbana, Ill., 1948 to date (biennial).

Coplans, John. *Pop Art USA*, Oakland Art Museum, Oakland, Calif., 1963.

———. *Roy Lichtenstein*, Pasadena Art Museum, Pasadena, Calif., 1967.

Demetrion, James T. *Allan Kaprow*, Pasadena Art Museum, Pasadena, Calif., 1967.

Elderfield, John. *Morris Louis*, Arts Council of Great Britain, London, 1974.

Finkelstein, Louis. *Painterly Representation*, Ingber Gallery, New York, 1975.

Fried, Michael. *Frank Stella: An Exhibition of Recent Paintings*, Pasadena Art Museum, Pasadena, Calif., 1966.

———. *Kenneth Noland*, Jewish Museum, New York, 1965.

———. *Morris Louis, 1912–1962*, Museum of Fine Arts, Boston, Mass., 1963.

———. *Three American Painters: Kenneth Noland, Jules Olitski, Frank Stella*, Fogg Art Museum, Harvard University, Cambridge, Mass., 1965.

Goossen, E. C. *The Art of the Real: USA 1948–1968*, Museum of Modern Art, New York, 1968.

———. *Ellsworth Kelly*, Museum of Modern Art, New York, 1973.

———. *Helen Frankenthaler*, Whitney Museum of American Art, New York, 1969.

Gordon, John. *Geometric Abstraction in America*, Whitney Museum of American Art, New York, 1962.

———. *Jim Dine*, Whitney Museum of American Art, New York, 1970.

Green, Samuel Adams. *Andy Warhol*, Institute of Contemporary Art, University of Pennsylvania, Philadelphia, 1965.

Greenberg, Clement. *Barnett Newman*, French and Company Gallery, New York, 1959.

———. *Post-Painterly Abstraction*, Los Angeles County Museum of Art, Los Angeles, Calif., 1964.

———. *Three New American Painters: Louis, Noland, Olitski*, Norman Mackenzie Art Gallery, Regina, Sask., Canada, 1963.

Heller, Ben. *Toward a New Abstraction*, Jewish Museum, New York, 1963.

Hopkins, Henry. *Milton Resnick: Selected Large Paintings*, Fort Worth Art Center, Fort Worth, Tex., 1971.

Hulten, K. G. Pontus. *The Machine as Seen at the End of the Mechanical Age*, Museum of Modern Art, New York, 1968.

Hunter, Sam. *Larry Rivers*, Poses Institute of Fine Arts, Brandeis University, Waltham, Mass., 1965.

———. *New Directions in American Paintings*, Poses Institute of Fine Arts, Brandeis University, Waltham, Mass., 1963.

Johnson, Ellen, J. *Painting/Sculpture—Dine, Oldenburg, Segal*, Art Gallery of Ontario, Toronto, 1967.

Kaprow, Allan. *18 Happenings in 6 Parts*, Reuben Gallery, New York, 1959.

———. "Notes on the Creation of a Total Art," *Allan Kaprow*, Hansa Gallery, New York, 1958.

———. "Some Observations on Contemporary Art," *New Forms—New Media I*, Martha Jackson Gallery, New York, 1960.

Klüver, Billy. *Nine Evenings: Theatre & Engineering*, Foundation for Contemporary Performance Arts in cooperation with Experiments in Art and Technology, New York, 1966.

———. *Some More Beginnings: An Exhibition of Submitted Works Involving Technical Materials and Processes*, Experiments in Art and Technology, New York, 1966.

Langsner, Jules. *Four Abstract Classicists*, Los Angeles County Museum of Art, Los Angeles, Calif., 1959.

MacAgy, Douglas. *Pop Goes the Easel*, Contemporary Arts Museum, Houston, Tex., 1963.

McChesney, Mary Fuller. A *Period of Exploration 1945–1950*, Oakland Museum Art Department, Oakland, Calif., 1973.

Marck, Jan van der. *Richard Stankiewicz and Robert Indiana*, Walker Art Center, Minneapolis, Minn., 1963.

Miller, Dorothy C. *Fifteen Americans*, Museum of Modern Art, New York, 1952.

——. *12 Americans*, Museum of Modern Art, New York, 1956.

——. *Sixteen Americans*, Museum of Modern Art, New York, 1959.

Mills, Paul. *Contemporary Bay Area Figurative Painting*, Oakland Art Museum, Oakland, Calif., 1957.

Moffett, Kenworth. *Jules Olitski*, Whitney Museum of American Art, New York, 1973.

Monte, James K. *Mark di Suvero*, Whitney Museum of American Art, New York, 1975–76.

Morris, Kyle. *Vanguard 1955*, Walker Art Center, Minneapolis, Minn., 1955.

Museum of Modern Art, New York, *The New American Painting*, 1959.

Nochlin, Linda. *Philip Pearlstein*, Museum of Art, University of Georgia, Athens, Ga., 1970.

Nordland, Gerald. *Richard Diebenkorn*, Washington Gallery of Modern Art, Washington, D.C., 1964.

——. *The Washington Color Painters*, Washington Gallery of Modern Art, Washington, D.C., 1963.

O'Hara, Frank. *Helen Frankenthaler*, Jewish Museum, New York, 1960.

Richardson, Brenda. *Frank Stella: The Black Paintings*, Baltimore Museum of Art, Baltimore, Md., 1976.

Robertson, Bryan. *Robert Rauschenberg: Paintings, Drawings, and Combines 1949–1964*, Whitechapel Art Gallery, London, England, 1964.

Rose, Barbara. *Claes Oldenburg*, Museum of Modern Art, New York, 1970.

Rubin, William S. *Frank Stella*, Museum of Modern Art, New York, 1970.

Sandler, Irving, Lucy Lippard, G. R. Swenson, and Waldo Rasmussen. *Two Decades of American Painting*, Museum of Modern Art, New York, 1966.

Sandler, Irving. *Concrete Expressionism*, New York University Art Collection, New York, 1965.

——. *Tanager Gallery*, Tanager Gallery, New York, 1959.

Seitz, William C. *The Art of Assemblage*, Museum of Modern Art, New York, 1961.

——. *Hans Hofmann*, Museum of Modern Art, New York, 1963.

Selle, Carol. *Larry Rivers Drawings 1949–1969*, Art Institute of Chicago, 1970.

Selz, Peter. *New Images of Man*, Museum of Modern Art, New York, 1959.

Siegal, Jeanne. *Kenneth Noland, Early Circle Paintings*, Visual Arts Gallery, School of Visual Arts, New York, 1975.

Smith, Gordon. *Mixed Media and Pop Art*, Albright–Knox Art Gallery, Buffalo, N.Y., 1963.

Sohm, Hans, ed. *Happenings & Fluxus*, Kölnischen Kunstverein, Cologne, Germany, 1970.

Solomon, Alan. *Jasper Johns*, Jewish Museum, New York, 1964.

——. *Painting in New York: 1944 to 1969*, Pasadena Museum of Art, Pasadena, Calif., 1969.

——. *Robert Rauschenberg*, Jewish Museum, New York, 1963.

——. *The Second Breakthrough: 1959–1964*, University of California, Irvine, Calif., 1969.

Steinberg, Leo. *Artists of the New York School: Second Generation*, Jewish Museum, New York, 1957.

Sweeney, James Johnson. *Sam Francis*, Museum of Fine Arts, Houston, Tex., 1967.

——. *Younger American Painters: A Selection*, Solomon R. Guggenheim Museum, New York, 1954.

——. *Younger European Painters: A Selection*, Solomon R. Guggenheim Museum, New York 1953–54.

Swenson, G. R. *The Other Tradition*, Institute of Contemporary Art, University of Pennsylvania, Philadelphia, 1966.

Tancock, John. "The Influence of Marcel Duchamp," *Marcel Duchamp*, Museum of Modern Art, New York, 1973.

Tuchman, Maurice, ed. *American Sculpture of the Sixties*, Los Angeles County Museum of Art, Los Angeles, Calif., 1967.

——. *New York School: The First Generation: Painting of the 1940s and 1950s*, Los Angeles County Museum of Art, Los Angeles, Calif., 1965.

Tucker, Marcia. *Al Held*, Whitney Museum of American Art, New York, 1974.

——. *Joan Mitchell*, Whitney Museum of American Art, New York, 1974.

Ventura, Anita. *Colorists 1950–1965*, San Francisco Museum of Art, San Francisco, Calif., 1965.

Waldman, Diane. *Kenneth Noland: A Retrospective*, Solomon R. Guggenheim Museum, New York, 1977.

——. *John Chamberlain*, Solomon R. Guggenheim Museum, New York, 1971.

Whitney Museum of American Art, Downtown Branch, New York, *Nine Artists/Coenties Slip*, 1954.

## PERIODICALS

Alloway, Lawrence. "Leon Golub: Art and Politics," *Artforum*, October 1974, pp. 66–71.

——. "Leon Polk Smith: Dealings in Equivalence," *Art in America*, July–August 1974, pp. 58–61.

———. "Sam Francis: From Field to Arabesque," *Artforum*, February 1973, pp. 37–41.

———. "Derealized Epic; James Rosenquist," *Artforum*, June 1972, pp. 35–41.

———. "Gesture into Form," *Art News*, April 1972, pp. 42–44.

———. "On Style: An Examination of Roy Lichtenstein's Development, Despite a New Monograph on the Artist," *Artforum*, March 1972, pp. 53–59.

———. "Frankenthaler as Pastoral," *Art News*, November 1971, pp. 66–68, 89–90.

———. "Rauschenberg's Graphics," *Art and Artists*, September 1970, pp. 18–21.

———. "The Man Who Liked Cats: The Evolution of Jasper Johns," *Arts*, September–October 1969, pp. 40–43.

———. "Popular Culture and Pop Art," *Studio International*, July–August 1969, pp. 17–21.

———. "Roy Lichtenstein," *Studio International*, January 1968, pp. 25–31.

———. "Art in Escalation: The History of Happenings: A Question of Sources," *Arts*, December 1966–January 1967, pp. 40–43.

———. "Apropos of Jim Dine," *Oberlin College Bulletin*, 23 (Fall 1965): 21–24.

———. "Leon Smith: New Work and Its Origin," *Art International*, April 25, 1963, pp. 51–53.

———. "Heraldry and Sculpture," *Art International*, April 1962, pp. 52–53.

———. "Easel Painting at the Guggenheim," *Art International*, Christmas 1961, pp. 26–34.

———. "Sign and Surface: Notes on Black and White Painting in New York," *Quadrum*, 9 (1960): 49–62.

———. "London Letter: Classicism or Hard Edge?" *Art International*, Vol. 4, No. 2–3 (1960): 60–63, 71.

Andersen, Wayne. "American Sculpture: The Situation in the Fifties," *Artforum*, Summer 1967, pp. 60–67.

Antin, David. "Alex Katz and the Tactics of Representation," *Art News*, April 1971, pp. 44–47, 75–77.

Arnason, H. H. "The New Geometry," *Art in America*, Vol. 48, No. 3 (1960): 54–61.

"Artists on the Current Scene: A Portfolio of Notable Paintings and Sculpture by American Artists," *Arts Yearbook*, 4 (1960): 141–168.

Ashbery, John. "Bell: Virtuosity Without Self-Interest," *Art News*, February 1970, pp. 44–45, 64–68.

———. "The Invisible Avant-Garde," *Art News Annual*, 34 (1969), 125–133.

———. "Brooms and Prisms," *Art News*, March 1966, pp. 58–59, 82–84 (on Jasper Johns).

———. "An Expressionist in Paris," *Art News*, April 1965, pp. 44–45, 63–64 (on Joan Mitchell).

Ashton, Dore. "Retrospective/Perspective 1961–1974," *Arts*, September 1974, pp. 34–39.

———. "Principles of Transitoriness," *Studio*, September 1973, pp. 91–92.

———. "Richard Diebenkorn's Paintings," *Arts*, December 1971–January 1972, pp. 36–37.

———. "A Planned Coincidence," *Art in America*, September–October 1969, pp. 36–47.

———. "An Interview with Marcel Duchamp," *Studio International*, June 1966, pp. 244–247.

———. "Helen Frankenthaler," *Studio International*, August 1965, pp. 52–55.

———. "Kelly's Unique Spatial Experiences," *Studio International*, July 1965, p. 40.

———. "Al Held: New Spatial Experiences," *Studio International*, November 1964, pp. 210–213.

———. "Recent Happenings and Unhappenings," *Studio International*, November 1964, pp. 220–223.

———. "Art USA, 1962," *Studio*, March 1962, pp. 84–95.

———. "Rauschenberg's Thirty-four Illustrations for Dante's Inferno," *Metro*, 2 (May 1961), 52–61.

———. "Perspective de la Peinture Américaine," *Cahiers d'Art*, 33–35 (1960): 203–220.

———. "La Sculpture Américaine," *XXᵉ Siècle*, 22 (1960): 85–91.

———. "New Images of Man," *Arts and Architecture*, November 1959, pp. 14–15.

———. "Gabriel Kohn," *Cimaise*, September–October–November 1959, pp. 58–65.

———. "Some Lyricists in the New York School," *Art News and Review*, November 22, 1958, pp. 3, 8.

———. "Art: Japanese Avantgardism," *Arts and Architecture*, November 1958, pp. 4–5, 34.

———. "Art," *Arts and Architecture*, September 1956, pp. 4, 6, 13, 35–36.

———. "Art," *Arts and Architecture*, March 1956, pp. 14–15, 43–44.

———. "Art," *Arts and Architecture*, February 1956, pp. 10–12.

———. "Art," *Arts and Architecture*, January 1956, pp. 10, 32–33.

———. "What Is Avant-Garde?" *Arts Digest*, 15 September 1955, pp. 6–8.

Baigell, Matthew. "American Painting: On Space and Time in the Early 1960's," *Art Journal*, Vol. 28, No. 4 (Summer 1969), 368–374, 387–401.

———. "American Abstract Expressionism and Hard Edge: Some Comparisons," *Studio International*, January 1966, pp. 10–15.

Baker, Elizabeth C. "Mark di Suvero's Burgundian Season," *Art in America*, May–June 1974, pp. 59–63.

———. "The Subtleties of Ellsworth Kelly," *Art News*, November 1973, pp. 30–33.

———. "The Chamberlain Crunch," *Art News*, February 1972, pp. 26–31, 60–61.

———. "Frank Stella: Perspectives," *Art News*, May 1970, pp. 46–49, 62–64.

———. "Morris Louis: Veiled Illusions," *Art News*, April 1970, pp. 36–39, 62–64.

Baldwin, Carl R. "On the Nature of Pop," *Artforum*, June 1974, pp. 34–38.

Bannard, Walter Darby. "Notes on American Painting of the Sixties," *Artforum*, January 1970, pp. 40–45.

Barber, Allen. "Making Some Marks," *Arts*, June 1974, pp. 49–51 (an interview with Grace Hartigan).

Baro, Gene. "The Art of Paul Feeley," *Studio International*, July 1968, pp. 24–28.

————. "American Sculpture: The New Scene," *Studio International*, January 1968, pp. 9–19.

————. "The Achievement of Helen Frankenthaler," *Art International*, September 20, 1967, pp. 33–38.

————. "Claes Oldenburg, or the Things of This World," *Art International*, November 20, 1966, pp. 41–43, 45–48.

————. "Paul Feeley: The Art of the Definite," *Arts*, February 1966, pp. 19–25.

Barozzi, Paolo. "Happenings à New York," *Metro* 3 (1961), 114–116.

Baron, Stephanie. "Matisse and Contemporary Art: 1950–1970," *Arts Magazine*, May 1975, pp. 66–67.

————. "Giving Art History the Slip," *Art in America*, March–April 1974, pp. 80–84.

Battcock, Gregory. "It Is," *Arts*, April 1974, pp. 31–33.

————. "Re-evaluating Abstract Expressionism," *Arts*, December 1969–January 1970, 46–48.

————. "Critique: Rauschenberg's New Clocks at Castelli," *Arts Magazine*, May 1969, p. 16.

————. "Helen Frankenthaler," *Art and Artists*, May 1969, pp. 52–55.

Baur, John. "The New Landscape: Three Directions," *Art in America*, June 1963, pp. 26–35.

Beck, Rosemarie. "In My Studio," *Perspectives on the Arts* (*Arts Yearbook* 5) (1961), 60–64.

Bell, Jane. "John Chamberlain: New Sculpture," *Arts*, June 1975, pp. 88–89.

Bell, Leland. "The Case for Derain as an Immortal," *Art News*, May 1960, pp. 24–27, 61–62.

Belz, Carl. "Fitting Sam Francis into History," *Art in America*, January–February 1973, pp. 40–45.

Benedikt, Michael. "Yoko Notes," *Art and Artists*, January 1972, pp. 26–29.

————. "Drexler's Dialectical Nudes," *Art News*, February 1966, pp. 50–51, 60.

————. "Youngerman: Liberty in Limits," *Art News*, September 1965, pp. 43–45, 54–55.

————. "Fairfield Porter: Minimum of Melodrama," *Art News*, March 1964, pp. 36–37, 66–67.

Benson, Legrace. "The Washington Scene (Some Preliminary Notes on the Evolution of Art in Washington, D.C.)," *Art International*, Christmas 1969, pp. 21–23, 36–42, 50.

Berkson, Bill. "Frank O'Hara and His Poems," *Art and Literature*, 12 (Spring 1967): 53–63.

————. "Ronald Bladen: Sculpture and Where We Stand," *Art and Literature*, 12 (Spring 1967): 139–150.

————. "Poet of the Surface," *Arts*, May–June 1965, pp. 44–50.

————. "Michael Goldberg Paints a Picture," *Art News*, January 1964, pp. 42–45, 65–67.

————. "Bluhm Paints a Picture," *Art News*, May 1963, pp. 38–41, 50–52.

Berkson, William. "Alex Katz's Surprise Image," *Arts*, December 1965, pp. 22–26.

————. "The Sculpture of Larry Rivers," *Arts*, November 1965, pp. 49–52.

Berrigan, Ted. "Painter to the New York Poets," *Art News*, November 1965, pp. 44–47, 71–72.

Betsch, Carolyn. "A Catalogue Raisonné of Warhol's Gestures," *Art in America*, May–June 1971, p. 47.

Borden, Lizzie. "Early Work of Agnes Martin," *Artforum*, April 1973, pp. 39–44.

Bowles, Jerry. "Helen Frankenthaler at the Whitney," *Arts*, March 1969, pp. 20–23.

Bowling, Frank. "If You Can't Draw, Trace," *Arts*, February 1971, pp. 19–21 (talks with Larry Rivers).

Brach, Paul. "Postscript: The Fifties," *Artforum*, September 1965, p. 32.

————. "Statement," *It Is*, 3 (Winter–Spring 1959): 26.

Burton, Scott. "John Button," *Art and Literature*, 11 (Winter 1967): 69–81.

————. "Anne Arnold's Animals," *Art and Literature*, 7 (Winter 1965), 122–135.

"John Cage in Los Angeles," *Artforum*, February 1965, pp. 17–19.

Cage, John. "26 Statements re Duchamp," *Art and Literature*, 3 (Autumn–Winter 1964): 9–10.

————. "On Robert Rauschenberg, Artist, and His Work," *Metro*, 2 (May 1961): 36–51.

Calas, Nicolas. "Jim Dine: Tools & Myth," *Metro*, 7 (1962): 76–79.

————. "Larry Rivers," *Art International*, March 1, 1961, pp. 36–39.

————. "ContiNuance," *Art News*, February 1959, pp. 36–39.

Campbell, Lawrence. "Dotted Light," *Art News*, April 1972, pp. 30–31, 71–73 (on Sally Hazelet).

————. "The Great Circle Route: Alexander Liberman," *Art News*, April 1970, pp. 52–57, 61–62.

————. "In the Mist of Life: Wolf Kahn, Passionate Landscapist of Hills and Barns," *Art News*, February 1969, pp. 42–43, 54.

————. "Paul Georges Paints a Nude," *Art News*, January 1966, pp. 52–55, 59–60.

————. "Lester Johnson on the Bowery," *Art News*, February 1964, pp. 46–47, 60–61.

————. "Five Americans Face Reality," *Art News*, September 1963, pp. 25–27, 54.

————. "Elaine de Kooning: Portraits in a New York Scene," *Art News*, April 1963, pp. 38–39, 63–64.

————. "Parker Paints a Picture," *Art News*, November 1962, pp. 40–43, 70–72.

————. "Lester Johnson Paints a Picture," *Art News*, March 1961, pp. 32–35, 51–55.

————. "Elaine de Kooning Paints a Picture," *Art News*, December 1960, pp. 40–44, 61–63.

————. "Reviews and Previews: 813," *Art News*, December 1960, p. 12.

————. "Blaine Paints a Picture," *Art News*, May 1959, pp. 38–41, 61–62.

————. "Resnick Paints a Picture," *Art News*, December 1957, pp. 38–41, 65–66.

————. "New Figures at the Uptown Whitney," *Art News*, February 1955, pp. 34–35, 67.

Carmean, E. A., Jr. "Morris Louis and the Modern Tradition: I: Abstract Expressionism," *Arts*, September 1976, pp. 70–75.

Carpenter, Ken. "To Re-examine the Work of Kenneth Noland," *Studio International*, July–August 1974, pp. 21–26.

Champa, Kermit S. "New Work of Helen Frankenthaler," *Artforum*, January 1972, pp. 55–59.

Chipp, Herschel B. "San Francisco," *Art News*, December 1957, p. 50.

————. "Diebenkorn Paints a Picture," *Art News*, May 1957, pp. 44–47, 54–55.

Cochrane, Diane. "Wolf Kahn: Updating Landscape Painting," *American Artist*, 38 (November 1974), pp. 58–63.

————. "Nell Blaine: High Wire Painting," *American Artist*, 37 (August 1973), pp. 20–25.

Coleman, Victor. "Look at My Product Notes, More or Less Specific on Jim Dine," *Arts Canada*, December 1970–January 1971, pp. 50–51.

Colt, Priscilla. "The Painting of Sam Francis," *College Art Journal*, Vol. 22, No. 1 (Fall 1962): 2–7.

Coplans, John. "Early Warhol: The Systematic Evolution of the Impersonal Style," *Artforum*, March 1970, pp. 52–59.

————. "The Earlier Work of Ellsworth Kelly," *Artforum*, Summer 1969, pp. 48–55.

————. "The Artist Speaks: Claes Oldenburg," *Art in America*, March–April 1969, pp. 68–75.

————. "Post-Painterly Abstraction: The Long-Awaited Greenberg Exhibition Fails to Make Its Point," *Artforum*, June 1964, pp. 4–9.

Crehan, Hubert. "Recent Attacks on Abstract Art," *It Is*, 1 (Spring 1958): 60–63.

————. "Is There a California School?" *Art News*, January 1956, pp. 32–35, 64–65.

————. "Edward Dugmore," *Arts Digest*, October 15, 1954, p. 9.

————. "A See Change," *Art Digest*, April 15, 1953, p. 5.

"Critics: They Know What They Like," *Art Digest*, March 1, 1952, pp. 8–9.

Cummings, Paul. "Interview with Fairfield Porter," *American Artist*, April 1975, pp. 34–39.

Davis, Douglas M. "Rauschenberg's Recent Graphics," *Art in America*, July–August 1969, pp. 90–95.

De Kooning, Elaine. "Kline and Rothko: Two Americans in Action," *Art News Annual*, 27 (1958), 86–97, 174–179.

————. "Pure Paints a Picture," *Art News*, June 1957, pp. 57, 86–87.

————. "Subject: What, How or Who?" *Art News*, April 1955, pp. 26–29, 61–62.

————. "Vicente Paints a Collage," *Art News*, September 1953, pp. 38–41, 51–52.

————. "Dickinson and Kiesler," *Art News*, April 1952, pp. 20–23, 66–67.

————. "David Smith Makes a Sculpture," *Art News*, September 1951, pp. 38–41, 50–51.

————. "Albers Paints a Picture," *Art News*, November 1950, pp. 40–43.

————. "Hans Hofmann Paints a Picture," *Art News*, February 1950, pp. 38–41, 58–59.

De Kooning, Willem. "What Abstract Art Means to Me," *Museum of Modern Art Bulletin*, 18 (Spring 1951): 4–8.

Denby, Edwin. "Katz: Collage, Cutout, Cut-up," *Art News*, January 1965, pp. 42–45.

————. "My Friend de Kooning," *Art News Annual*, 29 (1964): 82–99, 156.

Dorfles, Gillo. "Written Images of Cy Twombly," *Metro*, 6 (1962): 62–71.

————. "Rauschenberg, or Obsolescence Defeated," *Metro*, 2 (May 1961): 32–35.

Downes, Rackstraw. "What the Sixties Meant to Me," *Art Journal*, Vol. 35, No. 2 (Winter 1974–1975): 125–131.

Edgar, Natalie. "The Passing Crowd," *Art News*, January 1969, pp. 52–53, 65 (on Lester Johnson).

"Editorial: Letter to a Young Artist," *Art Digest*, March 15, 1953, p. 7.

Eisenhauer, Letty Lou. "Transformations from Nature," *Art and Artists*, November 1973, pp. 20–23 (on Bob Watts).

Elderfield, John. "Mondrian, Newman, Noland: Two Notes on Changing Style," *Artforum*, December 1971, pp. 48–53.

————. "Color and Area: New Paintings by Ellsworth Kelly," *Artforum*, November 1971, pp. 45–49.

Falk, Ray. "Japanese Innovators," *New York Times*, December 8, 1957, Sec. 2, p. 24.

Farber, Manny. " 'Insiders' and Others," *Arts*, January 1961, pp. 42–45.

————. "New Images of (ugh) Man," *Art News*, October 1959, pp. 38–39, 58.

Feinstein, Sam. "Jon Schueler: A Vision of Nature," *Art Digest*, March 1, 1954, pp. 14, 25.

Feldman, Morton. "The Anxiety of Art," *Art in America*, September–October 1973, pp. 88–93.

————. "Frank O'Hara: Lost Times and Future Hopes," *Art in America*, March–April 1972, pp. 52–55.

————. "Give My Regards to Eighth Street," *Art in America*, March–April 1971, pp. 96–99.

Ferren, John. "Epitaph for an Avant-Garde (The Motivating Ideas of the Abstract Expressionist

Movement as Seen by an Artist Active on the New York Scene)," *Arts*, November 1958, pp. 24–26.

———. "Stable State of Mind," *Art News*, May 1955, pp. 22–23, 63–64.

"Figurative Painters in California," *Arts*, December 1957, pp. 26–27.

Finch, Christopher. "Notes for a Monument to Claes Oldenburg," *Art News*, October 1969, pp. 52–56.

Finkelstein, Louis. "Al Held: Structure and the Intuition of Theme," *Art in America*, November–December 1974, pp. 83–88.

———. "Thoughts About Painterly," *Art News Annual*, 37 (1972): 9–24.

———. "Gotham News, 1945–1960," *Art News Annual*, 34 (1969): 114–123.

———. "Cajori: The Figure in the Scene," *Art News*, March 1963, pp. 38–41, 59–60.

———. "New Look: Abstract-Impressionism," *Art News*, March 1956, pp. 36–39, 66–68.

Finley, Gerald. "Louis, Noland, Olitski," *Artforum*, March 1963, pp. 34–35.

Fitzsimmons, James. "Stable Group Set a Smart Pace," *Art Digest*, February 1, 1954, pp. 11, 25.

———. "A Critic Picks Some Promising Painters," *Art Digest*, January 15, 1954, p. 10.

Folds, Thomas. "The New Images of the Chicago Group," *Art News*, October 1959, pp. 40–41, 52–53.

Forge, Andrew. "Anthony Caro: An Interview," *Studio International*, January 1966, pp. 6–9.

———. "An American Notebook," *Art and Literature*, 2 (Summer 1964), 40–48.

Fraser, Robert. "Dining with Jim," *Art and Artists*, September 1966, pp. 49–53 (an interview with Jim Dine).

Freilicher, Jane, and Alex Katz. "A Dialogue," *Art and Literature*, 1 (March 1964): 205–216.

Fried, Michael. "The Achievement of Morris Louis," *Artforum*, February 1967, pp. 34–40.

———. "Some Notes on Morris Louis," *Arts*, November 1963, pp. 22–27.

Friedman, B. H. "Towards the Total Color Image," *Art News*, Summer 1966, pp. 31–33, 67–68 (on Helen Frankenthaler).

Friedman, Ken. "Fluxus and Concept Art," *Art and Artists*, October 1972, pp. 50–53.

Friedman, Martin. "The Obsessive Images of Lucas Samaras," *Art and Artists*, November 1966, pp. 20–23.

———. "The Object Is Symbol," *Art News*, November 1965, pp. 32–35 (on George Ortman).

Fuller, Mary. "Was There a San Francisco School?" *Artforum*, January 1971, pp. 46–53.

———. "San Francisco Sculptors," *Art in America*, June 1964, pp. 52–59.

———. "Edward Corbett," *Art Digest*, January 1, 1954, pp. 21–23.

Fussiner, Howard. "The Use of Subject Matter in Recent Art," *College Art Journal*, Vol. 20, No. 3 (Spring 1961), 134–138.

Gablik, Suzi. "Meta-Trompe-l'Oeil," *Art News*, March 1965, pp. 46–48.

Gage, Otis. "The Reflective Eye," *Art Digest*, March 15, 1953, p. 4 (on Sculpture Panel at Club).

Gassiot-Talobot, G. "Hultberg," *Cimaise*, September–October 1961, pp. 12–19.

Geist, Sidney. "A New Sculptor: Mark di Suvero," *Arts*, December 1960, pp. 40–43.

———. "Stankiewicz: Miracle in the Scrapheap," *Art Digest*, December 1, 1953, p. 10.

———. "Ninth Street Moves Uptown," *Art Digest*, February 1, 1953, pp. 15–16.

Geldzahler, Henry. "Frankenthaler, Kelly, Lichtenstein, Olitski: A Preview of the American Selection at the 1966 Venice Biennale," *Artforum*, June 1966, pp. 32–38.

———. "Happenings: Theatre by Painters," *Hudson Review*, Winter 1965–1966, pp. 581–586.

———. "An Interview with Helen Frankenthaler," *Artforum*, October 1965, pp. 36–38.

———. "An Interview with George Segal," *Artforum*, November 1964, pp. 26–29.

———. "Interview with Ellsworth Kelly," *Art International*, February 15, 1964, pp. 47–48.

———. "Robert Rauschenberg," *Art International*, September 25, 1963, pp. 62–67.

Georges, Paul. "A Painter Looks at: (A) The Nude, (B) Corot," *Art News*, November 1956, pp. 38–41, 60.

Glaser, Bruce. "Modern Art and the Critics: A Panel Discussion," *Art Journal*, Vol. 30, No. 2 (Winter 1970–1971), 154–159 (Kozloff, Tillim, Rose).

——— (interviewer), and Lucy R. Lippard (editor). "Questions to Stella and Judd," *Art News*, September 1966, pp. 51–61. Glaser, Bruce (moderator). "Lichtenstein, Oldenburg, Warhol: A Discussion," *Artforum*, February 1966, pp. 20–24.

———. "The New Abstraction: A Discussion Conducted by Bruce Glaser" (with Paul Brach, Al Held, and Ray Parker), *Art International*, February 1966, pp. 41–45.

Glueck, Grace. "Odd Man Out: Red Grooms, The Ruckus Kid," *Art News*, December 1973, pp. 23–27.

———. "Rivers Paints Himself on the Canvas," *New York Times Magazine*, February 13, 1966, pp. 34–35, 78–83.

Goldin, Amy. "One Cheer for Expressionism: German Expressionism in a Show at Spencer Samuels," *Art News*, November 1968, pp. 48–49, 66–69.

———. "Beyond Style," *Art and Artists*, September 1968, pp. 32–35.

———. "Requiem for a Gallery," *Arts*, March 1966, pp. 25–29.

———. "Harold Rosenberg's Magic Circle," *Arts*, November 1965, pp. 37–39.

Goldwater, Robert. "Art Chronicle: Surfeit of the

New," *Partisan Review*, 29 (Winter 1962): 116–121.

———. "Reflections on the New York School," *Quadrum*, 7–8 (1960): 17–36.

———. "Everyone Knew What Everyone Else Meant," *It Is*, 4 (Autumn 1959): 35.

———. "La Sculpture Actuelle à New York," *Cimaise*, November–December 1956, pp. 24–28.

Golub, Leon. "2D/3D," *Artforum*, March 1973, pp. 60–68.

———. "A Critique of Abstract Expressionism," *College Art Journal*, 14 (Winter 1955): 142–147.

Goodman, Saul. "Brief Biography: Yvonne Rainer," *Dance Magazine*, December 1965, p. 110.

Goodnough, Robert. "Statement," *Art Now: New York*, Vol. 1, No. 4 (April 1969).

———. "About Painting," *Art and Literature*, 6 (Autumn 1965), 119–127.

———. "Postscript: The Forties," *Artforum*, September 1965, p. 32.

———. "Reviews and Previews: Second Annual," *Art News*, January 1953, p. 48.

———. "Kline Paints a Picture," *Art News*, December 1952, pp. 36–39, 63–64.

———. "Pollock Paints a Picture," *Art News*, May 1951, pp. 38–41, 60–61.

Goossen, E. C. "The Artist Speaks: Robert Morris," *Art in America*, May–June 1970, pp. 104–111.

———. "Helen Frankenthaler," *Art International*, October 20, 1961, pp. 76–79.

———. "The Philosophic Line of Barnett Newmann," *Art News*, Summer 1958, pp. 30–31, 62–63.

Goossen, Eugene Coons. "Color and Light," *Arts*, January 1974, pp. 32–41.

Greenberg, Clement. "Seminar II," *Art International* Summer 1974, pp. 72–74.

———. "Influences of Matisse," *Art International*, November 15, 1973, pp. 28–31, 39.

———. "Seminar I," *Arts*, November 1973, pp. 44–46.

———. "Necessity of 'Formalism,' " *Art International*, October 1972, pp. 105–106.

———. "Counter-Avant-Garde," *Art International*, May 20, 1971, pp. 16–19.

———. "Avant-Garde Attitudes: New Art in the Sixties," *Studio International*, April 1970, pp. 142–145.

———. "Anthony Caro," *Studio International*, September 1967, pp. 116–117.

———. "America Takes the Lead: 1945–1965," *Art in America*, August–September 1965, pp. 108–129.

———. "The 'Crisis' of Abstract Art," *Arts Yearbook: New York: The Art World*, No. 7 (1964), 89–92.

———. "Post Painterly Abstraction," *Art International*, Summer 1964, pp. 63–65.

———. "Art: How Art Writing Earns Its Bad Name," *Encounter*, December 19, 1962, pp. 67–71.

———. "After Abstract Expressionism," *Art International*, October 25, 1962, pp. 24–32.

———. "Modernist Painting," *Arts Yearbook*, No. 4 (1961): 109–116.

———. "Louis and Noland," *Art International*, May 25, 1960, pp. 26–29.

———. "Hans Hofmann: Grand Old Rebel," *Art News*, January 1959, pp. 26–29, 64.

———. "Sculpture in Our Time," *Arts*, June 1958, pp. 22–25.

———. " 'American-Type' Painting," *Partisan Review*, Vol. 22, No. 2 (Spring 1955), 179–196.

———. "Abstract and Representational," *Arts Digest*, November 1954, pp. 6–8.

———. "Renoir and the Picturesque," *Art News*, April 1950, pp. 32–35, 62–63.

———. "Art Chronicle: The New Sculpture," *Partisan Review*, 16 (June 1949): 637–642.

———. "Art," *The Nation*, April 16, 1949, pp. 453–454.

———. "The Present Prospects of American Painting and Sculpture," *Horizon*, London, October 1947, pp. 20–30.

———. "Art," *The Nation*, March 8, 1947, p. 284.

Greene, Balcomb. "A Thing of Beauty," *College Art Journal*, Vol. 25, No. 4 (Summer 1966): 364–369.

Guest, Barbara. "Helen Frankenthaler: The Moment and the Distance," *Arts*, April 1975, pp. 58–59.

———. "Fay Lansner: Deliberate Contraries," *Art News*, December 1963, pp. 36–37, 67.

Hahn, Otto. "Passport No. G2553000: United States of America," *Art and Artists*, July 1966, pp. 6–11.

Hamilton, George Heard. "Painting in Contemporary America," *Burlington Magazine*, 102, May 1960, pp. 192–197.

Hamilton, Richard. "Roy Lichtenstein," *Studio International*, January 1968, pp. 20–24.

Haney, William L. "What If?" *Art Journal*, Vol. 31, No. 2 (Winter 1971–1972): 173–174, 177.

Hansen, Al. "Life in Destruction," *Art and Artists*, August 1966, pp. 32–35.

Harithas, James. "Weather Paint," *Art News*, May 1972, pp. 40–43, 63.

Harrison, Jane. "On Color in Kenneth Noland's Paintings," *Art International*, June 1965, pp. 36–38.

Hauptman, William. "The Suppression of Art in the McCarthy Decade," *Artforum*, October 1973, pp. 48–52.

Hellman, Geoffrey T. "The Keys to Canaday," *Art in America*, Fall 1962, pp. 68–73.

Henry, Gerrit. "Views from the Studio," *Art News*, May 1976, pp. 32–36.

———. "The Artist and the Face: A Modern American Sampling," *Art in America*, January 1975, pp. 34–35.

Heron, Patrick. "The Americans at the Tate Gallery," *Arts*, March 1956, pp. 15–17.

Herrera, Hayden. "Pearlstein: Portraits at Face

Value," *Art in America*, January–February 1975, pp. 46–47.

Hess, Thomas B. "Pinup and Icon: Woman as Sex Object: Studies in Erotic Art, 1730–1970," *Art News Annual*, 38 (1972): 223–237.

———. "Larry Rivers' History of the Russian Revolution," *Art News*, October 1965, pp. 37, 58.

———. "Editorial: The Artist as a Company-Man," *Art News*, October 1964, p. 19.

———. "The Phony Crisis in American Art," *Art News*, Summer 1963, pp. 24–28, 59–60.

———. "Collage as an Historical Method," *Art News*, November 1961, pp. 30–33, 69–71.

———. "Editorial: The Many Deaths of American Art," *Art News*, October 1960, p. 25.

———. "Mixed Mediums for a Soft Revolution," *Art News*, Summer 1960, pp. 45, 62.

———. "Reviews and Previews: Jean Tinguely," *Art News*, April 1960, pp. 16, 54.

———. "U.S. Art, Notes from 1960," *Art News*, January 1960, pp. 24–29, 56–58.

——— "Homage to Nell Blaine," *Art News*, December 1959, pp. 34–35.

———. "In Praise of Folly," *Art News*, March 1959, pp. 24–27, 59–61.

———. "The Cultural-Gap Blues," *Art News*, January 1959, pp. 22–25, 61–62.

———. "The Year's Best: 1958," *Art News*, January 1959, pp. 44–45, 60–61.

———. "U.S. Sculpture: Some Recent Directions," *Portfolio*, 1 (1959), 112–127, 146–152.

———. "Reviews and Previews: New Faces This Month: Gutai," *Art News*, November 1958, p. 17.

———. "Inside Nature," *Art News*, February 1958, pp. 40–43, 59–65.

———. "For Spacious Skies, and All That," *Art News*, November 1957, pp. 28–31, 58–60.

———. "Reviews and Previews: New York Artists," *Art News*, Summer 1957, p. 20.

———. "Younger Artists and the Unforgivable Crime," *Art News*, April 1957, pp. 46–49, 64–65.

———. "Mutt Furioso: A Closet-Drama About the Whitney Annual of U.S. Painting and Sculpture," *Art News*, December 1956, pp. 22–25, 64–65.

———. "Monet: Tithonus at Giverny," *Art News*, October 1956, pp. 42, 53.

———. "Great Expectations, Part 1 and Part 2," *Art News*, Summer 1956, pp. 36–38, 59–62.

———. "U.S. Painting: Some Recent Directions," *Art News Annual*, 25 (1956): 73–98, 174–180, 192–199.

———. "Trying Abstraction on Pittsburgh," *Art News*, November 1955, pp. 40–42, 56–57.

———. "Mixed Pickings from Ten Fat Years," *Art News*, Summer 1955, pp. 36–39, 77–78.

———. "The New York Salon," *Art News*, February 1954, pp. 24–25, 56–57.

———. "De Kooning Paints a Picture," *Art News*, March 1953, pp. 30–33, 64–67.

———. "Cinemaconology and Realstraction," *Art News*, December 1952, pp. 24, 67.

———. "Miracle at Schenley Park," *Art News*, November 1952, pp. 28–30, 66–67.

———. "Invited Guests at the Whitney," *Art News*, December 1950, pp. 32–33, 63.

———. "Seeing the Young New Yorkers," *Art News*, May 1950, pp. 23, 60.

Higgens, Andrew. "Clement Greenberg and the Idea of the Avant-Garde," *Studio International*, October 1971, pp. 144–147.

Higgins, Dick. "Something Else About Fluxus," *Art and Artists*, October 1972, pp. 16–21.

Hodgins, Eric, and Leslie Parker. "The Great International Art Market," *Fortune*, December 1955, pp. 118–120, 150–169.

Hopkins, Budd. "Budd Hopkins on Budd Hopkins," *Art in America*, July–August 1973, pp. 90–93.

Hopps, Walter. "An Interview with Jasper Johns," *Artforum*, March 1965, pp. 32–36.

Hunter, Sam. "The Recent Work of Larry Rivers," *Arts*, April 1965, pp. 44–50.

———. "Abstract Expressionism Then and Now," *Canadian Art*, September–October 1964, pp. 266–269.

———. "Guggenheim Sampler: Abstract Painting Comes of Age in a Museum Exhibition of Fifty-four Younger Americans," *Art Digest*, May 15, 1954, pp. 8–9, 31.

"Is There a New Academy?" Part II, *Art News*, September 1959, pp. 36–39, 58–60.

"Is There a New Academy?" Part I, *Art News*, Summer 1959, pp. 34–37, 58–59.

"Is Today's Artist With or Against the Past?" Part II, *Art News*, September 1958, pp. 38–41, 58–63.

"Is Today's Artist With or Against the Past?" Part I, *Art News*, Summer 1958, pp. 26–29, 42–45, 54–58.

Johns, Jasper. "Thoughts on Duchamp," *Art in America*, July–August 1969, p. 31.

———. "Sketchbook Notes," *Art and Literature*, 4 (Spring 1965), 185–192.

———. "The Green Box," *Scrap*, 2 (December 23, 1960), 4.

Johnson, Ellen H. "Oldenburg's Poetics: Analogues, Metamophoses and Sources," *Art International*, April 1970, pp. 42–45.

———. "The Lichtenstein Paradox," *Art and Artists*, January 1968, pp. 12–15.

———. "Jim Dine and Jasper Johns: Art About Art," *Art and Literature*, 6 (Autumn 1965): 128–140.

———. "The Sculpture of George Segal," *Art International*, March 1964, pp. 46–49.

Johnston, Jill. "The New American Modern Dance," *Art and Literature*, 5 (Summer 1965), 118–133.

Josephson, Mary. "Warhol: The Medium as Cultural Artifact," *Art in America*, May–June 1971, pp. 40–46.

Jouffroy, Alain. "Jim Dine, Through the Telescope," *Metro*, 7 (1962), 72–75.

Judd, Donald. "Chamberlain: Another View," *Art International*, January 16, 1964, pp. 38–39.

"Judson: A Dance Chronology," *Ballet Review*, Vol. 1, No. 6 (1967): 54–72.

Kaprow, Allan. " 'Easy,' " *Art in America*, July–August 1974, pp. 73–75.

———. "The Education of the Un-Artist, Part III," *Art in America*, January–February 1974, pp. 85–91.

———. "The Education of the Un-Artist, Part II," *Art News*, May 1971, pp. 34–39, 62–63.

———. "The Education of the Un-Artist, Part I," *Art News*, February 1971, pp. 28–31, 66–68.

———. "The Shape of the Art Environment," *Artforum*, Summer 1968, pp. 32–33.

——— and Robert Smithson. "What Is a Museum?" *Arts Yearbook*, No. 9 (1967): 94–101 (a dialogue).

Kaprow, Allan. "Pinpointing Happenings," *Art News*, October 1967, pp. 46–47, 70–71.

———. "Death in the Museum," *Arts*, February 1967, pp. 40–41.

———. "Experimental Art," *Art News*, March 1966, pp. 60–63, 77–82.

———. "The Happenings Are Dead—Long Live the Happenings," *Artforum*, March 1966, pp. 36–39.

———. "Hans Hofmann, an Obituary," *Village Voice*, February 24, 1966, pp. 1–2.

———. "Should the Artist Become a Man of the World?" *Art News*, October 1964, pp. 34–37, 58–59.

———. "What Is an 'Environment'?" Statement and Drawing in "Eat," *Vogue*, April 1, 1964, p. 125.

———. "Segal's Vital Mummies," *Art News*, February 1964, pp. 28–31, 64–66.

———. "The World View of Alfred Jensen," *Art News*, December 1963, pp. 28–31, 64–66.

———. "An Artist's Story of a Happening," *New York Times*, Sec. 2, October 6, 1963, p. 17.

———. "Impurity," *Art News*, January 1963, pp. 30–33, 52–55.

———. "A Service for the Dead," *Art International*, January 1963, pp. 46–47.

———. "Happenings in the New York Scene," *Art News*, May 1961, pp. 36–39, 58–62.

———. "The Demiurge," *Anthologist* (Rutgers State University), 30 (Winter 1959), 4.

———. "Something to Take Place: A Happening," *Anthologist* (Rutgers State University), 30 (Winter 1959): 5–10.

———. "The Principles of Modern Art," *It Is*, Autumn 1959, pp. 51–55.

———. "The Legacy of Jackson Pollock," *Art News*, October 1958, pp. 24–26, 55–57.

Katz, Alex. "Rudolph Burckhardt: Multiple Fugitive," *Art News*, December 1963, pp. 38–41.

Kelly, Edward T. "Neo-Dada: A Critique of Pop Art," *College Art Journal*, Vol. 23, No. 3 (Spring 1964), 192–201.

Kirby, Michael, and Richard Schechner. "An Interview with John Cage," *Tulane Drama Review*, 10 (Winter 1965): 50–72.

Kirby, Michael. "The New Theater," *Tulane Drama Review*, 10 (Winter 1965): 23–43.

Klüver, Billy, and Simone Whitman. "Theatre and Engineering: An Experiment," *Artforum*, February 1967, pp. 26–33.

Kostelanetz, Richard. "Profile of Merce Cunningham," *Michigan Quarterly Review*, Vol. 14, No. 4 (Fall 1975), 363–382.

———. "The Two Extremes of Avant-Garde Music," *New York Times Magazine*, January 15, 1967, pp. 34–35, 52–58, 62–64.

———. "The Artist as Playwright and Engineer," *New York Times Magazine*, October 9, 1966, pp. 32–33, 109–110, 114, 119–124.

Kozloff, Max. "American Painting During the Cold War," *Artforum*, May 1973, pp. 43–54.

———. "Inwardness: Chicago Art *Since* 1945," *Artforum*, October 1972, pp. 51–55.

———. "Andy Warhol and Ad Reinhardt: The Great Accepter and the Great Demurrer," *Studio International*, March 1971, pp. 113–117.

———. "The Late Roman Empire in the Light of Napalm," *Art News*, November 1970, pp. 58–60, 76–78 (on Leon Golub).

———. "The Division and Mockery of the Self," *Studio International*, January 1970, pp. 9–15.

———. "Jasper Johns: Colors, Maps, Devices," *Artforum*, November 1967, pp. 26–31.

———. "Modern Art and the Virtues of Decadence," *Studio International*, November 1967, pp. 189–199.

———. "Mark di Suvero," *Artforum*, Summer 1967, pp. 41–46.

———. "Review: Assemblage, Environments & Happenings," *The Nation*, New York, July 3, 1967, pp. 27–29.

———. "The Critical Reception of Abstract-Expressionism," *Arts*, December 1965, pp. 27–33.

———. "Larry Rivers, Stuart Davis and Slang Idiom," *Artforum*, November 1965, pp. 20–24.

———. "An Interview with Friedel Dzubas," *Artforum*, September 1965, pp. 49–52.

———. "The Honest Elusiveness of James Dine," *Artforum*, December 1964, pp. 36–40.

———. "The Dilemna of Expressionism," *Artforum*, November 1964, pp. 32–35.

———. "Johns and Duchamp," *Art International*, March 20, 1964, pp. 42–45.

———. "The Impact of de Kooning," *Arts Yearbook*, No. 7 (1964), pp. 77–88.

———. "A Letter to the Editor," *Art International*, June 1963, pp. 88–92.

Kramer, Hilton. "30 Years of the New York School," *New York Times Magazine*, October 12, 1969, pp. 28–30, 89–102, 109–110, 117–120.

———. "Di Suvero: Sculpture of Whitmanesque Scale," *New York Times*, Sec. 2, January 30, 1966, pp. 25–26.

———. "The Strange Case of Harold Rosenberg," *Lugano Review*, Vol. 1, No. 2 (1965): 123–128.

———. "Notes on Painting in New York," *Arts Yearbook*, No. 7 (1964): 9–20.

———. "Art Chronicle," *Hudson Review*, 16 (Spring 1963): 96–101.

———. "A Critic on the Side of History: Notes of

Clement Greenberg," *Arts*, October 1962, pp. 60–63.

———. "Month in Review," *Arts*, November 1960, pp. 48–51.

———. "Constructing the Absolute," *Arts*, May 1960, pp. 36–43.

———. "Editorial: The Coming Political Breakthrough," *Arts*, January 1960, p. 13.

———. "Month in Review: Elmer Bischoff and the San Francisco School of 'Figuratives,' " *Arts*, January 1960, pp. 42–45.

———. "Editorial," *Arts*, December 1959, p. 15.

———. "Critics of American Painting," *Arts*, October 1959, pp. 26–31.

———. "Month in Review," *Arts*, September 1959, pp. 56–59.

———. "Month in Review," *Arts*, April 1959, pp. 44–47.

———. "Month in Review," *Arts*, February 1959, pp. 48–51.

———. "Editorial," *Arts*, February 1959, p. 13.

———. "Month in Review," *Arts*, January 1959, pp. 48–51.

———. "Report on the Carnegie International," *Arts*, January 1959, pp. 30–37.

———. "Month in Review," *Arts*, March 1957, pp. 46–49.

———. "Month in Review," *Arts*, December 1956, pp. 46–49 (on Stankiewicz).

———. "Month in Review," *Arts*, November 1956, pp. 52–55.

———. "As Artists See Themselves: The Stable Show," *Arts*, June 1956, pp. 14–17.

———. "Pittsburgh's International," *Arts*, November 1955, pp. 18–20.

———. "The New American Painting," *Partisan Review*, 20 (July–August 1953), 421–427.

Krauss, Rosalind. "How Paradigmatic Is Anthony Caro?" *Art in America*, September–October 1975, pp. 80–83.

———. "Rauschenberg and the Materialized Image," *Artforum*, December 1974, pp. 36–43.

———. "Painting Becomes Cyclorama," *Artforum*, June 1974, pp. 50–52.

———. "A View of Modernism," *Artforum*, September 1972, pp. 48–51.

———. "Problems of Criticism: Pictorial Space and the Question of Documentary," *Artforum*, November 1971, pp. 68–71.

Kroll, Jack. "Some Greenberg Circles," *Art News*, March 1962, pp. 35, 48–49.

———. "American Painting and the Convertible Spiral," *Art News*, November 1961, pp. 34–37, 66–69.

Kuspit, Donald B. "Golub's Assassins: An Anatomy of Violence," *Art in America*, May–June 1975, pp. 62–65.

Laderman, Gabriel. "Notes from the Underground," *Artforum*, September 1970, pp. 59–61.

Lanes, Jerrold. "Richard Diebenkorn: Cloudy Skies Over Ocean Park," *Artforum*, February 1972, pp. 61–63.

———. "Brief Treatise on Surplus Value; or, The Man Who Wasn't There," *Arts*, November 1959, pp. 28–35.

———. "Reflections on Post-Cubist Painting," *Arts*, May 1959, pp. 24–29.

Larson, Philip. "Robert Rauschenberg," *Arts*, April 1975, p. 78.

"L'Ecole du Pacifique," Débat entre Julien Alvard, Claire Falkenstein, Sam Francis, James Fitzsimmons et Michel Tapié, *Cimaise*, June 1954, pp. 6–9.

Leider, Philip. "Literalism and Abstraction: Frank Stella's Retrospective at the Modern," *Artforum*, April 1970, pp. 44–51.

———. "California After the Figure," *Art in America*, October 1963, pp. 73–83.

Levin, Kim. "Fifties Fallout: The Hydrogen Juke Box," *Arts*, April 1974, pp. 29–30.

Levine, Les. "Suffer, Suffer, Suffer: A Portrait of John Bernard Myers," *Arts*, April 1974, pp. 38–39.

———. "The Golden Years: Portrait of Eleanor Ward," *Arts*, April 1974, pp. 42–43.

———. "The Spring of '55: A Portrait of Sam Kootz," *Arts*, April 1974, pp. 34–35.

Lichtenstein, Gene. "10th Street: Main Street of the Art World," *Esquire*, September 1959.

Lippard, Lucy R. "Rudy Burckhardt: Moviemaker, Photographer, Painter," *Art in America*, March–April 1975, pp. 75–81.

———. "Constellation in Harsh Daylight: The Whitney Annual," *Hudson Review*, 21 (Spring 1968), 174–182.

———. "The Silent Art," *Art in America*, January–February 1967, pp. 58–63.

Liss, Carla. "Show Me Your Dances . . . Joan Jonas and Simone Forte Talk with Carla Liss," *Art and Artists*, October 1973, pp. 14–21.

Livingston, Jane. "Some Thoughts on 'Art and Technology,' " *Studio International*, June 1971, pp. 258–263.

Loftus, John. "The Plastic Arts in the Sixties: What Is It That Has Got Lost?" *College Art Journal*, Vol. 26, No. 3 (Spring 1967), 240–245.

Loring, John. "Oldenburg on Multiples," *Arts*, May 1974, pp. 42–45.

Love, Joseph. "The Group in Contemporary Japanese Art—Gutai and Jiro Yoshihara," *Art International*, Summer 1972, pp. 123–127.

Lucie-Smith, Edward. "An Interview with Clement Greenberg," *Studio International*, January 1968, pp. 4–5.

———. "Frank O'Hara, Poet and Museum Official: An Interview," *Studio International*, September 1966, pp. 112–113.

Malone, Patrick T., and Peter Selz. "Is There a New Chicago School?" *Art News*, October 1955, pp. 36–39, 58–60.

Marck, Jan van der. "George Brecht: An Art of Multiple Implications," *Art in America*, July–August 1974, pp. 48–57.

Martin, Henry. "An Interview with George Brecht,"

*Art International*, November 20, 1967, pp. 20–24.

Masheck, Joseph, and Robert Pincus-Witten. "Al Held: Two Views," *Artforum*, January 1975, pp. 54–56.

Masheck, Joseph. "Ellsworth Kelly at the Modern," *Artforum*, November 1973, pp. 54–57.

Mellow, James R. "The Flowering Summer of Nell Blaine," *New York Times*, Sec. 2, October 11, 1970, p. 23.

Merkert, Jörn. "Pre-Fluxus Vostell," *Art and Artists*, May 1973, pp. 32–37.

Midgett, Willard F. "Philip Pearlstein: The Naked Truth," *Art News*, October 1967, pp. 54–55, 75–78.

Mills, Paul. "Bay Area Figurative," *Art in America*, June 1964, pp. 42–45.

Moffett, Kenworth. "Noland," *Art International*, Summer 1973, pp. 22–23, 91–93, 100.

———. "Morris Louis: Omegas and Unfurleds," *Artforum*, May 1970, pp. 44–47.

Morris, Robert. "Notes on Sculpture: Part IV," *Artforum*, April 1969, pp. 50–54.

Müller, Gregoire. "Donald Judd: Ten Years," *Arts*, February 1973, pp. 35–42.

Munro, Eleanor C. "The Found Generation," *Art News*, November 1961, pp. 38–39, 75–76 (on Joan Mitchell).

———. "De Niro Works on a Series of Pictures," *Art News*, May 1958, pp. 38–41, 48–50.

———. "Explorations in Form: A View of Some Recent American Sculpture," *Perspectives, USA*, No. 16 (Summer 1956): 160–172.

———. "Private Faces in Public Places," *Art News*, December 1955, pp. 34–35, 67–68.

Musgrave, Victor. "The Unknown Art Movement," *Art and Artists*, October 1972, pp. 12–16.

Mussman, Toby. "A Comment on Literalness," *Arts*, February 1968, pp. 14–17 (on Rauschenberg).

Myers, John Bernard. "Junkdump Fair Surveyed," *Art and Literature*, 3 (Autumn–Winter 1964): 122–141.

Nemser, Cindy. "Interview with Helen Frankenthaler," *Arts*, November 1971, pp. 51–55.

"The New Abstraction," *Art International*, February 20, 1966, pp. 41–45 (a discussion conducted by Bruce Glaser with participants Paul Brach, Al Held, and Ray Parker).

Newman, Barnett. "The New York School Question," *Art News*, September 1965, pp. 38–41, 55–56 (interview with Neil A. Levine).

Nochlin, Linda. "The Realist Criminal and the Abstract Law II," *Art in America*, November–December 1973, pp. 96–103.

———. "The Realist Criminal and the Abstract Law I," *Art in America*, September–October 1973, pp. 54–61.

———. "The Ugly American: The Work of Philip Pearlstein," *Art News*, September 1970, pp. 55–57, 65–70.

Nodelman, Sheldon. "Sixties Art: Some Philo-

sophical Perspectives," *Perspecta 11, Yale Architecture Journal* (1967): 72–89.

Nordland, Gerald. "Robert Natkin," *Art International*, October 1969, pp. 53–55.

———. "Diebenkorn Retrospective in Washington," *Artforum*, January 1965, pp. 20–25.

Novik, Elizabeth. "Happenings in New York," *Studio International*, September 1966, pp. 154–159.

Nyman, Michael. "The Experimental Tradition," *Art and Artists*, October 1972, pp. 44–49.

O'Doherty, Brian. "Rauschenberg and the Vernacular Glance," *Art in America*, September–October 1973, pp. 82–87.

———. "Master of the Movement Manqué," *Arts*, April 1966, pp. 27–30.

Oeri, Georgine. "Edward Higgins," *Metro*, 1 (1960), 74–89.

O'Hara, Frank. "Alex Katz," *Art and Literature*, No. 9 (Summer 1966), 91–101.

———. "Larry Rivers: Why I Paint as I Do," *Horizon*, September 1959, pp. 94–102 (an interview).

———. "Porter Paints a Picture," *Art News*, January 1955, pp. 38–41, 66–67.

———. "Nature and New Painting," *Folder*, 3 (1954–1955), n.p.

Oldenburg, Claes. "Chronology of Drawings," *Studio International*, June 1970, pp. 249–253.

———. "America: War and Sex, Etc.," *Arts*, Summer 1967, pp. 32–38.

"Other 'Symbols' from the U.S.," *Metro*, 2 (1961), 93–94 (on Kenneth Noland).

"Our Country and Its Culture: A Symposium," *Partisan Review*, 19 (May–June 1952), 282–326.

Page, Robin, and Carla Liss. "George Brecht," *Art and Artists*, October 1972, pp. 28–33 (an interview).

Parker, Raymond. "Intent Painting," *It Is*, 2 (Autumn 1958), 8–9.

———. "A Cahier Leaf: Direct Painting," *It Is*, 1 (Spring 1958): 20.

Pearlstein, Philip. "Whose Painting Is It Anyway?" *Arts Yearbook: New York: The Art World*, No. 7 (1964), 129–132.

———. "Figure Paintings Today Are Not Made in Heaven," *Art News*, Summer 1962, pp. 39, 51–52.

———. "The Private Myth," *Art News*, September 1961, pp. 42–45, 62.

———. "The Symbolic Language of Francis Picabia," *Arts*, January 1956, pp. 37–43.

Perreault, John. " 'Classic' Pop Revisited," *Art in America*, March–April 1974, pp. 64–68.

Petersen, Valerie. "U.S. Figure Painting: Continuity and Cliché," *Art News*, Summer 1962, pp. 36–38, 51–52.

———. "Gabriel Kohn Makes a Sculpture," *Art News*, October 1961, pp. 48–51, 66–67.

———. "Young Americans, Seen and Heard," *Art News*, November 1960, pp. 36–37, 54–58.

Pincus-Witten, Robert. "Cy Twombly," *Artforum*, April 1974, pp. 60–64.

———. "George Segal," *Art and Artists*, January 1968, pp. 38–41.

———. "George Segal as Realist," *Artforum*, Summer 1967, pp. 84–87.

Plagens, Peter. "Sam Francis Retrospective in Houston," *Artforum*, January 1968, pp. 38–43.

Plaskett, Joe. "Some New Canadian Painters and Their Debt to Hans Hofmann," *Canadian Art*, Winter 1953, pp. 59–63, 79.

Pollett, Elizabeth. "Hans Hofmann," *Arts*, May 1957, pp. 30–33.

"Jackson Pollock: An Artists' Symposium, Part II," *Art News*, May 1967, pp. 26–29, 66, 69–72.

"Jackson Pollock: An Artists' Symposium, Part I," *Art News*, April 1967, pp. 28–33, 59–67.

Pomeroy, Ralph. "Pearlstein's Portraits," *Art and Artists*, September 1973, pp. 38–43 (an interview).

Popper, Frank. "Tinguely: Inspired Anarchist," *Art and Artists*, August 1966, pp. 12–15.

Porter, Fairfield. "Speaking Likeness," *Art News Annual*, 36 (1971): 40–51.

———. "The Education of Jasper Johns," *Art News*, February 1964, pp. 44–45, 61–62.

———. "David Smith: Steel into Sculpture," *Art News*, September 1957, pp. 40–43, 54–55.

———. "Jane Freilicher Paints a Picture," *Art News*, September 1956, pp. 46–49, 65–66.

———. "Stankiewicz Makes a Sculpture," *Art News*, September 1955, pp. 36–39, 62–63.

———. "Rivers Paints a Picture," *Art News*, January 1954, pp. 56–59, 81–83.

———. "Tworkov Paints a Picture," *Art News*, May 1953, pp. 30–33, 72–73.

Ragon, Michel. "L'Art Actuel aux Etats-Unis," *Cimaise*, March 1959, pp. 6–35.

Rainer, Yvonne. "Yvonne Rainer Interviews Ann Halprin," *Tulane Drama Review*, 10 (Winter 1965), 142–166.

"Random Order," *Location*, Vol. 1, No. 1 (Spring 1963), 27–31 (on Robert Rauschenberg).

Ratcliff, Carter. "Notes on a Transitional Period: Noland's Early Circle Paintings," *Art in America*, May–June 1975, pp. 66–67.

———. "Art Criticism: Other Eyes, Other Minds (Part V), On Clement Greenberg," *Art International*, December 1974, pp. 53–57.

———. "Joan Mitchell's Envisionments," *Art in America*, July–August 1974, pp. 34–37.

———. "Painterly vs. Painted," *Art News Annual*, 37 (1972): 129–147.

———. "Sam Francis: 'Universal Painter,'" *Art News*, December 1972, pp. 56–59.

———. "Mark di Suvero," *Artforum*, November 1972, pp. 34–42.

———. "New York Letter," *Art International*, September 20, 1971, pp. 68–72.

Rauschenberg, Robert. "The Artist Speaks," *Art in America*, May–June 1966, pp. 72–85.

———. "Oyvind Fahlström," *Art and Literature*, 3 (Autumn–Winter 1964): 219.

Raynor, Vivien. "Jasper Johns: 'I Have Attempted to Develop My Thinking in Such a Way That the Work I've Done Is Not Me,'" *Art News*, March 1973, pp. 20–22.

Read, Herbert. "The Disintegration of Form in Modern Art," *Studio International*, April 1965, pp. 144–155.

———. "Recent Tendencies in Abstract Painting," *Canadian Art*, August 1958, pp. 192–203, 242–243.

"The Realist Predicament, Past and Present Traditions of the National Scene," *Times Literary Supplement* (London), November 6, 1959, p. 29.

Reaves, Angela Westwater. "Claes Oldenburg, An Interview," *Artforum*, October 1972, pp. 36–39.

Reinhardt, Ad. "44 Titles for Artists Under 45," *It Is*, 1 (Spring 1958), 22–23.

———. "Twelve Rules for a New Academy," *Art News*, May 1957, pp. 37–38, 56.

Reise, Barbara. "Greenberg and the Group: A Retrospective View," *Studio International*, May 1968, pp. 254–257, and June 1968, pp. 314–315.

Restany, Pierre. "Jasper Johns and the Metaphysic of the Commonplace," *Cimaise*, September–October 1961, pp. 90–97.

Rexroth, Kenneth. "Americans Seen Abroad," *Art News*, Summer 1959, pp. 30–33, 52–54.

Rivers, Larry, and David Hockney. "Beautiful and Interesting," *Art and Literature*, No. 5 (Summer 1965): 94–117.

Rivers, Larry. "Life Among the Stones," *Location*, Vol. I, No. 1 (Spring 1963): 90–98.

——— and Frank O'Hara. "How to Proceed in the Arts," *Evergreen Review*, July–August 1961, p. 19.

Rivers, Larry. "A Discussion of the Work of Larry Rivers," *Art News*, March 1961, pp. 44–46, 53–55.

———. "Monet: The Eye Is Magic," *Art News*, April 1960, pp. 26–29, 60.

———. "Young Draftsmen on Master Draftsmen," *Art News*, January 1955, pp. 26–27.

Robbins, Daniel. "Morris Louis at the Juncture of Two Traditions," *Quadrum*, No. 18 (1965): 41–54.

———. "Morris Louis: Triumph of Color," *Art News*, October 1963, pp. 28–29, 57–58.

Robbins, Eugenia S. "Performing Art," *Art in America*, July–August 1966, pp. 107–111.

Robins, Corinne. "The Artist Speaks: Ronald Bladen," *Art in America*, September–October 1969, pp. 76–81.

———. "The Artist Speaks: Nicholas Krushenick," *Art in America*, May–June 1969, pp. 60–65.

Rose, Barbara. "On Chamberlain's Interview," *Artforum*, February 1972, pp. 44–45.

———. "Quality in Louis," *Artforum*, February 1972, pp. 44–45.

———. "The Graphic Work of Jasper Johns, Part II," *Artforum*, September 1970, pp. 65–74.

———. "The Airflow Multiple of Claes Oldenburg," *Studio International*, June 1970, pp. 254–255.

———. "The Graphic Work of Jasper Johns, Part I," *Artforum*, March 1970, pp. 39–45.

———. "The Origins, Life and Times of Ray Gun," *Artforum*, November 1969, pp. 50–57.

———. "Problems of Criticism, VI: The Politics of Art, Part III," *Artforum*, May 1969, pp. 46–51.

———. "Painting Within the Tradition: The Career of Helen Frankenthaler," *Artforum*, April 1969, pp. 28–33.

———. "Problems of Criticism, V: The Politics of Art, Part II," *Artforum*, January 1969, pp. 44–49.

———. "The Sculpture of Ellsworth Kelly," *Artforum*, Summer 1967, pp. 51–55.

——— and Irving Sandler. "Sensibility of the Sixties," *Art in America*, January–February 1967, pp. 44–57.

Rose, Barbara. "An Interview with Jack Youngerman," *Artforum*, January 1966, pp. 27–31.

———. "ABC Art," *Art in America*, October–November 1965, pp. 56–69.

———. "The Second Generation: Academy and Breakthrough," *Artforum*, September 1965, pp. 53–63.

———. "Looking at American Sculpture," *Artforum*, February 1965, pp. 29–36.

———. "Art Talent Scouts," *Art in America*, August 1964, pp. 18–19.

———. "Kenneth Noland," *Art International*, Summer 1964, pp. 58–61.

———. "How to Look at John Chamberlain's Sculpture," *Art International*, January 16, 1964, pp. 36–38.

———. "Dada Then and Now," *Art International*, January 25, 1963, pp. 23–28.

Rosenberg, Harold. "The Teaching of Hans Hofmann," *Arts*, December 1970–January 1971, pp. 17–19.

———. "The Image as Counterforce," *Art News*, February 1966, pp. 48–49, 64–65 (on Lester Johnson).

———. "Rivers' Commedia dell'Arte," *Art News*, April 1965, pp. 35–37, 62–63.

———. "After Next, What?" *Art in America*, April 1964, pp. 64–73.

———. "Hans Hofmann's 'Life' Class," *Portfolio and Art News Annual*, No. 6 (Autumn 1962), 16–31, 110–115.

———. "Critic Within the Act," *Art News*, October 1960, pp. 26–28.

———. "Tenth Street: A Geography of Modern Art," *Art News Annual*, 28 (1959), 120–143, 184–192.

———. "Hans Hofmann: Nature into Action," *Art News*, May 1957, pp. 34–36, 55–56.

———. "The American Action Painters," *Art News*, December 1952, pp. 22–23, 48–50.

Rosenblum, Robert. "Pop and Non-Pop: An Essay in Distinction," *Canadian Art*, January 1966, pp. 50–54.

———. "Pop Art and Non-Pop Art," *Art and Literature*, No. 5 (Summer 1965): 80–93.

———. "Jasper Johns," *Art International*, September 25, 1960, pp. 74–77.

———. "The New Decade," *Arts Digest*, May 15, 1955, pp. 20–23.

———. "Vanities of Impressionism," *Arts Digest*, October 1, 1954, p. 7.

Rosenstein, Harris. "The Colorful Gesture," *Art News*, March 1969, pp. 29–31, 68.

———. "Di Suvero: The Pressures of Reality," *Art News*, February 1967, pp. 36–39, 63–65.

———. "Climbing Mt. Oldenburg," *Art News*, February 1966, pp. 21–25, 56–59.

Roth, Moira and William. "John Cage on Marcel Duchamp: An Interview," *Art in America*, November–December 1973, pp. 72–79.

Roth, Moira. "Robert Smithson on Duchamp," *Artforum*, October 1973, p. 47 (an interview).

Rubin, William. "Ellsworth Kelly: The Big Form," *Art News*, November 1963, pp. 32–35, 64–65.

———. "Younger American Painters," *Art International*, Vol. 4, No. 1 (1960): 24–31.

———. "New Images of Man," *Art International*, Vol. 3, No. 9 (1959): 1–5.

———. "Pittsburgh's Carnegie International," *Art International*, Vol. 3, No. 1–2 (1959): 19–23.

———. "The New York Season Begins," *Art International*, Vol. 2, No. 8 (November 1958): 27–29.

———. "The New York School Then and Now, Part I," *Art International* Vol. 2, Nos. 2–3 (March–April 1958): 23–26; Part II, Vol. 2, Nos. 4–5 (May–June 1958): 19–22.

Rudikoff, Sonia. "New Realists in New York," *Art International*, January 25, 1963, pp. 39–41.

———. "Images in Painting," *Arts*, June 1960, pp. 40–46.

Russell, John. "Seated One Day at the I-Ching," *Art News*, January 1970, pp. 52–53, 71–72.

———. "Tenth Street and the Thames," *Art in America*, April 1964, pp. 74–76.

Sandler, Irving. "Hans Hofmann: The Pedagogical Master," *Art in America*, May–June 1973, pp. 48–55.

———. "Reinhardt: The Purist Blacklash," *Artforum*, December 1966, pp. 40–47.

———. "The Club," *Artforum*, September 1965, pp. 27–31.

———. "Expressionism with Corners," *Art News*, April 1965, pp. 38–40, 65–66.

———. "The New Cool-Art," *Art in America*, January–February 1965, pp. 96–101.

———. "Al Held Paints a Picture," *Art News*, May 1964, pp. 42–45, 51.

———. "In the Art Galleries," *New York Post*, June 16, 1963, p. 14 (an interview with Allan Kaprow).

———. "Ash Can Revisited: A New York Letter," *Art International*, October 25, 1960, pp. 28–30.

———. "American Construction Sculpture," *Evergreen Review* Vol. 2, No. 8 (Spring 1959): 136–146.

————. "Mitchell Paints a Picture," *Art News*, October 1957, pp. 44–47, 69–70.

Sawin, Martica. "Abstract Roots of Contemporary Representation," *Arts*, June 1976, pp. 106–109.

———— "Richard Stankiewicz," *Arts Yearbook: Paris/New York*, No. 3 (1959): 156–159.

————. "Month in Review," *Arts*, March 1959, pp. 46–49.

————. "Jan Müller: 1922–1958" *Arts*, February 1959, pp. 38–45.

————. "New York Letter," *Art International*, Vol. 3, No. 1–2 (1959): 45–46.

————. "Hyde Solomon," *Arts*, November 1958, pp. 38–43.

————. "In the Galleries: New York Artists Annual," *Arts*, June 1957, p. 49.

Sawyer, Kenneth. "Art Chronicle," *Hudson Review*, 5 (Spring 1957): 111–116.

Schapiro, Meyer. "The Liberating Quality of Avant-Garde Art," *Art News*, Summer 1957, p. 36–42.

————. "The Younger American Painters of Today," *The Listener*, January 26, 1956, pp. 146–147.

Schechner, Richard. "Is It What's Happening, Baby?" *New York Times*, June 12, 1966, Sec. 2, p. 3.

————. "Happenings," *Tulane Drama Review*, Vol. 10, No. 2 (Winter 1965): 229–232.

Schjeldahl, Peter. "Bluhm's Progress," *Art International*, May 1974, pp. 35, 58.

————. "Urban Pastorals," *Art News*, February 1971, pp. 32–33, 60–62.

Schmit, Tomas. "If I Remember Rightly," *Art and Artists*, October 1972, pp. 34–39.

Schorr, Justin. "Destination: Realism," *Art in America*, February 1964, pp. 116–118.

Schulze, Franz. "Chicago Popcycle," *Art in America*, November–December 1966, pp. 102–104.

Schuyler, James. "Frank O'Hara: Poet Among Painters," *Art News*, May 1974, pp. 44–45.

————. "Immediacy Is the Message? Fairfield Porter's New Works," *Art News*, March 1967, pp. 32–33, 68–70.

————. "The Painting of Jane Freilicher," *Art and Literature*, No. 10 (Autumn 1966): 147–159.

————. "Alex Katz Paints a Picture," *Art News*, February 1962, pp. 38–41, 52.

————. "Bell Paints a Picture," *Art News*, September 1958, pp. 42–45, 61–62.

Schwartz, Ellen. "A Conversation with Philip Pearlstein," *Art in America*, September–October 1971, pp. 50–57.

Schwartz, Sanford. "Myron Stout," *Artforum*, March 1975, pp. 38–43.

————. "Alex Katz So Far," *Art International*, December 15, 1973, pp. 28–30, 58.

Seckler, Dorothy Gees. "The Artist Speaks: Robert Rauschenberg," *Art in America*, May–June 1966, pp. 72–85.

————. "The Artist in America: Victim of the Culture Boom?" *Art in America*, December 1963, pp. 27–39.

————. "The Audience Is His Medium!" *Art in America*, April 1963, pp. 62–67.

————. "Folklore of the Banal," *Art in America*, Winter 1962, pp. 56–61, and August 1963, pp. 44–48.

————. "Chain of Generations—Contrast and Continuity," *Art in America*, Vol. 48, No. 1 (1960): 94–97, 122–132.

————. "Can Painting be Taught? (1) Beckman's Answer, (2) Hofmann's Answer," *Art News*, March 1951, pp. 39–40, 63–64.

————. "Can Painting Be Taught? Barnet Answers," *Art News*, November 1950, pp. 44–45, 64.

————. "Can Painting Be Taught? Ozenfant Answers," *Art News*, October 1950, pp. 44–45, 61.

Segal, George. "Bob Whitman and Things," *Art and Artists*, November 1972, pp. 16–19.

————. "George Segal on His Art," *Studio International*, October 1967, pp. 147–149.

Seitz, William. "Mondrian and the Issue of Relationships," *Artforum*, February 1972, pp. 70–75.

————. "The Relevance of Impressionism," *Art News*, January 1969, pp. 28–34, 43, 56–60.

————. "Problems of 'New Directions' Exhibitions," *Artforum*, September 1963, pp. 23–25.

————. "Assemblage: Problems and Issues," *Art International*, February 1962, pp. 26–34.

————. "Monet and Abstract Painting," *College Art Journal*, 16 (Fall 1956): 34–46.

Selz, Peter. "Between Friends: Still and the Bay Area," *Art in America*, November–December 1975, pp. 70–73.

————. "A Symposium of Pop Art," *Arts*, April 1963, pp. 36–45.

————. "A New Imagery in American Painting," *College Art Journal*, 15 (Summer 1956): 290–301.

Shapiro, David. "Imago Mundi," *Art News*, October 1971, pp. 40–41, 66–68.

————. "Strawberry Cake with the Psyche of a Good Camera," *Art News*, December 1970, pp. 30–33, 67–70.

————. "Jim Dine's Life-in-Progress," *Art News*, March 1970, pp. 42–46.

Siegel, Jeanne. "An Interview with James Rosenquist," *Artforum*, June 1972, pp. 30–34.

————. "Oldenburg's Places and Borrowings," *Arts*, November 1969, pp. 48–49.

————. "How to Keep Sculpture Alive In and Out of a Museum: An Interview with Claes Oldenburg on His Retrospective Exhibition at the Museum of Modern Art," *Arts*, September–October 1969, pp. 24–28.

————. "Some Late Thoughts of Marcel Duchamp: From an Interview with Jeanne Siegel," *Arts*, December 1968–January 1969, pp. 21–22.

Simon, Sydney. "George Sugarman," *Art International*, May 20, 1967, pp. 22–26.

————. "Larry Rivers," *Art International*, November 20, 1966, pp. 17–25.

Smith, Leon Polk. "A Statement from My Paintings," *Art Now*, Vol. 1, No. 8 (October 1969).

———— and Hayman D'Arcy. "The Paintings of

Leon Polk Smith," *Art and Literature*, No. 3 (Autumn–Winter 1964): 82–103 (a conversation).

Soby, James Thrall. "An Interview with Larry Rivers," *Saturday Review*, September 3, 1955, pp. 23–24.

Solomon, Alan R. "Jim Dine and the Psychology of the New Art," *Art International*, October 20, 1964, pp. 52–56.

——. "The New American Art," *Art International*, March 20, 1964, pp. 50–55.

——. "The New Art," *Art International*, September 25, 1963, pp. 37–41.

Stankiewicz, Richard. "The Prospects for American Arts," *Arts*, September 1956, pp. 16–17.

Steinberg, Leo. "Reflections on the State of Criticism," *Artforum*, March 1972, pp. 37–49.

——. "Jasper Johns," *Metro*, 4–5 (May 1962): 87–109.

——. "Month in Review," *Arts*, July 1956, pp. 25–28.

——. "Month in Review," *Arts*, June 1956, pp. 42–45.

——. "Month in Review," *Arts*, April 1956, pp. 42–45.

——. "Month in Review," *Arts*, January 1956, pp. 46–48.

Stiles, Knute. "Al Held," *Artforum*, March 1968, pp. 49–53.

Stuart, Michelle. "NO Is an Involvement," *Artforum*, September 1963, pp. 36–37.

Suzuki, Daisetz T. "Sengai: Zen and Art: Graphic Epigrams of a Buddhist Monk," *Art News Annual*, 27 (1958), 116–121, 193–196.

Swanson, Dean. "Nicholas Krushenick," *Art International*, April 20, 1968, pp. 31–33.

Swenson, G. R. "What Is Pop Art?" Part 2, *Art News*, February 1964, pp. 40–43, 66–67.

——. "What Is Pop Art?" Part 1, *Art News*, November 1963, pp. 24–25, 61–65.

——. "Rauschenberg Paints a Picture," *Art News*, April 1963, pp. 44–47, 65–67.

——. "The New American 'Sign Painters,'" *Art News*, September 1962, pp. 44–47, 60–62.

"Symposium: The Creative Process," *Art Digest*, January 15, 1954, pp. 15–16, 30–34.

"Symposium: The Human Figure," *Art Digest*, November 15, 1953, pp. 12–13, 32–33.

Tannenbaum, Judith. "A Poet in the Fifties," *Arts*, April 1974, pp. 46–47.

Tapié de Céleyran, Michel. "Mathieu Paints a Picture," *Art News*, February 1955, pp. 50–53, 74–75.

Thomsen, Barbara. "The Strange Case of Jules Olitski," *Art in America*, January–February, 1974, pp. 62–64.

——. "The Individual as a Crowd: Lester Johnson's Recent Paintings," *Art in America*, November–December 1973, pp. 110–111.

Thwaites, John Anthony. "Report on Documenta II," *Arts*, November 1959, pp. 44–49.

Tillim, Sidney. "A Variety of Realisms," *Artforum*, Summer 1969, pp. 42–47.

——. "The Reception of Figurative Art: Notes on a General Misunderstanding," *Artforum*, February 1969, pp. 30–33.

——. "Evaluations and Re-evaluations," *Artforum*, Summer 1968, pp. 20–23.

——. "The Katz Cocktail: Grand and Cozy," *Art News*, December 1965, pp. 46–49, 67–69.

——. "Further Observations on the Pop Phenomenon," *Artforum*, November 1965, pp. 17–19.

——. "The Figure and the Figurative in Abstract Expressionism," *Artforum*, September 1965, pp. 45–48.

——. "The Year of Jasper Johns," *Arts*, April 1964, pp. 22–26.

——. "Realism and 'The Problem,'" *Arts*, September 1963, pp. 48–51.

——. "The Present Outlook on Figurative Painting," *Perspectives on the Arts: Arts Yearbook*, 5 (1961): 37–59.

——. "Month in Review," *Arts*, April 1961, pp. 46–49.

——. "Month in Review," *Arts*, December 1960, pp. 44–47.

——. "Ellsworth Kelly," *Arts Yearbook*, *Paris/New York*, 3 (1959): 148–151.

——. "Month in Review," *Arts*, October 1959, pp. 48–51.

——. "What Happened to Geometry?" *Arts*, June 1959, pp. 38–44.

Towle, Tony. "Notes on Jim Dine's Lithographs," *Studio International*, April 1970, pp. 165–168.

"Trend to the 'Anti-Art,'" *Newsweek*, March 31, 1958, p. 94.

Tuchman, Phyllis. "POP!" *Art News*, May 1974, pp. 24–29.

——. "Ellsworth Kelly's Photographs," *Art in America*, January–February 1974, pp. 55–61.

——. "An Interview with George Segal," *Art in America*, May–June 1972, pp. 74–81.

——. "An Interview with John Chamberlain," *Artforum*, February 1972, pp. 38–43.

——. "An Interview with Jack Tworkov," *Artforum*, January 1971, pp. 62–68.

——. "George Segal," *Art International*, September 1968, pp. 51–53.

*Tulane Drama Review*, 10 (Winter 1965) (an issue on happenings and related events).

Tworkov, Jack. "A Cahier Leaf: Journal," *It Is*, 1 (Spring 1958): 25.

——. "The Wandering Soutine," *Art News*, November 1950, pp. 30–33, 62.

Tyler, Parker. "The Purple-Patch of Fetishism," *Art News*, March 1957, pp. 40–43, 52–53.

Varnedoe, Kirk. "Revision, Re-Vision, Re: Vision: The Status of Impressionism," *Arts*, November 1974, pp. 68–71.

Vaughan, David. "Diaghilev/Cunningham," *Art Journal*, Vol. 32, No. 2 (Winter 1974/75): 135–40.

Ventura, Anita. "Place and Show: The Stable," *Arts Digest*, May 1955, pp. 6–7, 31.

Vinklers, Bitite. "Why Not Dante? A Study of Rauschenberg's Drawings for the Inferno," *Art International*, Summer 1968, pp. 99–106.

Vogel, Lise. "Flexibility Verus Formalism," *College Art Journal*, Vol. 27, No. 3 (Spring 1968): 271–278.

Waldman, Diane. "Kelly Color," *Art News*, October 1968, pp. 40–41, 62–64.

Wasserman, Emily. "Yoko Ono at Syracuse: 'This is Not Here,' " *Artforum*, January 1972, pp. 69–73.

Weinstein, David. "Noland and Zox," *Art in America*, September–October 1973, pp. 94–96.

"Wholly American," *Times Literary Supplement* (London), November 6, 1959, p. 643 (an editorial).

Williams, Jonathan. "The Paintings of Dan Rice," *Art International*, Vol. 4, No. 1 (1960): 54–56.

Wilson, William. "Ray Johnson: New York Correspondence School," *Art and Artists*, April 1966, pp. 54–57.

Wright, Clifford. "Stankiewicz: Junk Poet," *Studio*, July 1962, pp. 2–5.

Young, Joseph E. "Jasper Johns: An Appraisal," *Art International*, September 1969, pp. 50–56.

# List of Illustrations

*Height precedes width in all dimensions given.*

1 Willem de Kooning, *Woman I*, 1950–52. Oil on canvas, 75⁷/₈″ x 58″. The Museum of Modern Art, New York.

2 Hans Hofmann, *Fantasia in Blue*, 1954. Oil on canvas. 60″ x 52″. Whitney Museum of American Art, New York. Gift of the Friends of the Whitney Museum of American Art. Photo: Geoffrey Clements.

3 Hans Hofmann, *Magenta and Blue*, 1950. Oil on canvas, 48″ x 58″. Whitney Museum of American Art, New York. Purchase. Photo: Geoffrey Clements.

4 Willem de Kooning, *Gotham News*, 1955. Oil on canvas, 69″ x 79″. Albright–Knox Art Gallery, Buffalo, New York. Gift of Seymour H. Knox.

5 Mark Rothko, *Four Darks in Red*, 1958. Oil on canvas, 102″ x 116″. Whitney Museum of American Art, New York. Gift of the Friends of the Whitney Museum of American Art, Mr. and Mrs. E. M. Schwartz, Mrs. S. A. Seaver, Charles Simon (and purchase). Photo: Geoffrey Clements.

6 Clyfford Still, *1950-A, No. 2*, 1950. Oil on canvas, 109″ x 93″. Hirshhorn Museum and Sculpture Garden, Smithsonian Institution, Washington, D.C. Photo: O. E. Nelson.

7 Barnett Newman, *Covenant*, 1949. Oil on canvas, 48″ x 60″. Hirshhorn Museum and Sculpture Garden, Smithsonian Institution, Washington, D.C.

8 Ad Reinhardt, *Number 87*, 1957. Oil on canvas, 72″ x 40″. The Museum of Modern Art, New York.

9 Jackson Pollock, *Number 27, 1950*, 1950. Oil on canvas, 49″ x 106″. Whitney Museum of American Art, New York. Purchase. Photo: Geoffrey Clements.

10 Franz Kline, *Mahoning*, 1956. Oil on canvas, 80″ x 100″. Whitney Museum of American Art, New York. Gift of the Friends of the Whitney Museum of American Art.

11 Larry Rivers and Frank O'Hara, *Stones*: Plate 8: "Melancholy Breakfast," 1957–60. Lithographs and wrapper, 15″ x 19¹/₈″. The Museum of Modern Art, New York. Gift of Mr. and Mrs. E. Powis Jones.

12 Grace Hartigan and Frank O'Hara, *What Fire Murmurs Its Seditions Beneath the Oaks*, 1953. Oil on paper, 48¹/₂″ x 38¹/₂″. Collection, Gertrude Kasle, Detroit, Michigan.

13 Norman Bluhm and Frank O'Hara, *Noel*, 1960. Gouache on paper, 19¹/₄″ x 14″. New York University Art Collection, Grey Art Gallery and Study Center. Photo: John D. Schiff.

14 Joan Mitchell, *George Went Swimming at Barnes Hole, but It Got Too Cold*, 1957. Oil on canvas, 85¹/₂″ x 78¹/₂″. Albright–Knox Art Gallery, Buffalo, New York. Gift of Seymour H. Knox.

15 Pierre Bonnard, *The Breakfast Room*, 1930–31. Oil on canvas, 62⁷/₈″ x 44⁷/₈″. The Museum of Modern Art, New York. Given anonymously.

16   Wolf Kahn, *Arnold's Place*, 1954. Oil on canvas, 28″ x 36″. Courtesy Grace Borgenicht Gallery, New York. Photo: Dan Brinzac, courtesy the artist.

17   Nell Blaine, *Harbor and Green Cloth, II*, 1958. Oil on canvas, 50″ x 65″. Whitney Museum of American Art, New York. Neysa McMein Purchase Award. Photo: Oliver Baker.

18   Claude Monet, *Water Lilies*, c. 1920. Oil on canvas, 78¹/₂″ x 235¹/₂″. The Museum of Modern Art, New York. Mrs. Simon Guggenheim Fund. Photo: Geoffrey Clements.

19   Philip Guston, *Dial*, 1956. Oil on canvas, 72″ x 76″. Whitney Museum of American Art, New York. Purchase. Photo: Geoffrey Clements.

20   Helen Frankenthaler, *Abstract Landscape*, 1951. Oil on sized, primed canvas, 69″ x 71⁷/₈″. Collection, the artist. Photo: Rudolph Burckhardt, courtesy the artist.

21   Helen Frankenthaler, *Mountains and Sea*, 1952. Oil on canvas, 86⁷/₈″ x 117¹/₄″. Collection, the artist. On loan to the National Gallery of Art, Washington, D.C. Photo, courtesy the artist.

22   Jackson Pollock, *Echo*, 1951. Oil on canvas, 91⁷/₈″ x 86″. The Museum of Modern Art, New York. Acquired through the Lillie P. Bliss Bequest and the Mr. and Mrs. David Rockefeller Fund.

23   Helen Frankenthaler, *Round Trip*, 1957. Oil on canvas, 70¹/₄″ x 70¹/₄″. Albright–Knox Art Gallery, Buffalo, New York. Gift of James I. Merrill.

24   Helen Frankenthaler, *Open Wall*, 1952–53. Oil on canvas, 53³/₄″ x 131¹/₈″. Collection, the artist. Photo: Rudolph Burckhardt, courtesy the artist.

25   Helen Frankenthaler, *Blue Territory*, 1955. Oil on canvas, 113″ x 58″. Whitney Museum of American Art, New York. Gift of the Friends of the Whitney Museum of American Art. Photo: Geoffrey Clements.

26   Helen Frankenthaler, *Trojan Gates*, 1955. Duco on canvas, 72″ x 48⁷/₈″. The Museum of Modern Art, New York. Gift of Mr. and Mrs. Allan D. Emil.

27   Helen Frankenthaler, *Mountain Storm*, 1955. Oil on canvas, 72″ x 48″. Andre Emmerich Gallery, New York. Photo: Ann Freedman.

28   Helen Frankenthaler, *Eden*, 1957. Oil on canvas, 103″ x 117″. Collection, the artist. Photo: Eric Pollitzer, courtesy the artist.

29   Helen Frankenthaler, *Basque Beach*, 1958. Oil on canvas, 58¹/₂″ x 69¹/₂″. Hirshhorn Museum and Sculpture Garden, Smithsonian Institution, Washington, D.C.

30   Joan Mitchell, *14th of July*, c. 1956. Oil on canvas, 60″ x 108″. Collection, Mr. and Mrs. Gifford Phillips, New York.

31   Joan Mitchell, *Hemlock*, 1956. Oil on canvas, 91″ x 80″. Whitney Museum of American Art, New York. Gift of the Friends of the Whitney Museum of American Art. Photo: Geoffrey Clements.

32   Joan Mitchell, *Mont St. Hilaire*, 1957. Oil on canvas, 80″ x 76″. The Lannan Foundation, Palm Beach, Florida. Photo: Lee Brian.

33   Joan Mitchell, *City Landscape*, 1955. Oil on canvas, 80″ x 80″. The Art Institute of Chicago. Gift of the Society for Contemporary American Art.

34   Alfred Leslie, *The Minx*, 1955. Oil on fiberboard, 56³/₄″ x 40¹/₂″. Collection, Mr. and Mrs. Sidney Kohl, Milwaukee, Wisconsin. Photo: John Lloyd Taylor.

35   Alfred Leslie, *Collage with Stripes*, 1956. Collage of ink, paper and oil paint, 24¹/₄″ x 18¹/₂″. Whitney Museum of American Art, New York. Anonymous gift. Photo: John D. Schiff.

36   Alfred Leslie, *Abstraction*, 1956. Oil on canvas, 48″ x 48″. Neuberger Museum, State University of New York at Purchase. Gift of Roy R. Neuberger. Photo: Geoffrey Clements.

37   Alfred Leslie, *Soldier's Medal*, 1959. Oil on canvas, 92″ x 119″. Albright–Knox Gallery, Buffalo, New York. Gift of Seymour H. Knox.

38   Michael Goldberg, *At Patsy's*, 1958. Oil on canvas, 59″ x 54″. Collection, Mr. and Mrs. Sidney Kohl, Milwaukee, Wisconsin. Photo: John Lloyd Taylor.

39   Michael Goldberg, *Summer House*, 1958. Oil on canvas, 89″ x 86″. Albright–Knox Art Gallery, Buffalo, New York. Gift of Seymour H. Knox.

40   Milton Resnick, *RR*, 1957. Oil on canvas, 36″ x 38″. New York University Art Collection, Grey Art Gallery and Study Center. Gift of Guy Weill. Photo: John D. Schiff.

41   Milton Resnick, *Low Gate*, 1957. Oil on canvas, 76″ x 68¹/₂″. Whitney Museum of American Art, New York. Gift of Mr. and Mrs. Guy A. Weill. Photo: Oliver Baker.

42   Milton Resnick, *Genie*, 1959. Oil on canvas, 104″ x 70″. Whitney Museum of American Art, New York. Photo: Geoffrey Clements.

43 Clyfford Still, *Untitled*, 1957. Oil on canvas, 112″ x 154″. Whitney Museum of American Art, New York. Gift of the Friends of the Whitney Museum of American Art (and purchase). Photo: Geoffrey Clements.

44 Ernest Briggs, *Untitled*, 1953. Oil on hemp canvas, 66″ x 37¹/₂″. Collection, the artist. Photo, courtesy the artist.

45 Ernest Briggs, *Untitled*, 1955. Oil on canvas, 57″ x 127″. Collection, the artist. Photo, courtesy the artist.

46 Edward Dugmore, *Untitled, 1951—Red*, 1951. Oil on canvas, 69¹/₂″ x 52″. The Maurice E. Odoroff Family Collection, Alexandria, Virginia. Photo, courtesy the artist.

47 Edward Dugmore, *Untitled, 1959—J*, 1959. Oil on canvas, 77¹/₂″ x 59″. Collection, the artist. Photo, courtesy the artist.

48 Jon Schueler, *Counterpoint*, 1953. Oil on canvas, 50″ x 48″. Collection, Rosemary Franck, West Nyack, New York.

49 Jon Schueler, *Snow Cloud and Blue Sky*, 1958. Oil on canvas, 80″ x 71″. Whitney Museum of American Art, New York. Gift of the Friends of the Whitney Museum of American Art. Photo: Oliver Baker.

50 Sam Francis, *Blue-Black*, 1952. Oil on canvas, 117″ x 76¹/₄″. Albright–Knox Art Gallery, Buffalo, New York. Gift of Seymour H. Knox.

51 Sam Francis, *Big Red*, 1953. Oil on canvas, 120″ x 76¹/₄″. The Museum of Modern Art, New York. Gift of Mr. and Mrs. David Rockefeller. Photo: Geoffrey Clements.

52 Sam Francis, *Red and Black*, 1954. Oil on canvas, 76³/₄″ x 38¹/₈″. The Solomon R. Guggenheim Museum, New York.

53 Sam Francis, *The Whiteness of the Whale*, 1957. Oil on canvas, 104¹/₂″ x 85¹/₂″. Albright–Knox Art Gallery, Buffalo, New York. Gift of Seymour H. Knox.

54 Sam Francis, *Shining Back*, 1958. Oil on canvas, 79³/₈″ x 53¹/₈″. The Solomon R. Guggenheim Museum, New York.

55 Sam Francis, *Abstraction*, 1959. Oil on canvas, 84″ x 50″. Whitney Museum of American Art, New York. Bequest of Udo M. Reinach. Photo: Geoffrey Clements.

56 Larry Rivers, *Double Portrait of Frank O'Hara*, 1955. Oil on canvas, 15¹/₄″ x 19¹/₈″. The Museum of Modern Art, New York. Gift of Stuart Preston.

57 Larry Rivers, *Molly and Breakfast*, 1956. Oil on pressed wood board, 47³/₄″ x 71³/₄″. Hirshhorn Museum and Sculpture Garden, Smithsonian Institution, Washington, D.C.

58 Jane Freilicher, *Portrait of John Ashbery*, 1954. Oil on canvas, approx. 42″ x 55″. Whereabouts unknown. Photo, courtesy the artist.

59 Jane Freilicher, *The Mallow-Gatherers*, 1958. Oil on canvas, 72″ x 72″. Collection, the artist. Photo: Rudolph Burckhardt, courtesy the artist.

60 Nell Blaine, *Autumn Studio II*, 1957–8. Oil on canvas, 45″ x 38″. Courtesy the Fischbach Gallery, New York. Photo: O. E. Nelson, courtesy the artist.

61 Willem de Kooning, *Marilyn Monroe*, 1954. Oil on canvas, 50″ x 30″. Neuberger Museum, State University of New York at Purchase. Gift of Roy R. Neuberger. Photo: Geoffrey Clements.

62 Fairfield Porter, *Katie and Anne*, 1955. Oil on canvas, 80¹/₄″ x 62¹/₈″. Hirshhorn Museum and Sculpture Garden, Smithsonian Institution, Washington, D.C.

63 Elaine de Kooning, *Scrimmage*, 1953. Oil on canvas, 25″ x 36″. Albright–Knox Art Gallery, Buffalo, New York. The Martha Jackson Collection.

64 Larry Rivers, *The Burial*, 1951. Oil on canvas, 60″ x 108″. Fort Wayne Museum of Art, permanent collection. Gift of the Gloria Vanderbilt Purchase Fund, donated by the American Federation of Art.

65 Larry Rivers, *Portrait of Frank O'Hara*, 1952. Oil on canvas, 30¹/₂″ x 26″. Promised gift of Mrs. Percy Uris to the Whitney Museum of American Art, New York. Photo: Geoffrey Clements.

66 Larry Rivers, *Washington Crossing the Delaware*, 1953. Oil on canvas, 83⁵/₈″ x 111⁵/₈″. The Museum of Modern Art, New York. Given anonymously.

67 Larry Rivers, *Double Portrait of Berdie*, 1955. Oil on canvas, 70³/₄″ x 82¹/₂″. Whitney Museum of American Art, New York. Anonymous Gift. Photo: Geoffrey Clements.

68 Larry Rivers, *The Studio*, 1956. Oil on canvas, 82¹/₂″ x 193¹/₂″. Minneapolis Institute of Arts. The John R. Van Derlip Fund.

69 Larry Rivers, *Berdie with the American Flag*, 1957. Oil on canvas, 20″ x 25⁷/₈″. William Nelson Gallery—Atkins Museum, Kansas City, Missouri. Gift of William Inge.

70    Larry Rivers, *ME*, 1959. Oil on canvas, 114¼″ x 177½″. Chrysler Museum at Norfolk, Virginia. Gift of Walter P. Chrysler, Jr.

71    Larry Rivers, *The Last Civil War Veteran*, 1959. Oil and charcoal on canvas, 82½″ x 64¹/₈″. The Museum of Modern Art, New York. Blanchette Rockefeller Fund.

72    Grace Hartigan, *"Rough Ain't It!,"* 1949–50. Mixed media on canvas, 40″ x 53″. Stolen, whereabouts unknown. Photo: Walter Silver, courtesy the artist.

73    Grace Hartigan, *The Persian Jacket*, 1952. Oil on canvas, 57½″ x 48″. The Museum of Modern Art, New York. Gift of George Poindexter.

74    Grace Hartigan, *Grand Street Brides*, 1954. Oil on canvas, 72″ x 102½″. Whitney Museum of American Art, New York. Anonymous gift. Photo: Geoffrey Clements.

75    Grace Hartigan, *New England, October*, 1957. Oil on canvas, 68¼″ x 83″. Albright–Knox Art Gallery, Buffalo, New York. Gift of Seymour H. Knox.

76    Grace Hartigan, *Sweden*, 1959. Oil on canvas, 83³/₄″ x 87½″. Whitney Museum of American Art, New York. Gift of Mr. and Mrs. Guy A. Weill. Photo: Geoffrey Clements.

77    Robert Goodnough, *The Struggle*, 1957. Oil on canvas, 44″ x 60″. Albright–Knox Art Gallery, Buffalo, New York. Gift of James I. Merrill.

78    Robert Goodnough, *The Frontiersman*, 1958. Oil on canvas, 67″ x 60″. Collection, Larry Aldrich, Ridgefield, Connecticut. Photo: Edward Meneeley.

79    Robert Goodnough, *Battle Landscape*, 1958. Oil on canvas, 65″ x 85″. New York University Art Collection, Grey Art Gallery and Study Center. Gift of Ingram Merrill Foundation Fund. Photo: O. E. Nelson.

80    Robert Goodnough, *Pink Reclining Nude*, 1959. Oil on Canvas, 53¼″ x 70″. Whitney Museum of American Art, New York. Gift of Andy Warhol. Photo: Geoffrey Clements.

81    Robert Goodnough, *Standing Figure*, 1960. Oil on canvas, 64″ x 63⁷/₈″. Brandeis University Art Collection—Rose Art Museum, Waltham, Massachusetts. Gift of James Goodman, New York. Photo: Mike O'Neil.

82    Jan Müller, *The Heraldic Ground*, 1953. Oil on jute, 14½″ x 41″. Estate of Jan Müller.

83    Jan Müller, *Double Circle Path #1*, 1956. Oil on jute, 38″ x 42″. Estate of Jan Müller. Photo: Rudolph Burckhardt.

84    Jan Müller, *The Temptation of St. Anthony*, 1957. Oil on canvas 79″ x 120³/₄″. Whitney Museum of American Art, New York. Purchase. Photo: Geoffrey Clements.

85    Jan Müller, *Faust, 1*, 1956. Oil on canvas, 68¹/₈″ x 120″. The Museum of Modern Art, New York. Purchase. Photo: Rudolph Burckhardt.

86    Jan Müller, *Jacob's Ladder*, 1958. Oil on canvas, 83½″ x 115″. The Solomon R. Guggenheim Museum, New York. Photo: Robert E. Mates.

87    Lester Johnson, *Mother and Children*, 1959. Oil on canvas, 34″ x 22″. Courtesy the artist. Photo: John D. Schiff, courtesy the artist.

88    Lester Johnson, *Profile with Tree*, c. 1959. Oil on paper, 26″ x 40″. Courtesy Zabriskie Gallery, New York. Photo: John D. Schiff.

89    Lester Johnson, *Three Men*, 1960. Oil on canvas, 53″ x 68″. Courtesy Zabriskie Gallery, New York. Photo: John D. Schiff.

90    Fairfield Porter, *Jimmy and John*, 1957–58. Oil on canvas, 36″ x 45½″. Courtesy Hirschl and Adler Galleries, Inc., New York. Photo: Paulus Leeser.

91    Fairfield Porter, *Red Wheel Barrow*, 1959. Oil on canvas, 40⁷/₈″ x 38½″. Courtesy Hirschl and Adler Galleries, Inc., New York. Photo: Paulus Leeser.

92    Alex Katz, *Luna Park*, 1960. Oil on canvas, 40″ x 30″. Collection, the artist. Photo: Rudolph Burckhardt.

93    Alex Katz, *Ada Ada*, 1959. Oil on canvas, 50″ x 50″. New York University Art Collection, Grey Art Gallery and Study Center. Gift of Mr. and Mrs. Samuel Golden Photo: Charles Uht.

94    Philip Pearlstein, *Rock Mound*, 1958. Oil on canvas, 44″ x 52″. Whitney Museum of American Art, New York. Gift of the Friends of the Whitney Museum of American Art. Photo: Oliver Baker.

95    Philip Pearlstein, *Positano I*, 1960. Oil on canvas, 66″ x 96″. Collection, Dorothy Pearlstein, New York. Photo: Eric Pollitzer, courtesy Allan Frumkin Gallery, New York.

96    Richard Diebenkorn, *Berkeley No. 37*, 1955. Oil on canvas, 70″ x 70″. Museum of Art, Carnegie Institute, Pittsburgh, Pennsylvania. Gift of Mr. and Mrs. Charles Denby.

97    Richard Diebenkorn, *Girl on a Terrace*, 1956. Oil on canvas, 71″ x 66″. Neuberger Museum,

State University of New York at Purchase. Gift of Roy R. Neuberger. Photo: Rudolph Burckhardt.

98    Leon Golub, *Damaged Man*, 1955. Lacquer and oil on canvas, 48″ x 36″. Collection, Mr. Gene R. Summers, Laguna Beach, California.

99    Leon Golub, *Colossal Heads (I)*, 1959. Lacquer on canvas, 81″ x 131″. Collection, Mr. Ulrich E. Meyer, Chicago, Illinois.

100    Richard Stankiewicz, *Untitled*, c. 1959. Steel, c. 48″ high. Courtesy Zabriskie Gallery, New York.

101    David Smith, *Hudson River Landscape*, 1951. Steel, 49½″ x 75″ x 16¾″. Whitney Museum of American Art, New York. Purchase. Photo: Geoffrey Clements.

102    John Chamberlain, *Essex*, 1960. Automobile body parts and other metal, relief, 108″ x 80″ x 43″. The Museum of Modern Art, New York. Gift of Mr. and Mrs. Robert C. Scull and Purchase Fund.

103    Mark di Suvero, *Barrell*, 1959. Wood and steel cable, 96″ high. Now destroyed. Photo: Rudolph Buckhardt, courtesy Richard Bellamy.

104    Richard Stankiewicz, *Natural History*, 1959. Welded iron pipes and boiler within wire mesh, 14¾″ x 34¼″ x 19¼″. The Museum of Modern Art, New York. Elizabeth Bliss Parkinson Fund.

105    Richard Stankiewicz, *Kabuki Dancer*, 1956. Cast iron and steel, 84″ x 24″ x 26″. Whitney Museum of American Art, New York. Gift of the Friends of the Whitney Museum of Modern Art. Photo: E. Nelson.

106    Richard Stankiewicz, *Figure*, 1952. Aluminum wire, 31″ x 14″ x 15″. Courtesy Zabriskie Gallery, New York.

107    Richard Stankiewicz, *Our Lady of All Protections*, 1958. Iron and steel, 51″ x 31″ x 32″. Albright–Knox Art Gallery, Buffalo, New York. Gift of Saymour H. Knox.

108    Richard Stankiewicz, *The Candidate*, 1960. Scrap metal and brass, 37″ high. Collection, Mr. and Mrs. Gifford Phillips, New York.

109    Richard Stankiewicz, *Untitled*, 1960. Steel, 50″ x 17″ x 19″. Collection, Hanford Yang, New York.

110    Jean Follett, *Lady with the Open Door Stomach*, 1956. Painted wood, gravel and metal, and assemblage, 46¾″ x 48″ x 3″. Whitney Museum of American Art, New York. Anonymous gift. Photo: Geoffrey Clements.

111    Jean Follett, *Many Headed Creature*, 1958. Assemblage: light switch, cooling coils, window screen, nails, faucet knob, mirror, twine cinders, etc., on wood panel, 24″ x 24″. The Museum of Modern Art, New York. Larry Aldrich Foundation Fund.

112    John Chamberlain, *Wildroot*, 1959. Enamelled steel, 66″ x 65″. Sammlung Karl Stroher im Hessischen Landesmuseum Darmstadt. Photo: Rudolph Burckhardt.

113    John Chamberlain, *Cord*, 1957. Steel, 16″ x 12″ x 10″. Courtesy Allan Stone Gallery, New York.

114    John Chamberlain, *Nutcracker*, 1958. Welded and painted steel, 50″ x 50″ x 30″. Courtesy Allan Stone Gallery, New York. Photo: Eric Pollitzer.

115    John Chamberlain, *Hudson*, 1960. Welded and painted steel, 27″ x 27″ x 12″. Courtesy Allan Stone Gallery, New York.

116    John Chamberlain, *Swannanoa*, 1959. Enamelled steel, 45¼″ x 64½″ x 35″; base: 20″ x 3½″ x 3½″. Courtesy The Mayor Gallery, London. Photo: O. E. Nelson.

117    Mark di Suvero, *Che Faro Senza Eurydice*, 1959. Wood, rope and nails, 84″ x 104″ x 91″. Private Collection, New York. Photo: Rudolph Burckhardt, courtesy Richard Bellamy.

118    Mark di Suvero, *For Sabater*, 1959. Wood and paint, approx. 96″ high. Now destroyed. Photo: Courtesy Richard Bellamy.

119    Mark di Suvero, *Hankchampion*, 1960. Wood and chains, 77½″ x 149″ x 105″. Whitney Museum of American Art, New York. Gift of Mr. and Mrs. Robert C. Scull. Photo: Geoffrey Clements.

120    Mark di Suvero, *Hand Pierced*, 1959. Bronze, 60½″ high. Private Collection, New York. Photo: Eric Pollitzer, courtesy Richard Bellamy.

121    Mark di Suvero, *Ladder piece*, 1961–62. Wood and steel, 75″ high. Private Collection. Photo: Rudolph Burckhardt, courtesy Richard Bellamy.

122    Robert Rauschenberg, *Canyon*, 1959. Combine painting, 86½″ x 70″ x 23″. Private Collection, New York.

123    Jasper Johns, *Painted Bronze*, 1960. Painted bronze, 13½″ x 8″ diameter. Collection, the artist. Photo: Rudolph Burckhardt, courtesy Leo Castelli Gallery.

124  Marcel Duchamp, *The Bride Stripped Bare by Her Bachelors Even* (large glass), 1915–23. Oil, varnish, lead foil, lead wire, and dust on two glass panels (cracked), each mounted between two glass panels, with five glass strips, aluminum foil, and a wood and steel frame, 109¼″ x 69¼″. Philadelphia Museum of Art. Bequest of Katherine S. Dreier.

125  Robert Rauschenberg, *White Painting (Seven Panels)*, 1951. House paint on canvas, 72″ x 128″. Collection, the artist. Photo: Rudolph Burckhardt, courtesy Leo Castelli Gallery.

126  Robert Rauschenberg, *Crucifixion and Reflexion*, 1950. Oil and collage on canvas, 51″ x 47½″. Andrew J. Crispo Collection, New York.

127  Robert Rauschenberg, *The Lily White* (formerly known as *White Painting with Numbers*, 1949), ca. 1950. Oil and pencil on canvas, 39½″ x 23½″. Collection, Mr. and Mrs. Victor W. Ganz, New York.

128  Robert Rauschenberg, *Charlene*, 1954. Oil, paper, fabric, wood, metal, on wood panels, 89″ x 112″. Stedelijk Museum, Amsterdam, The Netherlands.

129  Robert Rauschenberg, *Coca-Cola Plan*, 1958. Combine painting, 27″ x 26″ x 6″. Collection, Panza, Milan, Italy. Photo: Rudolph Burckhardt, courtesy Leo Castelli Gallery.

130  Kurt Schwitters, V-2, 1928. Collage of colored and printed papers with pen and ink and crayon, 5⅛″ x 3½″. The Sidney and Harriet Janis Collection. Gift to the Museum of Modern Art, New York.

131  Robert Rauschenberg, *Monogram*, 1955–1959. Construction, 48″ x 72″ x 72″. National Museum, Stockholm, Sweden.

132  Robert Rauschenberg, Illustration for Dante's *Inferno: Canto XXXI: The Giants*, 1959–60. Red pencil and graphite, gouache and transfer, 14½″ x 11½″. The Museum of Modern Art, New York. Given anonymously.

133  Robert Rauschenberg, *Bed*, 1955. Combine painting, 74″ x 31″. Collection, Mr. and Mrs. Leo Castelli, New York. Photo: Rudolph Burckhardt, courtesy Leo Castelli Gallery.

134  Robert Rauschenberg, *Factum I*, 1957. Combine painting, 62″ x 35½″. Collection, Panza, Milan, Italy. Photo: Rudolph Burckhardt, courtesy Leo Castelli Gallery.

135  Robert Rauschenberg, *Factum II*, 1957. Combine painting, 62″ x 35½″. Collection, Mr. and Mrs. Morton Neumann, Chicago, Illi-

nois. Photo: Rudolph Burckhardt, courtesy Leo Castelli Gallery.

136  Jasper Johns, *Target with Four Faces*, 1955. Encaustic on newspaper over canvas, 26″ x 26″, surmounted by four tinted plaster faces in wooden box with hinged front. Overall dimensions with box open, 33⅝″ x 26″ x 3″. The Museum of Modern Art, New York. Gift of Mr. and Mrs. Robert C. Scull.

137  Jasper Johns, *Flag*, 1958. Encaustic and collage on canvas, 42″ x 60″. Collection, Mr. and Mrs. Leo Castelli, New York. Photo: Shunk-Kender, courtesy Leo Castelli Gallery.

138  Jasper Johns, *False Start*, 1959. Oil on canvas, 67¼″ x 54″. Private Collection, New York. Photo: Rudolph Burckhardt, courtesy Leo Castelli Gallery.

139  Jasper Johns, *Painted Bronze (ale cans)*, 1960. Painted bronze, 5½″ x 8″ x 4¾″. Kunstmuseum Basel, collection Ludwig. Photo, courtesy Leo Castelli Gallery.

140  Jasper Johns, *Lightbulb II*, 1958. Sculp-metal, 3⅛″ x 8″ x 5″. Collection, the artist. Photo: Rudolph Burckhardt, courtesy Leo Castelli Gallery.

141  Jasper Johns, *Numbers in Color*, 1959. Encaustic and collage on canvas, 66½″ x 49½″. Albright–Knox Art Gallery, Buffalo, New York. Gift of Seymour H. Knox.

142  Jasper Johns, *Drawer*, 1957. Encaustic and assemblage on canvas, 30¾″ x 30¾″. Brandeis University Art Collection, Waltham, Massachusetts. Gevirtz-Mnuchin. Purchase Fund.

143  Jasper Johns, *Tennyson*, 1958. Encaustic and canvas collage on canvas, 73½″ x 48¼″. Des Moines Art Center. Coffin Fine Arts Trust Fund, 1971.

144  Allan Kaprow, *An Apple Shrine*, 1960. Environment. Photo: Robert R. McElroy.

145  Allan Kaprow, *George Washington Bridge (with Cars)*, 1955. Oil on canvas, 41½″ x 49¼″. Collection, Mr. and Mrs. Michael M. Peters, Stamford, Connecticut. Photo: Adrienne Campbell, courtesy the artist.

146  Allan Kaprow, *Woman Out of Fire*, 1956. Metal, paper and plaster covered with roofing cement, approx. 36″ x 24″ (plaster-covered wooden base missing in photo). Collection, the artist.

147  Allan Kaprow, *Hysteria*, 1956. Collage, painted rags, aluminum foil, 72½″ x 67¼″. Collection, Dr. Hubert Peeters, Bruges, Belgium. Photo: George Franklin Hurych, courtesy the artist.

148  Allan Kaprow, *Grandma's Boy*, 1957. Hinged assemblage; right panel: 18¹/₂″ x 15³/₄″ x ¹³/₁₆″, left panel: 16⁷/₁₆″ x 12³/₈″ x 1⁷/₈″. Collection, Rhett and Robert Delford Brown, New York. Photo: George Hurych, courtesy the artist.

149  Allan Kaprow, *Interchangeable Panels*, 1957–59. Assemblage with tar, paint, leaves, mirrors, lights, collage of paper, false fruit, aluminum foil. This is the Kiosk arrangement. The panels can be exhibited as a two-dimensional work and new panels can be added, 96″ x 204″. Collection, Dr. Hubert Peeters, Bruges, Belgium. Photo: Peter Moore, courtesy the artist.

150  Jim Dine, *Household Piece*, 1959. Assemblage with wood, canvas, cloth, iron, springs, oil and bronze paint, sheet copper, brown paper bag, mattress stuffing, plastic, 54¹/₄″ x 44¹/₄″ x 9¹/₄″. The Museum of Modern Art, New York. Gift of John W. Weber.

151  Claes Oldenburg, *Snapshots from the City*, 1960. Happening (from the street). Photo: Martha Holmes.

152  Robert Whitman, *E. G.*, 1960. Happening. Photo: Robert R. McElroy.

153  Claes Oldenburg, *Shirt*, 1960. Plaster and paint, 29¹/₈″ x 25¹/₄″ x 5″. Whitney Museum of American Art, New York. Gift of Andy Warhol. Photo: Geoffrey Clements.

154  Jim Dine, *The Valiant Red Car*, 1960. Oil on canvas, 54″ x 123″. Collection, The Martha Jackson Gallery, New York. Photo: O. E. Nelson.

155  Jim Dine, *The Smiling Workman*, 1960. Happening. Photo: Martha Holmes.

156  Red Grooms, *The Burning Building*, 1959. Happening. Photo: John Cohen.

157  Ellsworth Kelly, *Black Ripe*, 1956. Oil on canvas, 63″ x 59″. Private Collection. Photo: Eric Pollitzer.

158  Henry Matisse, *Bather*, 1909. Oil on canvas, 36¹/₂″ x 29¹/₈″. The Museum of Modern Art, New York. Gift of Abby Aldrich Rockefeller.

159  Piet Mondrian, *Composition in Red, Blue and Yellow*, 1937–42. Oil on canvas, 23³/₄″ x 21⁷/₈″. The Sidney and Harriet Janis Collection. Gift to the Museum of Modern Art, New York.

160  Leon Polk Smith, *May Twenty*, 1959. Oil on canvas, 68″ x 68″. Collection, the artist. Photo: John O. Schiff.

161  Myron Stout, *No. 3, 1957*, 1957. Oil on canvas, 26″ x 18″. Museum of Art, Carnegie Insti-

tute, Pittsburgh, Pennsylvania. Gift of Mr. Leland Hazard.

162  Ellsworth Kelly, *Atlantic*, 1956. Oil on canvas, 80″ x 114″. Whitney Museum of American Art, New York. Photo: Geoffrey Clements.

163  Ellsworth Kelly, *Aubade*, 1957. Oil on canvas, 80″ x 80″. Museum of Art, Carnegie Institute, Pittsburgh, Pennsylvania. Richard Mace Feldman Memorial Fund.

164  Ellsworth Kelly, *New York, N.Y.*, 1957. Oil on canvas, 73¹/₄″ x 91″. Albright–Knox Art Gallery, Buffalo, New York. Gift of Seymour H. Knox.

165  Ellsworth Kelly, *Bay*, 1959. Oil on canvas, 70″ x 50″. Collection, Joseph A. Helman, New York.

166  Ellsworth Kelly, *Green White*, 1959. Oil on canvas, 46″ x 60″. Private Collection. Photo: Geoffrey Clements, courtesy Leo Castelli Gallery.

167  Ellsworth Kelly, *Running White*, 1959. Oil on canvas, 88″ x 68″. The Museum of Modern Art, New York. Purchase. Photo: Geoffrey Clements.

168  Ellsworth Kelly, *Pony*, 1959. Painted aluminum, 31″ x 78″ x 64″. Collection, Mr. and Mrs. Miles Q. Fiterman, Minneapolis, Minnesota. Courtesy John C. Stoller & Co., Minneapolis, Minnesota.

169  Ellsworth Kelly, *Charter*, 1959. Oil on canvas, 95¹/₂″ x 60″. Yale University Art Gallery, New Haven, Connecticut. Gift of Helen W. Benjamin in memory of her husband, Robert M. Benjamin.

170  Ellsworth Kelly, *Blue, White*, 1960. Oil on canvas, 85″ x 68″. Art Gallery of Ontario, Toronto. Gift from the Women's Committee Fund, 1963. Photo: Oliver Baker.

171  Leon Polk Smith, *Anitou*, 1958. Oil on canvas, 56⁵/₈″ diameter. The Museum of Modern Art, New York. Gift of Dr. and Mrs. Arthur Lejwa.

172  Leon Polk Smith, *Expanse*, 1959. Oil on canvas, 68¹/₂″ x 74″. Whereabouts unknown. Photo: O. E. Nelson, courtesy the artist.

173  Leon Polk Smith, *Correspondence: Red Black*, 1960. Oil on canvas, 33″ x 27″. Whereabouts unknown. Photo: Oliver Baker, courtesy the artist.

174  Myron Stout, *Number 3*, 1954. Oil on canvas, 20¹/₈″ x 16″. The Museum of Modern Art, New York. Philip Johnson Fund. Photo: Rudolph Burckhardt.

175  Myron Stout, *Untitled*, 1954–55. Oil on canvas, 20″ x 14″. Collection, Mrs. and Mrs. Charles H. Carpenter, Jr., New Canaan, Connecticut. Photo: Rudolph Burckhardt, courtesy Richard Bellamy.

176  Morris Louis, *Point of Tranquility*, 1958. Acrylic on canvas, 101³/₈″ x 135″. Hirshhorn Museum and Sculpture Garden, Smithsonian Institution, Washington, D.C. Photo: Geoffrey Clements.

177  Barnett Newman, *Vir Heroicus Sublimis*, 1950–51. Oil on canvas, 95³/₈″ x 213¹/₄″. The Museum of Modern Art, New York. Gift of Mr. and Mrs. Ben Heller.

178  Morris Louis, *Tet*, 1958. Oil on canvas, 93¹/₂″ x 115¹/₂″. Whitney Museum of American Art, New York. Gift of the Friends of the Whitney Museum of American Art. Photo: Geoffrey Clements.

179  Morris Louis, *Untitled*, 1956. Acrylic on canvas, 83″ x 93″. Neuberger Museum, State University of New York at Purchase. Gift of Roy R. Neuberger.

180  Morris Louis, *Alpha*, 1960. Acrylic resin paint on canvas, 105¹/₂″ x 145¹/₂″. Albright–Knox Art Gallery, Buffalo, New York. Gift of Seymour H. Knox. Photo: Sherwin Greenberg.

181  Kenneth Noland, *Spread*, 1958. Oil on canvas, 117″ x 117″. New York University Art Collection, Grey Art Gallery and Study Center.

182  Kenneth Noland, *Turnsole*, 1961. Synthetic polymer paint on canvas, 94¹/₈″ x 94¹/₈″. The Museum of Modern Art, New York. Blanchette Rockefeller Fund.

183  Jules Olitski, *Isis Ardor*, 1962. Acrylic on canvas, 80″ x 66″. Harry N. Abrams Family Collection, New York. Photo: Eric Pollitzer.

184  Sally Hazelet Drummond, *Hummingbird*, 1961. Oil on canvas, 12″ x 12″. The Museum of Modern Art, New York. Larry Aldrich Foundation Fund.

185  Nicholas Krushenick, *East Hampton*, 1962. Liquitex on canvas, 60″ x 50″. Collection, the artist.

186  Alfred Jensen, *Family Portrait*, 1958. Oil on canvas, 75″ x 40″. Albright–Knox Art Gallery, Buffalo, New York. Martha Jackson Collection.

187  Alfred Jensen, *The Great Mystery II*, 1960. Oil on canvas, 50″ x 42″. Albright–Knox Art Gallery, Buffalo, New York. Gift of Seymour H. Knox.

188  Paul Brach, *Merlin*, 1959. Oil on canvas, 60″ x 50″. Collection, Dr. and Mrs. Robert D. Seely, New York.

189  Miriam Schapiro, *The Game*, 1960. Oil on canvas, 81″ x 90¹/₂″. Collection, the artist.

190  George Ortman, *Game of Chance*, 1959. Construction, canvas and oil-wax medium, 60″ x 60″. New York University Art Collection, Grey Art Gallery and Study Center. Photo: Charles Uht.

191  Raymond Parker, *Untitled*, 1956. Oil on canvas, 83″ x 49″. Whitney Museum of American Art, New York. Gift of the Uris Brothers Foundation Inc. Photo: Geoffrey Clements.

192  Raymond Parker, *P. 30*. Oil on canvas, 64″ x 68″. The Art Museum, Princeton University. Gift of Barbara Rose for the William C. Seitz Memorial Collection. Photo: Taylor & Dull, Inc.

193  Raymond Parker, *Untitled*, 1959. Oil on canvas, 68¹/₂″ x 69″. Albright–Knox Art Gallery, Buffalo, New York. Gift of Seymour H. Knox.

194  Al Held, *Untitled*, 1956. Oil on canvas, 66″ x 48″. Collection, the artist. Photo: Geoffrey Clements.

195  Al Held, *Untitled*, 1956. Oil on canvas, 108″ x 192″. Collection, Mara Held, Santa Monica, California. Photo: Geoffrey Clements.

196  Al Held, *Untitled*, 1960. Acrylic on canvas, 50″ x 45″. Private Collection, New York. Photo: Geoffrey Clements.

197  Al Held, *I-Beam*, 1961. Acrylic on canvas, 114″ x 192″. Collection, the artist. Photo: Rudolph Burckhardt.

198  Gabriel Kohn, *Pitcairn*, 1958. Wood, 22⁵/₈″ x 49¹/₂″ x 24¹/₂″. Albright–Knox Art Gallery, Buffalo, New York. Gift of Seymour H. Knox.

199  Gabriel Kohn, *Nantucket (Equatorial Trap)*, 1960. Wood, 26″ x 35″ x 23¹/₄″. Hirshhorn Museum and Sculpture Garden, Smithsonian Institution, Washington, D.C.

200  George Sugarman, *Six Forms in Pine*, 1959. Pine, approx. 96″ long. Collection, the artist.

201  George Sugarman, *Yellow Top*, 1960. Laminated wood, polychromed, 87¹/₂″ x 54″ x 34″. Walker Art Center, Minneapolis, Minnesota. Gift of the T. B. Walker Foundation.

202  George Sugarman, *Spiral Sculpture*, 1961. Laminated wood, fiberglass over wire mesh,

liquitex paint, 70″ x 60″ x 33″. Destroyed. Photo, courtesy the artist.

203  Ronald Bladen, *Untitled*, 1958–59. Oil on pressed wood board, 48″ x 36″. Collection, Connie Reyes, New York. Photo: Julio Ravello.

204  Ronald Bladen, *Untitled*, 1961. Paper collage, 36″ x 30″. Collection, Connie Reyes, New York. Photo: Walter J. Russell.

205  Ronald Bladen, *Untitled*, 1962. Painted wood construction 96″ x 72″. Collection, Connie Reyes, New York. Photo: Eric Pollitzer.

206  Helen Frankenthaler, *Mount Sinai*, 1956. Oil on canvas, 30″ x 30″. Neuberger Museum, State University of New York at Purchase. Gift of Roy R. Neuberger. Photo: Geoffrey Clements.

207  Joan Mitchell, *Untitled*, 1960. Oil on canvas, 71⅛″ x 63″. Philadelphia Museum of Art. Given by Mr. and Mrs. Joseph Sliska.

208  Larry River, *Berdie in a Red Shawl*, 1953. Oil on canvas, 53″ x 65″. Whitney Museum of American Art, New York. Lawrence H. Bloedel Bequest. Photo: Geoffrey Clements.

209  Grace Hartigan, *Shop Window*, 1955. Oil on canvas, 63″ x 81″. Neuberger Museum, State University of New York at Purchase. Gift of Roy R. Neuberger. Photo: Geoffrey Clements.

210  Alfred Leslie, *#3339 Fountain*, 1958. Oil on canvas, 60″ x 66″. Harry N. Abrams Family Collection, New York. Photo: Oliver Baker.

211  Robert Rauschenberg, *Winter Pool*, 1959. Combine painting with oil, paper, fabric, wood on canvas, with wood ladder, 88½″ x 58½″ x 3″. Collection, Mr. and Mrs. Victor W. Ganz, New York.

212  Robert Goodnough, *Summer III*, 1959. Oil on canvas, 50″ x 66″. Whitney Museum of American Art, New York. Gift of Mrs. Iola S. Haverstick. Photo: Geoffrey Clements.

213  Jasper Johns, *Flag Above White*, 1954. Encaustic on canvas, 22″ x 19″. Private Collection, New York. Photo: Rudolph Burckhardt, courtesy Leo Castelli Gallery.

214  Roy Lichtenstein, *Girl with Ball*, 1961. Oil on canvas, 60¼″ x 36¼″. Private Collection. Photo: Rudolph Burckhardt, courtesy Leo Castelli Gallery.

215  Andy Warhol, *Water Heater*, 1960. Synthetic polymer paint on canvas, 44¾″ x 40″. The Museum of Modern Art, New York. Gift of Roy Lichtenstein.

216  James Rosenquist, *Look Alive*, 1961. Oil on canvas, 67″ x 58⅛″. Harry N. Abrams Family Collection, New York.

217  David Park, *Four Men*, 1958. Oil on canvas, 57″ x 92″. Whitney Museum of American Art, New York. Gift of an anonymous foundation. Photo: Geoffrey Clements.

218  Philip Pearlstein, *Male and Female Models Sitting on the Floor*, 1962. Oil on canvas, 44″ x 50″. Courtesy Allan Frumkin Gallery, New York. Photo: Nathan Rabin.

219  Alex Katz, *The Red Smile*, 1963. Oil on canvas, 78″ x 120″. Collection, the artist. Photo: Rudolph Burckhardt.

220  Jim Dine, *Flesh Striped Tie*, 1961. Oil and canvas collage, 60¼″ x 50″. Hirshhorn Museum and Sculpture Garden, Smithsonian Institution, Washington, D.C. Photo: Geoffrey Clements.

221  George Segal, *Man at Table*, 1961. Plaster, wood, glass, 338″ x 305″ x 305″. Städtisches Museum Mönchengladbach, Germany. Photo: Eric Pollitzer, courtesy the artist.

222  Claes Oldenburg, *Red Tights with Fragment 9*, 1961. Muslin soaked in plaster over wire frame, painted with enamel, 69⅝″ x 34¼″ x 8¾″. The Museum of Modern Art, New York. Gift of G. David Thompson. Photo: Rudolph Burckhardt.

223  Frank Stella, *The Marriage of Reason and Squalor*, 1959. Oil on canvas, 90¾″ by 132¾″. Museum of Modern Art, New York. The Larry Aldrich Foundation Fund.

224  Frank Stella, *Coney Island*, 1958. Oil on canvas, 85¼″ x 78¾″. Yale University Art Gallery, New Haven, Connecticut. Gift of Larom B. Munson, B.A., 1951. Photo: Joseph Szaszfal.

225  Frank Stella, *Pagosa Springs*, 1960. Copper paint on shaped canvas, 99¼″ x 99¼″. Hirshhorn Museum and Sculpture Garden, Smithsonian Institution, Washington, D.C.

## Color Plates

PLATE I  Helen, Frankenthaler, *Jacob's Ladder*, 1957. Oil on canvas, 113 ⅜″ x 69⅞″. The Museum of Modern Art, New York. Gift of Hyman N. Glickstein. Photo: Rudolph Burckhardt.

PLATE II  Joan Mitchell, *Ladybug*, 1957. Oil on canvas, 77 ⅝″ x 108″. The Museum of Mod-

ern Art, New York. Photo: Rudolph Burckhardt.

PLATE III   Larry Rivers, *The Pool*, 1956. Oil, charcoal, and bronze paint on canvas, 103³/₈″ x
92⁵/₈″. The Museum of Modern Art, New
York. Gift of Mr. and Mrs. Donald Weis-
berger.

PLATE IV   Grace Hartigan, *River Bathers*, 1953. Oil
on canvas, 69³/₈″ x 88³/₄″. The Museum of
Modern Art, New York.

PLATE V   Robert Goodnough, *Laocoön*, 1958. Oil
and charcoal on canvas, 66³/₈″ x 54¹/₈″. The
Museum of Modern Art, New York. Photo:
Soichi Sunami.

PLATE VI   Robert Rauschenberg, *Rebus*, 1955. Oil,
pencil, paper, and fabric on canvas, 94″ x
144″. Collection, Mr. and Mrs. Victor Ganz,
New York.

PLATE VII   Jasper Johns, *Painting with Two Balls*,
1960. Encaustic and collage on canvas with
objects, 65″ x 54″. Collection, the artist.
Photo: Rudolph Burckhardt, courtesy Leo
Castelli Gallery.

PLATE VIII   Ellsworth Kelly, Rogue, 1956. Oil on
canvas, 34″ x 38″. Anonymous collection.
Photo: Eric Pollitzer, courtesy Leo Castelli
Gallery.

# Index

*Page numbers in italic refer to illustrations. Color Plates follow page 210.*

Albers, Josef, 33, 174, 236
Alloway, Lawrence, 265
*American Abstract Expressionists and Imagists* (show, 1961), 269, 271, 283
Amram, David, 21, 24
Andre, Carl, 309, 310
Area Gallery, 30, 41
Armory Show (1913), 163, 304
Arnason, H. Harvard, 271
Arp, Jean, 31, 36, 215, 218, 239, 247
Artaud, Antonin, 196
  *The Theatre and Its Double*, 196
*Art Digest* (*Arts Digest; Arts*), 258, 263–64, 269
*Art in America*, 264
*Art International*, 265
Artists Club. *See* Club
*Artists of the New York School: Second Generation* (show, 1957), 261
*Art News*, 280–81, 282
  criticism by artists and poets, 37, 258, 263
  Hess as editor and critic, 13, 258, 260, 263
  Johns painting on cover, 269
  on Kaprow, 199, 201
  Kaprow on Happenings, 211, 263, 269
  Kaprow on Pollock, 34, 203
  Porter on Stankiewicz, 147–48
  Rosenberg as critic, 258
  "Ten Best" shows, list of, 263
*Art News Annual: U.S. Painting: Some Recent Directions*, 260
*The Art of Assemblage* (show, 1961), 269, 292

*Arts. See Art Digest*
*Arts and Architecture*, 264
Ashbery, John, 21, 22, 37, 108, 115
  portrait of, by Freilicher, 92
Ashton, Dore, 264, 279, 286
*Atelier*, 17, 30
Avery, Milton, 94, 127

Bacon, Francis, 134
Barr, Alfred H., Jr., 265, 269, 282, 283
Bazaine, Jean, 10
Baziotes, William, 17, 30, 321
Beck, Julian, 305
Beck, Rosemarie, 269
Bell, Leland, 261, 263, 322
Bellamy, Richard, 24, 36
Bentley, Eric, 33
Bischoff, Elmer, 132, 271, 284, 297
Black Mountain College, 22, 23, 32, 33, 177
  Cage event (1952), 167–68, 174, 196
Bladen, Ronald, 41, 238, 247, 249–50
  *Untitled* (1958–59), *251*
  *Untitled* (1961), *252*
  *Untitled* (1962), *252*
Blaine, Nell, 36, 52, 259, 263, 322
  *Autumn Studio II*, *93*
  *Harbor and Green Cloth, II*, *54*
  shows and exhibitions, 36, 37, 38, 261, 264, 322
  mentioned, 31, 56, 90
Blesh, Rudi: *Modern Art USA*, 265

Bluhm, Norman, 35, 266, 322
  *Noel*, 40
Bonnard, Pierre, 6, 36, 52, 56, 100, 127, 259
  *The Breakfast Room*, 53
  shows and exhibitions, 52, 99, 103
Bosch, Hieronymus, 135
Brach, Paul, 38, 238, 258, 283, 322
  *Merlin*, 241
  mentioned, 31, 315
Braque, Georges, 6, 146
Brata Gallery, 30, 41, 249
Bread and Puppet Theater, 306
Brecht, George, 34, 41, 163, 196, 303
Briggs, Ernest, 35, 78, 322
  shows and exhibitions, 38, 261, 265, 322
  *Untitled* (1953), 80
  *Untitled* (1955), 80
Brodie, Gandy, 261, 322
Brook, Peter, 305
Brooklyn Museum: and EAT, 305
Brooks, James, 51, 321
Burckhardt, Rudolph, 37
Burnham, Jack, 305

Café Cino, 306
Café La Mama, 306
Cage, John: aesthetic and influence of, x, 22, 33–34,
    36, 41, 163–70 *passim*, 174, 176, 177, 180, 183,
    185, 196, 197, 205, 208, 293, 304, 305, 314; on
    Johns, 34, 163, 170, 185; on Kaprow, 34, 163,
    170, 196, 197; on Rauschenberg, 33–34, 163,
    165, 167, 170, 174, 176, 177, 180
  and Cunningham, 33, 163, 167, 168
  event at Black Mountain College (1952), 167–68,
    174, 196
  *4'33"*, 174
  influence on, 196; of Zen Buddhism, 167, 170, 196
  as teacher, 33, 34, 163, 196
  mentioned, 21, 31
Cajori, Charles, 38
Calas, Nicolas, 263
California School of Fine Arts, 32, 35, 78, 132
Callahan, Harry, 33
Camino Gallery, 30, 41
Campbell, Lawrence, 107, 258, 263
Campoli, Cosmo, 271
Canaday, John, 258–59, 281–82, 285
Carnegie Institute, 263
Carnegie International Exhibition, 264, 269
Castelli, Leo, 37, 258, 285
Leo Castelli Gallery, 38, 258, 269
Cavallon, George, 51
Cedar Street Tavern, 2, 15, 30, 32, 33, 37, 42
Cézanne, Paul, 6, 13, 36, 90, 229–30, 244, 280
Chaikin, Joseph, 306

Chamberlain, John, 33, 36, 140, 147, 152, 154–55,
    158, 293, 322
  *Card*, 155
  *Essex*, 144
  *Hudson*, 156
  *Nutcracker*, 155
  *Swannanoa*, 156
  *Wildroot*, 153
Chicago: monster painting, 133–36, 271
Childs, Lucinda, 305
Chipp, Herschel B., 133
City Gallery, 41
Club (Eighth Street Club; Artists Club), 2, 18, 30,
    31–32, 37, 38, 42, 99, 147, 203, 279, 282, 287,
    305. *See also* Ninth Street Show; Stable Gallery,
    Stable Annuals
  decline of, 285, 286
Cohen, George, 133, 271
Constructivism, 158
Corbett, Edward, 263
Cornell, Joseph, 31, 143
Corso, Gregory, 22, 24
Courbet, Gustave, 98, 299
  *Burial at Ornans*, 103
  *The Studio*, 108
Creeley, Robert, 22–23, 33
Crehan, Hubert: on abstract art and success, 286
  *and Art Digest*, 263–64
  on de Kooning, 94–95
  on Rauschenberg, 146
  on Stankiewicz, 143; 146–47
  on Still and California school, 78
Cubism, reaction to and influence of, 2, 6, 8, 10, 11,
    13, 56, 59, 62, 69, 78, 108, 116, 119, 143, 180,
    191, 198, 215, 218, 230, 231, 247, 310, 312, 313
Cunningham, Merce, 21, 33, 163, 205
  aesthetic and influence of, 163, 165–66, 168, 304
  and Cage, 33, 163, 167, 168

Dada, 143, 147, 148, 167, 168, 170, 183, 191, 196,
    293. *See also* Neo-Dada
Dahlberg, Edward, 33
Dali, Salvador, 189
Daphnis, Nassos, 269
David, Jacques Louis, 106
de Kooning. *See* Kooning, Elaine de; Kooning,
    Willem de
Delancey Street Museum, 41
Delacroix, Eugène, 106
Denby, Edwin, 37
de Niro, Robert, 263, 322
  shows and exhibitions, 32, 37, 38, 259, 261, 322
Denney, Reuel: *The Lonely Crowd*, 19
Devree, Howard, 258
Diebenkorn, Richard, 132, 284, 297, 322
  *Berkeley No. 37*, 133

Diebenkorn, Richard (*cont'd*)
  *Girl on a Terrace*, 134
  shows and exhibitions, 38, 261, 271, 322
Dine, Jim, 34, 207, 299, 301, 322–23
  *Car Crash*, 208
  *Flesh Striped Tie*, 301
  Happenings, 196, 197, 207, 208, 209, 304
  *Household Piece*, 202
  shows and exhibitions, 41, 323
  *The Smiling Workman*, 208, 209
  *The Valiant Red Car*, 207
  mentioned, x, 294, 306
di Suvero, Mark, 140, 143, 147, 154, 155, 158, 264,
    293–94, 323
  *Barrell*, 145
  *Che Faro Senza Eurydice*, 157
  *For Sabater*, 157
  *Hand Pierced*, 159
  *Hankchampion*, 158
  *Ladder piece*, 159
  shows and exhibitions, 155, 323
Dlugoszewski, Lucia, 21
*II Documenta '59*, 266–67, 272
Dodd, Lois, 38
Drummond, Sally. *See* Hazelet, Sally
Duberman, Martin, 22
Dubuffet, Jean, 134
Duchamp, Marcel, 163
  aesthetic and influence of, x, 69, 163, 164, 167,
    168, 169, 170, 183, 189, 197, 290, 314
  *The Bride Stripped Bare by Her Bachelors Even*
    (*Large Glass*), 168, 169
  Leonardo, *Mona Lisa*, defacing of, 177
  *Nude Descending the Staircase*, 163
  Readymades, 164, 183, 185, 189
Dugmore, Edward, 35, 78, 264, 323
  shows and exhibitions, 38, 261, 323
  *Untitled, 1951-Red*, 81
  *Untitled, 1959-J*, 81
Duncan, Robert, 22, 33
Dunn, Judith, 304
Dunn, Robert, 304
Dürer, Albrecht, 113
Dzubas, Friedel, 3, 15, 29, 62, 323
  shows and exhibitions, 32, 37, 38, 259, 261, 323

EAT (Experiments in Art and Technology), 305
Egan, Charles, 37
Charles Egan Gallery, 32, 37
Eighth Street Club. *See* Club
*Emerging Talent* (show, 1954), 259
Ensor, James, 125, 135
Environments, x, 198, 199, 201–05 *passim*, 283, 299
*European Art This Month*, 264
exhibitions and shows, 36–38, 41, 256, 258, 259, 260,
    265–69 *passim*, 271, 286, 322–25

Existentialism, 18, 48, 51, 73, 163
Experiments in Art and Technology (EAT), 305
*Expo '70* (Osaka): Pepsi-Cola pavilion, 305
Expressionism, 6, 99, 103, 125, 126, 131, 135, 158,
    193, 198, 220, 238

Fahlström, Oyvind, 305
Fautrier, Jean, 236
Fauvism, 2, 6, 10, 56, 100, 198
Feldman, Morton, 21
  on Cage, 164, 169–70
  on O'Hara, 37–38
Ferber, Herbert, 31, 142
Ferren, John, 1, 19, 321
  and Canaday, 281
  on Monet, 100
  on Rauschenberg, 147
  on the Stable Annual (1955), 279
*Fifteen Americans* (show, 1952), 265
Finkelstein, Louis, 31, 49, 51, 55–56, 57, 230, 263
Fitzsimmons, James, 264
Five Spot Café, 24
Flavin, Dan, 310
Fleischman Gallery, 41
Fluxus, 301–04
Follett, Jean, x, 140, 146, 152
  *Lady with the Open Door Stomach*, 152
  *Many Headed Creature*, 153
  shows and exhibitions, 41, 261
  mentioned, 36, 143, 199, 264
Forge, Andrew, 187
Forst, Miles, 36, 261, 323
*Fortune* (mag.): on the art market, 17
Francis, Sam, 78, 82, 85, 87, 323
  *Abstraction*, 87
  *Big Red*, 82, 84
  *Black in Red*, 82
  *Blue-Black*, 84
  *Emblem*, 87
  *Red and Black*, 85
  *Shining Back*, 87
  shows and exhibitions, 38, 82, 265, 266, 267, 323
  *Whiteness of the Whale*, 85, 86
Frank, Robert, 23–24
Frankenthaler, Helen, 59–60, 62, 65–67, 69, 71, 82,
    232–33, 236, 272, 292, 323
  *Abstract Landscape*, 59, 60
  *Basque Beach*, 68
  *Blue Territory*, 64
  *Eden*, 66, 67
  *Ed Winston's Tropical Gardens*, 59
  and Greenberg, 59, 62, 229
  Hofmann student, 33, 66
  influence of, 231, 292
  *Jacob's Ladder*, Plate I
  *Mountains and Sea*, 60, 61, 62, 231

Frankenthaler, Helen (*cont'd*)
   *Mountain Storm*, 65
   *Mount Sinai*, 262
   *Open Wall*, 64, 67
   Pollock and his influence, 15, 37, 59–60, 62, 65,
     69, 233
   Rose on, 67
   *Round Trip*, 63
   shows and exhibitions, 32, 37, 59, 259, 261, 266,
     267, 269, 323
   *Trojan Gates*, 64
   mentioned, ix, x, 31, 46, 51, 229, 264, 265, 291
Freilicher, Jane, 37, 263, 323
   on O'Hara, 37
   influence on, 52
   *The Mallow-Gatherers*, 93
   on painting process, 90
   on Pollock, 15
   *Portrait of John Ashbery*, 92
   on Schapiro, 35
   mentioned, 31, 263
French and Company Gallery, 229, 230, 269, 311
Fried, Michael, 311–12
Friedman, B. H., 265, 272
Fuller, R. Buckminster, 33
Futurists, 69, 143

Gage, Otis, 131
Garth, Midi, 21
Gaugh, Harry F., 33
Geist, Sidney, 147, 158, 258, 263
Giacometti, Alberto, 134
Ginsberg, Allen, 22, 24
   *Howl*, 24
Glarner, Fritz, 31
Glazer, Nathan: *The Lonely Crowd*, 19
Goldberg, Michael, 71, 75, 323
   *At Patsy's*, 76
   shows and exhibitions, 32, 37, 38, 259, 261, 264,
     266, 267, 269, 323
   *Summer House*, 76
   mentioned, x, 30, 31, 46, 51, 264, 282
Goldwater, Robert, 51–52, 281
Golub, Leon, 133, 135–36, 271
   *Colossal Heads (I)*, 136
   *Damaged Man*, 135
Gombrich, E. H.: on Rauschenberg, 165
Gonzalez, Julio, 151
Goodman, Paul, 33
Goodnough, Robert, 33, 116, 119, 121, 272, 323
   *Abduction*, 121
   *Abstraction*, 116
   art criticism, 37, 258
   *The Bathers*, 121
   *Battle Landscape*, 118
   *Calamity Jane*, 121

Goodnough, Robert (*cont'd*)
   *Carnival II*, 119, 121
   *Cha-Cha-Cha*, 119
   *The Chair*, 121
   *The Frontiersman*, 118, 119, 121
   *Laocoön*, 119, 121, Plate V
   *Pegasus*, 116, 121
   *Pink Reclining Nude*, 119
   on Pollock, 15
   *Rearing Horses*, 116
   shows and exhibitions, 32, 37, 259, 261, 263, 264,
     323
   *Standing Figure*, 120
   *The Struggle*, 117
   *Summer III*, 272
   mentioned, 31, 56, 263, 265, 291
Goossen, E. C., 222, 265
Gordin, Sidney, 282
Gorky, Arshile, 59, 65, 69, 82, 106, 321
Gottlieb, Adolph, 31, 321
   *Bursts*, 239
Goya, Francisco José de, 113, 115, 135
Great Jones Gallery, 41
Greenberg, Clement, 33, 35, 37, 55, 311
   aesthetic and influence of, 95–96, 259, 279, 283,
     311–12, 313, 314. *See also* color-field painting
     *below*
   " 'American-Type' Painting," 13, 269
   *Art and Culture: Critical Essays*, 271, 311
   and *Art International*, 265
   and color-field painting, 13, 228–32 passim, 269,
     271, 311, 314
   and Frankenthaler, 59, 62, 229
   on French painting, 73, 75
   on Goodnough, 116
   on Hofmann, 8
   on Impressionism, 52, 229–30
   on Johns, 186
   on de Kooning and his school, 312–13
   on Louis, 231–32
   on *Nation*, 35, 258
   and *Partisan Review*, 35, 258
   on Rivers, 103, 259
   shows and exhibitions arranged by, 229, 230, 259,
     263, 272, 311
   and Stable Annual, 260
Grillo, John, 35, 323
   shows and exhibitions, 36, 37, 38, 261, 323
Grooms, Red, 34, 41, 299, 301, 323
   *The Burning Building*, 210, *210*
   Happenings, 196, 197, 208, 210, *210*
   mentioned, x, 306
Gropius, Walter, 33
Grünewald, Matthias, 135
"guerrilla theater," 306
Guest, Barbara, 21, 22, 37, 148

Solomon R. Guggenheim Museum, 269
  *American Abstract Expressionists and Imagists*
    (1961), 269, 271, 283
Guston, Philip, 55, 264, 321
  *Dial*, 56
  influence of, 75, 191, 292, 294
  shows and exhibitions, 55, 267
  mentioned, x, 30, 37, 51


Hansa Gallery, 33, 35, 36, 37, 41, 198, 199, 258, 263
Hansen, Al, 34–35, 163, 196, 303
Happenings (and events), x, 183, 196–99, 201–03,
    205, 207–08, 210–11, 214, 283, 299, 301,
    303–04, 304–05, 305–06
  by Cage, at Black Mountain College, 167–68, 174,
    196
Hare, David, 30, 142
Hartigan, Grace, 71, 111, 113, 115–16, 264, 265,
    272, 323
  on corruptibility in art, 287
  *Grand Street Brides, 114*, 115
  *New England, October, 115*
  and O'Hara, 40, 115
  *The Persian Jacket, 113*
  *River Bathers*, 115, Plate IV
  *Rough Ain't It!, 112*
  *Shop Window*, 267
  shows and exhibitions, 32, 37, 113, 259, 261, 265,
    266, 323
  *Sweden, 117*
  *What Fire Murmurs Its Seditions Beneath the Oaks,
    40*
  mentioned, ix, x, 31, 46, 51, 90, 264, 291, 292
Hawkins, Erik, 21
Hay, Alex, 304, 305
Hay, Deborah, 304, 305
Hayter, Stanley William, 30, 322, 324
Hazelet (Drummond), Sally, 38, 236, 238
  *Hummingbird*, 238
Heizer, Michael, 310
Held, Al, x, 41, 214, 238, 244, 247, 249, 323
  *I-Beam*, 247
  shows and exhibitions. 38, 323
  *Untitled* (1956), *245*
  *Untitled* (1956), *245*
  *Untitled* (1960), *246*
  mentioned, 35, 307
Hess, Thomas B., 35, 37, 51, 90
  and *Art News*, 13, 258, 260, 261
  on Cage, 170
  on Hofmann, 8
  on de Kooning, 99
  on Newman, 13
  New York School and support of, 259, 261,
    279–80, 281

Hess, Thomas B. (*cont'd*)
  and Rauschenberg, 148
  on Stable Annual: (1954), 18–19, 279; (1956), 280
  U.S. Painting: *Some Recent Directions* selected by
    (show, 1955), 148, 260–61, 271
Higgins, Dick, 34, 35, 163, 196, 303, 304
Hofmann, Hans, 2, 3, 5, 6, 8, 10–11, 321
  *Fantasia in Blue, 6*
  influence on, 2, 6, 10, 13
  *Magenta and Blue, 7*
  as teacher and influence of, 2, 3, 5, 8, 33, 66, 75,
    99, 108, 116, 121, 149, 263. *See also* Hofmann
    School of Fine Arts
  mentioned, x, 106
Hans Hofmann School of Fine Arts, 2, 5, 8, 30, 32,
    33, 36, 37, 38, 116, 152, 198, 322, 323, 324, 325.
  *See also* Hofmann, Hans, as teacher and influence of
Holty, Carl, 8
Holtzman, Harry, 31
Hopper, Edward, 133
Howe, Irving, 285
Huelsenbeck, Richard, 31
Hultberg, John, 17, 35, 41, 264
Hunter, Sam: *Art Since 1945*, 265


Iglehart, Robert, 31
Impressionism, 11, 13, 52, 55, 56, 99, 103, 140, 191,
    280, 299
Indiana, Robert, 42
Ionesco, Eugene, 205
Ippolito, Angelo, 38, 99, 100, 261, 269
Isquith, Ben, 38, 236 .
*It Is* (mag.), 211, 264, 269


Jackson, Harry, 32, 259
Jackson, Martha, 258
Martha Jackson Gallery, 38, 258
  *New Media—New Forms* (1960), 269
James Gallery, 33, 41
Jane Street Gallery, 36, 37, 258, 259
Sidney Janis Gallery, 32, 55
Jenkins, Paul, 15, 38, 269
Jensen, Alfred, 38, 41, 238, 264
  *Family Portrait, 240*
  *The Great Mystery II, 241*
Jewish Museum: art and technology show, 305
  Johns showing at, 269
Joans, Ted, 24
Johns, Jasper, x, 110, 170, 183, 185–87, 189, 191,
    193, 263, 293, 296, 323
  *Coat Hanger*, 187
  *Drawer, 192*
  on Duchamp, 168
  *False Start*, 187, *188*
  *Flag, 186*

Johns, Jasper (*cont'd*)
  *Flag Above White, 294*
  influence of, 294, 296
  influence on, 183; of Cage, 34, 163, 170, 185
  *Jubilee,* 187
  *Lightbulb II,* 190
  *Numbers in Color,* 190
  *Painted Bronze,* 166
  *Painted Bronze (ale cans),* 187, *189*
  *Painting with A Ball,* 187
  *Painting with Two Balls,* Plate VII
  Rose on, 191
  *Shade,* 187
  shows and exhibitions, 38, 261, 268, 269, 292, 323
  *Target,* 269
  Target with Four Faces, 185
  *Tennyson,* 191, *192*
  *Three Flags,* 187
  White Flag, 191
  mentioned, 34, 164, 265
Johnson, Lester, x, 90, 125–27, 207, 323
  *The Hero,* 126
  *Mother and Children, 125*
  *My Love,* 126
  *Profile with Tree, 126*
  shows and exhibitions, 36, 38, 126, 261, 264, 323
  *Three Men, 128*
Johnson, Ray, 35
Judd, Donald, 154–55, 296, 310
Judson Church, 304
Judson Dance Theater, 304
Judson Gallery, 41, 201

Kahn, Wolf, 36, 52, 90, 261, 323
  *Arnold's Place, 53*
Kandinsky, Wassily, 59, 69, 100
Kanovitz, Howard, 24
Kaprow, Allan, 8, 34, 197–99, 201–05 *passim,* 207,
  208, 323
  *An Apple Shrine,* 197
  *Courtyard,* 208
  "18 Happenings in 6 Parts," 201–02
  Environments and Happenings, 196, 197, 198,
    201–05 *passim,* 207, 208, 208, 211, 263, 269,
    303, 306–07
  *George Washington Bridge (with cars),* 198
  *Grandma's Boy,* 200
  *Hysteria,* 200
  Hofmann student, 33, 198
  influence on, of Cage, 34, 163, 170, 196, 197
  *Interchangeable Panels,* 201
  on paintings, 5, 8, 283
  on Pollock, 34, 203
  on Schapiro, 35
  shows and exhibitions, 41, 198, 261, 323

Kaprow, Allan  (*cont'd*)
  *Woman Out of Fire,* 199
  mentioned, ix, x, 36, 264, 314
Karp, Ivan, 36
Katz, Alex, 127, 296–97, 297–98, 299, 323–24
  *Ada Ada, 130*
  *Luna Park, 129*
  shows and exhibitions, 38, 269, 324
  *The Smile,* 300
  mentioned, x, 90, 307
Kelly, Ellsworth, 214, 215, 218, 220, 222, 224, 226,
  239, 264, 324
  *Atlantic, 219,* 222
  *Aubade, 219*
  *Bar,* 222
  *Bay, 220*
  *Black Ripe, 215,* 222
  *Broadway,* 222
  *Charter, 224*
  *Cowboy,* 222
  *Gate,* 222
  *Green White, 221*
  *New York, N.Y., 219*
  *North River.* 222
  *Painting in Five Panels,* 222
  *Pony, 223*
  *Rebound (1956),* 218, 222
  *Rogue,* Plate VIII
  *Running White, 221*
  shows and exhibitions, 264, 268, 269, 324
  *South Ferry,* 222
  *Two Panels: Black and White,* 222
  *White Blue, 224*
  *Yellow Relief,* 222
  mentioned, x, 35, 42, 264, 283, 307
Kerouac, Jack, 22, 23, 24
  *On the Road,* 24
Kienbusch, William, 100
King, William, 38
Kirby, Michael, 208, 305–06
Kline, Franz, 48, 69, 85, 261, 292, 321
  influence of, 22–23, 33, 69, 127, 140, 154, 158,
    271, 292, 293
  *Mahoning,* 34
  mentioned, x, 1, 2, 17, 24, 31, 33, 37, 99, 177, 285
Klüver, Billy, 304, 305
Koch, Kenneth, 21, 22, 37, 108
Kohn, Gabriel, 247, 249, 264
  *Nantucket (Equatorial Trap),* 248
  *Pitcairn,* 248
  shows and exhibitions, 38, 267
Kooning, Elaine de, 37, 99, 263, 322
  art criticism, 37, 55, 258, 263
  on "beautiful" in art, 51
  on nature as subject for art, 96, 98–99

Kooning, Elaine de (cont'd)
  Scrimmage, 98
  shows and exhibitions, 32, 37, 38, 259, 261, 263,
    322
  mentioned, 33, 90
Kooning, Willem de, 2–3, 5, 6, 8–9, 9–10, 11, 48,
    94–95, 105, 110, 231, 292, 307, 321
  and Art News, 261
  Attic, 113
  and Cage, 164
  on Cubism, 11
  Excavation, 69, 113
  Gotham News, 9
  Greenberg on, 312–13
  Hess on, 99
  influence of, 2, 13, 15, 16, 36, 37, 51, 55, 69, 71,
    75, 103, 113, 127, 133, 140, 143, 154, 177, 180,
    236, 244, 271, 292, 293, 294; circle/"school,"
    ix, 2, 15, 16, 31, 35, 37, 38, 312–13
  influence on, 6, 8, 10, 13, 16, 103, 116, 180, 236
  Marilyn Monroe, 95
  Museum of Modern Art lecture, 3
  and Pollock, rivalry, 15–16, 37
  Rivers on, 99
  Woman series, 3, 5, 99; Woman I, 3, 4, 143
  mentioned, ix, x, 17, 24, 30, 31, 33, 65, 106, 285
Samuel Kootz Gallery, 32, 37, 229
  Emerging Talent (1954), 259
  New Talent (1950), 259, 263, 272
Kozloff, Max, 187
Kramer, Hilton, 131, 264, 286–87
  and Arts, 264
  on the Carnegie International Exhibition, 269
  gesture painting attacked by, 284, 297
  on Newman, 230
  on Stable Annual, 260
  on Stankiewicz, 152
Krauss, Rosalind, 310–12, 313
Krushenick, Nicholas, 41, 238
  East Hampton, 239

Lanes, Jerrold, 230–31
Lassaw, Ibram, 142, 147
Lebel, Robert, 163
Le Corbusier, 249
Léger, Fernand, 36, 149
Leider, Philip, 310, 312
Leonardo da Vinci: Battle of Anghiari, Rubens copy
    of, 116
  Mona Lisa, Duchamp defacing of, 177
Leslie, Alfred, 23, 71, 272, 324
  Abstraction, 73
  Collage with Stripes, 72
  The Minx, 72
  #3339 Fountain, 268

Leslie, Alfred (cont'd)
  Porter on, 71, 75
  shows and exhibitions, 32, 37 38, 71, 259, 261, 267,
    268, 324
  Soldier's Medal, 74
  mentioned, x, 31, 46, 51, 60, 291
Leutze, Emanuel, 105, 106
Lewitin, Landis, 131
Lichtenstein, Roy, 294
  Girl with Ball, 295
  mentioned, 299, 301, 306, 310, 314
Life (mag.), 256
Lippard, Lucy, 310
Lipton, Seymour, 142
Living Theater, 305–06
Los Angeles County Museum of Art, 305
Louis, Morris, 65, 214, 228, 231–32, 232–33, 235,
    236, 239, 269, 271, 310–11, 324
  Alpha, 234
  Florals, 233, 235
  Point of Tranquility, 229
  shows and exhibitions, 38, 229, 233, 235, 259, 269,
    271, 324
  Stripes, 235
  Tet, 232
  Unfurleds, 235
  Untitled (1956), 234
  Veils, 233
  mentioned, x, 265, 283, 307, 314

MacAgy, Douglas, 35
McClure, Michael, 22, 23
McCray, Porter, 266
Maciunas, George, 301, 304
MacLow, Jackson, 34, 35, 196, 303
  The Marrying Maiden, 305
McNeil, George, 321
Magritte, René, 186
Malina (Beck), Judith, 305
Manessier, Alfred, 10
Manet, Edouard, 299
March Gallery, 30, 41
Marin, John, 131
Marsicano, Merle, 21
Martin, Agnes, 42
Matisse, Henri: Bather, 216
  influence of and reaction to, 6, 52, 56, 100, 115,
    127, 133, 198, 216, 218, 220, 239
Maxfield, Richard, 303
Mayakowski, Vladimir, 169, 170
Metropolitan Museum: Pollock, Autumn Rhythm,
    purchased by, 286
Miller, Dorothy C., 265, 285
Miller, Henry, 146
Mills, C. Wright: White Collar, 19

Mills, Paul, 133
Minneapolis Institute of Art, 267
Miró, Joan, 59, 215, 218, 292
Mitchell, Fred, 38, 42
Mitchell, Joan, 49, 51, 69, 71, 263, 264, 272, 324
  *City Landscape*, 71
  *14th of July*, 68
  *George Went Swimming at Barnes Hole, but It Got
    Too Cold*, 50, 69, 71
  *Hemlock*, 70
  *Ladybug*, Plate II
  *Mont St. Hilaire*, 70
  shows and exhibitions, 32, 38, 259, 261, 263, 264,
    266, 267, 269, 324
  *Untitled* (1960), 262
  mentioned, ix, x, 24, 31, 35, 46, 51, 56, 60, 291,
    292
*Modern Artists in America* (mag.), 31, 259
Mondrian, Piet, 36, 69, 99, 116, 119, 127, 215, 218,
  226
  *Composition in Red, Blue and Yellow*, 216
Monet, Claude, 13, 52, 55, 75, 82, 99, 230
  *Nymphéas* (*Water Lilies*), 52, 54, 55–56, 57
Morris, Kyle, 99, 100, 261, 271
Morris, Robert, 296, 304, 310
Morris (Forti), Simone, 41, 304
Motherwell, Robert, 46, 48, 321
  *The Dada Painters and Poets*, 183, 196
  and *Modern Artists in America*, 31, 259
  *Spanish Elegies*, 239
  mentioned, 17, 29, 30, 31, 33, 177
Müller, Jan, 90, 121, 125, 198, 264, 324
  *Double Circle Path #1*, 122
  *Hamlet and Horatio*, 121
  *The Heraldic Ground*, 121, 122
  *Jacob's Ladder—of Hell and Conformity*, 121, 124
  *Of This Time—Of That Place*, 121
  *The Robe*, 121
  *The Search for the Unicorn*, 121
  shows and exhibitions, 36, 261, 269, 324
  *The Temptation of St. Anthony*, 121, 123
  *Walpurgisnacht—Faust*, 121; *Faust, I*, 123
  mentioned, x, 56, 264
Mumford, Lewis, 21
Munch, Edvard, 135
Munro, Eleanor C., 263
Museum of Modern Art, 82, 265–69 *passim*
  *The Art of Assemblage* (1961), 269, 292
  Bonnard retrospective, 52, 99, 103
  *II Documenta '59*, 266–67, 272
  and EAT, 305
  *Fifteen Americans* (1952), 265
  de Kooning lecture, 3
  Monet, *Nymphéas* (*Water Lilies*), purchase of, 52,
    54, 55–56, 57

Museum of Modern Art (*cont'd*)
  *The New American Painting* (1958), 82, 265,
    266–67, 272, 287
  *New Images of Man* (1959), 134, 268, 271
  *New Talent* (1950 on, series), 265
  *Paris Biennale* (1959), 267
  *Sixteen Americans* (1959), 268, 269, 272, 285, 292
  Soutine retrospective, 103
  Tinguely's *Homage to New York*, 292–93
  *12 Americans* (1956), 55, 82, 265, 271, 272. *See also*
    Barr, Alfred H., Jr.; O'Hara, Frank
Myers, John B., 15, 31, 36
  and de Nagy Gallery, 36, 37, 258
mythology, influence of, 121, 125, 136

Tibor de Nagy Gallery, 35, 36–37, 38, 258, 263
*Nation* (mag.): Greenberg criticism, 35, 258
*Nature in Abstraction* (show, 1958), 269
Nauman, Bruce, 310
Neel, Alice, 24
Neo-Dada (assemblage), x, 146, 148, 191, 196, 198,
  203, 210–11, 263, 268, 283, 292–93, 299
Nevelson, Louise, 268
*The New American Painting* (show, 1958), 82,
  265–66, 266–67, 272, 287
Newbill, Al, 99, 100
*New Images of Man* (show, 1959), 134, 268, 271
Newman, Barnett, 11, 218, 230–31, 310, 321
  *Covenant*, 12
  Hess on, 13
  influence of, x, 233, 239, 271, 283
  *Vir Heroicus Sublimis*, 231
  mentioned, 2, 8, 30, 31, 52, 55, 229, 230, 271
*New Media—New Forms* (show, 1960), 269
New School for Social Research, 34, 196, 303
*New Talent* (show, 1950, Kootz Gallery), 259, 263,
  272
*New Talent* (show series, 1950 on, Museum of
  Modern Art), 265
New York Artists Annuals. *See* Stable Gallery, Stable
  Annuals
New York City Audio-Visual Group, 34–35
*New York Times*: art criticism, 258–59, 264, 281–82
New York University, 30–31
*9 Evenings: Theatre and Engineering*, 304–05
*Ninth Street Show* (1951), 32, 259, 260, 263, 272
Noland, Kenneth, 214, 228, 231, 235–36, 239, 269,
  271, 310–11, 324
  shows and exhibitions, 37, 229, 235, 259, 269, 324
  *Spread*, 235
  *Turnsole*, 237
  mentioned, x, 33, 35, 265, 283, 307, 314
Nolde, Emil, 125, 135
Nonagon Gallery, 41

O'Doherty, Brian, 179–80, 285
O'Hara, Frank, 1, 21, 31, 37–38, 108
    art criticism, 22, 37, 99, 131, 263
    and Hartigan, 40, 115
    *Noel*, 40
    poetry, 23, 24, 37, 39, 40, 108
    on Porter, 127
    on Rauschenberg, 148, 180
    and Rivers, 39, 91, 104, 107, 108
    *Stones:* Plate 8: "Melancholy Breakfast," 39
    *What Fire Murmurs Its Seditions Beneath The Oaks*, 40
Oldenburg, Claes, 34, 140, 204, 207, 208, 301, 324
    Happenings, 196, 197, 204, 204, 207, 208, 301, 304
    *Red Tights with Fragment 9*, 303
    *Shirt*, 206
    shows and exhibitions, 41, 324
    *Snapshots from the City*, 204, 208
    mentioned, x, 143, 294, 306
Olitski, Jules, x, 214, 236, 314
    *Isis Ardor*, 237
Olson, Charles, 22, 23, 33, 167
Open Theater, 306
Oppenheimer, Joel, 22, 23
Ortman, George, 38, 41, 238, 324
    *Game of Chance*, 242
Ozenfant, Amédée: as teacher, 30, 116

Pace, Stephen, 261
Paik, Nam June, 303
Paris, School of, 10, 16, 73
Paris, study in, 16, 32, 35
*Paris Biennale* (1959), 267
Park, David, 132–33, 271, 284, 297
    *Four Men*, 297
Parker, Raymond, 48, 71, 73, 214, 238–39, 265, 282, 324
    on "direct painting," 47, 283–84
    on painter's attitude, 47–48
    *P. 30*, 243
    shows and exhibitions, 261, 324
    on Still, 11, 13
    *Untitled* (1956), 243
    *Untitled* (1959), 244
    mentioned, x, 31, 56, 271
Betty Parsons Gallery, 32, 37
*Partisan Review:* Greenberg criticism, 35, 258
    symposium, "Our Country and Our Culture," 20
Pasilis, Felix, 36, 261, 264, 324
Pavia, Phillip, 31–32, 264
Paxton, Steven, 304, 305
Pearlstein, Philip, 127, 131–32, 264, 296–97, 298–99, 324
    *Male and Female Models Sitting on the Floor*, 298

Pearlstein, Philip (*cont'd*)
    *Positano I*, 132
    *Rock Mound*, 131
    shows and exhibitions, 38, 127, 259, 264, 324
    mentioned, x, 307
Performance Group, 306
Phoenix Gallery, 41
Picasso, Pablo, 6, 52, 116, 146, 151, 292, 313
    *Ma Jolie*, 119
Poggioli, Renato, 313
Poindexter, Eleanor, 258
Poindexter Gallery, 38, 258
Pollock, Jackson, 15–16, 35, 116, 232–33, 256, 261, 321
    *Autumn Rhythm*, 286
    black-and-white paintings, 59, 99
    black paintings, 62
    "drip" painting, 11, 23, 52, 60, 69, 113, 199, 203
    *Echo*, 62
    and Frankenthaler, 37, 60, 62, 65. *See also* influence of *below*
    influence of, x, 15–16, 69, 75, 82, 113, 203, 231, 233, 239, 244; on Frankenthaler, 15, 59–60, 69, 233
    Kaprow on, 34, 203
    and de Kooning, rivalry, 15–16, 37
    *Number 27, 1950*, 14
    Rivers on, 15
    shows and exhibitions, 59, 265
    mentioned, ix, 2, 8, 17, 31, 52, 106, 285
Pollock, Lee Krasner, 37
Poons, Larry, 34, 35
Porter, Fairfield, 96, 127, 263, 324
    art criticism, 37, 258, 263
    *Jimmy and John*, 128
    on Johnson, 126
    *Katie and Anne*, 97
    on Katz, 127
    on Leslie, 71, 75
    *Red Wheel Barrow*, 129
    on Rivers, 106
    shows and exhibitions, 32, 37, 259, 261, 263, 264
    on Stankiewicz, 147–48
    mentioned, x, 90
Pousette-Dart, Richard, 321
primitive art, influence of, 18, 135, 136
Public Theater: *Hair*, 305
*Pull My Daisy*, 23–24

Rainer, Yvonne, 304, 305
Rauschenberg, Robert, x, 29, 146, 148, 152, 174, 176–77, 179–80, 183, 263, 272, 293, 324
    *Bed*, 180, 182
    black collages, 176, 177
    *Broadcast*, 180

Rauschenberg, Robert (cont'd)
  and Cage, 167, 174, 176. See also influence of below
  Canyon, 165, 177
  Charlene, 178, 180
  Coca-Cola Plan, 179
  "combine-paintings"/"combines," 100, 140, 170,
    177, 180, 183, 199, 205, 293
  Crucifixion and Reflexion, 174, 175
  Dante, Inferno, illustrations, 177, 180; Canto
    XXXI: The Giants, 182
  Dirt Painting: For John Cage, 176
  events and Happenings, 167, 174, 304, 305
  Factum I, 180, 183 184
  Factum II, 180, 183, 184
  Gombrich on, 165
  influence on, 174, 177, 180; of Cage, 33–34, 163,
    165, 170, 174, 176, 177, 180
  The Lily White (formerly White Painting with
    Numbers), 176
  The Man with Two Souls, 174
  Monogram, 181
  Rebus, Plate VI
  shows and exhibitions, 38, 261, 266, 267, 268, 269,
    292, 324
  Trinity, 174
  White Painting, 175
  white paintings, 174, 175, 176
  Winter Pool, 270
  mentioned, ix, 31, 33, 34, 143, 291
Reality (mag.), 94
Regionalism, 18, 94
Reinhardt, Ad, 11, 13, 15, 55, 278, 284, 321
  aesthetics, 94, 96, 309, 310
  influence of, 38, 236
  Modern Artists in America, 31, 259
  Number 87, 14
  as teacher, 35
  mentioned, 17, 31, 96
Rembrandt, 8
Remenick, Seymour, 261
Renoir, Pierre Auguste, 52, 100
Resnick, Milton, 51, 71, 75, 263, 324
  Genie, 79
  Low Gate, 77
  RR, 77
  shows and exhibitions, 32, 38, 259, 261, 263, 264,
    324
  mentioned, x, 8, 30, 31
Reuben Gallery, 41, 201, 299, 304
Rewald, John, 52
Rice, Dan, 265
Richards, Mary Caroline, 33, 167, 196
Riesman, David: The Lonely Crowd, 19
Rivers, Larry, 49, 98, 103, 105–08, 110–11, 263, 272,
    324
  Berdie in a Red Shawl, 266

Rivers, Larry (cont'd)
  Berdie with the American Flag, 108, 109
  The Burial, 103, 104
  Cedar Bar Menu, 110
  Double Portrait of Berdie, 106–07, 107
  Double Portrait of Frank O'Hara, 91
  Football Players, 103
  The Greatest Homosexual, 106
  Greenberg on, 103, 259
  Hofmann student, 33, 108
  influence on, 52, 103
  on de Kooning, 99
  The Last Civil War Veteran, 111, 112
  ME, 110, 111
  Molly and Breakfast, 92
  and O'Hara, 39, 91, 104, 107, 108
  on Pollock, 15
  The Pool, Plate III
  Portrait of Frank O'Hara, 104
  shows and exhibitions, 36, 37, 259, 261, 263, 265,
    324
  Stones: Plate 8: "Melancholy Breakfast," 39
  The Studio, 108, 109
  Washington Crossing the Delaware, 105, 105, 106,
    108
  mentioned, ix, x, 1, 17, 24, 31, 263, 264, 291
Robbe-Grillet, Alain, 314
Rose, Barbara, 314–15
  on Frankenthaler, 67
  on Johns, 191
Rose, Leatrice, 37
Rosenberg, Harold, 31, 37, 258
  "The American Action Painters" and action paint-
    ing, 35–36, 46–47, 48, 49, 197, 312
Rosenblum, Robert, 131, 265, 307
Rosenquist, James, 42, 294
  Look Alive, 296
Roszak, Theodore, 142
Rothko, Mark, 11, 13, 127, 321
  Four Darks in Red, 10
  influence of, x, 78, 82
  as teacher, 35
  mentioned, ix, x, 8, 30, 31, 55, 229, 230, 271
Rubens, Peter Paul, 8, 113
  Leonardo, Battle of Anghiari, copy of, 116
Rubin, William S., 265, 271, 283

Samaras, Lucas, 36, 41
Sander, Ludwig, 282–83
Sandler, Irving, 32, 265
San Francisco: figurative painting, 132–36 passim, 271
São Paulo (Brazil): Fourth Bienal, 265
  Fifth Bienal, 267
Saret, Alan, 310
Sartre, Jean Paul, 73
Satie, Erik, 196

Sawin, Martica, 78, 126
Schapiro, Meyer, 21, 35, 47, 48
    on ethical content in art, 18
    shows and exhibitions chosen by, 259, 261, 263,
        272
Schapiro, Miriam, 238
    *The Game*, 242
Schechner, Richard, 306
*School of New York: Some Younger Artists* (Friedman,
    ed.), 265, 272
School of Paris, 10, 16, 73
Schueler, Jon, 78, 264, 324
    *Counterpoint*, 82
    shows and exhibitions, 38, 261, 269, 324
    *Snow Cloud and Blue Sky*, 83
    on Still, 35
Schultze, Franz, 136
Schumann, Peter, 306
Schuyler, James, 21, 37
    on Bell, 263
    on Frankenthaler, 67
    on Johnson, 125–26
    on Katz, 127
    on Porter, 127
    Schwitters, Kurt, 143, 180, 293
    *V-2*, 181
Segal, George, 34, 36, 301, 324
    *Man at Table*, 302
    shows and exhibitions, 41, 261, 324
Seitz, William C., 143, 269, 285, 293
Selz, Peter, 134, 267, 271
Serra, Richard, 310
Siskind, Aaron, 33
*Sixteen Americans* (show, 1959), 268, 269, 272, 285,
    292
Smith, David, 142, 143, 267
    *Hudson River Landscape*, 142
Smith, Leon Polk, x, 214, 215, 218, 224, 226, 239,
    324
    *Antiou*, 225
    *Correspondence: Red Black*, 227
    *Expanse*, 226
    *May Twenty*, 217
Smith, Tony, 31, 37
Smithson, Robert, 310
Solomon, Hyde, 259, 261, 264, 325
*Some More Beginnings* (show, 1968), 305
Something Else Press, 303
Sonnier, Keith, 310
Soutine, Chaim, 6, 36, 100, 103, 127, 135
Stable Gallery, 32, 36, 38, 148, 258, 260–61, 263
    Stable Annuals, 32, 38, 260; (1953), 260; (1954),
        18–19, 279; (1955), 19; (1956), 280
    *U.S. Painting: Some Recent Directions* (1955), 148,
        260–61, 263, 271, 272
Stael, Nicolas de, 38

Stamos, Theodoros, 33, 321
Stankiewicz, Richard, x, 140, 143, 146–47, 147–48,
    148–49, 151–52, 199, 263, 293, 325
    *The Candidate*, 150
    *Fantastic Creatures and Satiric Poses*, 149
    *Figure*, 149
    Hofmann student, 33, 149
    *Kabuki Dancer*, 149
    *Natural History*, 147
    *Our Lady of All Protections*, 150
    *Secretary*, 151
    shows and exhibitions, 38, 41, 149, 264, 268, 269,
        292, 325
    *Untitled* (ca. 1959), *141*
    *Untitled* (1960), *151*
    mentioned, ix, 35, 36, 264, 284
Stefanelli, Joseph, 16, 31, 32, 259, 261
Steinberg, Leo: on Follett, 146
    on Goldberg, 75
    and Johns, 183
    on Rauschenberg, 146
Stella, Frank, 265, 307, 309–11, 325
    aesthetics, 284, 285
    black paintings, 307, 310
    *Coney Island*, 308
    influence of, 310
    influence on, 294, 296
    *The Marriage of Reason and Squalor*, 308
    *Pagosa Springs*, 309
    shows and exhibitions, 268, 285, 325
    mentioned, x, 283, 299, 314
Stewart, Ellen, 306
Still, Clyfford, 11, 13, 15, 78, 321
    influence of, x, 75, 78, 82, 233, 263, 271
    *1950-A, No. 2*, *12*
    Parker on, 11, 13
    Schueler on, 35
    as teacher, 35, 78, 133
    *Untitled* (1957), *79*
    mentioned, 2, 8, 17, 31, 52, 55, 229, 230
Stout, Myron, x, 214, 215, 218, 226, 264, 269
    *Number 3* (1954), 227
    *No. 3, 1957*, *217*
    *Untitled* (1954–55), *228*
Studio 35, 31
Subjects of the Artist School, 30, 31, 164
Sugarman, George, 41, 247, 249
    *Six Forms in Pine*, 249
    *Spiral Sculpture*, 251
    *Yellow Top*, 250
Surrealism, 41–42, 142, 143, 168, 180, 215, 218, 293
Suzuki, Daisetz T., 167, 196

Taeuber-Arp, Sophie, 215
Tanager Gallery, 30, 35, 38, 41, 258, 285
Theater of the Absurd, 205, 207

Thomson, Virgil, 21
Tiepolo, Giovanni Battista, 113
Tillim, Sidney, 284, 297–98, 313–14
*Time* (mag.), 258
*Times Literary Supplement*, 265, 267
Tinguely, Jean: *Homage to New York*, 292
Tobey, Mark, 82
Tomkins, Calvin, 167
Tomlin, Bradley Walker, 51, 55, 321
Tuchman, Maurice, 305
Tudor, David, 167, 305
*12 Americans* (show, 1956), 55, 82, 265, 271, 272
Tworkov, Jack, 321
    gesture painting defined, 278–79
    on style, 49
    on subject matter in art, 99
    mentioned, 2, 31, 33, 51, 177
Tyler, Parker, 263

*U.S. Painting: Some Recent Directions* (show, 1955), 148, 260–61, 271, 272

*Vanguard 1955* (show), 261, 271
Varèse, Edgard, 21
Velázquez, 113
Venice Biennale, 269
Vicente, Esteban, 2, 30, 33, 51, 321
Vlaminck, Maurice, 56, 198
Vostell, Wolf, 301
Vuillard, Jean Edouard, 52, 100, 127
Vytlacil, Vaclav, 177

Walker Art Center (Minn.): *Vanguard 1955*, 261
Ward, Eleanor, 258
Warhol, Andy, 294, 296
    *Water Heater*, 295
    mentioned, 299, 301, 306, 310, 314
Washburn, Gordon, 269
Weiss, Peter: *Marat/Sade*, 305
Westermann, H. C., 271
Whitman, Robert, x, 34, 36, 325
    E. G., 206
    Happenings, 196, 197, 206, 208, 210, 305
    shows and exhibitions, 41, 325
Whitney Museum, 269
    *Nature in Abstraction* (1958), 269
    Whitney Annual, 256
    *Young America 1957*, 269
    *Young America 1960*, 269
Whyte, William H., Jr.: *The Organization Man*, 19
Williams, Jonathan, 265
Wilson, Edmund, 22
Wolpe, Stefan, 21, 33
Woodruff, Hale, 31
Wright, Frank Lloyd, 269

Young, La Monte, 35
*Young America 1957* (show), 269
*Young America 1960* (show), 269
Youngerman, Jack, 35, 42, 264

Zadkine, Ossip, 149
Zen Buddhism, 167, 170, 196
Zurbarán, Francisco de, 113

## Icon Editions

Abercrombie, A./Architecture As Art   IN-159
Ades, D./Dali and Surrealism   IN-119
Arnell P., and Bickford T./Gwathmey Siegel,
    Architects   IN-145
Baigell, M./Concise History of American Painting &
    Sculpture   IN-85
Baigell, M./Dictionary of American Art   IN-78
Banham, R./Age of the Masters   IN-64
Barnett, J./Introduction to Urban Design   IN-114
Beck, J./Italian Renaissance Painting   IN-82
Blunt, A./Baroque and Rococo   IN-115
Broude, N., and Garrard, M./Feminism and Art History
    IN-117
Butler, R./Western Sculpture   IN-98
Carey, F., & Griffiths, A./The Print in Germany
    1880-1933   IN-151
Cathcart, L.L./American Still Life, 1948-1982   IN-131
Clark, K./The Gothic Revival   IN-48
Clark, K./Landscape into Art   IN-88
Clark, K./Introduction to Rembrandt   IN-92
Cole, B./Giotto and Florentine Painting   IN-71
Cole, B./The Renaissance Artist at Work   IN-129
Davidson, A./Early American Modernist Painting   IN-120
D'Oench, E.G., & Feinberg, J.E./Jim Dine Prints,
    1977-1985   IN-144
Edgerton, S. Y./Renaissance Rediscovery of Linear
    Perspective   IN-69
Eitner, L./An Outline of 19th Century European
    Paintiing   IN-126
Frascina, F., and Harrison C./Modern Art & Modernism
    IN-124
Frascina, F./Pollock and After   IN-147
Goldman, J./American Prints   IN-116
Goldwater, R./Symbolism   IN-95
Gowans, A./Images of American Living   IN-72
Greenhalgh, M./Classical Tradition in Art   IN-118
Hall, J./Dictionary of Subjects & Symbols in Art   IN-100
Hall, J./A History of Ideas and Images in Italian
    Art   IN-141
Harrison, C., & Orton, F./Modernism, Criticism,
    Realism   IN-142
Harrison, H./Larry Rivers   IN-146
Haskell, B./Milton Avery   IN-121
Henri, R./The Art Spirit   IN-138
Hibbard, H./Caravaggio   IN-128
Hibbard, H./Michelangelo Second Edition   IN-148
Highwater, J./Arts of the Indian Americas   IN-135
Honour, H., & Fleming, J./Dictionary of the Decorative
    Arts   IN-164
Honour, H./Romanticism   IN-89
Johnson, E./American Artists on Art   IN-112

Kahr, M./Dutch Painting in the Seventeenth Century
    IN-87
Kouwenhoven, J. A./The Columbia Historical Portrait of
    New York   IN-30
Lane, B. G./The Altar and the Altarpiece   IN-133
Lee, S. E./Chinese Landscape Painting   IN-10
Licht, F./Goya   IN-123
Loehr, M./Great Painters of China   IN-105
Mâle, E./Chartres   IN-149
Mâle, E./The Gothic Image   IN-32
Martin, J. R./Baroque   IN-77
Masterpieces of the Shin'enkan Collection   IN-160
Medley, M./Handbook of Chinese Art   IN-44
Novak, B./American Painting of the Nineteenth
    Century   IN-99
Osborne, R./Lights and Pigments   IN-113
Panofsky, E./Early Netherlandish Painting Vol. I   IN-2;
    Vol. II   IN-3
Panofsky, E./Studies in Iconology   IN-25
Panofsky, E./Renaissance and Renascences in Western
    Art   IN-26
Panofsky, E./Idea   IN-49
Rawson, J./Ancient China   IN-109
Robins, C./The Pluralist Era   IN-137
Rosenblum, R./Modern Painting and Northern Romantic
    Tradition   IN-57
Roskill, M./What Is Art History?   IN-74
Roth, L. M./Concise History of American Architecture
    IN-86
Roth, L. M./America Builds   IN-122
Roth, L.M./McKim, Mead & White, Architects   IN-136
Russell, J./The Meanings of Modern Art   IN-110
Sandler, I./The Triumph of American Painting   IN-75
Sandler, I./New York School   IN-94
Smith, L./Contemporary Japanese Prints   IN-153
Smith, L./The Japanese Print Since 1900   IN-130
Speight, C. F./Images in Clay Sculpture   IN-127
Stangos, N./Concepts of Modern Art   IN-104
Sterling, C./Still Life Painting   IN-96
Stoddard, W. A./Art and Architecture in Medieval
    France   IN-22
Stokstad, M./Medieval Art   In-132
Tafuri, M./Theories and History of Architecture   IN-108
Taylor, J./America as Art   IN-90
Venturi, R., & Brown, D.S/A View from the
    Campidoglio   IN-139
Weaver, M./The Photographic Art   IN-160
Wren, L., with Wren, D./Perspectives on Western
    Art   IN-154